THE SOCIETY FOR
POST-MEDIEVAL ARCHAEOLOGY
MONOGRAPH 2

Series Editor
DAVID BARKER

THE ARCHAEOLOGY OF
INDUSTRIALIZATION

THE ARCHAEOLOGY OF INDUSTRIALIZATION

Edited by

DAVID BARKER *and* DAVID CRANSTONE

Papers given at the Archaeology of Industrialization
Conference, October 1999, hosted jointly by

Association for Industrial
Archaeology

Society for Post-Medieval
Archaeology

MANEY

2004

© Authors and The Society for Post-Medieval Archaeology, 2004
www.spma.org.uk

For users in North America, permission is granted by the copyright owner for libraries and others registered with the Copyright Clearance Center (CCC) to make copies of any article herein. Payment should be sent directly to CCC, 222 Rosewood Drive, Danvers, MA 01923, USA. In the UK, the Copyright Licensing Agency, 90 Tottenham Court Road, London W1P 9HE is mandated to grant permission to make copies.

Statements in the volume reflect the views of the authors, and not necessarily those of the Society, editors or publisher.

ISBN   1 904350 01 1
ISSN   1740–4924

24304263

FRONT COVER
Coal. — Whimsey, or engine, drawing coal in the Staffordshire Collieries. Artist, W. H. Prior. Mid-19th-century engraving.

Published by Maney Publishing, Hudson Road, Leeds LS9 7DL, UK
www.maney.co.uk

Maney Publishing is the trading name of W. S. Maney & Son Ltd

Typeset, printed and bound in the UK by
The Charlesworth Group

CONTENTS

PAGE

Foreword vii

The Archaeology of Industrialization: Introduction
By MARILYN PALMER I

APPROACHES TO THE ARCHAEOLOGY OF INDUSTRIALIZATION

The Dialectic of Past-Present Relations
By DAVID UZZELL 5

Archaeological Science as an Aid to the Study of Post-Medieval Industrialization
By JUSTINE BAYLEY and DAVID CROSSLEY 15

INDUSTRY IN THE RURAL LANDSCAPE

Industrial Rural Settlements: Genesis, Character and Context 1550–1900
By RICHARD NEWMAN 25

Landscape, Economy and Identity: A Study in the Archaeology of Industrialization
By DAVID GWYN 35

Industrialization in the Countryside: The Roles of the Lord, Freeholder and Tenant in the Manchester Area, 1600–1900
By MICHAEL NEVELL and JOHN WALKER 53

Water Power in the Landscape: The Rivers of the Sheffield Area
By DAVID CROSSLEY 79

Woodland, Industry and Common Rights — A Conflict of Interest
By TOM GLEDHILL 89

LANDSCAPES OF MINING

The Mining Landscape of Cosgarne Common, Gwennap, Cornwall
By LYNN WILLIES 95

From Pick to Powder — Phases of Change in a North Pennine Landscape
By ALAN BLACKBURN 103

Metal Mining and Vegetational History of the Upper Rookhope Valley, Weardale, Northern Pennines
By TIM M. MIGHALL, LISA DUMAYNE-PEATY and STUART FREETH . . 119

SETTLEMENT AND THE URBAN LANDSCAPE

Social Archaeology: A Possible Methodology of the Study of Workers' Settlements based on the 18th- and 19th-Century Copper Industry of Swansea
By STEPHEN HUGHES 137
The Atlantic World and Industrialization: Contexts for the Structures of Everyday Life in Early Modern Bristol
By ROGER H. LEECH 155
Urban Industrial Landscapes: Problems of Perception and Protection
By PAUL BELFORD 165

ARTEFACTS AND INDUSTRY

Pathways of Change: Towards a Long-Term Analysis of the Ceramic Industry
By PAUL COURTNEY 181
The Industrialization of the Staffordshire Potteries
By DAVID BARKER 203

MATERIAL CULTURE AND SOCIAL CHANGE

Rural Burial and Remembrance: Changing Landscapes of Commemoration
By HAROLD MYTUM 223
'For Their Own Convenience': The Archaeology of 19th-Century Pub Tokens
By YOLANDA COURTNEY 241
Goods and Stores for the Workers: The Shaping of Mass Retailing in Late 19th-Century Ghent
By PETER SCHOLLIERS 257

THE INFLUENCE OF THE PAST ON THE PRESENT

Recording People and Processes at Large Industrial Structures
By ANNA BADCOCK and BRIAN MALAWS 269
Industrial Buildings and their Evaluation
By TAMARA ROGIC 291
Snail and Snail Shell: Industrial Heritage and the Reconstruction of a Lost World
By ERIK NIJHOF 299

CONCLUSION

The Archaeology of Industrialization — New Directions
By DAVID CRANSTONE 313
Index 321

FOREWORD

This volume, *The Archaeology of Industrialization*, is the outcome of the first joint conference of the two country's foremost societies devoted to the archaeological study of the early-modern and modern worlds, the Society for Post-Medieval Archaeology and the Association for Industrial Archaeology. Industrial archaeology and post-medieval archaeology have traditionally been seen as two separate disciplines, with different roots and very different intellectual interests, but in reality the two leading societies have many common goals.

The interest of the Association for Industrial Archaeology in industry and industrial development is self-evident, while the Society for Post-Medieval Archaeology's journal, *Post-Medieval Archaeology*, has always included papers on industrial subjects and excavation reports on industrial sites. Given these shared interests it is surprising that the two societies have not collaborated in this way previously and have not together assessed their respective contributions to this subject area. However, the results of this first joint venture, held in Bristol in 1999, are most encouraging, highlighting a high level of interest and demonstrating a breadth and vitality to the scholarship of the two groups.

The Archaeology of Industrialization explores the common ground between the two societies and their disciplines, and goes a long way towards breaking down barriers. The progress of industrialization and its impact upon modern society has a wide relevance, and in this volume twenty-three papers from Britain and Europe address the relationship between production and consumption and consider approaches to the study of manufacturing processes, trade, and the role of industrially-made material goods within society.

The two societies are grateful to the conference organisers, David Cranstone and Professor Marilyn Palmer, for their vision and energy which resulted in an event as successful as it was stimulating. This volume is the ultimate outcome of their endeavours in 1999 and earlier.

DAVID BARKER
President 1999, Society for Post-Medieval Archaeology

MICHAEL HARRISON
President 1999, Association for Industrial Archaeology

THE ARCHAEOLOGY OF INDUSTRIALIZATION: INTRODUCTION

By MARILYN PALMER

Industrialization is one of the key developments in the post-medieval British economy and society, and also one of the major contributions that Britain made to the rest of the world. This was recognized in the recent review of the selection of sites put forward for World Heritage status: 'Britain was the birth-place of industrialization which has shaped the modern world'.[1] As a result, three industrial sites in England, one in Wales and one in Scotland were added to the list of World Heritage sites in 1999 and 2000, and others are likely to join them in the next five years.

Industrialization is not, however, solely the product of that classic period usually known as The Industrial Revolution, dating from about 1760 to 1830 and characterized by innovative developments in power, transport and the organization of work. There is a long pre-history of industrialization in Britain, without which the widespread changes of the late 18th century would never have taken place. It was to explore this continuum that the Society for Post-Medieval Archaeology (SPMA) and the Association for Industrial Archaeology (AIA) came together at a conference in Bristol in 1999, organized by David Cranstone and Marilyn Palmer. Both societies were formed in the mid 20th century to explore what in the USA is termed 'historical archaeology', the inter-relationship between material culture and documentary evidence in understanding the recent past. As the eminent American historical archaeologist, James Deetz, has said, 'the combined use of archaeological and documentary materials should permit us to say something about the past that could not have been said using only one set of data'.[2] SPMA has always had a wider remit in terms of subject matter than AIA, as can be seen from David Crossley's seminal *Post-Medieval Archaeology in Britain*,[3] with chapters on church archaeology, fortifications and shipwrecks. Nevertheless, half the chapters in that volume do relate to industrial topics such as mining, glass and water-power. Early books on industrial archaeology,[4] on the other hand, concentrated exclusively on industrial and transport topics, although more recent ones[5] have taken a broader stance in looking at buildings, landscapes and landownership. Richard Newman's *The Historical Archaeology of Britain c. 1540–1900*[6] attempts to bring the two disciplines of post-medieval and industrial archaeology together, despite a separate chapter on the latter, the subject matter of which would perhaps have been better integrated into earlier chapters on house and home, landscapes and so on. This volume is another attempt to integrate what have been seen as two separate disciplines in the study of a topic common to them both, that of industrialization.

The contents of the volume have been enriched by four contributions from an earlier conference on 'Industry and Agriculture in the Northern Uplands', held jointly by SPMA and the Historical Metallurgy Society in 1995. The papers by Blackburn, Crossley, Gledhill, and Mighall *et al.* were originally written for this conference, and therefore to an earlier deadline and a slightly different remit to the remainder of the volume.

Turning to the content of the present volume, the first two contributions take different approaches to the interpretation of evidence about the past. David Uzzell's challenging article on the dialectic of past-present relations discusses the psychological processes which influence our understanding of the world, past and present: the perception of time and the social construction of knowledge. By contrast Justine Bayley and David Crossley aim to show that the wider application of scientific techniques to post-medieval investigations as well as those from earlier periods would be rewarded by significant new insights.

The next two sections of the book deal with landscapes, the first with industry in a rural context and the second with landscapes which are largely the product of metal mining activity. Landscape is, of course, often taken to mean natural scenery to which the onlooker reacts aesthetically, and is therefore devoid of human interference. But to the historian and the archaeologist, landscape is the physical manifestation of changes wrought by man in both space and time. It therefore includes buildings, not as discrete entities but in their relationship to one another and to their topographical setting. One of the major reasons for studying industrial landscapes is to transform a collection of individual structures into a coherent whole which has meaning in both cultural and technological terms. Culturally, these interrelationships can reveal systems of industrial organization often influenced by the nature of landownership and the existence of accepted social customs, as discussed by contributors to the section on industry in the rural landscape. Technologically, the interrelationship of buildings and features in the landscape is usually determined by sequences of industrial production, as in the landscapes of metalliferous mining and considerations of power sources. The task of the archaeologist is to analyse the industrial landscape in terms of both the spatial and the sequential relationships of structures and features in order to illuminate the process of industrialization.

Both post-medieval and industrial archaeologists have tended in the past to ignore urban landscapes, as Paul Belford rightly points out. Roger Leech's article takes us beyond Britain to consider how the global economy affected the development of one particular urban landscape, that of Bristol, while Stephen Hughes introduces the neglected topic of workers' housing in an attempt to persuade industrial archaeologists to look beyond the physical remains to the social constructs which lie behind them. He emphasizes how elements in the urban landscape such as workers', managers' and employees' housing, the development of workers' settlements and employers' estates, workers' Nonconformist chapels and employers' Anglican churches, are all related socially, economically and spatially to each other.

The next two sections of the book deal with the study of artefacts, perhaps the main component of the archaeological record, yet one neglected by industrial although not by post-medieval archaeologists. To many archaeologists, artefacts comprise the main body of evidence from which information about the lifestyles of past societies are derived. Variations in the type and distribution of artefacts indicate material change and prompt investigation into its causes. Industrial archaeologists, however, have chronicled the development of the means of production in terms of textile mills,[7] pot-kilns[8] and so on, but have so far paid little attention to the consequent effect of this development on the nature of the artefacts produced, and therefore of material change and consumption. This is clearly a field in which the two disciplines need to work together, as is shown by two papers on the ceramics industry in which both production and consumption are considered. This theme is also pursued by Harold Mytum in his study of rural burial grounds and their gravestones, looking both at changes in the production of gravestones and what their forms and inscriptions reveal about social change and motivation in the industrial period.

The final two papers in this section consider aspects of retailing, an important means of exchange in the modern period. Yolanda Courtney considers the use of pub tokens as evidence for social activities among the working class in the 19th century, while Peter Scholliers looks at the interest shown by workers in consumer goods before the First World War through a consideration of co-operative retailing in the important industrial city of Ghent in Belgium.

The final section of the book moves beyond the use of material culture to understand the process of industrialization, to a consideration of the value of industrial buildings and structures as components of the contemporary landscape. The concept of industrial heritage is one which is perhaps more familiar to industrial than post-medieval archaeologists, since the discipline of industrial archaeology grew out of an urgent need to protect survivals from the industrial past which were fast disappearing in the 1950s and 1960s. Industrial buildings and structures present particular difficulties for conservation: they are often vast in size, made of materials such as cast iron and steel which are difficult and expensive to preserve and, as in the case of the coal and textile industries, large numbers of similar structures have become redundant at the same time and selection criteria have had to be devized. Tamara Rogic looks at the legislative framework within which the survival of industrial structures has to be considered and points out that it is often not appropriate for their particular form and construction. Brian Malaws and Anna Badcock, both practizing industrial archaeologists, take as their theme the preservation by record of the processes which took place and the people who carried them out in large industrial works, using two large coking plants as case studies. Finally, Eric Nijhof continues this theme by urging us to look at the preservation and recording of industrial culture as a whole rather than individual buildings from particular trades and industries.

The book is concluded by David Cranstone, my fellow organizer of the Bristol conference, with some thoughts on future directions for the study of industrialization. He feels we should not lose sight of the importance of technology in our determination to delineate the social dimensions of the industrial past: and that archaeology could throw light on the processes of innovation and invention. At the same time, I feel that we should be looking beyond the monument, landscape and structure in an attempt to understand the aspirations and motivations of those who were responsible, both as entrepreneurs and members of the workforce, for the early industrialization of Britain. This volume brings together a wide-ranging collection of papers which shed new light on that important process.

Marilyn Palmer, School of Archaeological Studies, University of Leicester, University Road, Leicester, LEI 7RH, UK

NOTES

[1] DCMS 1999, 9.
[2] Deetz 1996, 32.
[3] Crossley 1990.
[4] Buchanan 1972; Raistrick 1972; Cossons 1975.

[5] Palmer & Neaverson 1998; Nevell & Walker 1999.
[6] Newman *et al.*, 2001.
[7] E.g. Giles & Goodall 1992.
[8] Baker 1991.

BIBLIOGRAPHY

Baker, D. 1991, *Potworks*, London: RCHME.

Buchanan, R. A. 1972, *Industrial Archaeology in Britain*, London: Pelican.

Cossons, N. 1975, *The BP Book of Industrial Archaeology*, Newton Abbott: David and Charles.

Crossley, D. 1990, *Post-Medieval Archaeology in Britain*, Leicester: Leicester University Press.

Deetz, J. 1996, *In Small Things Forgotten*, New York: Doubleday (revised edition, first edition New York: Anchor, 1977).

Department for Culture, Media and Sport 1999, *World Heritage Sites: The Tentative List of The United Kingdom of Great Britain and Northern Ireland* London: DCMS.

Giles, C. & Goodall, I. H. 1992, *Yorkshire Textile Mills: The Buildings of the Yorkshire Textile Industry 1770–1930*, London: HMSO.

Nevell, M. & Walker, J. 2000, *Tameside in Transition: the Archaeology of the Industrial Revolution in two North West Lordships, 1642–1870*, Tameside: Tameside Metropolitan Borough Council.

Newman, R., Cranstone, D., & Howard-Davis, C. 2001, *The Historical Archaeology of Britain c. 1540–1900*, Stroud: Sutton Publishing Ltd.

Palmer, M. & Neaverson, P. A. 1998, *Industrial Archaeology: Principles and Practice*, London: Routledge.

Raistrick, A. 1972, *Industrial Archaeology; An Historical Survey*, London: Eyre Methuen.

THE DIALECTIC OF PAST-PRESENT RELATIONS

By DAVID UZZELL

History is not the prerogative of the historian, nor even, as postmodernism contends, a historian's invention. It is, rather, a social form of knowledge; the work, in any given instance, of a thousand different hands. If this is true, the point of address in any discussion of historiography should not be the work of the individual scholar, nor yet rival schools of interpretation, but rather the ensemble of activities and practices in which ideas of history are embedded or a dialectic of past-present relations is rehearsed.

(R. Samuel, *Theatres of Memory, Volume 1: Past and Present in Contemporary Culture*, p. 8)

The interpretation of history and the archaeological record is inevitably subjective, and influenced by psychological processes. Clearly the more evidence that one has for the events of the past, the more accurate and reasonable an interpretation one can place on those events. But we know from eyewitness accounts in the present day that collecting evidence of what happened only days, hours or even minutes earlier can be remarkably unreliable. For example, asking six people to say what happened when a person was mugged on the street, how many muggers were there, what did they look like, can generate six different accounts of even straightforward descriptive information. Inferring motivation, cause and antecedents can be even more problematic. Hodder identified various problems in archaeology which would benefit, he suggested, from the contribution of historians, economists, anthropologists, sociologists and geographers.[1] Psychologists are not mentioned, yet the problems identified by Hodder in archaeology are at heart essentially psychological. This paper discusses two psychological processes which influence our understanding of the world, past and present: the perception of time and the social construction of knowledge.

In archaeology all inference is via material culture. Material culture is often the only evidence from which one can infer social organization and by extension psychological processes — psychological processes because it is typically assumed by archaeologists that material culture is a direct reflection of human behaviour. For example, one assumption commonly made by archaeologists is that the greater the similarity between artefacts in two separate places then the more frequent the interaction between the two human groups. But, as Hodder argues from evidence, the greater the interaction between peoples the *less* stylistic similarity is often found. Hodder's theory is that the distinctiveness of material culture is correlated with the degree of negative reciprocity between groups. In other words, in order to assert their

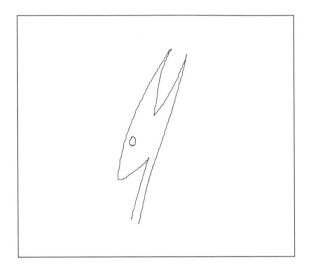

FIGURE 1. A bird or a deer? (after Hodder 1986).

own group identity — to differentiate themselves from others as increasing interaction breaks down distinctiveness — groups will produce different styles.[2] This can also operate within a group as a means to promote intra-group allegiances and social differences. In a class-ridden society like Britain one might, for example, expect burial practices to reflect such divisions, but the notable thing about burial grounds is their uniformity and implicit egalitarianism. This highlights the problem we face in inferring social organization from material culture. We have great difficulty doing it for the present, let alone the past.

The method of decoding the past is one of reading structure and process from the patterning of material culture. This approach is inevitably deterministic as it assumes material culture is a direct reflection of the social and physical environment. Artefacts, as Hodder states, are mute. We derive meaning from seeing artefacts in their temporal, spatial and functional context. There is a tendency to be deterministic in another sense as well. The processual approach to archaeology minimizes the role of the individual who makes the artefact, and instead looks at the societal system behind the individual and the artefact. The system becomes so pervasive and powerful that the individual becomes powerless. But as Hodder notes, each pot is made by an individual. Archaeology raises the question 'what is the relationship between the individual and society?'. This problem is no less familiar in psychology.[3]

It has been maintained by some archaeologists in the past that material remains speak for themselves. There was no need for theory, because interpretation was self-evident from the data. However, if one is to move beyond the descriptive, then one cannot make sense of data outside a theoretical framework. Taking an example from prehistoric art, our interpretation of the drawing may have important implications for how we interpret what else is going on in the picture and the nature of the society's technological development and social organization (Fig. 1).

The hypothetico-deductive approach common in the behavioural sciences is mirrored by the interpretive process engaged in by individuals when trying to make sense of the world. As the psychologist or archaeologist only understands behaviour through a theoretical framework, so do individuals interpret the world about them in the context of their own experiential theories about social relationships, places and people-environment relations. These theories inevitably and necessarily inform their interpretation of the past as well. We all draw upon our own contemporary social and cultural context to understand the past. The theories we use to interpret the past depend upon our own contemporary social and cultural context. Trigger, Leone and Uzzell have shown how changing interpretations of the past depend on changing social and cultural contexts in the present.[4] We use the past for particular social and ideological goals. In other words, like the relationship between human behaviour and material culture, theory and evidence have to be seen within particular social and cultural contexts.

CAN WE KNOW THE PAST?

How can we know the past? Our universe is being explored and revealed from the solar system to the mind. But regardless of how much research we undertake, our knowledge and experience of the past will always be incomplete. As Lowenthal (1985) remarks 'Unlike geographically remote places we could visit if we made the effort, the past is beyond reach'. John Keegan (1988), in *The Face of Battle*, tried to vault this temporal dimension by arguing that the battlefield accounts of veteran soldiers he taught at the Royal Military Academy at Sandhurst surely corresponded to the same experiences of those soldiers who had fought on the Somme, at Waterloo and at Agincourt:

> Since both danger and bravery in its face are absolutes — an arrow kills as certainly as a machine-gun and the courage to risk death by either takes an equal amount out of a man — the picture of the aristocracy of combat's ordeal to which my Sandhurst veterans had opened my eyes must have, I realized on reflection, a universal and permanent validity. What I had learnt about the inner nature of the Second World War was therefore also the key to understanding the First World War, the Napoleonic Wars, the Hundred Years War and the wars of antiquity.[5]

His argument is that if the experience of battle and war is 'universal and permanent', then surely we can have some insight into the past by accessing it through the present? Keegan argues that 'true history of the wars of the past' can be found by searching in 'the testimony of eye-witnesses for evidence of the sort of experiences I knew living warriors had thought central to their battlefield ordeal'. Does entering the minds of the present-day soldier open a door on the past? At first this seems highly plausible but, of course, as Samuel argues, 'history is a social form of knowledge; the work . . . of a thousand different hands'.[6] Therefore one cannot separate knowledge and understanding from the social context in which it is constructed. That social context is overwhelming formulated in our present-day culture, institutions and relations.

Writers such as Hewison and Wright quite justifiably question whether we can truly access the past.[7] Lowenthal puts forward a number of seemingly insuperable obstacles for us that firmly challenge the notion that we can know the past.[8] What is now known as the *past* was not what anyone experienced as the *present*. There is a sense in which we know the past better than those who experienced it. We have the benefit of hindsight and we know the outcome of the story: 'Knowing the future of the past forces the historian to shape his account to come out as things have done'.[9] Equally though, no historical account can ever capture what is the infinite content of an event. Most of the information generated by an event — whether it is at the individual or group level, or whether it is cognitive, affective or behavioural information — is not recorded: that which is recorded is also only a record of the past. Furthermore, we can only verify accounts of the past through other accounts. Historical knowledge, however well authenticated, is subjective and subject to the biases of its chronicler who is susceptible to the psychological processes of selective attention, perception and recall. To confound matters even more, selective attention, perception and recall affect what we, the chronicler's audience, make of this historical interpretation. Despite sincere attempts at authenticity, neither those who provide interpretations of the past nor those who receive them can avoid loading them with their own 20th-century perspectives. We cannot recreate the past or provide a 'truly authentic experience', since visitors' perceptions of the past will be influenced by their present-day attitudes and values.

TIMESCALE

A second factor affecting our understanding of the past is the timescale over which events are assessed.[10] The recession that affected Britain in the early 1990s could be interpreted as a temporary downturn in the economy. On the other hand and taking a longer term perspective, the economic boom of the late 1980s and then another in the late 1990s might be seen as evidence for the continual cycle of boom and slump which have been a feature of the British economy since 1945. Taking an even longer-term and Marxist analysis, the 1990s recession could be regarded as evidence of the predictable and inevitable death throe of late capitalism throughout western economies, the span of which extends over at least two centuries. Changing the temporal framework necessarily not only changes the geographical framework but also opens up the possibility of alternative social, economic, political and cultural interpretations.

Time and space in this form of analysis interact. The Cuban Missile Crisis is typically interpreted as the focus of a major clash between the United States and Russia. If we set the Cuban Missile Crisis in a larger time frame, say between 1939 and 1999, we can see it as demonstrating how alliances and allegiances between states can change over time so that Russia and the United States can be allies against the fascists in 1945 but in ideological conflict with each other less than ten years later. If we take a longer term perspective still, we might see the East-West conflict as the most recent manifestation of global geopolitics which extends back to the Greek and Roman Empires and may soon be replaced by a North-South conflict.

THE SEPARATION OF TIME

The third influence of time on our understanding of the past is the time-space that separates us from the events of the past. The meaning and resonance of events from the past changes as time separates us from those events. An illustration is provided by three examples of military events occurring 50, 80 and 700 years ago, which have been described in more detail elsewhere.[11]

The first case study relates to the massacre by the Nazis of virtually all the men, women and children from the village of Oradour-sur-Glane, near Limoges, in France in May 1944. Suspected of harbouring resistance fighters who had a few days earlier ambushed a German patrol, all the men of the village were taken to various houses, garages and public spaces and summarily executed. Following this, all the women and children were rounded up, taken to the Church, barricaded in and grenades were then thrown into the building which was then torched. Over 640 villagers were killed and the village destroyed. It was decided after the war that the village should not be rebuilt, but rather a new village constructed on the outskirts. The old village was turned into a national memorial by the French Government as a permanent reminder of what had happened.

Today, it is possible to visit the village and walk down the destroyed streets and into the shell of the church. In the mid 1980s a guide, related to one of the villagers who had been killed, took visitors around the town and explained in detail the chronology of events. It is also possible to buy various guidebooks and leaflets which graphically depict with contemporary photographs what happened. There is additional interpretation in the form of a small museum which contains the personal effects of those who were immolated. Returning to the village after a period of several years it seemed that there was a subtly different atmosphere. Maybe it was the tourist detritus that could be found on the ground, or maybe it was the presence of more young families. Whatever the cause, the place itself seemed to have changed from being a memorial to a day trip destination. It also changed from being an affective to a cognitive experience. For many French people (and non-French people, too) who had experienced the war the name Oradour-sur-Glane has a powerful resonance and is a highly significant and poignant moment in the French collective memory. Clearly this is not the case now for all visitors. Although the French authorities originally decided that, through the interpretation, visitors should not be spared the horror of what happened, one suspects that the anger and anguish will slowly be muted. The numbers for whom Oradour-sur-Glane provides a cathartic experience are declining.

The second example of the way in which time affects the emphasis which is placed by interpreters on events, and consequently what those event are made to mean to us is illustrated by reference to the major conflict in the second decade of the 20th century. Not many years ago, the presentation and interpretation of the First World War displays at the Imperial War Museum came in for criticism because it seemed that war was reduced to simply being a story about the application of technological and industrial developments to the slaughtering of millions, as if the most significant aspect of the First World War was the military technology. This museum was not alone in this kind of presentation — quite the contrary, it was the norm. Recently, however, the displays have been transformed with a successful attempt to interpret the 'meaning and significance' of the war in its many dimensions. But there are still many museums around the world where the sartorial elegance of the soldiery and the impressiveness of the instruments of war assume as much significance as, if not more than, their purpose and effect. As we go back in time we seem to be more willing to ignore suffering and treat events in a more disinterested way as if they are from a 'foreign country'.[12]

The third example illustrates that as we go further back in time not only are the emphases of history changed but history itself can become rewritten or forgotten altogether. At the time when the first study research on Oradour-sur-Glane was undertaken the interpretation of Clifford's Tower in York did not just minimize the history but failed even to tell the story of the 'ethnic cleansing' of the Jewish population of that city in the wave of anti-Semitic riots which occurred in various parts of the country after the Crusades, some 700 years ago. The interpretation of the Tower's history focused on who had lived there, its changing role over the centuries and its building materials, but no mention was made of the fact that the Jews of York were corralled into the Tower, and when faced with annihilation, committed suicide. Those who did not die at their own hands were tricked into opening the Tower's gates on the promise of clemency, but were then slaughtered. In the case of Clifford's Tower, it was not a case so much of history being re-written but rather history being forgotten. The displays at Clifford's Tower have since been changed by English Heritage. However, how many other heritage sites are there where shameful events of our past are forgotten altogether because they are seen to be so temporally distant that it is expedient to forget their occurrence?

CONSTRUCTING THE PAST

The issue of time and the social construction of the past acquire added significance when one considers that the construction of the past is now a major part of the tourism and leisure industry. Museums, visitor and heritage centres, stately homes, reconstructed villages, historical re-enactments, battlefield sites are all places where visitors come to re-live, to understand and to construct the past. Heritage interpretation is the name of this activity and it now includes a sizeable array of tools and techniques to transport the visitor back in time.

Visitor centres, old mines and factories and other such settings are places where visitors, especially the elderly, can tell their grandchildren about *The Way We Were*, as the Wigan Pier Experience used to be termed, but is now called the *Opie's Museum of Memories*. Middleton and Edwards suggest, however, that museums are not necessarily places for the reconstruction of memories, but places where visitors come to negotiate cultural meaning.[13] Some, like Hewison, go so far as to suggest that many museums do not provide an informative view of the past, but rather a symbolic view.[14] It can also be therapeutic and cathartic. For young people, it is a world they have never known, yet having viewed the interpretive displays or with the aid of 'first-person interpretation' experienced life in a mine or a factory or in the Napoleonic army, they can now be said to know the past. The re-presentation of the past becomes the memories of the future.

The museum and interpretive centre can be seen as a place where people come to understand themselves. If the museum is to be socially meaningful then it will be about the visitor. Gottesdiener suggests that the museum must be a place which puts the citizen back in society.[15] This is fundamental because it lies at the heart of how we acquire knowledge and understanding of the world and of ourselves. There are at least two approaches that we can take to the acquisition of knowledge and meaning. The traditional approach suggests that meaning and significance are self-evident from the object itself. In a museum, it used to be conventional to label objects with minimal information. We have now moved on, of course, to suggest that meaning is not always self-evident and that is why we need interpreters. But one is replacing one objectification and reification process by another. A subjective interpretation of the world is presented *as if* it is objectively true. The individual's role is still one of correctly identifying the meaning of the object as re-presented by the interpreter. The assumption is still that the exhibition designer will have a direct influence on a totally passive audience. In a sense, interpretation becomes a form of manipulation and therapy.

Alternatively, we can see knowledge as socially constructed. This perspective regards the audience as actively making sense out of the interpretation and relating it to their experience and world-view. The difference between these two positions is essentially one of meaning-taking *versus* meaning-making. Frameworks of meaning intervene between us and the object or place. It is these frameworks of meaning — the perceptions and attitudes of individuals and groups, and how events, practices and the environment mean — that have to be and should be interpreted.

For Gottesdiener, the consequence of placing the visitor rather than the exhibition at the centre of the learning experience and treating knowledge as a social construction is that the visitor becomes the author of the exhibition.[16] Each new visitor will bring to the museum a different reading or interpretation of the exhibits. The visitor starts to construct, psychologically, the exhibition. One consequence of this is that each exhibition becomes a mirror in which to reflect the visitor's own attitudes, values and beliefs. Perhaps this means that the visitor is unable to step back and take a wider perspective on society and culture. It does imply that the exhibition designer, and indeed the archaeologist who furnishes the artefacts, may lose his or her assumed autonomy. It challenges the idea that museums are simply agents of political and ideological propaganda and inculcation.[17]

CONCLUSION

Lowenthal argues there are three levels of historical analysis — memories, historical records and artefacts, which in turn correspond to the three academic disciplines of psychology, history and archaeology.[18] It was suggested above that the meanings of places change over time. Places, artefacts and events move from being a memory to being an historical record and archaeological site. Any interpretation of the recent past should draw as much on the analytical tools of the psychologist as the more conventional analytical tools of the historian and archaeologist. It is highly doubtful whether we can access the past through the present in the sense that Keegan intimates, but there are clearly still ways in which the psychologist might work alongside the archaeologist in order to make sense of the past. We might not be able to enter the minds of the 18th-century soldier, the 9th-century Viking invader or the 1st-century farmer, but by understanding those psychological processes which are contingent upon the socio-cultural context and those which may be independent (that is, the concern of evolutionary psychology) psychologists might be able to inform the work of archaeologists and the work of those whose aim is to present archaeological findings to the public.

David Uzzell, Department of Psychology, University of Surrey, Guildford, Surrey GU2 7XH, UK

NOTES

[1] Hodder 1986.
[2] Dittmar 1992.
[3] Breakwell 1991.
[4] Trigger 1980; Leone 1978; Uzzell 1989.
[5] Keegan 1988, 10.
[6] Samuel 1994, 8.
[7] Hewison 1987; Wright 1985.
[8] Lowenthal 1985.
[9] Ibid.
[10] Uzzell 1998.
[11] Uzzell 1989.
[12] Hartley 1953.
[13] Middleton & Edwards 1990.
[14] Hewison 1987.
[15] Gottesdiener 1993.
[16] Ibid.
[17] Hooper-Greenhill 1991.
[18] Lowenthal 1985.

BIBLIOGRAPHY

Breakwell, G. M. 1992, 'Integrating Paradigms, Methodological Implications', in Breakwell, G. M. & Canter, D. (eds), *Empirical Approaches to Social Representations*, Oxford: Oxford University Press.

Dittmar, H. 1992, *The Social Psychology of Material Possession*, Hemel Hempstead: Harvester Wheatsheaf.

Gottesdiener, H. 1993, *La Visite du Musée: Les interactions visiteur-environnement*, Note de Synthèse présentée pour l'habilitation à diriger des recherches, Université Paris X-Nanterre.

Hartley, L. P. 1953, *The Go-Between*, Harmondsworth: Penguin.

Hewison, R. 1987, *The Heritage Industry: Britain in a Climate of Decline*, London: Methuen.

Hodder, I. 1986, *Reading the Past*, Cambridge: Cambridge University Press.

Hooper-Greenhill, E. 1991, *Museum and Gallery Education*, Leicester: Leicester University Press.

Keegan, J. 1988, *The Face of Battle*, London: Barrie and Jenkins.

Leone, M. 1978, 'Time in American Archaeology', in Redman, C. *et al.* (eds), *Social Archaeology: Beyond Subsistence and Dating*, New York: Academic Press.

Lowenthal, D. 1985, *The Past is a Foreign Country*, Cambridge: Cambridge University Press.

Middleton, D. & Edwards, D. 1990, *Collective Remembering*, London: Sage.

Samuels, R. 1994, *Theatres of Memory, Volume 1: Past and Present in Contemporary Culture*, London: Verso Press.

Trigger, B. 1980, 'Archaeology and the Image of the American Indian', *American Antiquity*, 45, 662–76.

Uzzell, D. L. 1989, 'The Hot Interpretation of War and Conflict', in Uzzell, D. L. (ed.), *Heritage Interpretation: Volume I: The Natural and Built Environment*, London: Belhaven Press.

Uzzell, D. L. 1998, 'Interpreting Our Heritage: A Theoretical Interpretation', in Uzzell, D. L. & Ballantyne, R. (eds), *Contemporary Issues in Heritage and Environmental Interpretation: Problems and Prospects*, London: The Stationery Office, 11–25.

Wright, P. 1985, *On Living in an Old Country: The National Past in Contemporary Britain*, London: Verso.

ARCHAEOLOGICAL SCIENCE AS AN AID TO THE STUDY OF POST-MEDIEVAL INDUSTRIALIZATION

_____

By Justine Bayley *and* David Crossley

INTRODUCTION

Archaeological investigations dealing with the medieval and earlier periods routinely use a wide range of scientific techniques. These applications are well known and understood, and have been in use for a considerable time. Brothwell and Higgs edited a collection of papers covering the techniques then available,[1] and the more recent literature demonstrates the quality and quantity of information now contributed to archaeology by scientific studies.[2] In contrast, there is in general far less use of archaeological science where sites date to the post-medieval and early modern periods. A recent collection of papers on post-medieval archaeology, *Old and New Worlds*,[3] reinforces this point; only a handful of the 42 papers have any scientific content.

This paper will explore some reasons for this fundamental difference of approach, and will aim to show that the wider application of scientific techniques to post-medieval investigations would be rewarded by significant new insights. The potential exists but is often unrecognized and thus unrealized.

THE POST-MEDIEVAL WORLD

In the post-medieval period, economic changes that started in the later Middle Ages continued to affect every area of the lives of ordinary people, and the rate of change increased steadily from the 16th century onwards. Whyte argues that the driving force was the trebling of population from the 16th to the 19th century which encouraged the commercialization of agriculture, the growth and structural change of towns, and developments in the technology and scale of many industries.[4] Mechanization and industrialization affected both rural and urban economies, and the balance shifted from a predominantly rural society to one that, by the early 19th century, was dominated by urban populations and industry.

Many of the early studies of the post-medieval period were carried out by economic historians, to whom historical sources were seemingly abundant, so archaeological techniques, especially excavation, were normally considered inappropriate. More recently it has become accepted that the historical documents which are most likely to survive can lack information on many aspects of society and economy, and that industrial processes and the sites where they were carried out are rarely adequately described. Archaeology has thus gradually been accepted as a vital complement to archive-based historical studies, although the emphasis has often been on field survey and the examination of surviving structures, rather than on excavation which can be a source of samples for environmental investigation. Archaeological investigations can also provide a check on the biases inherent in documentary sources.

Compared with earlier periods, post-medieval archaeology has until recently had different priorities and has tended to ask different questions of the archaeological record, often those where scientific techniques have little to offer.[5] There has been an emphasis on research, often archive-directed, on urban sites whose post-medieval levels in fact have great potential for excavation. However, it has to be recognized that the nature of urban archaeological deposits is not the same as in earlier periods, as taphonomic processes such as rubbish disposal altered with the increasing density of occupation. Now that the need for excavation rather than bulldozing of post-medieval layers is accepted, the potential of scientific techniques can be more widely realized. However, the results obtained will depend on asking the right questions at the research design stage — which is the crux of the matter at any period.

INDUSTRIALIZATION AND ITS EFFECTS ON THE LANDSCAPE

The centuries between 1300 and 1750 saw changes in methods in rural industries. At the beginning of the period, the post-Black Death shortage of labour encouraged mechanization. This movement continued in the post-medieval period as markets for manufactured goods and larger-scale methods of production developed, particularly those which also resulted in improvements in quality. The competitive market for the products of woodlands during the 16th and 17th centuries encouraged the development of technologies that could use mineral fuels, and eventually led to the relocation of industries to the coalfields. These changes in methods of production can be seen as the beginnings of industrialization, though that term should strictly be reserved for non-domestic production.

The intensive use of woodlands for fuel over the period 1500–1800 is marked by the growth of regenerative coppicing. So far no investigations are known to have taken place into the effect of differing cycles of cropping on pollen production, reflected in pollen diagrams. It is important to be aware of the needs of the industries to which particular woodlands were dedicated: the young growth used by the iron and steel industries for charcoal contrasted with the more mature wood used by glass-makers and potters.

Much early mechanization, particularly in rural areas, was water-powered. Little attention has been paid to the environmental effects which the increase in the number of water mills would have had; their proliferation gave rise to landscape changes, particularly where their density was high to the point of overcrowding, as in the Cotswolds and the Pennines. The most visible alteration would have been changes of river-courses, and the creation of leats and races; these affected overall drainage patterns as well as changing the local flora and fauna. The scale and speed of these environmental changes can be determined using the techniques of botanical reconstruction which are commonplace for the prehistoric period.

As industry became more urbanized, growing town populations put pressure on agricultural production, reflected in landscape changes. The need to raise output led to the intake of waste, for example, the draining of marshland and enclosure of uplands for improved grazing, and to improvements in crop yields by consolidation and enclosure of former open fields. These landscape changes should be detectable from the study of botanical remains, and specifically of pollen sequences from lakes or bogs. Bell and Dark have shown there is a growing body of data and synthesis about historic period rural environments, although none of the examples they cite are from the post-medieval period.[6] This may be due, in part at least, to the vulnerability of upper levels in wetland deposits.

There is, however, more definite evidence for improvements in animal husbandry, and some suggestion of importing livestock. The increase in the size of cattle and sheep bones reported from a number of sites in England is probably linked with the Agricultural Revolution. This archaeological evidence supports the view that these improvements — the industrialization of agriculture — began in the 16th century, rather than from the mid 17th or 18th centuries when literary sources show that improved farming was being encouraged.[7] Studies of the mid 16th- to mid 17th-century bones from Camber Castle[8] show that much of the beef came from veal calves, which may reflect a shift from oxen to horses for power and a greater interest in cow milk.

DATING THE POST-MEDIEVAL

Most of the scientific techniques that are used to date the medieval and earlier periods can also be used in the post-medieval. Magnetic dating is far more precise than at earlier periods as that part of the calibration curve comes from direct observations. This precision could, potentially, sequence a series of high-temperature industrial features, though it is the date of the last firing, not the first, which can be determined.

Thermoluminescent dating of ceramics is also good, as the errors are a percentage of the age and so are smaller for more recent samples. For example, the error on a date of 1700 is $\pm$ 30 years at 1 sigma but a date of 1900 would have an error of only $\pm$ 10 years.[9] Chimney pots can be shown to be Tudor originals or 19th-century copies, and the dating of bricks is now a possibility — to show for instance whether partition walls are original or later additions. These types of information can be vital in deciding whether to list a particular building, or how to repair it.

Dendrochronology is a further success story; it has given precision to the Great Rebuilding of the 16th and 17th centuries. The change from oak as the main construction timber in the mid 17th century means that many later buildings cannot yet be dated using the technique. The conifers which then came into use were imported and master chronologies are not yet complete for all the common sources.[10] That for Baltic pine is well advanced, but timber imported from the New World is not yet datable by dendrochronology. Once reliable master curves are available, all sorts of structural timber, from pit props to components of large industrial complexes, will be datable — bringing precision to the interpretation of building sequences.

Radiocarbon dating is one scientific dating technique that is not often useful. This is because there is a plateau in the calibration curve for the period AD 1500–1650, and another from AD 1650–1950. Dates of such imprecision are rarely useful in the post-medieval period. An exception is dating the chemically-bound carbon in iron and steel, which has the potential to show whether the metal was smelted using charcoal or coke.

INDUSTRIES IN THE POST-MEDIEVAL PERIOD

The laboratory examination of samples from industrial sites has been demonstrated to be important in furthering our understanding of technological change. Some problems ideally require work on sizeable assemblages of residues, but the current pattern of archaeological fieldwork can make this difficult. Recently there have been few rescue excavations on early industrial sites, in part an effect of the procedures brought about by PPG 16. Hence, sampling of residues either from field walking or from near-surface contexts, or from small-scale interventions, can be significant. The variable survival of residues, caused by degradation and recycling, can affect the results obtained. Among the industries developing in the post-medieval period, those producing iron, lead and glass provide illustrations of these general points.

Iron

The excavations on British iron-smelting sites which have taken place since 1965, and the examinations of excavated materials which have followed, have clarified the nature of the variations in smelting technology. At the bloomery site at Rockley, Yorkshire (c. 1500–c. 1640) there was excellent evidence for the roasting of ores, substantial survivals of the smelting and reheating hearths, although no satisfactory evidence was found for a water-powered forging hammer. There was surprisingly little bloomery slag, which has now been explained by the evidence for subsequent re-smelting of this slag in the adjacent blast furnace (see below). At Muncaster Head, Cumbria (17th century), the use of high-quality haematite ore was demonstrated. Scientific studies also showed that a surprisingly large amount of slag had solidified within the furnace, an unusual technology for the period.

There have been numerous excavations on the sites of early blast furnaces.[11] From this resource of published work, and the specialist reports which it contains, there now exists a body of knowledge of the character of products and residues which enables sites to be identified and techniques to be evaluated from sampling, often of surface scatters. The range of slags produced by bloomeries and blast furnaces is well established, and can be related to ores and products. In both the bloomery and the blast furnace, material of particular value comes from the end of a smelt, retained in the base of the furnace hearth, which can contain ore, metal and slag, the slag on occasion showing prints from charcoal, the assemblage presenting a microcosm of smelting practice. A recent case is the examination of ore, slag and metal from

Rockley, which has indicated that bloomery slags had been added to the blast furnace-charge, giving credence to a late 18th-century description of the operation of this furnace, whose archive source is now lost.[12] This was the period when most ironmasters adopted coke as a fuel: the archaeological evidence which is generally sought for this change is a higher level of sulphur in coke-smelted iron than in the product of the charcoal blast furnace, but another approach is by radiocarbon dating (as mentioned above), using samples of cast iron.

A problem which persists is the difficulty of separating some kinds of bloomery wastes from those found at finery forges. Much of the slag from the bloomery is easily distinguishable, with hard black or grey-black surfaces showing evidence of viscous flow. However, some wastes from bloomeries can resemble finery cinder, a problem which scientific analyses may be able to resolve.

An aspect of iron working which has been studied for the Roman and medieval periods, and which is as relevant to the post medieval, is the characterization and distribution of hammer scale at forge sites. The distinction of spheroidal hammer scale, the result of forge-welding, from flake scale, derived from shaping of iron under the hammer, provides a way of distinguishing the nature of work carried out at a forge.

The nature and quantity of surviving slags is not necessarily indicative of the processes carried out at a particular site. In the case of iron, recycling of slags is known to have occurred. Bloomery slag could contain sufficient iron to be attractive to operators of blast furnaces, as at Rockley, noted above. Secondly, after the closure of ironworks, slags were frequently used as hard-core; indeed the end of the charcoal iron industry came at a time when road construction by turnpike trusts made use of slag deposits as quarries. Again, taking the case of Rockley which went out of use c. 1800 after a short phase using coke, the scarcity of surrounding slag deposits is matched by the construction of local colliery railways, along which there can be found scatters of blast furnace slag.

These examples suggest that the mismatch between known uses of a site and the surviving slags can be a problem, though once the possibilities are appreciated misleading interpretations can be avoided. Scientific analysis and identification of slags can, however, expand knowledge about a site and the processes carried out there. An example is the work on the excavated debris from Derwentcote cementation furnace, which identified other iron-working processes in addition to cementation, adding to the previously known uses of the site.[13]

Lead

Although far less well known than developments in iron technology, there were radical changes in methods of smelting lead. Bole-hearth smelting was succeeded by the water-powered ore-hearth in the second half of the 16th century, the latter to be largely replaced by the coal-fired natural-draught cupola over the 18th century. Changes in tin smelting are analogous, the water-powered blowing house being introduced late in the Middle Ages and being replaced by reverberatory induced draught furnaces in the 18th century.[14]

Most of our present knowledge of lead smelting is based on documentary evidence supplemented by field survey, largely from Derbyshire and the north Pennines, which provides a framework for the change from the bole-hearth and blackwork-oven to the ore-hearth and slag-hearth.[15] Scientific techniques have so far contributed relatively little, although the potential is considerable. Two projects which have demonstrated useful directions for future work involve geochemical investigations. Wild and Eastwood showed that the areas down-wind from bole sites had high levels of lead contamination in the soil.[16] If applied in reverse, the lead content of soils could be used to map the sites of bole hills, many of which are difficult to identify on the ground as many of the slags have been removed for later re-smelting. Secondly, the discovery of water-powered ore-hearth sites of the 16th and 17th centuries has been assisted by geochemical sampling of stream silts.[17]

Newly introduced smelting technologies could extract further lead from the slags of older processes. Care therefore needs to be taken in the interpretation of any analytical work on slag samples; they may be either the raw materials or the products of the site on which they are found. Science does not have all the answers!

Glass

Analytical investigations of the debris from glass-working sites have the potential to help understand the nature of the processes being carried out. Glass furnaces normally yield a range of residues, of four types. There are, firstly, the glasses themselves; some are materials which have been shaped and then discarded, largely due to breakage during the annealing process, or glass which has become waste at the time of blowing, the 'knock-offs' from blowing or gathering irons. Lumps of glass which have never been gathered are found, broken from crucible bases when the latter have been separated from their settings in the furnace. Secondly, glass-like materials, sometimes misleadingly named slags, result from the clearance of impurities floating on the top of the batch in the crucible, and have a bubbly appearance. There are, thirdly, fragments of furnace structure, of stone or clay, which may bear accumulations of spilled glass. Finally, crucible fragments often bear traces of glass, and may be of sufficient size to establish the form of the pot.

At different times in the life of a glass works the balance between these types of finds will vary. The ability of the glass-maker to recycle glass led to the removal of much of the glassy residues soon after their deposit, creating a bias towards the products of the last phase of use of a site. Even the product of this final operation may have been reduced if the site has been scavenged by a neighbouring maker. Consequently, the balance between glass and other materials was liable to be altered at an early stage, but subsequent land-use, particularly with modern agricultural equipment, leads to the pulverization of glasses and clay furnace fragments. Hence, crucible, the most durable material, is apt to be over-represented, although even this becomes fragmented. Broken crucible does however often continue to bear glass residues, which, despite the effect of interaction of glass and ceramic at the interface, can provide the best glass sample on severely eroded sites.

The scientific approach to problems of glass technology needs to be set within an understanding of the changes which took place over the post-medieval period. At the end of the Middle Ages there was small-scale glass production in England, of vessel and flat glass of poor quality by comparison with continental imports. Examination of residues has suggested, but not fully established, the reasons for the apparently poor durability of the medieval and early 16th-century English glasses, and for their variability in composition.[18]

The products of immigrant workers, appearing in the quarter century after 1567, are distinctive, and by the end of the 16th century glass of fine appearance and durability, hitherto imported, was generally available from English sources. The reasons for the superiority of immigrant methods have not received sufficient attention, and there is a need for examination of a substantial sample of glasses of late 16th-century English manufacture to establish the reasons for the consistency with which quality was maintained. There is also a need for further examination of crucibles of this period, to determine the sources of refractories, in those woodland regions remote from the fire-clays of the coal measures.

The major change of the early 17th century was the introduction of coal as a fuel, necessitating a change in the technology of furnaces, which took place rapidly between 1610 and 1620. Excavations of early and mid 17th-century furnaces, at Kimmeridge, Dorset,[19] Denton, Lancashire and Red Street, Staffordshire,[20] have clarified the features of furnace-design. Sites of the subsequent period, 1650–1820, have shown further developments in furnaces and crucibles.[21] The documented use of lead in glass has been demonstrated analytically.[22] Nevertheless, more sampling remains to be done, particularly directed towards examination of the early lead glasses immediately following Ravenscroft's experiments of the 1670s.

CONCLUSIONS

The archaeology of the post-medieval period enjoys the ability to correlate physical with written evidence. In cases where both sources exist, and are mutually illuminating, it is possible to create baselines for further research on sites or materials where the evidence is fragmentary, for this and earlier periods. In setting up such a framework based on complementary written and physical evidence, science-based research plays a vital role.

This paper has demonstrated that scientific techniques have already contributed substantially to the archaeology of the post-medieval and early modern periods. This is true not only for those disciplines discussed above but for others, such as the study of human skeletal remains.[23] It is to be hoped that future investigations of the material remains of these periods will utilize scientific techniques more fully than they have previously done, and so unlock their unrealized potential to expand our knowledge of the more recent past.

ACKNOWLEDGEMENTS

We would like to thank Alex Bayliss, Gill Campbell and Sebastian Payne for helpful discussions while writing this paper.

Justine Bayley, English Heritage Centre for Archaeology, Fort Cumberland, Fort Cumberland Road, Eastney, Portsmouth PO4 9LD, UK
David Crossley, ARCUS, University of Sheffield, Department of Archaeology, West Court, 2 Mappin Street, Sheffield S1 4DT, UK

NOTES

1 Brothwell & Higgs (eds) 1969.
2 E.g. Bayley 1998.
3 Egan & Michael 1999.
4 Whyte 1999.
5 Gaimster & Stamper 1997; Egan & Michael 1999.
6 Bell & Dark 1998.
7 Albarella & Davies 1994.
8 Connell & Davies 1997.
9 Aitken 1990.
10 Groves 1997.
11 Crossley 1990, 156–69.
12 Starley in Crossley 1995, 410–13.

13 McDonnell in Cranstone 1997, 93–102.
14 Gerrard 2000.
15 Kiernan 1988.
16 Wild & Eastwood 1992.
17 Crossley & Kiernan 1992.
18 Crossley 1967; Mortimer 1997.
19 Crossley 1987.
20 Hurst Vose 1994.
21 Ashurst 1970; Ashurst 1987.
22 Cable 1987.
23 Mays 1999.

BIBLIOGRAPHY

Aitken, M. J. 1990, *Science-based Dating in Archaeology*, Harlow: Longman.

Albarella, U. & Davies, S. 1994, 'Mammals and birds from Launceston Castle, Cornwall: decline in status and the rise of agriculture', *Circaea* 12, 1–156.

Ashurst, D. 1980, 'Excavations at Gawber glasshouse near Barnsley, Yorkshire', *Post-Medieval Archaeology* 4, 92–140.

Ashurst, D. 1987, 'Excavations at the 17th-18th-century glasshouse at Bolsterstone, Yorkshire', *Post-Medieval Archaeology* 21, 147–226.

Bayley, J. (ed.) 1998, *Science in Archaeology: an agenda for the future*, London: English Heritage.

Bell, M. & Dark, P. 1998, 'Continuity and change: environmental archaeology in historic periods', in Bayley, J. (ed.), *Science in Archaeology: an agenda for the future*, London: English Heritage, 179–93.

Brothwell, D. & Higgs, E. S. (eds) 1969, *Science in Archaeology*, London: Thames and Hudson.

Cable, M. 1997, 'Glass Technology at Bolsterstone', in Ashurst 1987, 217–23.

Connell, B. & Davies, S. J. M. 1997, 'Animal bones from Camber Castle, East Sussex, 1963–1983' (unpublished Ancient Monuments Laboratory Report 107/1997).

Cranstone, D. 1997, *Derwentcote Steel Furnace*, Lancaster: Lancaster Imprints.

Crossley, D. W. 1967, 'Glass making at Bagot's Park, Staffordshire in the 16th century', *Post-Medieval Archaeology* 1, 44–83.

Crossley, D. W. 1987, 'Sir William Clavell's glasshouse at Kimmeridge, Dorset: the excavations of 1980–81', *Archaeological Journal* 144, 340–82.

Crossley, D. W. 1990, *Post-Medieval Archaeology in Britain*, Leicester: Leicester University Press.

Crossley, D. W. 1995, 'The blast furnace at Rockley, South Yorkshire', *Archaeological Journal* 152, 381–421.

Crossley, D. W. & Kiernan, D. T. 1992, 'The lead smelting mills of Derbyshire', *Derbyshire Archaeological Journal* 112, 6–47.

Egan, G. & Michael, R. L. (eds) 1999, *Old and New Worlds*, Oxford: Oxbow.

Gaimster, D. & Stamper, P. (eds) 1997, *The Age of Transition: the Archaeology of English Culture 1400–1600*, Oxford: Oxbow.

Gerrard, S. 2000, *The Early British Tin Industry*, Stroud: Tempus.

Groves, C. 1997, 'The dating and provenancing of imported conifer timbers in England: the initiation of a research project', in Sinclair, A., Slater, E. & Gowlett, J. (eds), *Archaeological Sciences 1995*, Oxford: Oxbow (Monograph 64), 205–11.

Hurst Vose, R. 1994, 'Excavations at the 17th-century glasshouse at Haughton Green, Denton near Manchester', *Post-Medieval Archaeology* 28, 1–71.

Kiernan, D. T. 1988, *The Derbyshire Lead Industry in the Sixteenth Century*, Chesterfield: Derbyshire Record Series 14.

Mays, S. 1999, 'The study of human skeletal remains from English post medieval sites', in Egan & Michael (eds), 331–41.

Mortimer, C. 1997, 'Analysis of the Glass', in Welch 1997, 38–43.

Welch, C. M. 1997, 'Glass-making in Wolseley, Staffordshire', *Post-Medieval Archaeology* 31, 1–60.

Whyte, I. 1999, 'The historical geography of Britain from AD1500: landscape and townscape', in Hunter, J. & Ralston, I. (eds), *The Archaeology of Britain*, London: Routledge, 264–79.

Wild, M. & Eastwood, I. 1992, 'Soil contamination and smelting sites', in Willies, L. M. & Cranstone D. (eds), *Boles and Smeltmills*, Matlock: Historical Metallurgy Society, 54–57.

Willies, L. 1992, 'Problems in the interpretation of cupola lead smelting sites', in Willies, L. M. & Cranstone, D. (eds), *Boles and Smeltmills*, Matlock: Historical Metallurgy Society, 40–42.

INDUSTRIAL RURAL SETTLEMENTS: GENESIS, CHARACTER AND CONTEXT 1550–1900

By Richard Newman

Industry was responsible for the creation of more new settlements and the modification of existing ones than any other process in the post-medieval period. Best known of the non-urban settlements are the planned hamlets and villages deliberately designed and constructed to accommodate the workforce of a local enterprise such as at Styal, Cheshire, or Copley, near Halifax, Yorkshire. This paper will not deal with these settlements but with the more organic and unplanned growth of rural settlements which were not purposely created by an industrialist, but which nevertheless originated, or at least substantially evolved, in the period 1550–1900 as a consequence of industrialization. This paper is not based on the results of any excavation work but on documentary research and the, often fairly cursory, analysis of upstanding fabric. It will not present the results of systematic research or of one cohesive project and is not intended to be comprehensive in its representation of rural industrial settlements, as it deals with settlements from only two discrete areas, the Forest of Dean in Gloucestershire and the Lancashire/Westmorland border. It is little more than a set of observations concerning the shape, form, fabric and character of settlements. These have been made over many years and result, often incidentally, from various campaigns of research. Even so, some attempt is made at examining three basic questions:

— why do industrial settlements occur where they do?
— what are the characteristics of non-urban industrial settlements, and can meaningful typologies be compiled of these characteristics?
— what are the factors that influenced the appearance and topologies of these settlements?

There are a number of similarities between the two chosen study areas, besides their familiarity to the author. Both regions were throughout the post-medieval period, as today, primarily rural areas with limited urban development. They were physically and psychologically marginal, border areas.[1] They were situated on the periphery of major urban centres of economic activity, Bristol and south Lancashire. Both regions had direct access to the sea and also contain much woodland and have mineral deposits that are towards the bottom end of commercial viability.

SQUATTER SETTLEMENTS IN THE FOREST OF DEAN

The Forest of Dean was a royal forest in west Gloucestershire. It was never disafforested and remains in Crown hands today. The central core of the Forest was heavily wooded in the late 16th century, but on the margins, the area was settled and farmed with stretches of manorial common woodland. These areas of land were held by the manorial lord but rights to their use were invested in all the tenants of the manor. By the 17th century many of these areas of woodland had been denuded of trees as a consequence of the common grazing of animals by manorial tenants. These tenants had the right to take wood in various forms. The constant removal of trees, with the prevention of regeneration because of the grazing of the young spring by the commoners' animals, meant that gradually the woodland cover was doomed to extinction. The trees were removed and without improvement the land only supported rough grazing. The manorial lords could not enclose parts of the commons to allow woodland regeneration or to improve land quality, because to do so would have infringed the rights of the commoners.

The late 16th- and early 17th-century population increase, combined with regionally varying social factors, exerted pressure on existing settlement and tenurial systems, helping to create a body of landless poor. Those who did not inherit property, but remained tied to the land, laboured for others. Unmarried farm workers were often quartered on the farm, but once married required their own home. However, their employers, usually farmers, were reluctant to spend money on housing their workers and so they were left to fend for themselves. Thus land was available for settlement and a demand existed for it. The landless squatted on the commons. This happened widely in the Forest of Dean area. The early 17th-century traveller and commentator, John Norden, noted that whenever he crossed 'great and spacious wastes, mountains and heaths', he found new dwellings; in Gloucestershire, for example, he encountered 'very many cottages raised upon the forests'.[2]

These squatter settlements in west Gloucestershire would not have lasted for long nor have developed into the huge sprawl of settlements that today encircle the central core of the Forest of Dean without two additional factors: the encouragement of squatting by the manorial lords, and the potential for smallholders to seek by-employment in industrial enterprises. Throughout west Gloucestershire manorial court presentments record fines being paid for encroachments. These were relatively low and paid annually, so clearly were not financial punishments but rents. A squatted common was more valuable to the manor than an unsettled one — after all, the manorial lord hardly lost out by allowing squatting; it was his tenants whose rights were infringed who suffered. In some cases manorial lords assisted directly in the erection of cottages on the common. In the late 18th century Lord Bathurst had quarries at Pillowell and he paid for a cottage to be built on the common waste to house a quarry worker.[3]

Where settlements were discouraged by manorial lords their long-term survival was doubtful. A squatter settlement grew up on the edge of Yartleton Woods, seemingly around a glasshouse erected in 1598 (Fig. 1); a 1624 survey of the manor notes only one of the encroachments as recent.[4] Called Glasshouse Green, the

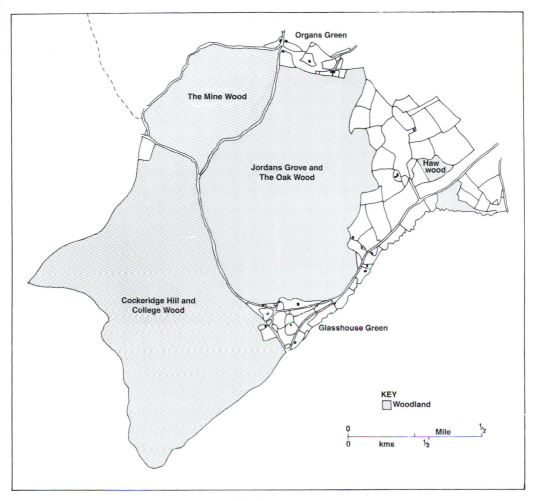

FIGURE 1.   Glasshouse Green in 1775.

settlement appears not to have met any resistance from the manorial lord. Then in 1632 the lord of the manor introduced a sixteen-year enclosure and coppice cycle into the woods to facilitate his growing interest in the charcoal blast furnace industry and immediately appears to have set about discouraging the encroachments. In 1638 he built a new blast furnace at Newent and Yartleton Woods were intended to be one of the principal sources of fuel supply, so it is hardly surprising that in 1639 the glasshouse seems to have gone out of business.[5] The squatter settlement at Glasshouse Green, nevertheless, survived throughout the 18th century and excavations there have shown that the glasshouse was replaced by a pottery.[6] The settlement did not grow or thrive, however, and had disappeared by 1839.[7]

Throughout the Forest of Dean area in the 16th to 18th centuries by-employment was sought by squatters in the various small-scale industries, such as woollen cloth, glass, paper, iron, brass, stone quarrying and above all cider, which were scattered throughout the region. The one to two acre encroachments were difficult to utilize for anything other than subsistence. By turning their plots over to orcharding, the squatters could still grow vegetables or quarter animals whist also producing a cash crop. Apples were sold to factors representing commercial cider mills such as that based in Newnham.[8]

Whilst the situation described can account for the development of settlements such as Woolaston Woodside or Gorseley Common with their widely scattered and extensive encroachments, as well as many smaller squatter encroachments, it cannot account for the development of the densely-settled and large settlements ringing the central core of the Forest of Dean, such as Berry Hill, Drybrook and Milkwall. Although affected by the conditions described thus far they owed their origins to the neglect of the woodlands by the Crown authorities and the Forest of Dean's tradition of free mining.

In the 17th century, government maladministration had led to the removal of much of the tree cover by 1700.[9] This allowed squatter developments to arise along the borders of the Forest. During the 17th century periodic purges of the 'cabbiners', as they were known, prevented the formation of permanent settlements, but for much of the 18th century government interest in the Forest was lacking, and by 1787 there were 582 cottage encroachments in the Forest of Dean.[10] Because of the tradition of free mining in Dean, whereby anyone born in the Hundred of St Briavells who had worked for a year and a day in a Dean colliery was entitled to open their own pit anywhere within the Forest, 6% of the encroachments on the edge of the Forest included a coal pit.[11] Most of the other pits situated deeper in the Forest were owned by people squatting on the edge of the Forest.

In Dean 13% of the 'cabbins' in 1787 were described as insubstantial structures built of mud, turf or in some cases rush.[12] Comparison of 17th- to 18th-century floor plans of squatter cottages with known cottages of husbandmen and other poor inhabitants of rural settlements, indicates that squatter's floor space was smaller than that of other social classes, often being no more than 15m.^{2}. Most of the cottages were single storey. Even so, there are some substantial, well-apportioned stone and timber squatter cottages built in the 17th and 18th centuries that survive today.

Most surviving squatter houses, however, are 19th century in date and it is likely that it is not until then that durable structures were generally built. In the early 19th century the commons were enclosed and as a result the encroachments were legalized. The squatted areas of the Forest core were also legalized. Legal recognition of holdings prompted the rebuilding of cottages in a more durable form. Often this rebuilding was accompanied by an insertion of a date stone demonstrating confidence in the future and pride in the newly acquired permanence of their holdings. The legal recognition of the holdings prompted their integration into an established settlement hierarchy. The Forest core was given parochial status and both there and in the squatted commons surrounding it Nonconformist chapels were established to serve the newly legalized communities.

Those squatter settlements that owed their existence at least in part to the availability of local industrial employment formed a highly distinctive type of settlement pattern. The encroachments were for the most part piecemeal, opportunistic and individualistic, and in this way reflected the nature of the small-scale industrial enterprises in which the squatters were employed. The settlements were amorphous, exhibited little evidence of planning, lacked community centres but instead were a collection of accreted, individually settled, properties. Many of the plots are large, terraced houses are for the most part absent, and the houses do not conform to any single plan or style type, rather they are individualistic and pragmatic adaptations and combinations of vernacular traditions influenced by various architectural fashions. These settlements acted as the foci for settlement growth driven by the development of the coke-fired iron industry and the increasing scale of the coal industry in the 19th century, even spawning one new industrial town, Cinderford. Consequently during the 19th century the haphazardly developed housing stock of previous centuries was added to by industrialist-sponsored rows of cottages and commercial developments.

INDUSTRIAL HAMLETS IN DEAN AND THE LANCASHIRE/WESTMORLAND BORDER

Another form of industrial settlement within the Forest of Dean area was the industrial hamlet. This was usually a subsidiary settlement of medieval origin within a manor and/or parish. Often situated in a steep valley with excellent provision for water power, they had become a focus for water-powered enterprises by the 17th century; Lydbrook and Redbrook are classic examples of such settlements. Both these settlements had excellent communications via the rivers Wye and Severn to Bristol, and this is reflected in Redbrook's late 17th-century incarnation as an adjunct to Bristol's copper industry. Here, and at similar sites, an increasing number of mills strung out along a valley acted as nuclei for settlement growth. The mill sites were valuable locations and as one enterprise failed so the mill sites were taken up and adapted to new purposes. Thus many sites went through a succession of uses as, for example, grist mills, fulling mills, iron forges, copper works and paper works.[13]

In the north Lancashire/Westmorland border area too is a group of settlements that can best be described in terms of their post-medieval evolution as industrial hamlets: Galgate, Holme Mills, Milnthorpe and Carnforth. Milnthorpe in particular shares many features with settlements like Lydbrook and Redbrook, though differences in geomorphology ensured that it lacked the valley-based ribbon development exhibited by the Dean settlements. Milnthorpe is situated on the present A6, the former turnpike road and coach route from Lancaster northwards. It is widely known as Westmorland's only port, being close to the mouth of the River Bela as it enters Morecambe Bay. Milnthorpe was a hamlet in the parish of Heversham and its medieval origins are somewhat given away by its name. It already appears to have had some importance by the end of the Middle Ages, since both a market and fair were held there. A water-powered bloomsmithy was established in Milnthorpe between 1650 and 1655.[14] By c. 1716 the bloomsmithy site had become a paper mill. Later in the 18th century two cotton mills were erected, one of which had also been converted to a paper mill by 1777, with the other having burnt down by 1816.[15] Only one paper mill existed in 1860 and by the end of the 19th century this had been

FIGURE 2.   The late 18th-century silk mill at Galgate; the 19th-century mill is in the background.

converted into a comb mill which employed about 70 people in 1912.[16] Throughout the 18th and early 19th centuries Milnthorpe continued to act as an entrepôt for Westmorland, holding goods in warehouses for transhipment to towns like Kendal. The port ceased to operate in the mid 19th century after the construction of the viaducts which enabled the Furness Railway to link with the London and North Western Railway (L&NW).

As in Milnthorpe, it was the presence of medieval water mills that acted as an attraction to industry at Galgate. Galgate is also a settlement on the present A6, taking its name from this route that was known as the Galloway *gata* throughout the medieval period. A hamlet appears to have been known by the name Galgate within the township of Ellel, south of Lancaster, as early as 1605.[17] Archaeological evidence suggests occupation in the area, perhaps associated with a tannery as early as the 14th century.[18] By *c.* 1912 Galgate was described as a considerable, important and populous village. Its growth appears to have been directly attributable to the establishment of a silk mill there in 1792 and claimed by Pevsner, erroneously, to be the oldest surviving one in England.[19] It is one of a number of silk spinning mills established in the Lancaster area in the late 18th and early 19th centuries (Fig. 2).

During the 19th century two more silk mills were added to it and a cotton mill was also erected, though this enterprise had failed and the mill had been pulled down by 1895.[20] In 1912 silk spinning was said to employ 300 people within the township of Ellel, or about 20% of the population, whilst many others were claimed to work in the Ellel Crag limestone quarry, although, interestingly, the VCH asserted that in 1911 the majority of the inhabitants of Galgate were employed in agriculture.[21]

Galgate was chosen as the base of a silk-spinning enterprise because it had the site of a corn mill of medieval origin which could be converted. The site lay adjacent to the Turnpike road. More importantly it was planned in 1790 to build a canal from Lancaster to Preston that would pass through Galgate. Indeed, when the Lancaster Canal opened in 1797, the opening ceremony included a symbolic exchange of limestone from Lancaster for coal from Preston which took place at the Galgate wharves.[22] The significance of Galgate was later recognized by the establishment of an L&NW railway station there which may have stimulated further growth. The importance of industry to the growth of Galgate in the 19th century has ensured that the settlement today has a quasi-urban character, as it has a number of terraces of industrial workers' housing.

Three miles to the south-east of Milnthorpe lies Holme Mills, a hamlet of the township and chapelry of Holme. In 1819 the Lancaster Canal section to Kendal via Holme was opened. Adjacent to the canal were two linen mills, established in the later 18th century on the approximate site of a medieval corn mill.[23] Sometime before 1860 the mill was partially destroyed by fire and linen manufacture ended, but the mill was rebuilt and converted to cocoa-mat and matting production. In 1912, 200 people were employed in this endeavour.[24] The effect of the canal and the subsequent opening of the linen mill is to some extent reflected in the population development of Holme in the 19th century. In 1811 the township had 283 inhabitants, within ten years this leapt to 420 and by 1851 had increased to 1,154.[25] Much of this new population appears to have been housed in the wholly new settlement of Holme Mills which grew up around the linen mill.

Carnforth, north of Lancaster, was a hamlet of Warton, a failed medieval borough. It existed in the medieval period when it may have been, like Ellel, a centre of pottery production. By the 18th century Carnforth appears to have been a sizeable settlement with about 40 resident families. It seems to have been a relatively impoverished settlement, however, since most houses were thatched, many were single storey and at least one was heated by an open hearth.[26] Its main claim to any prominence was that it lay along the Lancaster-Kendal turnpike road, the modern A6. In 1792 Carnforth became a settlement on the Lancaster Canal. This stimulated production from local gravel pits and may also have helped to encourage the mining of local haematite for paint, a venture which met with only limited success.[27] The real expansion of Carnforth did not start, however, until 1857 when it became a junction for the Furness Railway with the Lancaster-Carlisle Railway, the latter becoming the L&NW in 1861.[28]

These transport links made Carnforth a prime site for the establishment of a new industrial enterprise. In 1865 an ironworks was erected there, which by 1873 consisted of three blast furnaces and two Bessemer steel converters. The works continued until 1929.[29] The ironworks remained the primary employer in the area, though the railway further stimulated gravel production and by 1912 a blouse factory had opened which employed 140 people, 'mostly girls' and presumably the daughters, sisters and wives of the ironworkers. The impact of the ironworks can be clearly seen in the census figures for Carnforth. Between 1821 and 1851 the population remained remarkably stable at around 295; by 1861, following the arrival of the railway, it had increased to 393; by 1871 it was 1,091; and by 1901, 3,040.[30] The large workforce requirement of the ironworks ensured that Carnforth grew much larger than the other settlements under consideration and consequently it did achieve urban status in 1895.[31]

All four settlements grew in the 19th century with Milnthorpe and Carnforth achieving administrative and political independence, although Galgate and Holme Mills did not. For their growth they depended on one or two primary industries. They are all nucleated settlements with both Holme Mills and Galgate being restricted in size by the cost of land the mill owners had to purchase to erect workers' housing. In the early 19th century houses were built by the mill owners at Galgate and it seems also at Holme Mills for their workforce. At Carnforth both the railway and the ironworks built workers' housing in the late 19th century, though the majority of the housing was built as private developments of terraces of through-passage houses.[32] At Milnthorpe the more gradual development of the settlement, and indeed its commercial decline from the mid 19th century with the closure of the port and the decline of water-powered mills, ensured that 19th-century terraces are absent. Rows of 19th-century cottages are present, but they are accretions of often individually built dwellings infilling restricted spaces. The only evidence of the effect of past industry on the fabric of the settlement are the many former warehouses.

Aside from housing, industry brought other features into the settlements. None of them had any provision for worship before the 19th century. Nonconformist chapels were established at Galgate, Carnforth and Milnthorpe. An Anglican church was built in Milnthorpe in 1838. Holme had a church erected in 1839 which also served Holme Mills, and Carnforth's church was completed in 1873. Galgate, Carnforth and Milnthorpe all had gasworks established in the 19th century.

These four settlements all grew from hamlets lying close to other settlements to which they were subordinate in the local settlement hierarchy. Each had early mill sites and/or other associations with medieval industries. Industrial activity enabled each to grow into nucleated settlements with characteristics distinct from neighbouring non-industrial settlements. Like Lydbrook and Redbrook in Gloucestershire, they all benefited from communication links, three were on the Lancaster Canal, three on the Lancaster-Kendal turnpike road and all lay close to the L&NW railway. Milnthorpe was the most distinct in that it grew earlier as a result of water-powered industries and went into decline by the mid 19th century. In this way it was more similar to the industrial hamlets of west Gloucestershire.

CONCLUSION

As a settlement type industrial hamlets are very different in character to the squatter settlements of west Gloucestershire. The contrasts are primarily a result of the differences in industrial activity and the way in which it was organized and the nature of the land holding prior to the development of the settlement. The comparison of these different settlement types indicates that a typology of post-medieval industrial rural settlements based on readily identifiable criteria could be compiled and that it would provide a useful model for studying the development of such settlements. It is clear that industrialization was the major driving force in the development of new, and in the radical alteration of established, rural settlements during the post-medieval period. By the onset of the 21st century all the settlements considered in this paper had lost their dependence on industry as a *raison d'être*. The squatter settlements of west Gloucestershire had become the desirable addresses for executives working in Bristol and Newport, and the industrial hamlets of the Lancashire/Westmorland border the preferred abodes of the now largely de-industrialized area's single largest employer, Lancaster University.

Richard Newman, Victoria House, 6 Police Square, Milnthorpe, Cumbria LA7 7PY, UK

NOTES

[1] Newman, in prep.
[2] Porter 1978, 1.
[3] Newman 1988, 369.
[4] Ibid.
[5] Ibid., 177.
[6] Vince 1977.
[7] Newman 1988, 371.
[8] Newman 1983.
[9] Hart 1995.
[10] Newman 1988, 372.
[11] Ibid.
[12] Newman 1988, 375.
[13] Hart 1971.
[14] Phillips 1977.
[15] Bingham 1987; Newman 1999.
[16] Bulmer 1912, 536

[17] Farrer & Brownbill 1914, 96.
[18] LUAU 1996; Drury 1998.
[19] Pevesner 1969; Beedon 1991.
[20] LUAU 1996, 7.
[21] Bulmer 1912, 267–69; Farrer & Brownbill 1914, 96.
[22] Phillpotts 1993, 41.
[23] Somervell 1930, 99.
[24] Bulmer 1912, 485.
[25] Whellan 1860, 885.
[26] LUAU 1998, 108.
[27] Moseley *et al.* 1969; Ashmead & Peter 2000.
[28] Harris 1960.
[29] Newman 1999, 15.
[30] Farrer & Brownbill 1914, 166.
[31] Harris 1960.
[32] Harris 1960.

BIBLIOGRAPHY

Ashmead, R. & Peter, D. 2000, 'Warton Crag mines', *Keer to Kent* 43, 16.

Bingham, R. K. 1987, *The Chronicles of Milnthorpe*, Milnthorpe: Cicerone Press.

Breedon, R. E. 1991, 'Galgate silk mills: a study of the development of mill architecture', *Over-Wyre Historical Journal* 6, 39–48.

Bulmer, J. (ed.) 1912, *T Bulmer & Co's History Topography and Directory of Lancaster & District*, Preston: T. Snape & Co.

Drury, D. 1998, 'Archaeological Investigations at Tanhouse Holm Field, Galgate', *Contrebis* 23, 41–43.

Farrer, W. & Brownbill, J. (eds) 1914, *The Victoria County History of the County of Lancaster* 8 (VCH).

Hart, C. 1971, *The Industrial History of Dean. With an Introduction to its Industrial Archaeology*, Newton Abbott: David & Charles.

Hart, C. 1995, *The Forest of Dean. New History 1550–1818*, Stroud: Alan Sutton Publishing Ltd.

Harris, A. 1960, 'Carnforth, 1840–1900: the rise of a north Lancashire town', *Transactions of the Historical Society of Lancashire and Cheshire* 112, 105–19.

LUAU 1996, 'Land off Church Lane, Lancashire, Assessment Report' (unpublished client report).

LUAU 1998, 'Lancashire Extensive Urban Archaeological Survey, Assessment Report' (unpublished client report).

Moseley, C. M., Ashmead, P. & Cumpsty, P. 1969, *The Metalliferous Mines of the Arnside-Carnforth Districts of Lancashire and Westmorland*, Northern Cavern and Mine Research Society Individual Survey Series 3.

Newman, R. 1983, 'The effect of orcharding and the cider industry on the landscape of West Gloucestershire *c* 1600–1800', *Transactions of the Woolhope Naturalists Field Club* 54, 202–14.

Newman, R. 1988, 'The Development of the Rural Landscape of West Gloucestershire *c* 1550–1800' (unpublished PhD thesis, University of Wales).

Newman, R. 1999, 'Iron working and mining enterprises', *Keer to Kent* 38, 14–15.

Newman, R. in prep., 'Industrialisation at the margins: industrial origins and development along the Lancashire-Westmorland border', in Nevell, M. (ed.) *From Farmer to Factory Owner: The Archaeology of Industrialisation in North West England*.

Pevsner, N. 1969, *The Buildings of England. North Lancashire*, Harmondsworth: Penguin.

Phillips, C. B. 1977, 'William Wright: Cumbrian Ironmaster', *Transactions of the Lancashire and Cheshire Antiquarian Society* 79, 34–45.

Phillpotts, R. 1993, *Building the Lancaster Canal*, London: Blackwater Books.

Porter, J. 1980, *The Making of the Central Pennines*, Ashbourne: Moorland Publishing Company Ltd.

Somervell, J. 1930, *Water-Power Mills of South Westmorland*, Preston: Titus Wilson & Son.

Whellan, W. 1860, *The History and Topography of the Counties of Cumberland and Westmoreland*, Pontefract: W. Whellan & Co.

Vince, A. G. 1977, 'Newent Glasshouse', *CRAAGS Occasional Papers* 2.

LANDSCAPE, ECONOMY AND IDENTITY: A STUDY IN THE ARCHAEOLOGY OF INDUSTRIALIZATION

By DAVID GWYN

INTRODUCTION

This paper sets out an approach to the archaeology of a particular locality in north Wales, in which landscape evidence for the past is considered in the light of economic organization and social identity. It goes on to suggest ways in which such an approach can contribute to a broader understanding of historic landscape and society.

The locality chosen for study is Moel Tryfan, an area of upland historically exploited for both industry and agriculture, in the modern-day county of Gwynedd. It is roughly triangular in plan. To its north-east it falls steeply to the rural defile of the Gwyrfai valley. To its south it falls to the Nantlle valley, an area which in the 19th century saw intense industrialization as slate veins were opened out, and where recognizably industrial settlements, the villages of Pen y Groes, Tal y Sarn, Nantlle and Drws y Coed, came into being. To the west it slopes more gently to the Arfon plain; it is with this area, as well as the upland itself, that we are concerned (Fig. 1).

It is a remarkable survival. From the Lôn Wen, the 'white lane' which winds through the purple heather of the unenclosed moorland, the prospect is of the Irish Sea, and, spread out below, the Foryd, a sheltered bay at the mouth of the Menai straits, not far from Edward I's castle and town of Caernarfon. On the fertile lands near the coast is Glynllifon (SH 457554), home of the Lords Newborough, with its mausoleum and toy forts, built to discourage George Washington from invading. Around these are the larger yeoman farms, yielding, the higher up the slope one's eye travels, to progressively smaller cottages and smallholdings, until eventually cultivation ceases altogether. Twisting up through the tiny fields in corkscrew curves reminiscent of Colorado or Darjeeling is the trackbed of the North Wales Narrow Gauge Railway and its quarry tributaries. Here and there the topography defeated even the sanguine engineer who surveyed this route, forcing him to revert to the traditional counter-balanced inclines with their familiar slate drumhouses at the summit, until by one means or another the rails reached the quarry stackyard. The skyline is dominated by the enormous tips of rubble which are a feature of the slate industry (Fig. 2).

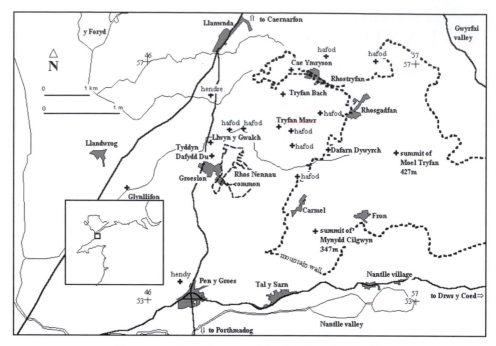

FIGURE 1.   Location map: Moel Tryfan, Gwynedd.

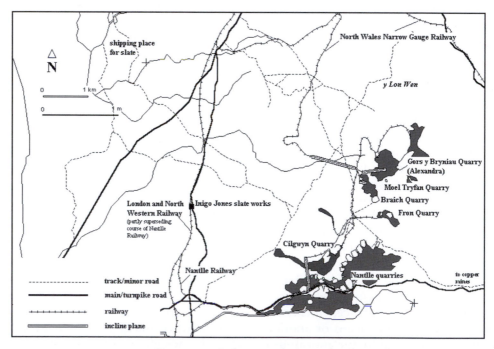

FIGURE 2.   Industry and transport.

The quarries of north Wales dominated the production of roofing material and architectural slabs world-wide in the 19th century, and attracted substantial levels of capital. Yet their context was always rural, and nowhere more so than here, within a dual economy of quarry and small-holding. In the words of one of its historians, '. . . a good number of hands skilled in gauging rock and wielding chisel and mallet could also perform with a long scythe in one of the bands that on July mornings would, standing in line, swathe their way through hilly hay fields.'[1]

As Britain underwent industrialization, economic dislocation, spiralling corn prices and technical innovation forced sudden changes to the margins of cultivation, just as they also located new industries in remote areas. The relationship between the agricultural and the technical economy has been little investigated,[2] but what is clear is that in many places mines, mills or quarries came into being or developed only because it was also possible to extend cultivation into hitherto marginal areas. In Cardiganshire, the revival of lead mining in the 19th century sustained the pastoral economy of the uplands.[3] Similar settlements existed in the coal-producing areas of south Wales, in the lead-mining areas of the Pennines and in the early textile industry of Lancashire and Cheshire.[4]

Moel Tryfan therefore retains many of the characteristics of a once common type of landscape, a type which, because it bears the mark of agriculture as well as industrialization, should furnish evidence for both continuity and disjunction. Recent studies have stressed environmental continuity, emphasizing the role of topography in use of resources, or of land-ownership,[5] or seeking the origins of industrialization in, for instance, the weakness of trade guilds.[6] For this reason, Moel Tryfan is likely to repay study. Furthermore, a wealth of documentation survives both about the area's changing economy and also about the ways in which those who dwelt within this landscape lived their lives and were themselves conscious of change. This makes it possible to set the written record against the archaeological resource in an attempt to establish whether or not they are congruent with each other, and what interactions might become possible between them.

LANDSCAPE

Location

Moel Tryfan is situated in the modern county of Gwynedd, in the former county of Caernarvonshire, and the historic *cantref* (hundred) of Arfon in north Wales. It is divided between the communities, formerly the civil parishes, of Llandwrog, Llanwnda and Betws Garmon.

Land-tenure

Place-name evidence indicates the focus of settlement in the medieval period — *hendre* and *hendy* on the plain (hendre = 'old township', hendy = 'old [principal] house'), the *hafodydd* on the slopes (hafod = 'summer pasture') — implying enclosure to about the 700ft contour, where by the 18th century the mountain wall defined the common land. Here the farmers grazed their sheep, undisturbed by the Crown as the nominal owner, and here also were the slate quarries of Ochr y Cilgwyn, which had been exploited since before the Conquest by local partnerships. A smaller patch of common also survived at Rhos Nennau, at the break of slope.

By the mid 18th century, when documentation becomes sufficiently comprehensive to permit a detailed picture of land-tenure in the area, these holdings formed part of various gentry estates — Vaynol, Bryncir, Garnons, Cefnamwlch and Bryntirion.[7] They exercised little control over their properties, and several of them were to die out or sell up in the later 18th or early 19th century.

A more important family were the Wynns (ennobled as the Lords Newborough in 1776), whose Glynllifon demesne lay nearby. But their largest estates lay elsewhere in north Wales, and in local terms they were hardly more active than their neighbours. In 1745 John Wynn obtained a Crown lease to exploit the quarries, but made very little attempt to do so.[8] Had he actively exploited the permission, he and his descendants might have played a leading role in the development of the slate industry. As it was, a clash of commercial and social rivalries ensued, in which the Crown turned its back on the Wynns, and in 1800 leased out the quarries to a syndicate of Caernarfon businessmen, of which the leading light was a lawyer, John Evans.[9]

The situation was further complicated by the fact that, around this time, younger sons of the farms on the lower slopes, many of whom were already working in the quarries, began to settle beyond the mountain wall. Already by the mid 18th century landlords, tenants and freeholders in the area had begun the process of encroachment on the commons by carving adjuncts of existing farms on the common land. Complex traditions governed the right of encroachment; a tenant-farmer might find that his landlord claimed an encroachment the farmer had made, but an encroachment could not be claimed by an estate if it did not directly adjoin a part of the estate. It therefore became traditional to leave a narrow 'buffer zone' between the two, and whilst this might itself be swallowed up by the estate, the encroachment itself was regarded as the farmer's property outright. By custom, no such buffer zone was needed between old encroachment and new encroachment.

A different phase was initiated in 1798 when one William Edwards enclosed a plot of four acres on the moor, despite objections from Squire Lloyd of Tryfan Bach. Over the next twenty-five years much of the surviving common land was covered with small enclosures, some adjoining each other, some completely separate, some springing up along the trackways with little or no land attached to them, evolving gradually into the villages of Rhostryfan, Rhosgadfan, Carmel and Fron.[10]

Matters reached a head in 1826–27, when Lord Newborough's bill to enclose the commons was thrown out by a Parliament of landowners following representations by the quarrymen themselves — not without some deft wire-pulling by John Evans, who had no desire to see the land around the quarries he leased pass from the Crown.[11]

The Commissioners of Woods and Forests acknowledged a *fait accompli* by giving the commoners the option of buying their smallholdings for a price that would have represented no more than a year or two's rent for a tenancy, or else paying a quitrent.[12] The pattern of landownership thereby established has survived to this day,

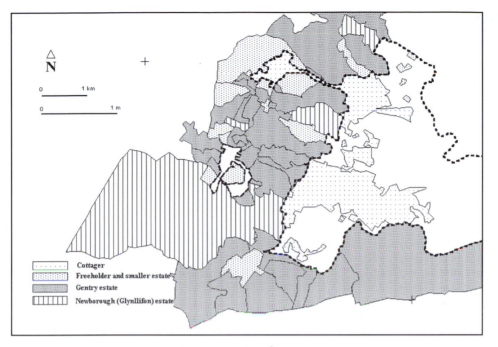

FIGURE 3. Land-tenure.

with the Crown as the largest single landowner within the area but with hundreds of pockets of non-crown land (Fig. 3).

The other major development came in the aftermath of the opening of the national railway network at the foot of the slope in 1866, when Lord Newborough released land on Grugan farm for building, under strict conditions, in the immediate vicinity of the station.[13] The result was the neat rows which make up the village of Groeslon — Glynllifon, Grugan, Gladstone and Rathbone terraces — and one of the area's two Anglican churches.

Building typology and spatial distribution

The house of greatest social consequence within the area is Glynllifon, where in 1751 Sir John Wynn rebuilt a house of *c*. 1600 as 'a moderate sized brick mansion', to be rebuilt again between 1836 and 1848.[14] One other had pretensions to gentility — Tryfan Mawr, the home of the Griffiths family, a 17th-century structure with an 18th-century house to the north.

Amongst the farms and cottages, the variation in the size of holdings is reflected in the size of dwellings. Only very rarely is polite influence visible — as at Llwyn y Gwalch (SH 4745 5638), a 55-acre holding, where the house windows are set in a lancet recess. The adjacent farmhouse, Tyddyn Dafydd Du on the Cefnamwlch estate (SH 4747 5610), is a compact double-fronted 18th-century house on a 21-acre holding. Within the mountain wall, the dominant pattern is the *crog-lofft* (a two-cell dwelling,

FIGURE 4.   The patrician landscape; Lord Newborough's seat at Glynllifon.

FIGURE 5.   The tenant-farmer landscape; Llwyn y Gwalch farmhouse on the Bryntirion estate.

in which one of the cells is divided in two by a floor at eaves level), frequently with lateral extensions, and a variety of free-standing structures. This type of dwelling was the dominant vernacular in both purely agricultural regions and in proto-industrial areas of north Wales, and examples continued to be constructed until the mid 19th century.[15]

Other domestic building types are also common. Here and there, short two-up-two-down terraces stand by themselves in small enclosures, removed from other buildings — the work of speculative builders who in the 1860s and 1870s decided that there was more money to be made out of house-building than out of keeping sheep. More substantial houses are to be found in the villages, in some cases adorned with decorative ironwork, the dwellings of shop-keepers, ministers or of quarry stewards.

Variants are to be found in the villages of Rhosgadfan, where a curious pattern of houses derived from the *crog-lofft* tradition but in a later 19th-century idiom survives alongside a road going up a hillside. Radiating out on one side of the road are a series of contour lane-ways, with one such dwelling at the point of junction (SH 4985 5775). Possibly these were intended to be part of a larger speculative development, in which only the first in what was meant to be a longer row was ever constructed.

Another variant is the *ty botal inc* ('ink-bottle house') at Rhostryfan (SH 5052 5698). The pyramid-roofed central chimney house derives in Welsh terms from Renaissance gentry dwellings,[16] but it also proved an effective way of cramming four families into a small space, one in each corner, whilst preserving the appearance of a *cottage ornée*, a style used by the Newborough estate.[17]

This particular building is also unusual in being built of coursed granite. Otherwise, building material is almost invariably stone gathered off the fields, except in Groeslon, where there is more use of brick, such as the fine range of shops centred on 'Gladstone House', with its polychromatic patterns (SH 4747 5587).

ECONOMY

Agriculture

Even by the standards of 18th- and 19th-century Wales, few of the farms were large. Llwyn y Gwalch at the foot of Moel Tryfan was amongst the largest, having not only a farm-yard, as an adjunct of arable farming, but also a mill. Most holdings include a pig-sty, and sometimes an outbuilding large enough for one animal. Those of more than 25 acres tend to have a barn and cow-house.[18] The small-holdings were on a lesser scale still; the 'humble petition' drawn up on the cottagers' behalf in 1826 emphasized that their dwellings lay on parts considered too wild for cultivation, 'but which your petitioners by incessant labour early and late during their other hours at the Quarries have so far cleared of stones, manured and cultivated as to make them produce Potatoes, in many cases slight crops of Corn and in some cases afford the means of supporting one or two cows'.[19] Eighty years later, the story was much the same:

> The land was poor . . . It had to be constantly cosseted and cared for, or else it would revert to soggy marsh choked with reeds . . . There was no money to be made out of it, but it helped feed us: butter, eggs, bacon and buttermilk, excellent buttermilk it was too, which my mother could sell at eight quarts for a penny.[20]

FIGURE 6. The cottagers' landscape: Ty'n Llwyn near Rhosgadfan.

FIGURE 7. Free trade and yellow brick; Gladstone House in Groeslon.

Few of the encroachment holdings would have been capable of supporting a family by itself, and in practically every case some of its members worked in the quarries. For this reason, the agricultural economy fared badly as the slate industry declined, particularly after the Wall Street Crash. Difficulties in obtaining dole for anyone who had even small amounts of land led to many small-holdings being abandoned in the 1930s. Many of the dwellings associated with them are now either derelict, or second homes, or have been bought up by incomers, attracted by the low prices. Unemployment remains high, job opportunities few and the housing stock poor.

Industry

The industrial development of the area in the 18th century was driven not by the patricians but by groups of working quarrymen-farmers. In 1738 the agent of the Penrhyn estate, where West Indian sugar profits were later to be reinvested in the slate industry with spectacular results, complained that the quarrymen of Ochr y Cilgwyn were underselling them in the London markets.[21] The available evidence suggests a thriving local slate industry, based around family units,[22] generating profits which were reinvested elsewhere in Caernarvonshire, Anglesey and Merioneth. Methusalem Jones (1731–1810), born at Tyddyn Dafydd Du, became tenant at Cefn Eithin, a farm nearby, but also worked as a quarryman in Cilgwyn, as a publican in Caernarfon, where he became a burgess, as a housebuilder in Amlwch on Anglesey, when the copper mines were in their glory, and as a shipper at the Foryd, where Cilgwyn slate was dispatched to London and elsewhere.[23] Much of this independence, and freedom to control when and how one worked, survived long after capitalized partnerships began to take over the quarries from 1800 onwards, and drove many a quarry manager to despair.

From 1800 onwards the initiative passed to partnerships and ultimately limited companies from outside the area, which took over not only Cilgwyn but also the quarries which had been opened elsewhere on the commons — Braich, Fron, Moel Tryfan and Gors y Bryniau. This made possible levels of investment that would have been beyond Methusalem and his friends. The quarries soon developed from hillside benches into deep pits, which required machinery, in the shape of railways, horse-whims, pumps, and the water wheels and wind mills to drive them. These made their appearance in the early years of the 19th century, followed by steam from around mid century, to pump, wind and above all to power cutting mills. Electricity made its way to the quarries after the establishment of the North Wales Power and Traction Company's hydro-plant at Cwm Dyli, in 1906.

Though the quarries continued to expand until the 1890s, the economics of the following century were harsher, and the financial collapse of 1929–30 dealt the area a blow from which it never recovered. The processing of slate, now brought in from mid Wales, continues at the Inigo Jones slab mill near Groeslon (SH 4708 5513) and some sporadic quarrying went on into the 1970s, but the industry had long been a pale shadow of its former self. Much of the working was in the black economy, with informal partnerships either quarrying in the pits themselves or re-working the rubble heaps and buildings for useable slate rock, leaving their mark in form of their tiny

FIGURE 8.   Near Fron, showing the course of the quarry railway and road. (Courtesy of Gwynedd Archives)

FIGURE 9.   In primitive shelters such as this, quarrymen reprocessed slate rubble; Cilgwyn Quarry.

irregular huts, and the piles of fine trimming waste around them. A reduction in the price of timber, which made it possible to use smaller roofing slates, made it worth looking again at much of the rock which had been flung to one side in earlier days. Higher building standards which required damp-course slates also came to their rescue. In many respects, the industry was reverting to its 18th-century characteristics, with small gangs of quarrymen taking over where limited companies failed.

Transport

The oldest transport routes in the immediate area long predate the Industrial period. An old drover's road which crossed Moel Tryfan also connected the copper mines at Drws y Coed with the harbour at the Foryd, and may have been used to ship ore in remote times. The Dafarn Dywyrch (SH 5013 5628, 'thatched tavern', though it had been slated time out of mind) was strategically placed to slake any thirst.[24] Pack horses, carrying perhaps 64 slates, picked their way down the slopes and along this road to the Foryd until well into the 19th century,[25] overlapping with more sophisticated means of transport. In 1796 the 560 quarrymen of Moel Tryfan and the Nantlle valley depended on no less than 183 carters, carrying perhaps 18cwt at a time, using either narrow- or broad-wheeled single-axle carts.[26] This situation prevailed until the railways arrived.

The railways fall into several distinct types. The 3ft 6in. gauge Nantlle Railway of 1828 sent out branches to Cilgwyn quarry (post-1841) and Fron (1868), operated by horse or counter-balance incline. This was partly superseded by a conventional locomotive-worked line between 1866 and 1872. A 2ft gauge passenger-carrying branch line was built in 1878–79, reaching Bryngwyn on gradients of 1/35 and curves as tight as $33\frac{3}{4}$ chains radius, whence even steeper branches led to the quarries.[27]

As with other aspects of the industrialization of the area, transport technology eventually turned full circle. By 1935 the volume of traffic generated by the quarries had fallen so low, and rolling stock was in such a poor condition, that a slate wagon was taking two and a half days to reach the standard-gauge railway from Cilgwyn quarry. A petrol lorry could do the job in twenty minutes, and the quarries reverted to road transport.

IDENTITY

Facts and fictions

Moel Tryfan and its environs produced some remarkable writers of prose fiction, and a number of able historians. Richard Hughes Williams, 'Dic Tryfan', (1878?–1915), a pioneer of the short story, published *Straeon y Chwarel* ('Quarry Tales') in the early years of the 20th century.[28] Also from Rhosgadfan was Kate Roberts (1891–1985), a Cilgwyn quarryman's daughter, one of the finest Welsh novelists of the 20th century, whose writing returns time and time again to her formative years at Cae'r Gors. Kate Roberts in particular, though she took as her theme the 'square mile' of memory and of the daily round,[29] touched the universal themes of loss and of hope, of endurance

" Mae'n caru ei wlad, mae'n Gymro pur,
Wrth drin y graig hefo'r ebill dur."

FIGURE 10.   Craft, skill and nation: 'A Welshman pure, he loves his land / As he works the rock with his drill of steel'. From Dic Tryfan, *Straeon y Chwarel*.

and of aging, in a sparse narrative in which the influence of both Maupassant and Chekhov is evident. The name she gave her autobiographical writings was *Y Lôn Wen*, 'The White Lane' which runs from Pen y Groes in Nantlle across the commons to the Gwyrfai valley.[30]

A different literary tradition is represented by the Revd William Hobley (1858–1933), whose *Hanes Methodistiaeth Arfon* ('The History of Methodism in Arfon'), published in stages from 1910 to 1924, is a detailed account of when, where, how and by whom each Calvinist chapel in the area was established, and who worshipped there, drawn from the chapels' own records or from the *Drysorfa*, the Methodist magazine. Here and there, tales from the unredeemed world found their way into Hobley's narrative, such as Griffith Jones Tyddyn Heilyn sneaking into the pub cellar to tap the barrels through a straw, but for the most part he studiously avoided anything that could cause embarrassment to his neighbours.[31] Much of our knowledge of farming practice and custom comes from the writings of Gilbert Williams (1874–1966), a primary school headmaster. Williams was the local historian through and through — Carmel held less interest for him than Rhosgadfan, and the wider world he completely ignored. Yet even as a youth he had started questioning his older neighbours about the encroachments of the very early 19th century, and about traditions that went back much further.[32]

Not only do sources such as these provide the historical details which are otherwise missing in a vernacular landscape, but are themselves testament to a strong sense of identity, and of immanence within place. Yet just as the landscape itself evolved, so this identity also was fluid and multi-faceted, open to challenge from without and within.

Contestation

When in 1798 William Edwards prevailed over Squire Lloyd of Tryfan Bach, and was allowed to retain occupancy of his enclosure on the moor unmolested, he defiantly named it Cae Ymryson, 'field of dispute' (SH 4944 5762).[33] The landscape of Moel Tryfan was in this sense a contested one from the very start, and was to be fought over again in the 1820s, when the cottagers resisted Lord Newborough's enclosure bill. The settlements were, or came to be, acts of defiance in themselves. Their own traditions and codes, already evident in the rules governing enclosure in the 18th century, marked them off from the authority of the great house. Furthermore, the comradeship of quarrymen, and the reliance on neighbours at harvest time, sustained an identity implicitly contrasted with the rentier culture of the nucleated settlements, and with transactional relationships based on speculation and property-as-income. In the village of Groeslon, at the foot of the slope, capital is apparent not only in the ample shops themselves but also in the purchased bricks of which they are built, unlike the stones gathered from the fields which went into the cottage walls. Even the names of the terraces here — 'Gladstone' and 'Rathbone' — proclaim the virtues of free trade,[34] whereas the cottages endlessly compound the words for 'moor', 'bog', 'sheepwalk', and 'mountain'.

Yet the landscape was contested within the culture of the quarry-cottagers as well. When in 1837 temperance enthusiasts talked a young couple out of serving beer at their wedding, the barrel that had been set aside for the feast was ceremonially carted up in a quarry wagon to where Saint Twrog was reputedly buried on the mountain top, and there interred. From this time forth, teetotal weddings were the rule.[35] The amusements which beguiled the first generation of cottagers, the harp-playing and the dancing in the fields,[36] gave way long before the end of the 19th century, here as elsewhere in Wales, to the narrow rule of the deacons, and to the stern cadences of visiting preachers.

Religion

John Jones asked where the chapel was to be, and Eleazer Owen replied that it was for him to say. 'Well, if that is so,' said he, 'then in this place the chapel shall be,' striking the ground with his stick. And where he struck the ground, there the chapel was built. And this was in the year 1826.[37]

Thus Hobley describes how, in Mosaic fashion, the great preacher John Jones of Tal y Sarn decided on the site of Carmel chapel, from which the village is named. Three meeting houses had been built by the following year — doubtless plain and unadorned structures, as early chapels were.[38] Thereafter increasingly substantial and architecturally sophisticated places of worship continued to be built, even after the last Welsh religious revival, in 1904.[39] They, and their schoolrooms, vestries and caretaker's houses, bear witness not only to the faith of their congregations, but also to the surplus which made it possible to pay for them, and even, paradoxically, to the consumerism of the later 19th century, evident in their stylized façades and lavish interiors.[40] The culture of Protestant Nonconformity — the old dissent of the Baptists and the Independents, the new dissent of the Wesleyans and the Calvinistic Methodists — was genuinely popular, sustained and largely accepted by the great majority of the population. Yet tensions and ambiguities were present in the religious culture also. Kate Roberts's best–known novel, *Traed mewn Cyffion*, 'Feet in Chains', opens in 1880 with the young wife, Jane Gruffydd, listening to a sermon on the slopes of Moel Tryfan, delivered from the back of a cart because the chapel cannot accommodate all who have come to listen; yet by the early years of the 20th century she, or the narrative voice which is rarely entirely separate from her consciousness, recognizes that things have changed:

> Their grandfathers and grandmothers — the pioneers of the Nonconformist causes scattered on the hillsides — had a profound knowledge of theology. There was devotion and self-sacrifice in their religion. But the grandchildren had lost the spirit of devotion and there was little call for sacrifice. They continued to study theology, but only coldly, as something removed from their lives . . . The young were placated by calling Christ a Socialist. Yet this too was a matter for the intellect, not one of belief. Their interest moved from Christ the Redeemer to Christ the Example.[41]

Politics

The changing nature of religious identity informed patterns of political belief and activity. The commoners cheerfully resorted to riot, destruction of property and sheep-maiming to further their aims in the early 19th century, but the nonconformist emphasis on respectability encouraged a temperate reformism, which found its voice in the Liberal party. The Social Gospel of the later 19th century, with its emphasis on the Sermon on the Mount rather than on the Pauline Epistles, increasingly fed into the work of the Independent Labour Party.

Not surprisingly, given both the semi-independent nature of slate quarrying and the independence which owning one's own small-holding conferred, trade unionism was particularly militant. There were disputes in Moel Tryfan in 1892, 1896, 1899 and 1906, and at Gors y Bryniau (Alexandra) from November 1913 to March 1914.[42]

Craft, skill and technology

The identity the commoners forged for themselves, their independence and political and religious radicalism, derived not only from the freedoms which being the owner

FIGURE 11. Men and machine; William Williams on the footplate of *Lilla* with rubble wagons at Cilgwyn Quarry. (Courtesy of Gwynedd Archives)

of one's own soil conferred but also from the traditional freedom of the slate quarry worker. I use the ungendered word advisedly, since there is evidence that the women of Moel Tryfan were economically involved as 'masters' in the 1770s. It is likely, though unproven, that women managed the pack animals, and later the carting, an extremely lucrative trade. With the railways, this changed; in an increasingly technological world, the quarries came to be managed by men. Women were expected to work the small-holdings; Kate Roberts records quarrymen's resentment if their wives even looked out for them on their way home, so complete had the separation of roles become.[43] The women in her fiction have no idea of what sort of place the quarry was, though they were expected to prepare the lunch tins, and to send their husbands out in a newly-bleached white fustian jacket.[44]

CONCLUSIONS

'Whatsoever then, he removes out of the state that Nature hath left it in, he hath mixed his labour with it, and joined to it something that is his own, and thereby makes it his property.' The words are Locke's,[45] but Jane Gruffydd says as much and more, as she pauses on the Lôn Wen to look over to the quarry, and its tip:

> . . . crawling down the mountain like an adder. From a distance, the slate waste looked good, shining in the sunlight. This was the quarry where Ifan's father had been killed. Who emptied the first rubble wagon over that tip-end there? He was in his grave by now, that was sure. And who would be the last to tip a load of rubble over the top?

> And what was the use of dreaming like this? There was something sad in the in the whole prospect, the quarry, the village and the mountain all mixed up together.[46]

Those who created and evolved this landscape invested not only their economic role in it, embodied in the quarryman pushing the wagon, but also their identity; even their lives — Jane's father-in-law is killed in the quarry. The richness of her intuited response contrasts with the arid concentration on material evidence for production which is the mark of much industrial archaeology.

This approach to landscape archaeology places the technical culture of economic change within a pattern of broader social change. As we have seen, it is from the poorer farms occupying the slopes, and not from the patrician sites on the best land, that there come the developments which shifted the economic margin and brought into being the colonies beyond the mountain wall, the quarries and the cottages. As is the nature of colonies, these display many of the salient characteristics of the landscape from which they came, exemplified in the vernacular character of their dwellings. As is also the nature of colonies, they in turn changed and enriched their originating settlements.

But a landscape archaeology of industrialization can and should move beyond the task of recording the material culture of a changing economy, important though that is. The archaeological and the written record are not alternative forms of evidence but are inextricably bound up with each other as cultural products; to consider them in their relation with each other makes possible an approach to the ways in which landscape and economy mediate identity. Landscape is actual space, but it is also discursive space, in which cultural and ideological priorities are expressed. Landscape features — a cottage, a field, a chapel, a quarry, a railway embankment — constitute elements of an infinitely complex pattern of economic organization; yet their significance can only be articulated if we acknowledge also the social discourses of identity — of being, belonging and alienation — which they mediate and by which they exist.

ACKNOWLEDGEMENTS

I would like to acknowledge the help and assistance of my wife Marian, of John Roberts, Gwynedd Archaeological Trust, of Judith Alfrey, Cadw: Welsh Historic Monuments, and of Dafydd Glyn Jones, Reader in Welsh at the University of Wales, Bangor. Thanks are also due to the members of my evening class in local history at Groeslon, who first made me think about the Moel Tryfan area. Diolch iddynt oll.

David Gwyn, Govannon Consultancy, Nant y Felin, Llanllyfni Road, Pen y Groes, Caernarfon, Gwynedd LL54 6LY, UK

NOTES

[1] Jones 1982, 19.
[2] Newell & Walker 1999, 1–14.
[3] Vaughan 1966, 247.
[4] Pollard 1997, 221–54.

[5] Alfrey & Clark 1993.
[6] Pollard 1995, 225–28.
[7] University of Wales, Bangor, Bangor MSS 9747.
[8] Caernarfon Record Office, XD2/12964.

[9] University of Wales, Bangor, Porth yr Aur MSS 27559.

[10] Williams 1983, 75–78.

[11] Dodds 1990, 78–79.

[12] Public Record Office CRES 2/1576, letters of John Williams to Office of Woods and Forests, 5 and 18 April 1827, UWB Bangor MSS 46, 118.

[13] CRO, XD2/6656–57, 6659.

[14] Royal Commission on Ancient and Historic Monuments of Wales 1960, 186.

[15] Smith 1988, 310–15.

[16] Smith 1988, 240–41.

[17] Exemplified in a row at Llandwrog and the house "'r Uncorn' ('one chimney') at Blaenau Ffestiniog.

[18] Alfrey 1999, 13–17.

[19] UWB, Porth yr Aur 13277.

[20] Roberts 1960, 29.

[21] UWB, Penrhyn 1967.

[22] In 1782, for instance, Cilgwyn quarry consisted of fourteen small pits. Apart from Cloddfa Cocsith, which was worked by one 'master' and three boys, all the others were worked by between four and twelve 'masters', some of them women, and an invariably smaller number of labourers and boys, a total of 128 persons (NLW, Glynllifon 84, 55–57v, 69v).

[23] Williams, Lewis 1987, 6–9. According to tradition, he was first man to learn of slate veins at Blaenau Ffestiniog, and this through supernatural revelation. The following day he walked there to open a quarry — an unusual example of an origin-myth for an industrial community.

[24] Richards 1970.

[25] UWB, Bangor MSS 46.

[26] Pritchard 1935, 88–89, 19, 42–44.

[27] Bradley 1992, 131–39, 186–87, 200, 262–63, 332–33.

[28] See Dictionary of Welsh Biography.

[29] The 'square mile' (milltir sgwar) is a phrase much used in Welsh to denote the area of the daily round, and more particularly of fiction set within it.

[30] Roberts 1960.

[31] Dictionary of Welsh Biography; Hobley 1910, 238.

[32] CRO, W. Gilbert Williams papers.

[33] CRO, X/WGW/8.

[34] W. E. Gladstone (1809–98), Liberal statesman; William Rathbone (1819–1902), businessman, philanthropist, Liberal MP for the county, 1880–95, shareholder in Moel Tryfan Quarry — Dictionary of Welsh Biography and pers. comm., Mrs Bridget Gledhill, Pwllfanogle.

[35] CRO, WGW/11/5, p. 52.

[36] Williams 1983.

[37] Hobley 1910, 241.

[38] Dodds 1990, 78.

[39] CRO, XM Maps 6162 21.

[40] Jones 1996, 50–130.

[41] Roberts 1936. Traed mewn cyffion = 'feet in stocks'; see Book of Job cap. XIII v. 27.

[42] Jones 1982, 199, 304–05.

[43] Roberts 1960, 34.

[44] Roberts 1924, 4.

[45] Locke 1690, bk II, cap. 5.

[46] A slightly different translation of this passage is to be found in Jones 1980, 22.

BIBLIOGRAPHY

Alfrey, J. & Clark, C. 1993, The Landscape of Industry: Patterns of Change in the Ironbridge Gorge, London and New York: Routledge.

Alfrey, J. 1999, 'A new look at conservation values', Heritage in Wales 12, 13–17.

Bradley, V. J. 1992, Industrial Locomotives of North Wales, London: Industrial Railway Society.

Dictionary of Welsh Biography 1955, London: Cymmrodorion.

Dodds A. H. 1990, The Industrial Revolution in North Wales, Wrexham: Bridge Books.

Hobley, W. 1910, Hanes Methodiastiaeth Arfon: Dosbarth Clynnog, Cyfarfod Misol Arfon.

Jones, A. 1996, Welsh Chapels, Stroud: Sutton.

Jones, J. I. 1980, Feet in Chains (trans. of Traed mewn Cyffion), Ealing: Corgi.

Jones, R. M. 1982, The North Wales Quarrymen 1874–1922, Cardiff: University of Wales Press.

Locke, J. 1690, Two Treatises of Civil Government bk II, cap. 5.

Newell, M. & Walker, J. 1999, Tameside in Transition, Ashton-under-Lyne: Tameside Metropolitan Borough Council.

Pollard, S. 1995, Marginal Europe, Oxford: Clarendon.

Pritchard, D. D. 1935, The Slate Industry of North Wales: A Study of the Changes in Economic Organization from 1780 to the Present Day (University of Wales MA thesis, 1935).

Roberts, K. 1936, Traed Mewn Cyffion, Aberystwyth: Gwasg Aberystwyth.

Roberts, K. 1960, Y Lôn Wen, Denbigh: Gwasg Gee.

Roberts, K. 1924, *Rhigolau Bywyd*, Aberystwyth, Gwasg Aberystwyth.

Royal Commission on Ancient and Historic Monuments of Wales 1960, *Inventory of Caernarvon-shire*, London: HMSO.

Smith, P. 1988, *Houses of the Welsh Countryside*, London: HMSO.

Vaughan, C. (Cledwyn Fychan) 1966, 'Lluestai Blaenrheidol', *Ceredigion*, 246–63.

Williams, W. G. 1983, *Moel Tryfan i'r Traeth*, Pen y Groes: Cyhoeddiadau Mei.

Williams, M. C., Lewis, M. J. T. 1987, *Pioneers of Ffestiniog Slate*, Penrhyndeudraeth, Snowdonia National Park.

Unpublished Sources

University of Wales Bangor
   Bangor MSS.
   Penrhyn MSS.
   Porth yr Aur MSS.
National Library of Wales
   Glynllifon 84.
   XD2 (Glynllifon papers).
   X/WGW (Gilbert Williams papers).
Public Record Office
   CRES papers.

INDUSTRIALIZATION IN THE COUNTRYSIDE: THE ROLES OF THE LORD, FREEHOLDER AND TENANT IN THE MANCHESTER AREA, 1600–1900

By MICHAEL NEVELL *and* JOHN WALKER

PREFACE

This paper summarizes some of the results of a long-term study into the history and archaeology of modern Tameside (Fig. 1) which have been published in eight volumes. The final two volumes of that study dealt explicitly with the problem of industrialization from an archaeological viewpoint. Those works were a response to a widespread call for archaeology to make a distinctive contribution to the study of the later period.

The approach adopted in the later volumes was one that might be described as traditional or classical save that we also attempted to relate the findings to more modern theoretical ideas. Space precludes a full exposition of the approach and the detailed results of over eight years fieldwork. However, this information and much more appears in the full series on Tameside.[1]

INTRODUCTION

Whilst there are many modern studies of the industrial development of the cities and towns of England, there are comparatively few by archaeologists which deal with the rural fringes where the contrast between pre-industrial and industrial society were often most dramatic. One aim behind undertaking the Tameside project was to attempt to describe from an archaeological viewpoint the way in which two long-lived landscape units, the lordships of Ashton and Longdendale, were changed by industrialization.

In comparison to the other modern boroughs that surround Manchester, Tameside and its Lordships (Fig. 2), contained no real urban centres prior to industrialization. The industrial growth in this area was therefore both more dramatic and less constrained than in other parts of the Manchester region.

The study area lies on the eastern side of the Mersey Basin, centred 18km. east of Manchester on the south-western flanks of the Pennines, and encompasses the middle reaches of the Tame and Etherow valleys. It is an area of physical contrasts, with wide lowland clay plains dominating the western half of the area whilst in the east there

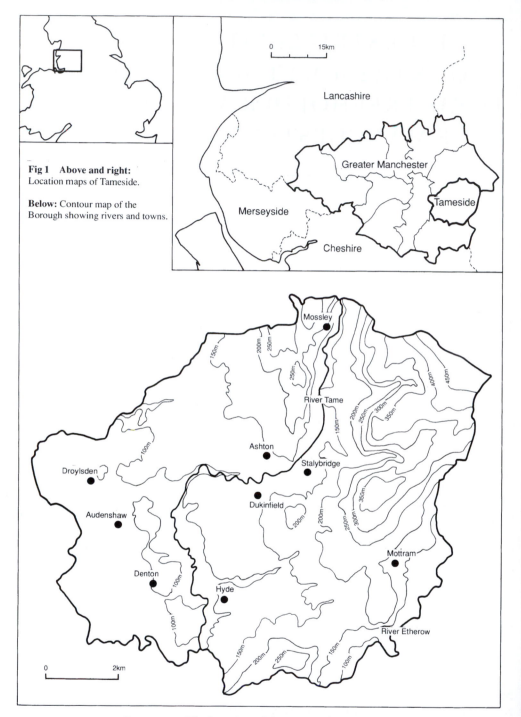

Fig 1 Above and right: Location maps of Tameside.

Below: Contour map of the Borough showing rivers and towns.

FIGURE 1.   The location of the Tameside study area.

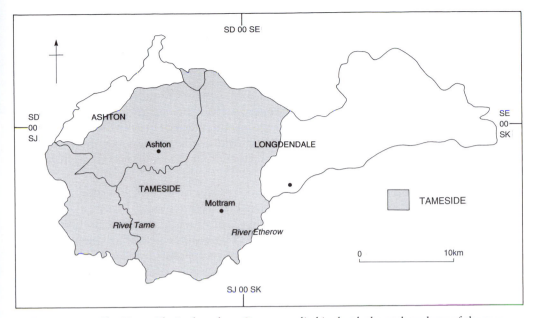

FIGURE 2. The Tameside Archaeology Survey studied in depth the archaeology of the two lordships of Ashton-under-Lyne and Longdendale. These were not co-terminous with the modern Borough of Tameside, but they did provide the landscape and historical framework for this study of the origins of industrialization in this part of the north-west.

are many steep-sided river valleys. The eastern two thirds lie between 76.2m. and 496.2m. above sea level upon the shales and sandstones of the Millstone Grit and Coal Measures. This eastern zone also contains the Longdendale valley which provided an historic access route through the Pennines. Throughout the study area the soil quality is generally poor, rainfall high and the valleys subject to rapid flooding.[2]

By the 18th century the area was part of the centre of an extensive international industrial complex primarily based upon cotton.[3] Aikin's contemporary description of the Tameside area in late 18th century is marked by contrasts; the township of Mottram, for instance, is described as having twelve large manufactories, but also a greater number of small mixed farms, the tenants of which eked out an existence through cottage industry combined with farming.[4]

CURRENT ARCHAEOLOGICAL THEORY AND THE INDUSTRIAL REVOLUTION

The study of the changes produced by industrialization has resulted in a wide range of economic analyses and explanations ranging from grand theory and macro-economic studies of statistical measures, down to detailed studies of regions and individual industries.

The contributions to the debate made by archaeologists have tended to lean towards studies of the mechanics, or physical character, of individual industries or structures. This trend amongst archaeologists is understandable given the volume of available historical data and the depth of the theories of economic historians. As English Heritage has observed, this trend may have meant that the contribution of archaeologists to the debate on the validity and origins of the Industrial Revolution has not been as great as it could have been.[5]

In recent years archaeology has moved towards providing its own insights into the processes and effects behind the transition from an agrarian to an industrial society. Three important studies have addressed the issue of the transition to a proto-industrial society in the period 1348 to 1642, and whilst some went on to look at aspects of the period 1642 to 1870, all took the view that the transition to an industrial society took considerable time.

Post-Medieval Archaeology in Britain, by David Crossley (1990), brought together the results of large numbers of individual archaeological studies conducted on remains dating from 1500 to 1800 and shows that much of the basic archaeological framework for these centuries is now in place. The volume also illustrates that local variations were often significant and that various types of archaeological remains seldom figure in the historical record.[6]

An Archaeology of Capitalism, by Matthew Johnson (1996), is the most explicitly theoretical of the volumes and appears to echo a wider trend in archaeology in explaining how the rise of the concept of the individual, seen by some as crucial to industrialization, can be demonstrated by changes in a wide range of physical remains.

Industrial Archaeology, Principles and Practices, by Marilyn Palmer and Peter Neaverson (1998), attempts to widen the horizons of the industrial archaeologist by relating industries to their associated housing and transport networks, and by placing aspects of the material culture of industrial production in its social context. The authors introduce ideas about the social controls which are both explicit and implicit in the architecture and spatial organization of industrial buildings, and the way in which social relations were both constructed and expressed in the housing built to accommodate those involved in industrial production.

In addition to these complete volumes, there has been a wide range of articles and smaller studies on the archaeology of England in the more recent centuries. The volume *The Familiar Past?*, edited by Sarah Tarlow and Susie West (1999), brought together recent contributions by some of the archaeologists involved in studying the period in Britain. In their contributions to this work Brooks, Buckham, Mytum and Tarlow explore in different ways aspects of the relationship between the material culture of the period and its social structure. Giles, Gould, Leech, Lucas, Johnson and Williamson demonstrate the relationship between structures (their layout and planning) and contemporary social issues, whilst Pennell does the same for diet. In the same volume Keith Matthews discusses how a classical archaeological approach to the study of the period is both in its infancy and still questioned.

In her summary of present progress Tarlow draws attention to areas where archaeologists are trying to make a contribution.[7] Great attention is being paid to how individuals in the past established and demonstrated their identity in various material ways such as building plans or funerary monuments. Tarlow also emphasizes that an archaeological approach demands or requires, by the nature of the discipline, the use of long timescales and broad concepts of a type that are not usually found in historical studies. In the same volume, Charles Orser, in examining the progress of historical archaeology in Britain and America, calls for a new form of archaeology centred upon four main concepts: a global view, an emphasis upon past social relations, the study of social relationships across space and through time, and a willingness to comment upon today by drawing from the recent past.[8] This current study, because of the insight gained in the companion volume, follows Orser's call by emphasizing social relations and their development through time. Elsewhere, Kate Clark, in a summary of developments in industrial archaeology, has also called for archaeology to consider how best it can contribute to a study of the period.[9]

In Manchester we took up the challenge of trying to present an archaeological understanding of the Industrial Revolution between the years 1600 and 1900. In general we have approached the subject in the same way as traditional, classically trained, archaeologists might study the Roman Empire, that is through charting and grouping sites by type, and using historical sources only to illustrate archaeological perceptions.

It is important to realize that this approach was quite distinctive in three ways — an emphasis on material remains, an holistic approach and a form of broad-brush analysis. This stress upon material remains was essential if archaeology was to make a contribution in its own right to the origins of industrialization in this area since the discipline remains the study of material culture. An holistic approach meant treating the period in the same way as we might treat the remains of the Bronze Age by giving in the initial phases of the study equal weight and importance to all elements of the physical remains. Broad-brush analysis tends to be a natural consequence of the study of any material culture and its results are presented in the rest of this paper.

Such an approach raises many issues but in this particular case we were fortunate in that we had already produced a series of volumes on the history, historic personalities, buildings and even folklore of the area which acted as a form of 'independent check' on the broader archaeological insights.

THE ARCHAEOLOGICAL DATABASE

Fieldwork and research confirmed that the archaeology of the study area, from the period 1348 to 1642, was distinct, being dominated by the remains of isolated farms and the homes of the owners of manors. In the first part of that study we examined a map of the late 16th-century Staley estate (Fig. 3), noting how the sites recorded corresponded with the known archaeological evidence for this area in the 16th and early 17th centuries. The map shows a pre-industrial landscape consisting of a major hall and isolated farms, lying amongst enclosed fields, some of which contained ridge and furrow. Beyond the limits of the fields lay the open moors or commons containing the remains of Buckton Castle, a cairn, a turf pit and a slate quarry. Allowing access between the two zones was a series of lanes and moor gates. Staley Hall, the manorial centre, appears as a large multi-gabled, multi-storeyed structure, apparently capable of housing many people, adjoined on one side by a field surrounded by a vertical

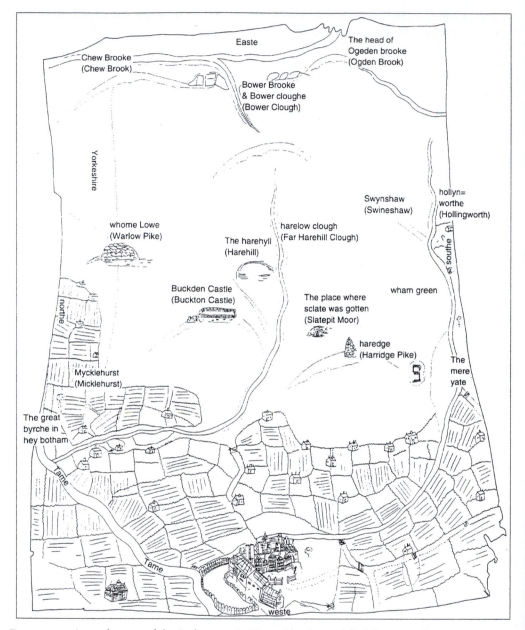

FIGURE 3.   An early map of the Staley area in Tameside. A simplified drawing of the 16th-century map of part of the Staley estates which was drawn for the Booth family, lords of Ashton and Dunham Massey. It shows a pre-industrial landscape consisting of a major hall and isolated farms lying amongst enclosed fields, some of which contain ridge and furrow, beyond which lies the open moors. This evidence is supported by the archaeological data from the area and confirms the distinctive nature of the archaeology of the region prior to industrialization. (After LRO DDX 350/21). (Courtesy of the County Archivist, Lancashire Record Office)

plank fence typical of a park pale. Other structures were all simple tenant houses with different arrangements of windows and chimneys, each surrounded by fields.

The archaeology of the period from 1642 to 1870 within the Ashton and Longdendale lordships is as distinct as that for the three centuries before 1642. It was dominated by two new archaeological site types: the textile site, of which 274 were established in Tameside between 1763 and 1907, and the terraced house, of which thousands of examples still survive from the period 1790 to 1870.

These patterns were tested and confirmed by a considerable number of individual building surveys allied to a campaign of dendrochronological dating. In addition to this data there have been a number of archaeological excavations at sites such as Ashton Old Hall, Dukinfield Hall, Denton Hall, Mottram village, the Black Bull Inn, the Haughton Green glassworks and later colliery, and the field boundaries and tracks of Werneth Low. Individual reports on this work and on continuing excavations at the early colliery site of Fairbottom Bobs are available from the University of Manchester Archaeology Unit.

The first problem was to characterize or group this new information and new sites in some sort of meaningful or generally acceptable fashion. In order to categorize much of the archaeological material and to provide a common frame of reference we used the archaeological site descriptions and monument category classifications contained within English Heritage's and the Royal Commission's *Thesaurus of Archaeological Monument Types*.

Using the *Thesaurus*, over 100 new types of archaeological site established in the Ashton and Longdendale lordships between 1600 and 1900 were identified (Fig. 4). These new sites fall, according to the schema within the *Thesaurus*, into one of fifteen major monument types: agricultural and subsistence monuments; civil monuments; commemorative monuments; commercial sites; defensive sites; domestic sites; education sites; monuments associated with gardens, parks and open spaces; those connected with health and welfare; industrial monuments; institutional monuments; recreational sites; religious, ritual and funerary sites; transport sites; and those monuments associated with water supply and drainage.

These new sites range from ice houses, such as the fine 18th-century example in the grounds of Broadbottom Hall; hatting plank shops, such as that on Joel Lane in Gee Cross built in the late 18th century; pumping engine houses, such as at Fairbottom Bobs near Park Bridge, probably from the 1780s (Fig. 5); to transport networks such as the Manchester to Ashton Canal, built in the 1790s, or the Manchester to Sheffield railway, built in the 1840s. However, the three most common of these new archaeological sites were: the terraced workers' house, of which the earliest surviving buildings are probably the row of six cottages in Broadbottom known as Summerbottom, built in 1790; the textile site, of which 274 sites are known, the earliest surviving purpose-built mill being Gerrards Wood Mill in Hyde, erected in the early 1790s; and the farmstead, of which 273 sites are known, one of the more notable being Old Post Office Farm, built in 1692 by one of the many wealthier tenant farmers in the area (Fig. 6).

Using the *Thesaurus* together with the findings made during the research for the earlier eight volumes, which included targeted archaeological fieldwork, it is possible

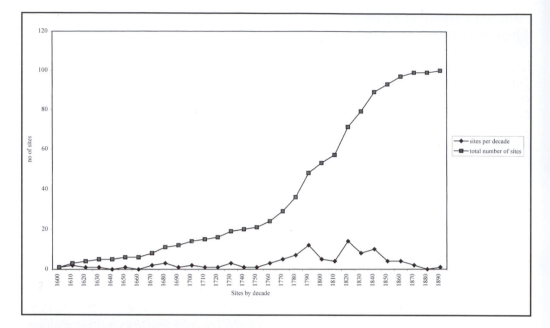

FIGURE 4.   The introduction of new types of archaeological site into the lordships of Ashton and Longdendale: a cumulative graph based upon English Heritage's and the Royal Commission's *Thesaurus of Archaeological Monument Types*.

FIGURE 5.   Excavations of the foundations of Fairbotton Bobs, a mine pumping engine from the late 18th century. This view shows the foundations for a later wagon boiler which replaced an early hay-stack boiler. The remains of the base of the chimney stack can be seen in the top left-hand corner and the site of the original Newcomen-style beam engine to the right of this.

FIGURE 6.   Old Post Office Farm, Mottram-in-Longdendale. Built in 1692 by a local yeoman tenant farmer, Nicholas Wagstaffe, it is a fine example of a Pennine farmhouse of this period. It is a two-bay, two-storey, baffle-entry building with a fine stone porch coped and decorated with ball finials and kneelers. The front elevation, overlooking the later Market Street, is symmetrical with mullion windows on either side of the porch. The interior contains wattle and daub partitions on both floors.

to draw a graph of when different types of site were first constructed within the study area. As the great majority of sites survived for long periods, it is more helpful to draw a cumulative graph showing how the total range of sites expanded through time. Figure 4 shows the pattern of introduction of new types of site in the area and how the range of sites expanded.

The slope of the graph is S-shaped with a long period in which new types of sites were gradually developed followed by phases of more rapid change. Such S-shaped (sigmoidal or logistic) growth curves are found in many cases of population growth. We can divide such graphs into four main phases:

1. The adaptive phase, in which change is slow;
2. The expansionary phase, a period of rapid growth with positive feedback;
3. The consolidatory phase, in which growth is less rapid and negative feedback becomes more common;
4. Maturity.

The study of growth curves is dominated by ecological theory,[10] and if we accepted some of these insights we might conclude that the graph of new archaeological type sites from the Tameside area is typical of a population where investment in developing new sites (population members) is high and that ultimately the total range is restricted by some form of complex constraint.

Having categorized the broad changes in the local material culture within the study area the problem then was to offer some form of insight into the pattern that had emerged. The *Thesaurus* only divides sites into groups or individual entities on the basis of a combination of site function and recognized archaeological typologies. The volume does not attempt to cross-relate the archaeological entities to any aspect of the contemporary context.

Having established a broad pattern of development in sites and site types, we used the *Lands and Lordships* volume[11] to explore different contemporary contexts which might fit this pattern. Analysis of environmental and population change did not throw any light on this pattern. However, perhaps the most significant discovery of the whole project was that each new type of site could be related to a distinct local social class and that in each case these new forms related directly to the traditional sphere of influence of each social class.

A difficult issue arising from this approach was to be sure that we could reasonably assign 'ownership' of sites to the right class. In a typical local manor such as Hattersley, a tenant was responsible for building his own house and in the early part of the period could use certain materials obtained from the common land. It might seem, therefore, that the house was the tenant's property but, in fact, if he lost his tenancy, he also lost the house and it became the property of the landowner. However, there is evidence that most tenants thought of themselves as quite secure in their tenancies. In practice, the relationship between tenant and owner was a relationship deeply anchored in custom and few tenants lost control of the houses they built. In every similar case where we have allocated control over the development of different types of sites, we have tried to balance the evidence of tradition and legal documents and only allocated 'control' of a site to a group where we could be reasonably satisfied that they had a combined influence on the building of the site and its form that was greater than that of any other group.

The pattern of site development in relation to social class (Fig. 7) is as follows:

The Lord's Archaeology (Table 1): 28 new archaeological type sites, spread across thirteen monument classes, associated with the landholders during the period under study, manorial halls and town halls being the most prominent.

The Freeholder's Archaeology (Table 1): 48 new archaeological type sites, spread across ten monument classes, associated with the freeholders in this period, the country house and the textile complex (Fig. 8) being the most prominent.

The Tenants' Archaeology (Table 1): 24 new archaeological type sites, spread across just five monument classes, associated with the tenants in this period, the weaver's cottage (Fig. 9) and the farmstead being the most prominent.

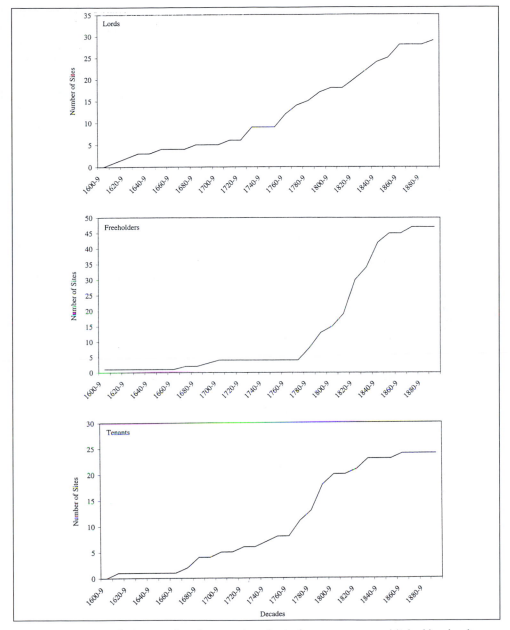

FIGURE 7. Cumulative graphs of new archaeological monuments established by the three social groups — lords (top), freeholders (centre) and tenants (bottom) — which do not show the same growth patterns. Whilst those for the freeholders and tenants show an S-shaped growth pattern, that for the lords shows almost a straight-line growth, suggesting constant investment on their part. The reason for this may lie in the fact that the lords always had large financial resources to draw on throughout the period 1600–1900, whereas the freeholders and tenants did not.

FIGURE 8. Castle Street Mills, Stalybridge. These were built by George Cheetham (1757–1826), a tenant farmer from Newton-in-Longdendale, in the period 1805–21. The success of the family was secured by the establishment of Bankwood Mills in 1832–34, the largest mill complex in Stalybridge. The family built Eastwood House, set in 20 acres of grounds, in the late 1820s on the fringes of the town next to the Bankwood Mill complex, marking their arrival as the wealthiest of the Stalybridge cotton mill-owners.

TOWARDS A LOCAL MODEL OF INDUSTRIALIZATION

This archaeological model combined with the earlier historical research allowed us to create a 'narrative' about the nature of the Industrial Revolution as it occurred in two lordships on the edge of the Pennines.

In the 16th century the two lordships of Ashton and Longdendale were marginal land. The backwater nature of the area meant that there was a lack of central direct control and absent lords. The patchy quality of the landscape and the absent lords meant that there developed a short, and dispersed, social hierarchy based upon land and social rights. These social groups of the lords, freeholders and tenants each gave birth to the distinct range of sites that characterized the area, and its archaeology, in the 17th century.

This community evolved into a remarkably open society with a keen interest in new opportunities to gain additional resources. Access to these resources was strongly

FIGURE 9. Weavers' cottages to the rear of the Gunn Inn in Hollingworth. The three-storey high and multi-light windows are characteristic features of handloom weavers' cottages, 63 examples of which can still be found within the Lordships of Ashton and Longdendale. These were built by John and Ann Morehouse, of the Gunn Inn, in, according to a datestone on the buildings, 1781. Land Tax returns in the late 1790s and early 1800s list the occupants of the cottages as cotton workers.

influenced by existing social and economic rules. The lords could generate additional income by exploiting the resources they controlled, such as stone and minerals, agricultural tenancies and (because they had some money) innovative capital projects. To the freeholders, their more limited rights, coupled with a desire to maintain social status, meant that in general additional income would have to come from agriculture. For the tenants, weak control meant that industry was a source of largely untaxed income and any innovations were not controlled by strong local guilds or effective national legislation.

Other factors may also have made the area particularly suitable for industrial development, such as, for example, large areas of free land in the river valley bottoms, a tradition of families working as one economic unit, a cheap and effective transport system, a society used to operating on credit and trust, and a local tradition of Puritanism.

The causes that quickened the pace of change between 1750 and 1820 remain unclear, although the increase in the range and number of archaeological sites is obvious. To anyone living within the central portion of that curve, roughly 1750 to 1820, the experience would be one of rapid and revolutionary change, even though the pattern of growth, when studied as a whole, would foster the impression of cyclical development. Surprisingly, the pattern of development in archaeological sites follows that laid down by the earlier social structure of the lords, freeholder and tenant. At the forefront of the development of new industrial sites were the tenants. The archaeological sites of the tenants show not a revolution but a gradual evolution as material prosperity increased as a whole. Whilst agriculture increased in efficiency ultimately the old medieval freeholders, with their strong reliance on farming, declined. They were replaced by a new form of freeholder interested not only in agriculture but also in industry. The lords, on the other hand, were responsible for, or involved with all the major new capital and strikingly innovative projects which involved administrative, legal and social control or infrastructure. The roles of the lord were in time taken over by the new Victorian local government.

A THEORETICAL BASIS

Having categorized the remains and provided an 'explanatory narrative' three significant tasks remain to be addressed:

— testing the validity of the categorization technique that was used;
— relating the narrative to existing models;
— testing the appropriate model (if possible).

The validity of the categorization technique

In compiling the graph we have classified as 'new' the archaeological remains defined as sites in the *Thesaurus* because of their distinct nature and form. There is the possibility that many types of sites defined in the *Thesaurus* should not really been seen as distinct but merely as elaborations of older forms. Whilst, for instance, the local 17th-century glassworks at Haughton Green was a totally new type of site introduced by immigrants, how should one view the emergence of the terraced house? From one viewpoint the local evidence suggests that it is the end of a chain that began with the labourer's room in the farm, which was superseded by individual worker's cottage which, in turn, led on to the development of the terrace. A similar process of elaboration is shown particularly well in the clothing industries, schools and the church.

There were hatting industry sites in Denton, such as Woolfendens, which in the 1870s consisted of a factory, workers' housing and three villas for the owner and his two sons. Today we might classify these remains as separate interrelated sites, each arising out of a particular tradition. In fact, they all originate from the phased growth of what originally consisted of a single farmhouse. In that dual-economy structure we would have found, around 1830, rooms for the owner, rooms for the labourers and a central room (often called 'the house' in local wills) for industrial activity. With the growth in prosperity there is a gradual pattern of expansion in the working area by adding a workshop in 1860 and building a factory in 1873, followed by the creation of separate cottages for the workers and new homes for the family.[12]

Schools also show a process of increasing elaboration with increasing wealth; the first references are to masters without separate buildings, a phase which is followed by the construction of small buildings and, eventually, by large-scale structures.

Contrary to some widespread opinions, the introduction of pews in churches marks not some new social order, but the elaboration of the old. The order of seating on the benches of the pewless Ashton church was, in 1422, already strictly controlled before the introduction of the pews. The 'new' pews were, initially at least, merely a more elaborate and expensive expression of an earlier system.

To try and resolve this problem of whether or not a site is really 'new' is extremely difficult. Recourse to the historical documents does not necessarily help simply because they are selective about what they record, factories, for instance, receiving a great deal more attention than stone quarries. At this stage we simply have to note the problem and rely upon the validity of the *Thesaurus*.

Relationship to other models

The cornerstone of this study is that the archaeological remains that have been classified can be further 'explained' by linking them to particular social groups. This concept of linking distinct types of remains to distinct social classes implies that the sites were constructed or shaped by the economic, political or social needs of these groups. This implication means that an attempt should be made to relate these archaeological conclusions to some wider body of social theory such as Closure Theory. This school of thought was suggested by Weber and has been developed by a number of recent scholars. For instance Rigby used and elaborated Closure Theory to explain developments during the later medieval period.[13]

Closure Theory concentrates upon how individuals within society attempt to bolster their position by acting as a group. To strengthen their position such groups make use of exclusion and usurpation. Exclusion involves the exercise of power downwards to control or restrict others, whilst usurpation involves lower groups wresting new rights from more powerful groups. This theory attempts to focus not only on competition between different classes but also on competition within particular classes. It draws attention to three main modes of power, economic, coercive (such as political, legal and military force), and ideological, that are used within and between groups to enhance or maintain their position. Rigby's work demonstrates how that approach is useful in classifying and categorizing the various developments in the medieval economy and society of England.

In many ways Weber's approach was similar to that developed by Karl Marx, but to Weber the causal factor in social change was not always the economy. To Weber, identifying the causes of change depended upon an analysis of each case and in each case the cause could be different.[14] Social groupings would establish or justify their power by appealing to or using one of the following factors:

— legal or traditional factors;
— ideology, morals or charismatic factors;
— rational or economic factors.

From our earlier studies it is clear that all such factors were used locally throughout the industrial period to foster the position of the various social groups.

The groups that we defined (lordships and manors, freeholds, and tenancies) could all be seen as quite distinctive methods of trying to achieve a sustainable relationship within a changing world. The adaptive strategies of each group were influenced by social factors that strengthened their position but also constrained or influenced their options for adjusting to change. Manors relied on various methods of exploiting the population, their access to capital and their traditional rights; freeholds pursued agricultural efficiency or growth; and tenancies concentrated upon finding a mechanism, such as crafts, that was not easily exploited by others.

Not all the strategies of adaptation were equally successful. The early agricultural freeholds declined and were replaced by new freeholds created by successful tenants who acquired their wealth through industry. It seems clear that these new freeholds, with only a partial reliance on agriculture, were designed to enhance the social position of their owner. Some lacunae in the pattern of archaeological remains also become more easily understood. The early coal pits, whilst following the best shallow seams, show gaps in their distribution which coincide with tenanted land. The reasons seem clear in that the local lord who controlled coal exploitation encouraged digging, but not where it could lead to complaints or claims from established tenants.

In recent years some sociologists and historians have brought the study of complex social networks to a level beyond that presented here.[15] Wetherell has, for instance, felt able to justify the view that in the past:

— all people were interdependent;
— that links or relations between people channelled resources;
— that the structure of these relations both eased and constrained actions;
— that the pattern of that structure defined economic, political and social structure.[16]

It is a view that this study tends to confirm. We might suggest that the proto-industrial culture of the north-west was different and made up of a small range of distinct groups with their own interests. These small groups can not only be detected in the archaeological record, but actually shaped that record to a considerable extent by the pursuit of their own distinct strategies designed to seize the opportunities presented by growth.

To some archaeologists, many of the conclusions presented thus far may be seen as fatally flawed. One reasoned criticism might be that we have presented just one interpretation, derived as much from our own unavoidable prejudices as from the facts, of a past that is ultimately unknowable. Another criticism might be that if we wish to adopt an approach based upon social groups it could be argued that it would have been better to present a multifaceted analysis in which equal weight was placed upon other groups such as the poor, women or the religious sects. All those groups appear in the local archaeological record and such a criticism has some merit. In a partial defence it should be noted that however important those groups were they did not dominate or shape as much of the archaeological record as the three major groups of manorial lord, freeholder and tenant.

It could also be argued that we should have placed greater emphasis upon the impact of new ideas such as the Enlightenment and shown how the creation of totally new sites, such as canals, was only possible through the widespread adoption of the new belief that the application of reason could solve contemporary problems.

As the past is probably unknowable and interpreted through our current perceptions, all these criticisms have some validity. By producing eight volumes which range from traditional archaeological texts to local hagiography and on to local mythology, we hope we have provided information for those who wish to develop other interpretations.

To an extent this use of a traditional archaeological approach, coupled with more modern theory, can go some way to providing a distinctive contribution to the wider debate. Pat Hudson provided an analysis of all the major trends in historians' thinking about the Industrial Revolution.[17] By simplifying, or perhaps over-simplifying, the historical models described by Hudson we can divide these trends into three main classes:

— hypotheses about the nature or form of the Revolution;
— hypotheses about the way the Revolution worked;
— hypotheses about the causes of the Revolution.

In terms of its nature the Industrial Revolution has variously been seen as short and dramatic, long and evolutionary, cyclical, patchy, widespread or part of a world-wide imperial phenomenon. The workings of the Revolution have been seen as taking place in clear progressive stages or as the result of a series of positive feedback loops working in a less predictable fashion. The causes of the Revolution have been variously seen as technological growth, trade growth, capital growth, imperial growth or even (now somewhat discredited) heroic entrepreneurs.

In recent years attention has also turned to the view that the Industrial Revolution mainly took place in marginal areas and that to an extent in Britain the revolution was unreal.[18] The latter point seems to find favour among many modern social commentators who see British industrialists as never really being interested in industry but seeing it merely as a mechanism to obtain sufficient wealth to become part of the landed or cultural élite.

It was the detailed work of the economic historians, particularly in the late 1980s, that allowed the Industrial Revolution to be seen not as a revolution brought about by technology, but as a broad process of growth throughout the economy as a whole.[19]

Paul Courtney, who is both historian and archaeologist, has recently emphasized that new studies suggest that the Industrial Revolution was both an intensely regional affair and a period of steady long term growth.[20]

The approach adopted here has something to contribute, from the archaeological evidence, to each of these insights. The S-shaped pattern of growth in new types of sites means that viewing the revolution as broad or short would appear equally valid depending upon the time frame one elected to study.

The way that detailed histories of successful tenant families show their striving for land echoes the view that industrialization might merely be a mechanism not an

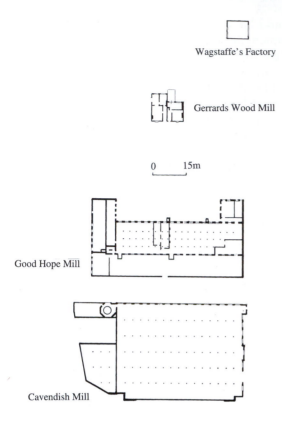

Wagstaffe's Factory

Gerrards Wood Mill

0   15m

Good Hope Mill

Cavendish Mill

FIGURE 10. The changing shape of the mill complex in Tameside: mill plans from 1786–1906. The design of the earliest purpose-built cotton spinning mills was almost identical to that of the silk mills of mid 18th-century Congleton and Macclesfield: that is a well-lit, uncluttered, floor area large enough for the efficient accommodation of processes and storage. The small scale of these initial structures allowed the wealthier tenant farmers of the study area, such as the Wagstaffes (Wagstaffe's Factory, c. 1786) and Ashtons (Gerrards Wood Mill, early 1790s), to invest in their construction. However, the introduction of new power technologies, such as bigger water wheels and steam power (Good Hope Mill, 1824–50), put these complexes beyond the financial reach of the farmer by 1820. Thereafter, the elaboration of mill design was driven by changes in cotton machinery design and changes in construction techniques, which meant that mills got bigger and bigger (Cavendish Mill, 1886).

end in itself. The suggestion that sites show elaboration more often than invention coupled with the basic pattern of development lends support to the idea of steady long-term growth (Fig. 10).

The unique pattern of the local social structure and landscape also echoes Courtney's emphasis on the importance of local factors.

The Closure Theory approach does not explain the causes of the revolution but merely suggests how the opportunities for growth in the area were exploited by different social groups on the basis of both their own self-interest and their traditional rights, to give rise to an ever more elaborate material culture.

An analysis derived from archaeology of the type used in this article has inherent limitations. The blunt and somewhat impersonal nature of the discipline means that the history of people and groups is rarely revealed. In this article we have used individual histories only where necessary to explore the archaeological argument; an approach that compares poorly with the benefits of a truly historical approach demonstrated in such classic works as Bythell's study of the local weavers.[21]

Clearly, there are various criticisms that could be offered of this narrative derived from archaeology coupled to sociology by the use of a selective approach to historical sources. Perhaps the criticism that carries most weight is that Closure Theory, and this article, might be taken to imply that social groups must close membership to

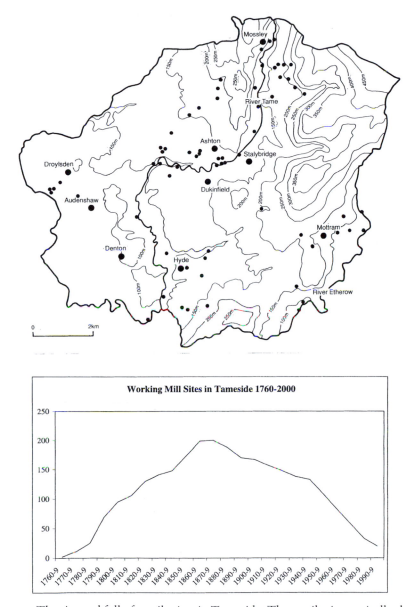

FIGURE 11. The rise and fall of textile sites in Tameside. The textile site, typically the cotton spinning mill, but also including the printing and dyeing works and woollen mills, was the second most common site in the period 1642–1870, with 274 sites known within the Tameside area, 67 of which were established before 1800 (see map above), and over 1,400 known in the Greater Manchester area. It was one of the type sites introduced in this period. Most were the property of the new industrial freeholder class by the mid 19th century. This bell-shaped graph shows the rise and fall in the numbers of operating textile mills in the Tameside area between 1763 and 1999. This is a pattern of growth and decline that can be paralleled in other areas in the region, notably Manchester and Oldham.

those trying to enter them. How is it possible for Tameside tenants, such as the Ashton family of Hyde, to become freeholders and ultimately lords if the driving force behind each group is to close off access to those from below, to keep what they hold? We might explain the Ashton case by saying that by this time the control of the lords had already passed to the industrialists, but this ignores the still potent social power of lords today. We could emphasize that there must have been occasions when it was easier to include new members into a group rather than promote conflict. A more satisfying view is to recognize that whilst we have explained much of the pattern of the archaeological remains by reference to social groups, there are exceptions. In the end Closure Theory and the approach we have adopted for the Manchester area are useful as a way of describing the changes that took place but their role in explaining the cause of those changes remains unclear, yet might be sought amongst such exceptions.

Even if an analysis based upon Closure Theory proves to have severe limitations the concept of treating the period as a whole and simply charting the typological and chronological development of sites will remain (Fig. 11), we hope, a cheap and effective method of creating a base from which archaeology can make a distinctive contribution.

Michael Nevell and John Walker, University of Manchester Archaeological Unit, Architecture Building, Oxford Road, Manchester M13 3PL, UK

TABLE 1
LIST OF THE FIRST APPEARANCE OF NEW MONUMENT TYPES, 1600–1900

This list has been compiled from the work conducted on the seven volumes of *the History and Archaeology of Tameside* series. Listed are the earliest known dates for new monument types introduced into the area between 1600 and 1900, as defined in the *Thesaurus of Monument Types*, published by English Heritage and the Royal Commission on the Historical Monuments on England. The initials GMSMR refer to the *Greater Manchester Sites and Monuments Record*, held at the University of Manchester. The numerals following GMSMR are the unique identifier for the individual site records which can be consulted on request at the Greater Manchester Archaeological Unit, University of Manchester. L = Lords, F = Freeholders, T = Tenants.

Agriculture and Subsistence

F 1690s threshing barn, brick, Audenshaw Lodge GMSMR 806
T 1700 cow house, stone, Meadowcroft Fold GMSMR 832
T 1837 laithe house, Widowscroft Farm GMSMR 937
L 1840s model farm, Hyde Hall, Hyde GMSMR 762

Civil

L 1636 court house GMSMR 8201
L 1718 stocks, Gee Cross GMSMR 621

L 1823 public square, Henry Square, Ashton GMSMR 3256
L 1831 town hall, Stalybridge GMSMR 5895

Commemorative

L 1655 commemorative stone (Holland monument at St Lawrence's) GMSMR 973
T 1680 external gravestone, Mottram Church GMSMR 812

Commercial

F 1787–1803 shop (fixed retail shop), 120 Stamford Street, Ashton GMSMR 6165
F 1820 savings bank, Warrington Street, Ashton GMSMR 745
F 1825 grain warehouse, Stalybridge corn mill GMSMR 3588
F 1828 wholesale warehouse, Peak Forest Canal, Hyde GMSMR 639
L 1830 market hall, Ashton GMSMR 752
F 1847 shopping arcade, Market Avenue, Ashton GMSMR 5853

Defence

L 1841 barracks, Ashton GMSMR 2195

Domestic

F 1604 date stone (building inscription) GMSMR 785
F 1672 farmhouse, brick, Red Hall GMSMR 8159
T 1676 labourers' cottages, Hodgefold GMSMR 950
T 1682 hamlet, Gee Cross GMSMR 622
T 1742 rainwater head, Old Street, Ashton GMSMR 823
T 1755 double (depth) house, Oakdene GMSMR 1008
L 1762–87 workers' cottages, brick, Dukinfield Circus GMSMR 3531
L 1770 country house, Dukinfield Lodge GMSMR 756
T 1772 handloom weavers' cottages, stone, Wednesough Green GMSMR 3448
F 1784–95 workers' village, Red Pump Street, Hyde GMSMR 3513
F 1787–1803 town house, no 121 & 135 Stamford Street, Ashton GMSMR 977
L 1780s circus, Stamford Street, Ashton GMSMR 6165
F 1790 terraced workers' housing, Summerbottom GMSMR 939
F 1794 split level (cellar) house, Hollingworth GMSMR 3448
F 1800s ice house, Broadbottom Hall GMSMR 759
F 1812 detached house, Croft House, Ashton GMSMR 965
F 1817 through to light terrace houses, Old Street, Broadbottom GMSMR 3508
F 1820s gate lodge, Mottram Old Hall GMSMR 826
F 1820s courtyard terrace houses, Stalybridge GMSMR 3583
F 1820s steeped terrace houses, Well Row, Broadbottom GMSMR 3508
F 1830s backyard, Gair Street, Hyde GMSMR 3513
F 1840s back-to-back houses, Ashton GMSMR 3526
F 1840s semi-detached house, Hyde GMSMR 3513
F 1850s tunnel back terraces, Croft Street, Hyde GMSMR 3513
F 1850s, managers house, Dean Terrace, Park Bridge GMSMR 749
F 1877 villa house, The Hollies, Ashton GMSMR 6165

Education

L 1623 church school, Mottram Grammar GMSMR 819
F 1793 Sunday School, Moravian settlement GMSMR 628
F 1841 day school, St Paul's, Stalybridge GMSMR 1062
F 1856 Mechanics' Institute building, Ashton GMSMR 3526
L 1891 public library, Ashton GMSMR 803

Gardens, Parks & Urban Spaces
L 1865 public park, Stamford Park GMSMR 9175

Health & Welfare

L 1850 hospital, Ashton GMSMR 9175
L 1868 Turkish baths, Stalybridge GMSMR 3583

Industrial

T 1614 coal pit, Mottram Moor GMSMR 3369
L 1615 glass works, Haughton GMSMR 3319
T 1722 mine shaft, Crickety Lane, Ashton GMSMR 3526
L 1735 horse engine, Denton GMSMR 6290
L 1771 atmospheric engine house (Newcomen), Hague Colliery GMSMR 6284
T 1777 printing works, Shepley GMSMR 8139
T 1779 water-powered textile spinning mill (cotton), Throstle Nest, Ashton GMSMR 6351
T 1784 ironworks, Park Bridge GMSMR 6078
T 1790/3 steam-powered textile spinning mill (cotton), Old Soot Poke GMSMR 3583
T 1792 brick & tile making site works, Dukinfield GMSMR 6269
T 1796–97 hand-powered textile spinning mill, Dry Mill GMSMR 6301
T 1805 bleach works, Hodge Mill, Broadbottom GMSMR 6348
T 1808 copperas Works, Bardsley GMSMR 183
F 1810 iron forge, Park Bridge GMSMR 6078
F 1812 gas works, Carrfield Mill, Hyde GMSMR 3431
F 1822 gas storage tank, Ashton Gas Works GMSMR 2272
F 1827 fire-proof textile mill, Copley mills GMSMR 3379
F 1820s weaving shed, Bayley Field Mill, Hyde GMSMR 3430
T 1823 pottery kiln, Pot House Farm, Matley GMSMR 5803
T 1839 hatters workshop, Joel Lane, Gee Cross GMSMR 6326
T 1868 hat factory, Howe & Sons, Denton GMSMR 481

Institutional

L 1730 workhouse, Ashton GMSMR 9175

Recreational

F 1870s theatre, Ashton GMSMR 6165

Religious, Ritual & Funerary

F 1707 nonconformist chapel, Dukinfield Old Chapel GMSMR 624
F 1784 Moravian settlement, Dukinfield GMSMR 628
F 1791 Methodist Chapel, Mottram GMSMR 815
L 1821 Commissioners church, St Peter's, Ashton GMSMR 5899
F 1838–39 Catholic church, St Peter's, Stalybridge GMSMR 5899
L 1865 cemetery chapel, Dukinfield GMSMR 9157

Transport

L 1683 road bridge, stone, Broadbottom GMSMR 3508
L 1732 toll road, Manchester to Saltersbrook GMSMR 823
T pre-1781 coaching inn, Gunn Inn GMSMR 934
L 1792–97 canal, Ashton to Manchester GMSMR 6361
L 1794–99 canal roving bridge, Peak Forest Canal GMSMR 975
T 1790s tramway, Parkbridge GMSMR 629
T 1790s tramway tunnel, Parkbridge GMSMR 2253
F 1790s lock-keeper's cottage, Droylsden GMSMR 646
L 1800 aqueduct, Stakes Aqueduct GMSMR 975
F 1820s toll house, Woodend Toll Bar Cottage GMSMR 634
F 1833 canal boat house, Droylsden GMSMR 646
F 1837–45 railway, Ashton & Woodhead GMSMR 949
F 1842 railway station building, Broadbottom GMSMR 6169
F 1842 station master's houses, Broadbottom GMSMR 6169
F 1843 railway goods shed, Broadbottom GMSMR 6169
F 1845 railway viaduct (brick), Ashton GMSMR 740

Water Supply & Drainage

L 1761 weir, Woolley Mill GMSMR 8175
L 1762–87 water tank, Dukinfield Circus GMSMR 3531
F 1808 water pipe, Flowery Field, Hyde GMSMR 9160
F 1825 reservoir, Tombottom Reservoir, Ashton GMSMR 5877

NOTES

[1] Burke & Nevell 1996; Nevell 1991, 1992, 1993, 1994; Nevell & Walker 1998, 1999.
[2] Nevell & Walker 1998, 17–32.
[3] Aikin 1795.
[4] Ibid., 458, 472.
[5] English Heritage 1997, 45.
[6] Crossley 1990, 2.
[7] Tarlow 1999.
[8] Orser 1999.
[9] Clark 1999.
[10] Allaby 1996; Colinvaux 1993; Smith & Smith 1998.

[11] Nevell & Walker 1998.
[12] Holding 1986.
[13] Rigby 1995.
[14] Weber 1927.
[15] Griffin & Van Der Linden 1998.
[16] Wetherell 1998.
[17] Hudson 1992.
[18] Pollard 1997, 10–17.
[19] Crafts 1989, 25–43; Davies 1989, 44–68.
[20] Courtney 1997.
[21] Bythell 1969.

BIBLIOGRAPHY

Aikin, J. 1795, *A Description of the Country Thirty to Forty Miles round Manchester*, London.

Allaby, M. 1996, *Basics of Environmental Science*, London: Routledge.

Burke, T. & Nevell, M. D. 1996, *A History and Archaeology of Tameside. Volume 5: Buildings of Tameside*, Ashton-under-Lyne: Tameside Metropolitan Borough Council with the University of Manchester Archaeological Unit and the Greater Manchester Archaeological Unit.

Bythell, D. 1969, *The Handloom Weavers*, Cambridge: Cambridge University Press.

Clark, K. 1999, 'The workshop of the world: the industrial revolution', in Hunter, J. & Ralston, I. (eds) 1999, *The Archaeology of Britain. An Introduction from the Upper Palaeolithic to the Industrial Revolution*, London: Routledge.

Colinvaux, P. 1993, *Ecology*, Chichester: John Wiley and Sons.

Courtney, P. 1997, 'The tyranny of constructs', in Gaimster & Stamper (eds), 9–24.

Crafts, N. F. R. 1976, 'English economic growth in the eighteenth century: a re-examination of Deane and Cole's estimates', *Economic History Review* 29, 226–35.

Crossley, D. 1990, *Post-Medieval Archaeology in Britain*, Leicester: Leicester University Press.

Davies, J. A. 1989, 'Industrialization in Britain and Europe before 1850: New Perspectives and Old Problems', in Mathias, P. & Davis, J. A. (eds), *The First Industrial Revolutions*, Cambridge: Blackwell Ltd, 44–68.

English Heritage 1997, *English Heritage Research Agenda*, London: English Heritage.

Gaimster, D. & Stamper, P. (eds) 1997, *The Age of Transition. The Archaeology of English Culture 1400–1600*, Oxford: Oxbow.

Griffin, L. J. & Van Der Linden, M. (eds) 1998, *New Methods for Social History*, International Review of Social History 43, 1998 Supplement.

Holding, T. 1986, 'An Archaeological Survey of the Hatting Industry in Denton' (unpublished MS copy in Tameside Local Studies Library).

Hudson, P. 1992, *The Industrial Revolution*, London: Edward Arnold.

Johnson, M. 1996, *An Archaeology of Capitalism*, Oxford: Blackwell.

Nevell, M. D. 1991, *A History and Archaeology of Tameside. Volume 2: Tameside 1066–1700*, Ashton-under-Lyne: Tameside Metropolitan Borough Council with the Greater Manchester Archaeological Unit.

Nevell, M. D. 1992, *A History and Archaeology of Tameside. Volume 1: Tameside Before 1066*, Ashton-under-Lyne: Tameside Metropolitan Borough Council with the Greater Manchester Archaeological Unit.

Nevell, M. D. 1993, *A History and Archaeology of Tameside. Volume 3: Tameside 1700–1930*, Ashton-under-Lyne: Tameside Metropolitan Borough Council with the Greater Manchester Archaeological Unit.

Nevell, M. D. 1994, *A History and Archaeology of Tameside. Volume 4: The People Who Made Tameside*, Ashton-under-Lyne: Tameside Metropolitan Borough Council with Greater Manchester Archaeological Contracts.

Nevell, M. D. & Walker, J. S. F. 1998, *A History and Archaeology of Tameside. Volume 6. Lands and Lordships in Tameside: Tameside in Transition 1348–1642*, Ashton-under-Lyne: Tameside Metropolitan Borough Council with the University of Manchester Archaeological Unit.

Nevell, M. & Walker, J. 1999, *A History and Archaeology of Tameside. Volume 7. Tameside in Transition 1642–1870: The Archaeology of the Industrial Revolution in Two North-West Lordships*, Ashton-under-Lyne: Tameside Metropolitan Borough Council with the University of Manchester Archaeological Unit.

Orser, C. E. 1999, 'Negotiating Our "Familiar" Past', in Tarlow & West (eds), 273–85.

RCHME 1996, *Thesaurus of Monument Types*, London: Royal Commission on the Historical Monuments of England,.

Palmer, M. & Neaverson, P. 1998, *Industrial Archaeology, Principles and Practice*, London & New York: Routledge.

Pollard, S. 1997, *Marginal Europe. The Contribution of Marginal Lands Since the Middle Ages*, Oxford: Clarendon Press.

Renfrew, C. & Bahn, P. 1996, *Archaeology. Theories, Methods and Practice*, 2nd edition, London: Thames and Hudson.

Rigby, S. H. 1995, *English Society in the Later Middle Ages. Class, Status and Gender*, London: Macmillan.

Smith, R. L. & Smith, T. M. 1998, *Elements of Ecology*, 4th edition, Harlow: Benjamin Cummings & Co.

Tarlow, S. 1999, 'Strangely Familiar', in Tarlow & West (eds), 263–72.

Tarlow, S. & West, S. (eds) 1999, *The Familiar Past? Archaeologies of Later Historical Britain*, London and New York: Routledge.

Ward, J. T. & Wilson, R. G. (eds) 1971, *Land and Industry: the Landed Estate and the Industrial Revolution*, London: David & Charles.

Weber, M. 1927, *General Economic History*, New York: Greenberg.

Wetherell, C. 1998, 'Historical Social Network Analysis', in Griffin & Van Der Linden (eds), 125–44.

WATER POWER IN THE LANDSCAPE: THE RIVERS OF THE SHEFFIELD AREA

By DAVID CROSSLEY

HISTORICAL INTRODUCTION

Five rivers flow through the modern city of Sheffield (Fig. 1), and during the industrialization of the region all have been intensively used for power. The Don has two local tributaries, the Loxley and the Sheaf, each of which has its own feeders, the Rivelin in the case of the Loxley and the Porter flowing into the Sheaf. The total length of these streams within the modern city boundaries totals about 30 miles (48km.), over which 115 mill sites are known.[1] The catchment comprises the high gritstone moors to the west of Sheffield, and the Coal-Measure lands to the east of this ridge. The relatively steady release of water provided by peat moorland favours mill operation, and the geology of the Coal Measures has provided sites for weirs where outcrops of hard rock are crossed by the streams.

Water power, for grinding and forging, was one of several factors which assisted the development of cutlery and edge-tool manufacture, for which the district is well known. However, many trades had begun as hand skills, only requiring power as the scale of manufacture grew. Basic to the early growth of the industry were the availability of fuel, from coppice-woodland and from coal deposits, of labour, in a region where secondary employments added to income from agriculture,[2] of iron ore, smelted to provide bar iron for objects such as nails, and of better grades of iron and steel imported through the Humber from the Baltic. In addition, the Coal Measures provided refractory sandstone and clay for hearths and furnaces, as well as stone suitable for blade-grinding.

At the end of the Middle Ages, the power of the local rivers was used for traditional mills. Records currently known suggest that there were corn mills at Sheffield, Bradfield, Bradway, Brightside, Ecclesall, Norton, Owlerton and Wadsley. There was also a mill for fulling cloth at Bradway. The earliest reference to powered grinding of metal goods is the lease in 1496 of a wheel on the Sheaf, likely to be Moscar Wheel. The middle decades of the 16th century saw a good deal of construction of grinding wheels. The circumstantial evidence is strong: John Leland, writing *c.* 1540, commented on the numerous smiths and cutlers in Hallamshire, and in the second half of the 16th century the metal trades appear to have outgrown the regulation of the manorial court, leading to the foundation of the Company of Cutlers in 1624. Much of the riverside property of the Sheffield area belonged to the manor of the Earls of Shrewsbury, but it is unfortunate that the estate rentals do not survive for

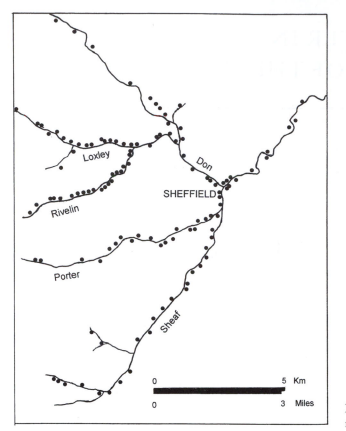

FIGURE 1. Sheffield and its rivers.

the years before 1581. At the start of the existing series, the section covering wheel-rents contains fourteen entries; it is not yet certain when these mills were built, although it is known that Lescar Wheels on the Porter were in use in the 1540s, and the surviving Shepherd Wheel, upstream, had been built by the 1560s. From the 1580s there is consistent information about the wheels on the Shrewsbury estates; rentals, and the survey of Sheffield manor made in 1637,[3] show that by that date there were about 30 wheels. There is less information about neighbouring estates, on the upper reaches of the Don, Loxley, Porter and particularly the Sheaf. This southernmost river became significant in the 17th century: the former lands of Beauchief Abbey possessed several suitable sites for mills, and the upper reaches were used for the smelting of lead in water-powered ore-hearths, much as in the other valleys of the north Derbyshire gritstone region.[4]

Of particular significance was the century after 1680, notably the years from c. 1720 to 1790. As is shown in the survey of 1794, all available sites on the rivers were developed, and in certain cases, notably on the Don, multiple mills were built. Construction took place on the less accessible upper reaches; this applies on the Rivelin (Fig. 2 and accompanying table) where numerous sites can be seen from the

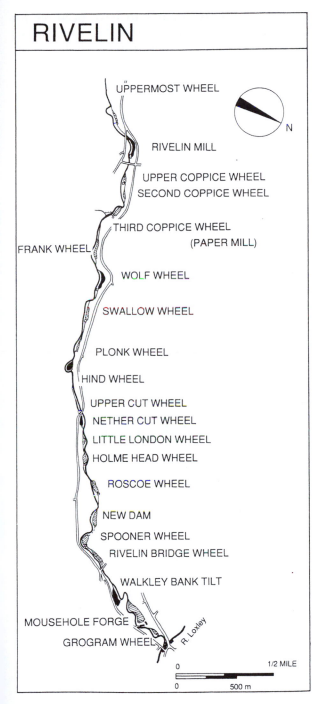

The earliest known dates for sites on the Rivelin:
Uppermost 1751
Rivelin Mill 1632
Upper Coppice 1736
Second Coppice 1736
Third Coppice 1758
Frank 1737
Wolf 1722
Swallow 1692
Plonk 1737
Hind 1581
Upper Cut 1749
Nether Cut 1719
Little London 1752
Holme Head 1742
Roscoe 1725
(New Dam 1853)
Spooner 1637
Rivelin Bridge 1724
Walkley Bank 1751
Mousehole 1632
Grogram 1620

FIGURE 2. Map of the Rivelin.

lease books of the Norfolk (previously Shrewsbury) estates to have been let for construction at this time. The number of wheels built on this and other streams is a comment on the development of the metal trades in Sheffield as a whole, amply demonstrated by recent research.[5]

1794 saw the use of water power at its maximum. Thereafter, a number of pressures worked for reduction of the numbers of mills. Steam power was increasingly used for grinding, forging and rolling. Near the centre of the town, rising land-values made the sites of mill-buildings, dams and ponds attractive for development. The landowner's view of the profitability of mills is shown early in the 19th century, when several were put up for sale by the Norfolk estate, which saw these as having less potential than property elsewhere. Some mills were not easy to dispose of, particularly in the depression which followed the Napoleonic wars, and they either stayed in Norfolk hands on short leases, or passed through series of ownerships. Several mill-sites on the Loxley and Rivelin were affected by the development of water resources for urban supply. Mill owners were objectors to the Water Works Bill of 1831, and debate continued over their rights in face of pressures for improved drinking-water for the town. The Sheffield Water Company purchased wheels on the Rivelin in the 1850s: several of these went out of use soon afterwards, although others maintained a precarious existence to the end of the century, worked on short tenancies.

There was some revival of the use of water power on the Loxley in the second half of the 19th century. Ironically this appears to have been prompted by the disastrous flood of 1864, when the bursting of Dale Dyke reservoir dam destroyed most of the buildings along the floor of the valley. Compensation paid by the water company led some owners to rebuild, and sites such as Low Matlock (Fig. 3) were redeveloped in a radical fashion. Indeed, only five sites were not reinstated: three were at the western end of the valley on ground used for Damflask reservoir, the site of Upper Cliffe Wheel was used to extend the Low Matlock dam, and Ashton Carr Wheel, one of the earliest sites on the Loxley, was never rebuilt.

As with many instances of industrial decline, the final years of the use of water power in and around Sheffield have left few records. One pointer is contained in rate-book entries, for when the head and fall of water, important for rating-valuation, ceased to be recorded, there is an inference that the wheels had been abandoned. Contemporary lists of mills support these conclusions: those on the Don were recorded in 1874 and 1895; there is a list of wheels on the Don, Loxley and Rivelin in 1907 in the Norfolk estate papers, and a comprehensive survey was published by W. T. Miller in 1936. The report of the *Council for the Conservation of Sheffield Antiquities* (1956) shows only the wheels at Sharrow Snuff Mill (Porter), Loxley Old Wheel and Storrs Mill (Loxley) in use, the Low Matlock rolling mill wheel having recently been disconnected. Abbeydale scythe works was yet to be repaired and developed as a museum, Shepherd Wheel, also, was yet to be put in order as a museum, and Malin Bridge corn mill had ceased to be used.

WATER POWER IN THE LANDSCAPE

The intensity with which water power was used on the Sheffield rivers can still be demonstrated on the ground, particularly in the upper reaches of the Loxley, Rivelin,

FIGURE 3. Low Matlock rolling mill, Loxley: rebuilt in 1882 after the destruction of the pre-existing forge during the flood of 1864.

Porter and Sheaf, where dams and channels have left numerous earthworks which have not been obscured by later development. There are important contemporary surveys and maps, which provide guides to layout, notably those in the collection of the Fairbanks. The latter were surveyors in Sheffield over the crucial period of water-power development in the 18th century, and provided evidence in the course of disputes over water rights in the early decades of the 19th century. In addition, local collections of late 19th-century photographs show landscapes of earthworks, ponds and buildings in valleys such as the Rivelin, which are now more heavily wooded.

The Don and its tributaries show the typical Pennine methods of harnessing abundant water. The normal practice was to use a by-pass layout rather than to construct a cross-valley dam. In fact Mayfield corn mill and Forge Dam, both at the head of the Porter valley, and Limbrick Wheel, a post-1864 reconstruction on the Loxley, are the only examples of cross-valley configuration. Forge Dam, whose earthworks survive and still hold water, shows the weaknesses of the system, the overflow weir bearing the force of storm water and the pond being severely silted.

The classic by-pass system employed a weir to deflect water, through a head-goit into a pond, known locally as the dam, set parallel with the river and confined by a bank which ran for the length of the pond. The bank generally turned towards the hillside adjacent to the mill, and was often reinforced by the back wall of the mill building. After water had passed through the mill, it was returned to the river by a tail goit with sufficient fall to ensure that water did not impede rotation of the wheel. There were numerous variations on the by-pass layout, resulting from pressures on siting. Compromises resulted from the overcrowding which is shown by the 1794 list of sites: in many places, notably on the Don, it was difficult to build adequate weirs because of insufficient fall between mills. So, as on the Rivelin, a shared weir would serve more than one site, the dams and wheels being placed in tandem without intermediate return of water to the river, the tail goit of one mill forming the head-goit to the next. In some cases two mills would be set alongside each other, as at Olive Wheel (Loxley), where a single dam feeds two wheels, set in adjacent wheel-pits (Fig. 4).

The standard elements of mill earthworks can be illustrated from surviving examples; of particular value are the strings of sites which survive on the Loxley, Rivelin and Porter, many of which are easy of access. The weir is the element which frequently remains where other features have been lost. It was typically built at an angle across the stream, to deflect water towards the entry to the head-goit. Construction was of pitched stonework, set in clay between top and bottom kerbs. The height of the top kerb regulated the amount of water admitted to the head-goit, but it also affected the flow in the river, sometimes hindering the egress of water from up-stream wheels. The height could be varied by the use of detachable wash-boards, edge-set planks mounted in wrought-iron fittings on the top of the weir. Weirs were liable to deterioration, stages of which can be shown on these rivers. The top kerbs could be displaced by flood-borne debris, and were reinforced by iron staples leaded into mortices. The lower kerbs were less vulnerable, and were rarely stapled; indeed some were of timber, which may survive under water. The sloping face of the weir deteriorated as stones were displaced, particularly if vegetation were established on the upstream end of the weir, over which water might only flow intermittently. Displacement has also taken place when vegetation, ultimately trees, has become established on silt deposited on the upstream side of the top kerb: roots have spread beneath the kerb and have loosened stones in the face. In attempts to prevent this, slabs were laid on the upstream side of some weirs, enabling silt to be removed. An interesting example, with a secondary kerb at the upstream edge of the slabs, can be still be seen at Roscoe Wheel, and is depicted on a Fairbank plan of 1830 (Fig. 5). In the 19th century many traditional weirs appear to have been replaced by stronger designs: on the Don and the Loxley there are examples where slopes have been divided into bays, separated by ashlar ribs.

Head-goits are usually marked by the substantial masonry of the entry to the channel adjacent to the weir, and by remains of shuttles formerly controlling the flow of water. The goit ran along the contour of the hillside, and frequently took in water on the way to the dam, from small tributaries intercepted by construction of the channel, or from field-drains. The dam itself was the key to the efficiency of the mill, and construction and maintenance were major commitments. It was necessary to build a substantial bank between the reservoir and the river, often supported on the river side by a massive wall. The storage area was increased by quarrying into the hillside, and the pond-bottom was lined with puddled clay to minimize leakage of water back to the river. Maintenance of the clay was important, and required periodic

FIGURE 4. Olive Wheels, Loxley: the left-hand wheel powered the grind-stones; the wheel on the right was for a paper mill.

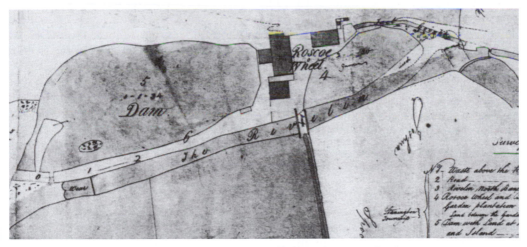

FIGURE 5. Roscoe Wheel in 1830. (Sheffield Archives: Fairbank Bra 118S.)

drainage and removal of silt and vegetation. An indication of how this was done is the siting of deep drainage shuttles along the lengths of dams: these allowed water to be released, and their substantial ashlar-faced structures are prominent survivals.

There is a striking variation in the size of dams on these rivers. In some cases the amount of water-storage was apparently important to patterns of work, whilst in others the dams were little more than side-channels serving as buffers against short-term variations in flow due to irregular release from upstream wheels. We can contrast the building of additional storage capacity for the Ponds sites at the lower end of the Sheaf, the second dam at Wadsley Forge on the Don, or the mid-19th-century New Dam at Spooner Wheel on the Loxley, with sites on the Loxley such as Upper Slack Wheel, Birley Meadows Wheel or Malin Bridge Wheel, where there was little or no storage capacity. The dam usually narrowed at its down-stream end, forming the fore-bay, which was often massively reinforced in stone. From the fore-bay the water flowed into the pentrough, to supply the wheel. The back of the pentrough was set into the dam wall behind the wheel-pit, and comprised a box built of timber or, in the 19th century, of cast iron plates. The penstock, the shuttle at the wheel end of the pentrough, was raised and lowered by rack and pinion, controlled by levers from within the mill. Working examples can be seen at Abbeydale and at Shepherd Wheel, and much of the mechanism survives at Low Matlock rolling mill.

For the field-worker, the identification of tail-goits, downstream from mills, can be of importance in confirming the location of sites which have been largely destroyed. It is also important to grasp the importance of maintaining a deep channel with a good flow of water away from the wheel. Sheffield has a number of examples where tail-goits are particularly long and prominent. This was due to physical or property constraints which led to difficulty in accommodating dam systems which would give adequate head for overshot or pitch-back wheels, but where it was feasible to dig a lengthy tail-goit. Hence it was possible to mount an overshot wheel at a low level and to design a long outlet channel with a fall which was adequate, but less steep than that of the river. The outfall was placed at a point where the water levels coincided. This can be seen at certain Rivelin examples, notably Third Coppice, Holme Head and Rivelin Bridge: in the case of the last two, the races are separated from the stream by, respectively, a prominent line of edge-set stone slabs, and by a narrow wall of stone blocks, both structures being secured by wrought-iron staples along the top. On the Porter, Sharrow snuff mill gives a remarkable demonstration of this strategy, the tail-goit leaving the deep wheel-pit in a culvert which tunnels beneath the river, to discharge at a distant point on the opposite bank, downstream.

WATER WHEELS

No pre-19th-century water wheels survive in Sheffield, but the likely design of those installed by earlier millwrights can be deduced from examples excavated elsewhere in Britain.[6] In Sheffield the configuration of the water wheel is rarely stated before the end of the 18th century, but something can be deduced from figures for the fall of water. Such information comes from the list made in 1794, from 19th-century surveys, and from rate-book entries. Where the fall is recorded as more than ten feet it is likely that an overshot or pitch-back wheel would be used, rather than an undershot or low-breast wheel. Low falls, of two to three feet, suggest undershot wheels, although these must have been rare. In fact, one undershot wheel does survive, at Malin Bridge corn mill, a site too confined to accommodate a dam. There are overshot wheels at Abbeydale (the blower wheel), Low Matlock, Olive and Shepherd Wheels, and at Sharrow snuff mill. There are also two pitch-back wheels at Abbeydale. There are cases where it is possible to deduce the form of the wheel from the masonry of the wheel-pit. Curved stonework at the back of the pit, designed to fit closely to the wheel and indicating a pitch-back design, can be seen at Roscoe Wheel on the Rivelin and Broadhead Wheel on the Loxley.

In the 19th century, there were improvements in the design and construction of water wheels, and this is seen in Sheffield. There are a number of local surveys in which details of wheels can be found, and by 1830 it was common for estimates of horse-power to be made. Precise evaluation of mill design arose in part from the choice of uses to which sites could be put during urban development, and also to the increasing availability of small steam engines as alternative power sources. Apart from attention to the efficiency of wheels, seen in detailed changes of design, the increase in the use of iron in their construction led to greater durability. By the middle of the 19th century most new or replacement wheels were of iron, as shown by the examples which post-date the 1864 Loxley flood at Low Matlock and Olive Wheels. Even so, some composite wheels, of timber and iron, did survive, notably at Abbeydale and at Malin Bridge. Sheffield millwrights do not seem to have adopted new designs which became popular elsewhere. There are no known examples of suspension wheels, although there were some cases of drive through toothed rings on the periphery of wheels. The reuse of water wheel pits for water turbines is so far only known in one case, a turbine installed in 1901 at Whirlow Wheel.

CONCLUSIONS

The landscape evidence for the use of water power survives particularly well on the rivers flowing through Sheffield. Mill sites are closely linked to the industries which characterized the economy of the district, and although many are in rural surroundings, there was always a close relationship with the urban trades. The forging and grinding of objects made in the town were put out to craftsmen using water power, and the growth of urban population led to the development not only of the long-established corn mills, but to the use of water for production of materials such as paper. Water mills should be seen as one component of an early industrial landscape; they should be related not only to sources of raw materials such as woodlands, mines or quarries, but to the houses and farms of those who, before the 19th century, worked in the grinding wheels and forges on a part-time basis.

David Crossley, ARCUS, University of Sheffield, Department of Archaeology, West Court, 2 Mappin Street, Sheffield S1 4DT, UK

NOTES

[1] Crossley *et al.* 1989.
[2] Hey 1972.
[3] Harrison 1908.

[4] Kiernan 1989; Crossley & Kiernan 1992.
[5] Hey 1991; Flavell 1996.
[6] Crossley 1991, 147–52.

BIBLIOGRAPHY

Crossley, D., Cass, J., Flavell, N. & Turner, C. 1989, *Water Power on the Sheffield Rivers*, Sheffield: University of Sheffield.

Crossley, D. 1991, *Post-Medieval Archaeology in Britain*, Leicester: Leicester University Press.

Crossley, D. & Kiernan, D. T. 1992, 'The lead smelting mills of Derbyshire', *Derbyshire Archaeological Journal* 112, 6–47.

Flavell, N. 1996, 'The Economic Development of Sheffeild and the Growth of the Town c. 1740–1820' (unpublished PhD thesis, University of Sheffield).

Harrison, J. (1908 edn) *An Exact and Perfect Survey and View of the Manor of Sheffield, 1637*, ed. by Ronksley, J., Sheffield.

Hey, D. G. 1972, *The Rural Metalworkers of the Sheffield Region*, Leicester: Leicester University Press.

Hey, D. G. 1991, *The Fiery Blades of Hallamshire*, Leicester: Leicester University Press.

Kiernan, D. T. 1989, *The Derbyshire Lead Industry in the Sixteenth Century*, Chesterfield: Derbyshire Record Series 14.

Miller, W. T. 1936, *The Water Mills of Sheffield*, Sheffield: Pawson and Brailsford.

WOODLAND, INDUSTRY AND COMMON RIGHTS — A CONFLICT OF INTEREST

By TOM GLEDHILL

Wood was an essential raw material for the lead industry of the 17th to 19th centuries in Swaledale. For the earlier part of this period wood was used both as a fuel for smelting and for lining shafts. Wood used for smelting was sometimes kiln dried to form white coal[1] or chopwood.[2] The documentary evidence for this is supported by the material remains of wood drying kilns.[3] The presence of platforms used for making charcoal in proximity to these suggests that charcoal may have been used for re-smelting lead rich slags. Large-diameter wood referred to as grove or groove timber was used to line shafts and adits. 'Stoprice' was brushwood used to stop the gaps between groove timbers. Additional wood was required for specialist purposes such as rails, and planking for constructing leats and washing floors. Although planks were often softwood imported from abroad, the remainder of these woodland products were supplied from local woods, mainly within the Dale.[4]

A study of the documentary record reveals that many of the woods which supplied the industry were managed as coppices.[5] Although wood ceased to be of primary importance as a fuel for smelting during the 18th century, it was still used in large quantities in the mines. Coppice management of the woods therefore continued into the 19th century. The decline in the use of wood for fuel may have caused a change in the length of coppice rotation. Coppice rotations employed for growing groove timber tend to be long, such as the 25 years recorded for the woods round Downholm Park in the 18th century.[6] Rotations for chopwood are likely to have been shorter than this. Coppice woodlands continued to be important to the lead industry into the 19th century, and their distinctive remains can still be seen in much of lower Swaledale.

This mainly documentary picture of Swaledale's woods gives the impression that woodlands managed as coppices for the lead industry were predominant. This is misleading as the documentary record tends not to record the more traditional exploitation of woodland by the agricultural community.[7] This is best reflected in the landscape itself. The landscape of upper Swaledale is divided into a number of small territorial units, each with a hamlet and an associated walled common pasture. Thus the pasture associated with Ivelet is Ivelet Side, that of Satron is Satron Side and so on (Fig. 1). Some of these pastures are partly wooded, Rowlieth Wood in Low Row

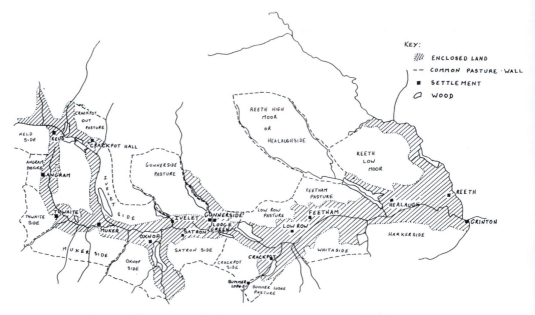

FIGURE I.   Common pastures in Upper Swaledale.

Pasture being a good example. These common pastures are of considerable antiquity. They are recorded in a 17th-century court case.[8] It seems likely that the medieval monastic and secular vaccaries were based on the same territorial units, as their names are those of the modern hamlets. The hamlets belonging to Harkerside and Whitaside have long disappeared from the map, but the remains of the hamlet of 'Harkey' can still be discerned within the modern fields.[9] These cow pastures appear to have been rather more wooded in the past. Medieval records of woodmen living on Whitaside suggest that this area may have been relatively wooded at the time.[10] More concrete evidence is available for Ivelet Side. Most of the lower slopes of this common pasture are covered in charcoal platforms, extending far outside the modern limits of Ivelet Wood. Excavation of one of these platforms produced charcoal radiocarbon-dated to the 17th century.[11] It thus seems likely that much of the post-medieval woodland in upper Swaledale was subject to common rights of pasture.

These were not necessarily the only rights exercised by the agricultural community. Rights to wood for domestic and agricultural purposes were common in the Middle Ages, and often survived into post-medieval times. These rights were called 'bootes'. There were thus houseboote for building and maintaining farm properties, fireboote for firewood, ploughboote, waineboote, hedgeboote and so on. The situation in the manor of Healaugh in the early 17th century is recorded in a court case relating to a dispute over tenant rights. The lord of the manor was allowed wood 'for the repair of his mills and mines only, and the tenants for the repair of their houses, fences and for firing as they have been accustomed'. Neither lord nor tenant were to sell or waste any.[12]

The vast bulk of the woodland in upper Swaledale was either on tenant land or on common pasture. The effect of this was that exploitation was not determined by outright ownership, but by a complex web of different rights. On the common pastures coppicing was ruled out by the rights to pasture. On tenant land coppicing was only possible with the good will of the tenant. As the lead industry expanded, a closer definition of rights was needed. Thus in 1618 an agreement between the Lords Wharton and their tenants of the manor of Muker allowed the tenants to fell wood and trees in hedgerows on their land and to sell them to any other of the tenants of the lordship or manor, but not to others. Timber was available from the woods for maintaining their farm by delivery of the bailiff. Underwood (i.e., wood from pollards, coppice wood and other small branches) was available to them as had traditionally been the case. The Lords Wharton were allowed to reserve woods for the use of the mines, excepting the needs of the tenants for timber.[13] This agreement probably represents the limit of what could be achieved within the existing system of common rights. It is important as much for what it leaves out as for what it contains. Most importantly the agreement does not allow the Lords Wharton to enclose any part of the common pastures. The large areas of woodland on the commons could therefore be felled for use in the mines and mills, but the subsequent regrowth could not be protected from browsing stock.

The effects of the limitations imposed on the exploitation of woodland for the mines is reflected in several different contexts. In the documentary record references to the desirability of planting woodland on demesne land,[14] and to the possibility of paying tenants more than the going rate for carriage in order to encourage them to care for, and coppice their woods,[15] reflect the difficulties in organizing efficient woodland management. Tenant opposition to industrial exploitation is illustrated by the following event recorded in 1677: 'Ant. Metcalf and some others cut up all the wood of their tenements that the lord might not have the wood.'[16]

The consequences of the difficulty in organizing woodland management of wooded commons are illustrated by an archaeological study of Ivelet Wood. This wood formerly covered most of the lower slopes of Ivelet Side. This is reflected by the distribution of 50 charcoal platforms and a number of wood drying kilns, which have been dated to the 17th century. Growth ring analysis of charcoal retrieved by excavation of one of the charcoal platforms has shown that the wood used in the last firing was at least 50 years old. This suggests that the woodland was not coppiced. Indeed the lack of a defined upper age limit for the trees used implies that there was no regular harvesting of the wood. If this is typical of the common woods of upper Swaledale then they can hardly have played a major role in supplying the lead industry.[17]

It is also possible to see the effects of the defence of common rights in the landscape. In part this is reflected by the continued existence of common woodlands such as Ivelet and Rowlieth Woods. It can also be illustrated by place-names. Certain place-names such as Spring and Hag strongly reflect the presence of coppice woodland.[18] These can be mapped to gain an impression of the importance of coppicing in a given area. If this is done for Swaledale it is immediately apparent that names with these elements are very common in lower Swaledale, to the east of Reeth,

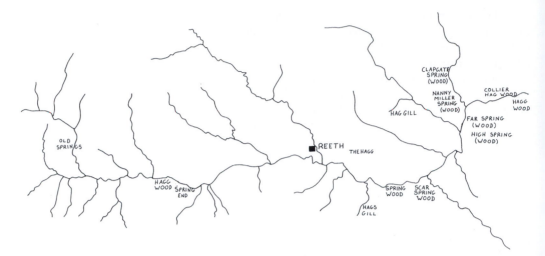

FIGURE 2. 'Hag' and 'spring' names in Swaledale.

but very rare in upper Swaledale, to the west of Reeth (Fig. 2). This contrast corresponds exactly to a change in the landscape organization of the Dale. The western area is organized around hamlets with individual common pastures as illustrated above. To the east the settlements are more conventional villages which had large open fields in the medieval period and which had been largely enclosed by the 17th century. Woodland in this area was therefore privately owned, and not generally subject to common rights.

The 1995 *Industry and Agriculture* conference presented the challenge to cross the boundaries between industrial archaeology, social history, and the study of the landscape. This attempt to do so has emphasized that the expansion of industry occurred within an inhabited and exploited landscape. In consequence the effects of industry on that landscape must be understood in terms of the interaction between industrial needs and the existing social framework. In the case of upper Swaledale the expansion of commercial coppicing appears to have been severely restricted by the social landscape organized around common rights, which survived the medieval period. In contrast, the woodlands of lower Swaledale had long been privatized and played a vital role in supplying the lead industry with wood.

Tom Gledhill, 1 Hylton Terrace, Rookhope, Bishop Auckland, Co. Durham DL13 2BB, UK

NOTES

[1] Crossley 1993.
[2] Raistrick 1982, 54–55.
[3] Gledhill 1992.
[4] Ibid.

[5] Ibid.
[6] North Yorkshire County Record Office, file ZBO.
[7] The pattern of rural rights and customs in Northern England is described by Winchester 2000.

[8] Ashcroft 1984, 42–43.
[9] Pers. comm., Andrew Fleming.
[10] Lancaster 1912, 254.
[11] Gledhill 1994, 372.
[12] Ashcroft 1984, 52–53.
[13] Ibid., 57–58.

[14] Ibid., 127.
[15] Ibid., 143.
[16] Ibid.
[17] A full report of the investigation of Ivelet Wood can be found as Appendix 2 in Gledhill 1994.
[18] Gledhill 1994, 164, 175–86.

BIBLIOGRAPHY

Ashcroft, M. Y. (ed.) 1984, *Documents Relating to the Swaledale Estates of Lord Wharton in the Sixteenth and Seventeenth Century*, North Yorkshire County Record Office Publications No. 36.

Crossley, D. W. 1993, 'White coal and charcoal in the woodlands of north Derbyshire and Sheffield', in Beswick, P., Rotherham, I. D. & Parsons, J. (eds), *Ancient Woodlands, their Archaeology and Ecology, a Coincidence of Interest*, Landscape Conservation Forum 67.

Gledhill. T. D. 1992, 'Smelting and woodland in Swaledale', in Willies, L. & Cranstone, D. (eds), *Boles and Smeltmills: Report of a seminar on the history and archaeology of lead smelting held at Reeth, Yorkshire*, Historical Metallurgy Society Ltd., 62–63.

Gledhill, T. D. 1994, 'A Woodland History of North Yorkshire' (unpublished PhD thesis: University of Sheffield).

Lancaster, W. T. (ed.) 1912, *The Chartulary of Bridlington Priory*, Leeds.

Raistrick, A. 1982, *The Wharton Mines in Swaledale in the 17th Century*, North Yorkshire County Record Office Publications 31.

Winchester, A. J. L. 2000, *The Harvest of the Hills: Rural Life in Northern England and the Scottish Borders, 1400–1700*, Edinburgh: Edinburgh University Press.

Archive Material

Bolton Castle Estate survey book for 1765–66.

THE MINING LANDSCAPE OF COSGARNE COMMON, GWENNAP, CORNWALL

By LYNN WILLIES

Cosgarne (nowadays Cusgarne) Common was the location of two of Cornwall's greatest copper mines, operating mainly between *c.* 1760 and 1870 when smaller mines were consolidated into two great setts, Consolidated Mines and United Mines (Fig. 1). At the time of their decline, *c.* 1860, these were further consolidated into a smaller, temporarily profitable mine, Wheal Clifford: the whole of the copper mines on the Common then became known as Clifford Amalgamated. The mines occupy an area about 3km. long and a little over 1km. wide.[1]

Cosgarne Common is a ridge extending east from the elevated granite outcrop known as Carn Marth. It is bounded on the north side by the Wheal Maid Valley and Stream and on the south by the Hicks Mill Stream, the waters of both derived mainly from Carn Marth. On the eastern margin, these run, at Haile Mills and at Point respectively, into the valley of the River Carnon, which is not far above sea level. The lodes are mainly found in the killas, indurated shales and siltstones belonging to the Mylor Series, but there are many instances where these are cut through by igneous dykes called elvans, which emanated from the underlying granite. The ground is much faulted; some of these faults host mineralized lodes, though others, of later date, are filled with clays and are known as fluccans.

An important effect on mining resulted from isostatic sea level changes which first created over-deepening and then flooding of the valleys resulted in the ria coastline. The over-deepening of the Carnon River has allowed groundwater penetration to a much greater depth than today's valley floors, transporting mobile copper minerals to greater depths (the oxidation and reduction enrichment zones) but also enhancing grades of the less mobile tin in the resultant shallow gossans. Thus the copper-bearing sections of lodes near the Carnon Valley are at depths requiring steam-pumping for access, whilst those further away, flanking Carn Marth, could be worked earlier with simpler drainage methods.

There is a great multiplicity of lodes,[2] but the two major systems run roughly east-west, one belonging to United, the other to Consolidated. Parallel lodes to these are found also to the north of the Wheal Maid Valley, worked by several other major mines, including, notably, the Poldice, Killifrith and Wheal Busy setts. This district, more than any other, saw the greatest developments of the Boulton and Watt engine,

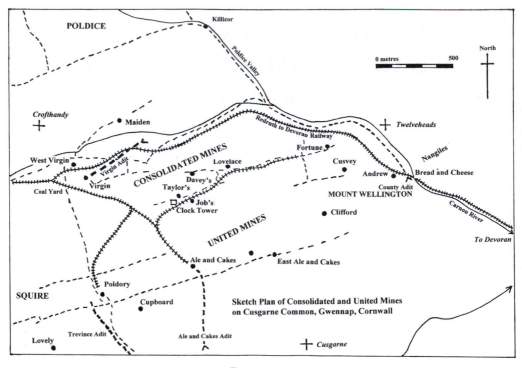

FIGURE 1.

and its successor, the Cornish engine. Southwards the lower ground, though not entirely unaffected by mining, has substantially fewer mines, most of which are obscured by the rampant vegetation of the area. The major lodes also continue to both east and west, beyond the River Carnon and towards Camborne respectively; many of these also sustained very large-scale mining operations.

At the western end of the Common was the Manor of Trevince, owned wholly and continuously by the Beauchamp family. This area was ultimately to become known as Wheal Squire, though previously it was divided into a substantial number of separate titles. Cosgarne Common was divided into two parts, east and west, with slightly different Lords, usually four in all,[3] with Beauchamp having an interest in the western part. The boundaries between Trevince and Cosgarne, and between the east and west parts of Cosgarne, were delineated by lines of stone posts, as were many of the setts and bounds laid out by the miners and tinners. Most of these have now disappeared, some very recently, but the locations are often shown on the 1st and 2nd Edition OS large scale maps.

A BRIEF HISTORY OF THE LANDSCAPE

Prior to the major development of copper mining, the Common, apart from areas utilized for rough grazing, was largely given over to tin working. This involved the

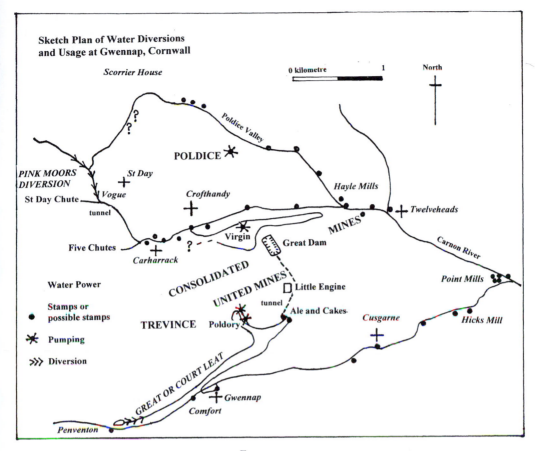

Sketch Plan of Water Diversions and Usage at Gwennap, Cornwall

FIGURE 2.

use of water for streaming the tin in alluvial and shode deposits and its working to shallow depths on suitable lodes. Much material needed to be crushed or stamped to release the fine tinstuff and this was done at a score or so of small-scale, water-powered, tin stamps and associated dressing floors. These utilized a complex system of leats and channels along the rivers and also involved diversion of water over substantial distances by means of larger leats, notably the 2km. long Great or Court Leat in the Hicks Mill valley (certainly in use some years before 1784)[4] and a still-functioning diversion under the watershed (1680s or possibly earlier)) from Pink Moors and Tolcarne, near Vogue at St Day into the Wheal Maid system (see Fig. 2 for both diversions and known stamp mill sites on the two streams).

The rights to work tin were long established and the area was divided into renewable bounds of relatively small size, following either lodes or the river valley floors, or both. Within these areas the ground was turned over again and again, with the original course of the rivers, for instance, being determined by sets of parallel posts set equidistant on the banks. For the right to work, the bounders paid the land/mineral owner a proportion of the ore and a rent for any stamp mill they operated. Some of the stamped waste was stored in heaps but much appears to have been discharged into the river system, ending in the Carnon and, ultimately, in the tidal estuary of the Fal at Devoran (which was eventually overwhelmed for shipping purposes by the amount of silt from the Carnon). Bounds could be individually owned, but by the 19th century — and probably much earlier — the bounds were usually divided amongst a number of owners each with a small part.[5]

Relatively little tin was mined at depth, though the claimed depth of nearby Poldice, worked by a water wheel since the 1680s, by the 1720s was over 100 fathoms (180m.).[6] This should warn us not to under-estimate the abilities of miners to follow a good lode, even before steam power. With the development of large-scale copper mining, tin-working took a lesser part, and was probably suppressed where feasible by the copper mine. However some tin-working continued throughout and, ironically, was probably the last work done on Clifford Amalgamated.[7]

The resultant landscape of tin mining, where not subsumed into the larger effects of copper mining, is seen in the broad relict working bed of the very small streams, traces of leats and dumps, and mounds at former stamp mill sites. One substantial area of tin open-working between Wheal Fortune and Wheal Lovelace (NGR SX 751 421) has lines of closely-spaced small mounds resulting from excavation of a working face in illuvium about 100m. long and 2m. high. It is clear that a line of men have sorted tinstones from the illuvium and cast the waste on to the heaps behind them. Similar features in the course of production were noted on a recent visit to Mexico.

Copper mining seems to have commenced near the end of the 17th century, probably in Trevince at the Wheal Lovely Lode, and further north around Wheal Busy at Chacewater:[8] both were well away from the over-deepened areas and access would have been possible down to the rich secondary copper ores. In the early 18th century, John Coster, a Bristol merchant and smelter, took an interest in both areas. He seems to have introduced, or financed the development of, substantial drainage levels (one was approaching Wheal Lovely in 1723–24) and the use of somewhat larger and more efficient water wheels than hitherto used. The area of Trevince and the adjacent area of the Common (Cupboard Hill and Ale and Cakes) seem to have been worked by his Metals Company until the mid century, though not on a very substantial scale by later standards. Apart from the leats and water wheels, the most conspicuous features of such working were the small shafts with hand windlasses and the fewer larger shafts with horse-whims mounted on the waste heaps.

The great event which led to large-scale working was the discovery of rich copper ore at Wheal Virgin in 1757. This was not a 'two-week wonder' discovery based on £100 expenditure as many have claimed, but the result of several years driving and considerable expense on a drainage adit from the Wheal Maid Valley.[9] If it had not been discovered then, it would have been discovered soon after, since an even deeper drainage adit was already driving, since 1748. This was the brainchild of the 'Great William Lemon' whose fortune came from a good marriage and the very profitable working of Wheal Fortune at Ludgvan near Penzance, and his mining manager John Williams. Beginning with a short section to Killicor Mine up the Carnon Valley en route to Poldice from just above Point, a branch was driven from near Haile Mills to Virgin and, a little later, from there to the mines on Cupboard Hill and in Trevince. The Poldice or Great Adit, now the County Adit, was driven on to drain some scores of mines and has a total length of some 50km.[10]

Events at Virgin were too promising to wait for the new adit. Between 1758 and 1777 seven Newcomen Engines were installed on Virgin and adjacent mines and two or three more on the mines over the hill, all later pumping into the new adit. The need for co-ordinated drainage was undoubtedly the driving force behind consolidation of individual titles into the Consolidated Mines and the United Mines which took place about 1770. This involved men such as Thomas 'guinea a minute' Daniels who was trustee to Lemon's heirs, and John Vivian, who formed a series of interlocking partnerships to work the mines.

It was the seven engines at Virgin and nearby Wheal Maid, now within the Consolidated title, which were replaced from 1778 by five Boulton and Watt types onwards of greater power and efficiency, with a further three being installed at Poldory and at Ale and Cakes at United. Watt installed his first rotary winding engine at Wheal Maid in 1785.[11] Unfortunately the production of vast amounts of copper at Thomas Williams' Parys Mountain in Anglesey took the gloss, and profit, from these adventures, and Boulton and Watt found themselves in litigation with the Cosgarne Mines, in which they themselves were also shareholders, over refusals to pay engine royalties and the employment and encouragement of 'pirates' such as the Hornblowers, Bull and Trevithick.[12]

By the turn of the century, both United and Consolidated were struggling. Consolidated was 'knacked' (closed) about 1809, but United continued, controlled by the now locally powerful Williams family — successors to Lemon's agent, John Williams, employing William Sims to convert the existing Watt engines there and at Wheal Squire to compound types.[13]

In 1819 John Taylor took control of Consolidated. He had proved himself in employment with the Duke of Bedford by driving the Tavistock Canal tunnel and in discovering and working Wheal Friendly there (near Morwellham). He had gone to London and had attracted a group of 'friends' or speculators to assist him in mining adventures. Whilst in London he had become acquainted with the engineer Woolf, and with him as engineer installed three unprecedentedly huge single-acting engines at Consolidated. After an initial expense of some £65,000, he brought the mines into profit and, after repayment of capital, brought profits of about half a million pounds to himself and friends by 1839.[14] Further profits were made by opening the Devoran railway in 1824, which served the Cosgarne Mines, and went as far as Redruth-Camborne providing them with a southern maritime connection with the port on the Fal. In 1823 Taylor took over United, financing it with the profits from Consolidated. He appointed a 21-year-old book-keeper from his London office as agent (the same age as Taylor had been when first employed by the Duke of Bedford) and employed Hocking and Loam (Woolf's 'boys') as engineers — all with resounding success.

In 1839 Consolidated was lost by Taylor to the Williams family as the result of a series of shenanigans which enraged the *Mining Journal* and helped to further convince London investors (if further convincing was needed) of the iniquities of the Cornish managements. The plant was sold to Williams for £65,000 and the money soon invested in a deep drainage scheme at East Ale and Cakes, hitherto largely unexploited at depth. Here Taylor installed Cornwall's most efficient engine, named, of course, after himself, which continuously provided a duty of over 100 million (foot-pounds per bushel of coal), and soon after, the second man-engine to be installed in Cornwall. The adventure was another considerable success. By 1850 Consolidated and United were again struggling and Taylor seized an opportunity to dispose of United to Williams for some £90,000. The Williams family were not entirely unsuccessful, but overall their management proved unable to provide the drive, finance and horse-power needed for successful working and, following further amalgamations to form Clifford Amalgamated, the whole enterprise, with 65 steam engines on site, was sold off for £12,000 in 1870.[15]

Subsequent workings have been relatively small. At Trevince an arsenic works relied mainly on the halvans (discarded material on waste heaps) for ore and at East Ale and Cakes the Gwennap United company set up a steam-powered plant for retreatment of tips for tin and arsenic in 1895, but this lasted in operation only a year or so. Small scale working for tin and wolfram took place around the war years and inter-war years at Trevince and at Mount Wellington (at the west and east ends of the setts respectively) and in the 1970s and 1980s dredging took place on the Carnon and deep mining at Mount Wellington.[16] For disposing of tailings, large dams were built in the Wheal Maid Valley, obscuring many earlier details, and other areas have been planted with the iniquitous fir. Today much of the east side of the Common has been designated for heritage preservation and an application for World Heritage Status is being progressed. The old railway is to become a cycleway and footpaths are being provided through the area. The remainder of the Common has fared less well, being rescued from what planners think of as dereliction by an industrial estate, scrap metal recovery, a waste disposal site and (at the East Ale and Cakes site), a 'banger racing track'.

The contemporary area, a natural heathland, at its height was thus characterized by the large-scale mines at surface, with huge dumps, most of which were surmounted by the engines and boiler houses, lines of open fronted dressing sheds, horse gins, smithies and carpenters' shops, count houses, changing sheds and water leats and dams, including a 'great dam' on the hill top to which water was pumped using the 'Little Engine'. The individual sites, where they could be differentiated, were linked by a network of paths and the single-track horse-operated railway system which branched from the Redruth-Devoran main line running up the valley side and floor. Amongst the buildings, at the most conspicuous point since it overlooked all the major areas of surface working, was the clock tower, built around 1825, possibly partly to control the single track railways, partly to govern the hours of work, but mainly, in retrospect at least, to symbolize the complete industrialization of the mining process and the protelarianization of the once independent Cornish miners.

Surviving mining plans and sections of the area — more than 67 at the last count with some several metres long — show not only the now totally hidden underground landscape, largely as a rectangular grid of workings, but also the surface features described above in a colour wash along the top. By combining this evidence with the surviving features, it is possible to build-up an image of the area both surface and underground to an unusual degree of satisfaction.

Growth of vegetation and destruction from other causes severely limits what can be seen today. The excavation of a stamp mill site at Cupboard Hill by the Cornwall Archaeological Unit[17] allowed a quick glimpse of a dressing floor, now buried, almost exactly as depicted by Pryce in 1778. However, the clock tower survives, which is unique in British metal mining, and in all there are half a dozen more or less surviving engine houses and chimneys, including Taylor's pumping and winding engine-houses and the Cusvey pumping engine house on Consolidated, and the Little Engine, Garlands and Gwennap at United. Some shafts are still apparent (and often still open) with their mounds, and some leats and, especially, the Great Dam survive. Seen from St Day on a summer evening, the Common still rises dramatically above the valley floors and is clearly a mining landscape, which is now almost assured of a maintained survival.

ACKNOWLEDGEMENTS

This account results from research in progress on a fuller description of the Consolidated and United Mines from work initially conducted in part with colleagues from Wessex Archaeology, notably Phil Andrews and Roland Smith. I am especially grateful to Cornwall Environmental Services Ltd (CES) who have funded some of the research into the area, and to the staff at the Cornwall Record Office, the Courtney Library at the Royal Museum of Cornwall (RIC) and the Cornwall Studies Library at Redruth. Justin Brooke has been kind enough to share some of his current research with me, and I have benefited from his substantial mining deposit in the Cornwall Record Office. I am also grateful for the co-operation of Anna Lawson-Jones of the Cornwall Archaeological Unit, for the excavation and report at the Cupboard Hill Stamps.

As a general guide to the area I recommend Ken Brown and Bob Acton's *Exploring Cornish Mines*, and for details of the development of steam power there and some of the controversies surrounding it and the mines, the series of Jennifer Tann's articles in the *Transactions of the Newcomen Society*.

Lynn Willies, Peak District Mining Museum, Matlock Bath, Derbyshire DE4 3NR, UK

NOTES

1 See Brown & Acton 1994 for a general account and guide to the area.
2 Thomas 1819; Dines 1956.
3 See, for example, CRO, WH2102.
4 Lawson-Jones & Willies 1998, 34–36.
5 See John Williams' Bound Books, RIC/16/7;7A.
6 Hamilton Jenkin 1981, 9.
7 CRO, MRO/R103/10.
8 See notes by Brooke, CRO, DDX745.

9 CRO, WH2096.
10 Buckley 1989.
11 See Farey 1971 for copious details.
12 Tann 1980.
13 Farey 1981.
14 Lemon 1969, 70.
15 Hamilton Jenkin 1981, 23.
16 Brooke 2000.
17 Lawson-Jones & Willies 1998.

BIBLIOGRAPHY

Borlase, W. 1758, *Natural History of Cornwall*, Oxford: W. Jackson.
Brooke, J. 2000, 'Mount Wellington Mine, Gwennap, Cornwall', *Mining History* 14:4, 23–30.

Brooke, J. 2001, *The Kalmeter Journal*, Truro: Twelveheads Press.

Brown, K. & Acton, R. S. 1994, *Exploring Cornish Mines*, Truro: Landfall Publications.

Buckley, J. A. 1989, 'The Great County Adit: A model of cooperation', *J. Trevithick Soc.* 16, 2–21.

Dines, H. G. 1956 (reprinted and amended 1988), *The Metalliferous Mining Region of South-West England*, London: HMSO.

Farey, J. 1971, *A Treatise on the Steam Engine (1827)*, 2 vols, Newton Abbot: David and Charles.

Hamilton, Jenkin A. K. 1981, *Mines and Miners of Cornwall. VI Around Gwennap*, Bracknell: Forge Books.

Lawson-Jones, A. & Willies, L. 1998, 'Research and Excavation at a Tin Stamping Site, Cupboard Hill, United Downs, Cornwall', *Mining History* 13:5, 33–49.

Lemon, Sir C. 1838, *The Statistics of the Copper Mines of Cornwall*, reprinted in Burt, R. (ed.) 1969, *Cornish Mining: Essays on the Organisation of Cornish Mines and the Cornish Mining Economy*, 31–48, Newton Abbot: David and Charles.

Pryce, W. 1778, *Mineralogia Cornubiensis*, 1972 edition, Truro: Bradford Barton.

Tann, J. 1980, 'Mr Hornblower and His Crew: Watt Engine Pirates at the end of the 18th century', *Trans. Newcomen Soc.* 51, 95–109.

Tann J. 1996, 'Riches from Copper: The Adoption of the Boulton and Watt Engine by the Cornish Mine Adventurers', *Trans. Newcomen Soc.* 67, 27–51.

FROM PICK TO POWDER — PHASES OF CHANGE IN A NORTH PENNINE LANDSCAPE

By ALAN BLACKBURN

Although much of the contents of this paper applies to the whole of Weardale, the main focus is on the mines of the Rookhope Valley. Weardale lies in the far west of County Durham, within the north Pennine uplands, and comprises all the land within the watershed of the river Wear from Wolsingham (NGR, NZ076 373) west to the top of the watershed above Killhope at 746m. AOD. The Rookhope Valley forms a fairly steep-sided tributary valley, some 11km. in length, on the north side of Weardale.

In reviewing the information on the history of the Rookhope Valley, in an attempt to clarify it from the aspect of landscape change, and to encompass the minutiae of details into a more easily interpreted overview, it became apparent that there were periods where the changes to the landscape were of a consistent nature, even if the changes themselves were quite dynamic. For example, there might be a period during which the mines were being developed by hand mining with shaft windlasses. This period might last for say eighty years, before a new type of development becomes noticeable, which again spreads across the mining field over a period of time. Each period, or phase, therefore, represents the time during which a particular sequence, or type of change occurs. For some phases, the type of changes will be few, and their impact on the landscape relatively minor, whereas another phase, involving the adoption of higher technology methods, might have a lot of changes, with a considerable impact on the landscape.

In reviewing the history of a period or phase, it is often possible to identify some reasons for the adoption of the particular changes of that period. These reasons can usually be clarified into what might be called the elemental forces of mining, that is the available technology, the social organization of the miners, and the economic conditions. For any given phase these three forces interact, but further study of the phases shows that there is always one dominating or driving force, which will control or limit the type of changes that can occur in that phase.

The dates given for the phases are inevitably approximate, and mark the decade in which the changes of the next phase start to appear.

THE MOORMASTER PHASE, 1560s–1680s

The first phase of post-medieval mining starts on or about 1566, when the first Moormaster of the Weardale mining field, of which Rookhope was a part, was

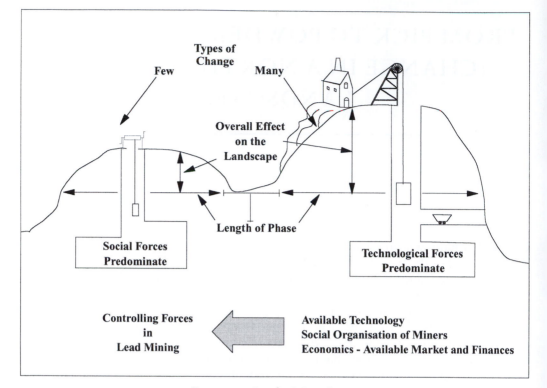

FIGURE 1. Lead mining phases.

appointed.[1] The field was part of the huge land possessions of the Bishop of Durham, and a change in the bishop, to a distinctly radical one, produced a change in the operation of the bishop's mining field. A Moormaster was introduced who leased the field from the bishop, and a set procedure was adopted for the operation of the field by the Moormaster. These procedures became the unwritten rules by which the mining field was run over the next 120 years. The principal features were that while the Moormaster administered the field, and received all the lead ore produced at a controlled price, which he was free to smelt and sell, he did not operate the mines. They were financed and run by groups of miners and investors who sub-leased them, by means of a tack note, from the Moormaster. Each of these groups was completely independent from the others, so that the mining field consisted of a large number of separately run mines.

It is important to note that a particular form of social organization resulted in a widely fragmented mining field, thus making it the dominant force in the Moormaster phase. Its effects were to lock up the mines in such a way that, for nearly 130 years, very few advances in technology could be used. For instance, some of the devices used on the Continent could have given advances in pumping and winding but were not adopted because most of these required a larger scale of business to become viable. It also prevented the use of large scale extractive hushing, a technically simple process

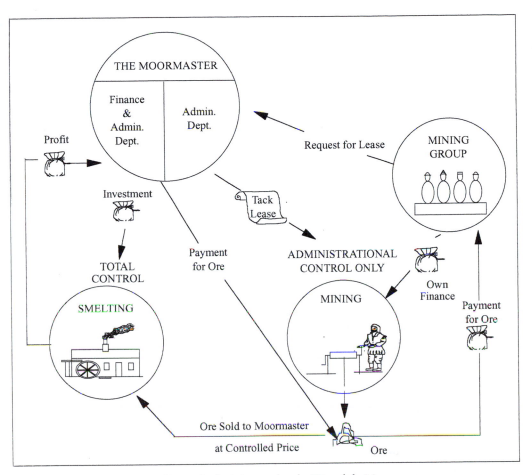

FIGURE 2. Control of mining under the Weardale Moormaster.

which could not take place because of the many individual tacks up and down the vein getting in the way.

In fact, the Moormaster system seems to have been devised in such a way as to prevent any one group becoming dominant. Either that, or the procedures that were adopted, probably to a large extent borrowed from earlier medieval mining, produced this result without those involved actually realizing their long term effects.

Whatever the reasons, the result of this exercise in individual private enterprise was a landscape that was characterized by a scattering of shafts and levels, with the occasional exploratory trench dug to find or open the vein, which might later have a shaft sunk in it. Over each shaft there would have been a windlass or stowes for raising ore or water, with the ore being dressed on knockstones which, together with the waste heaps and a primitive washing place, were usually kept close to the shaft.

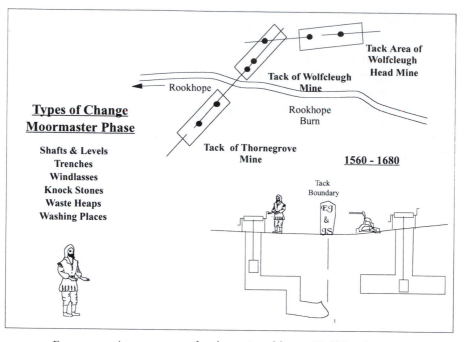

FIGURE 3. Arrangement of tacks at site of future Wolfcleugh Mine.

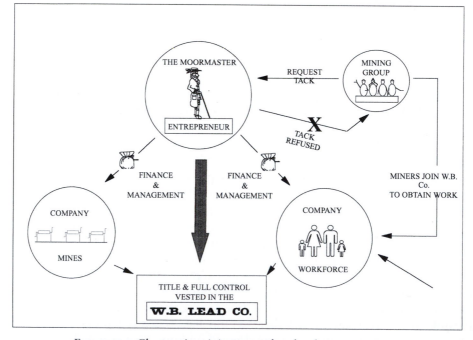

FIGURE 4. Changes in mining control under the entrepreneur.

One example of this phase in the valley, shown in the accompanying drawing, is that of a site called Wolfcleugh, on which there were in 1679 three active mine tacks, Wolfcleugh Head, Wolfcleugh and Thornegrove.

THE ENTREPRENEURIAL PHASE, 1680S–1740S

The next phase starts in 1688, and is called the Entrepreneurial phase, for the simple reason that nobody else could possibly have achieved the radical social changes brought about in this phase. These changes could not have been undertaken by the miners, investors, or even the traditional Moormasters; they really had to be guided by one person with considerable forward vision. In short, they had to be done by an entrepreneur, and the name of that entrepreneur was William Blackett, founder of the W. B. Lead Company. In fact it took three generations of William Blacketts from 1688 to 1725 to engineer this change, and few details of the period survive, but fortunately that is not critical, because in 1725 the first of the W. B. Co. account books to survive starts, and it is clear that a radical change has taken place. In a dramatic move, the rights of the miners to lease and run their own mines, enshrined in various practices for several centuries, had disappeared. They had been turned, in an exceedingly short time, into that most desirable of technological icons - a company workforce. Now they had to work in the W. B. Co. mines, under the supervision of the company's agents. They retained a tiny vestige of their former pride, in that they were allowed to take on work in gangs, called partnerships, of their own choosing. But if they still had hopes of making a lot of money from a successful strike they were to be sadly mistaken; the work bargaining system operated by the company was carefully weighted against them.

The echoes of these radical social changes probably went far deeper into the social fabric of the dale than the production of a workforce. During the 17th century the number of tackers steadily increased, and mining became a growth industry. Many new people moved into the dales; most of them were relatively affluent investors, or miner/investors keen to get a stake in the mines. The reason for the inflow of investors is a throwback many centuries old, when the bishop had agreed to let his tenants take leases on the mines. This persisted into the Moormaster period, so in order to participate in this thriving industry where anyone with some capital was free to try and make their fortune, it was necessary to become a tenant of the bishop. The result of this rule was that both the miners and investors lived in the dale, so that all the profits of the mines were by and large retained and spent within the dale. After the coming of the company, apart from subsistence wages for the workers, the mining profits were taken out of the dale, into the hands of an increasingly wealthy merchant/industrialist. This left the dale with a population whose social mix was radically changed as the gentlemen investors left the dale, leaving only those miners and people who were prepared to work for the subsistence wages paid by the company. Thus the area became impoverished by the company taking the mining profits, and the investors removing themselves and their wealth.[2] When, or indeed whether, the indigenous population recovered its internal wealth and its social mix is not known,

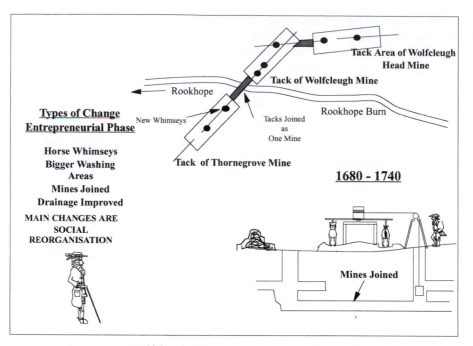

FIGURE 5. Wolfcleugh Mine: entrepreneurial phase, 1680–1740.

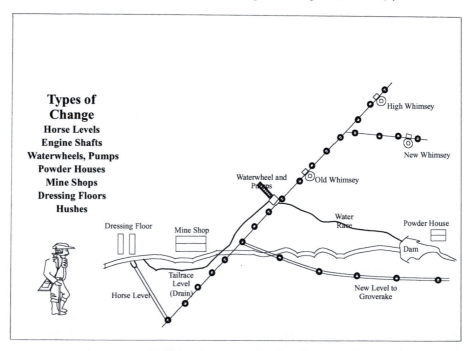

FIGURE 6. Wolfcleugh Mine: industrial phase 1740–1820.

but the effects of the coming of the company must have echoed through the dale for many long years. Arguably, they still do.

The landscape changes typical of the Entrepreneurial phase were quite subtle, and do not reflect the significance of the social changes needed to bring them about. Now that the W. B. Co. had total control of its mines, it proceeded to do what would have been impossible under the old system, it started to link them together, with immediate benefits in ventilation, drainage, winding, and underground transport. These improvements then led to the adoption of strategic shafts as main haulage shafts, and they were fitted with horse gins or whimseys, which could wind heavier loads from greater depths than the old windlasses. None of these changes used any particularly new technology, all that was involved in this phase was to use the advantages of scale that could be made once the old mining system had been disposed of.

At Wolfcleugh, the three separate tacks had been joined into one single mine, with two winding shafts fitted with horse gins. This is the period from which the name of Wolfcleugh mine as a single entity can be attributed.

THE INDUSTRIAL PHASE 1740S-1810S

The Entrepreneurial phase was not a long phase, but its sweeping social changes left a homogenous mining field ready to accept the newly emerging technologies of the next phase, the Industrial phase.[3] During this phase, the dominant influence on lead mining in Weardale was technology. One of the greatest advances in underground mining was brought about by the introduction of blasting powder, which was in use in a small way in the Rookhope Valley around 1730. By 1750 it was in common use, which resulted in the speed of mining being considerably increased, especially in the harder and deeper rocks that were now being worked. This sudden increase in potential output enabled other new ideas to be introduced. The first wooden rails and horse drawn tubs in the area were installed before 1760 in nearby Coalcleugh mine, where a new long, wide and high level was driven especially for the purpose. The success of this led to the adoption of rails and the introduction of horse levels to most of the larger Weardale mines by the end of the century. The development of the mines continued at a high pace, with many internal levels being opened up for rails and tubs. New advances were also made in pumping, which combined with new drainage levels enabled the mines to go much deeper. Ventilation was improved with the introduction of the water blast, and by the turn of the century hand-operated air blowers were being introduced.

Wolfcleugh became in this phase the largest mine in the Rookhope Valley, and it received a horse level in 1770. Work was also started on a new long level towards Groverake, which it reached by about 1790. This proved a success, and shortly afterwards the new Groverake mine began to operate independently. On the surface, apart from the new adits and shafts, there were significant changes to the landscape. The new horse level brought out large quantities of ore, so a dressing floor was built near it. The first of what would become typical mine buildings started to appear, when a mine shop was built in 1766. The other notable building was the first of the powder houses in the valley, built in 1769. A waterwheel for pumping was built sometime around 1770; and to supply water, a low dam was built across the Rookhope burn. To supply it, water leats were built to collect water from either side of the valley. Because it now controlled large tracts of mining land, and equally importantly, it did not have to pay compensation for any damage to them, the W. B. Co. were now able to introduce hushing. The first hushing in the Rookhope Valley was started by Joseph Fraser and partners in 1758 at a place not far from the head of the valley, and although these hushes had ceased operating by the turn of the century, they left one legacy to the valley; the area is still known today as Fraser's Hush.

Although the industrial phase was dominated by the technological changes, there were still a few social changes taking place. In general, these amounted to a tightening of the control the company had over its workforce, and in particular, over its managers. At the end of the Entrepreneurial phase, around 1730, the mine and mill agents saw themselves as quasi-owners of their own domains, able to not only hire and fire men at will, but in many cases to practice dubious methods of raising further finance for themselves, such as the sale of candles, tools, horses, and even beer, at inflated rates to the miners or the company. The agents were used to working on their own, and not used to accounting for their expenditure to a superior manager. In fact the accounts of the then senior mill agent were never sorted out, except to the point where Sir William Blackett agreed to pay off his outstanding debts. Many of these agent's accounts were late reaching the chief agent, some over a year late, making production of the company accounts very difficult.

By the turn of the century the accounting procedure was much improved, and the private practices had largely been eliminated. Essentially what had happened was that a gradual process of pressure to conform, with the occasional removal of unwanted men, had enabled the chief agent to mould his previously disparate gang of agents into a new necessity for progress; he had made them into company men.

THE MECHANIZATION PHASE 1810s–1930s

The Industrial phase lasted for some 70 years, and in the next phase the driving force of technology still remained dominant, but there was to be a significant change in its application. In the industrial phase, technology had enabled men to do work that could not have been done before, but it was all essentially labour intensive. In the mechanization phase, new power sources were made available that could produce far greater power than had been available before. The use of these new power sources enabled a new breed of men, the engineers, to design and build machines that could do the work of many men. The newest and most significant power source was the steam engine. Already in use in the north-east coalfields, its introduction to the Weardale lead mines was much more problematical. The engineers of the W. B. Co. decided that the cost of transporting large amounts of coal into the area made the engines less promising than in the coalfields. They decided that, with a plentiful supply of water, the best prime mover to use was the water wheel. Much bigger and more efficient versions were made, which were used to operate better pumps and shaft winders, and the mechanization of the dressing floor was begun. This eventually led,

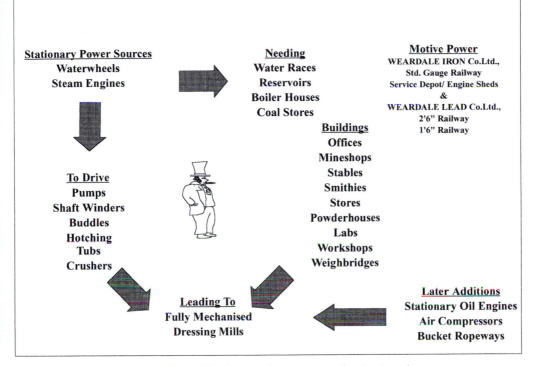

Stationary Power Sources
Waterwheels
Steam Engines

Needing
Water Races
Reservoirs
Boiler Houses
Coal Stores

Motive Power
WEARDALE IRON Co.Ltd.,
Std. Gauge Railway
Service Depot/ Engine Sheds
&
WEARDALE LEAD Co.Ltd.,
2'6" Railway
1'6" Railway

Buildings
Offices
Mineshops
Stables
Smithies
Stores
Powderhouses
Labs
Workshops
Weighbridges

To Drive
Pumps
Shaft Winders
Buddles
Hotching
Tubs
Crushers

Leading To
Fully Mechanised
Dressing Mills

Later Additions
Stationary Oil Engines
Air Compressors
Bucket Ropeways

FIGURE 7.   Typical landscape changes — mechanization phase.

near the end of the century, to the fully enclosed processing plant, of which three were built in the valley.

Although not strictly connected with lead mining, mention should be made of another arrival in the valley that was to make considerable changes to the landscape. In 1846, the Weardale Iron Co. brought its railway into the valley via a 1.8km. rope-hauled incline. By 1865 it had spread up and down the valley, and large ironstone quarries were opened on the valley sides. The company also took over Rispey mine, which it worked with the aid of a stationary steam engine. This was a very short lived bonanza; by 1880 the quarries had all closed down, although the railway continued to operate for about 40 years. Coinciding with the end of iron mining, the lead mines hit a bad recession. In previous phases, these had always been short term positions from which the industry would recover, but this time the dominating influence of technology was being challenged by economic forces. To put it simply, the available market had started to decline, while supplies of cheaper lead from overseas were now readily available. The W. B. Co. felt the pressure most, and when, after an acrimonious few years of discussions, the Ecclesiastical Commissioners insisted on a substantial increase in the mining lease, the company decided — in 1883 — to close down all its mining operations and leave Weardale, almost two hundred years after its first lease.

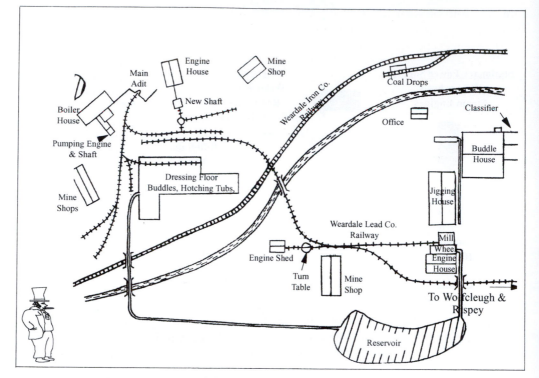

FIGURE 8.   Groverlake Mine: mechanization phase, 1820–1920.

The late 19th-century enthusiasm for investing in mining companies helped support two new ventures. First was the Rookhope Valley Mining Company, who littered the landscape at Stotsfieldburn with a plethora of machinery, including Cornish-style pumping engines, and steam-powered winders and dressing floors, before going into unavoidable decline due to an overestimate of the workable ore body.[4] The second, and ultimately more important, was the Weardale Lead Company, who took over the mines of the W. B. Co. in 1883.

By the turn of the century, the influence of economic forces was almost dominant, the Rookhope Valley Mining Company had gone, and the Weardale Lead Company was struggling. Fortune, however, was at hand, as with the apocryphal last pickstroke of the last man working on the last shift before closure at Boltsburn mine, a massive new ore body was found, and the Weardale Lead Company had a reprieve. Such was the size and quality of the Boltsburn flats that the company could once again compete on the world market. Over the next 30 years the company built a large new ore processing plant with labs, offices, and workshops at Boltsburn, together with new mine shops, and even a mine manager's house. Another narrow gauge line was built to feed the smelt mill from the plant, while coal for the steam boilers which powered the shaft winders and provided compressed air for the mine, was brought in on the railway. Even when the railway was closed shortly after the First World War, the company output was such that it built a cable operated bucket-way two miles down the valley, to take the ore to the railway in the main valley.

Clearly there were numerous changes to the landscape in this phase, a small sample of which can be seen from a drawing of Groverake mine, which was only really started around 1800, and which gives some idea of the speed of change of the period. By 1860, when the Weardale Iron Company's standard gauge railway came up the valley, it had a water wheel operated pump and the reasonably large dressing floor had nine hotching tubs. On either hillside above the mine were ironstone quarries with rope inclines down to the main railway, By about 1885 it had a new fully enclosed crushing and dressing plant on the other side of the river, and by about 1895 another one had been built at Rispey, and a narrow gauge railway took ore to it from Groverake Steam pumping and winding engines were also installed around this time, together with a new haulage shaft, and various shops and offices were built.

THE DESTRUCTION PHASE 1930S-2000

Because of its last minute discovery of a new ore body, the Weardale Lead Company was able to prosper for about another 30 years. But for lead mining in general, economic forces were now the dominating force, and a strong negative influence. As soon as the Boltsburn flats were worked out, in 1931, the company had no choice but to close. It was simply not a viable option to raise substantial funds against a deeper exploration for unproven ore bodies. The market for lead was now considerably smaller than it was at the turn of the century, and still contracting. Ironically, it was the indiscriminating influence of the new technologies that turned the new industries towards steel, and away from lead.

From this point in time the valley, and most of the north Pennines, went into an industrial decline, and entered the last phase of lead mining, the destruction phase. Although the lead mines were now no longer viable, the phase was punctuated by occasional periods of small scale re-opening of the mines for fluorspar. This industry probably reached its peak sometime around 1970, and at the time of writing has stopped, with the closure of Groverake mine (by then the last in the north Pennines) in the late 1990s.

For most of this phase the mines remained abandoned, a state which can be said to take two forms, active and passive. Active abandonment usually takes place straight after closure, but can be resumed at any time. This involves the removal of anything of value for resale or scrap, and in some cases, further destruction by robbing of building materials. It also includes any form of landscaping. Passive abandonment leaves the site subject only to the long term decay of the north Pennine weather system, which can also induce cases of mine workings collapsing, producing new surface changes in the form of sinks, sometimes of quite a large size.

At any particular time during abandonment, the difference between the natural landscape and the state of the derelict mines, could be termed the residual effect of lead mining on the landscape.

THE LEAD MINING PHASES 1550–2000

At the end of each growth phase, there is an overall effect on the landscape. If it were possible to measure this, then it would be possible to draw a graph of the changes on the landscape due to lead mining. For the 19th-century phases, it is theoretically possible to get quite an accurate measurement from maps, documents and field evidence. However, the time that would be required to produce these measurements was not available to me, so in order to pursue the ideas in this paper, a different way of obtaining a rough estimate of the actual area affected by mining was tried.

In 1683 a list of all the tacks known to have been worked in the Rookhope Valley from the time of the first Moormaster was given in evidence for an Exchequer court case, the total being 41 tacks. The commonest size of tack was approximately 400 x 40m. This gives an area disturbed by mining of 0.66km.^{2}. Since the total area of the Rookhope Valley is a very approximate 30km.^{2}, the total direct effect on the landscape of the Moormaster phase is about 0.22%. Using this figure as a basis, the effect of the changes of the other phases was estimated against the Moormaster phase. The effect of the Entrepreneurial phase was estimated as the same as the Moormaster phase, with the Industrial phase four times that, and the Mechanization phase four times the Industrial phase. The total effect of all the phases on the landscape, at its peak, is,

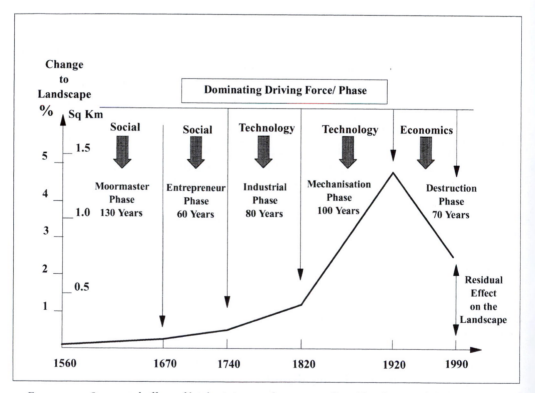

FIGURE 9. Suggested effect of lead mining on the post-medieval landscape of the Rookhope Valley.

according to these figures 4.8%, or about 1.5km.^{2}. Bearing in mind that this does not include the many quarries of the Weardale Iron Company, nor their railway, this result is a not unreasonable ballpark figure, and at least gives an idea as to the way that lead mining has changed the landscape.

The resulting graph shows the rate of change as a straight line, which is an obvious simplification, as the true spread of these changes would be subject to economic forces. When examined against the 50 to 100 years of the phases, however, these fluctuations are less significant than they might appear. For instance, periods of recession are not uncommon in mining as are periods of high growth. Both can be quite powerful, but the strongest effects of them rarely last longer than, say, ten years, before resuming a more normal level. While it would be desirable to show these fluctuations, their effect on the long-term rate of change is not thought to be particularly significant.

There remains one important factor to bear in mind when assessing the total effect on the landscape, and that is that this analysis only refers to the visible landscape. If such a concept as the invisible landscape exists, then the total effect on the underground or invisible landscape will be far in excess of that on the visible landscape. If it does not currently exist, it may be necessary to invent it, as with a knowledge of the invisible landscape, it may be possible to explain, or even predict, such occurrences as the collapse of land or buildings into old mine workings, or the causes of groundwater pollution.

THE LEAD MINING CYCLE

Having produced this graphical overview of the changes to the Rookhope Valley landscape caused by lead mining, perhaps in time it might be possible to look at earlier phases. This might make it possible to look at the whole cycle of lead mining, from the prehistoric to the present day. Clearly finding data for these earlier phases would be difficult, but possibly a backwards extrapolation from previous phases may give an indication of the size of the industry, and even that could be a helpful indicator for future research.

The complete cycle, at whatever point the final phase is examined, leaves an impact on the environment in the form of the residual effect. This negative effect on the landscape could possibly be changed, or at least given a different interpretation, if mining preservation is considered. The growth in the preservation of mining and industrial sites is continuing and this process will stabilize the residual effect from further long term decay. The most interesting part of this is that these newly preserved sites are now part of a new phenomenon, tourism, and perhaps much of the residual effect of the mining cycle could now be transferred to a growth phase of a new cycle, the industrial tourism cycle of the north Pennines.

POST CONFERENCE THOUGHTS

I was greatly encouraged by the very positive reception given to this paper at the Industry and Agriculture conference in 1995, and I would like to thank everyone for

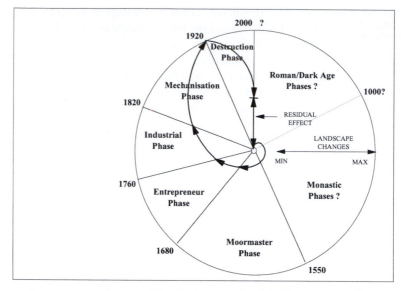

FIGURE 10. The overall lead mining cycle of the Rookhope Valley.

their comments both during and immediately after the conference. For publication, I have decided to make no significant changes to the paper as it was presented (apart from updating the final phase of closure), although I remain very conscious of the fact that in order to produce the graph of the post-medieval lead mining phases, I had to estimate the growth of the phases subsequent to the Moormaster phase, leaving me with a graph whose later phases were based on very subjective evidence. However, it was either that, or no graph, and I felt this visual illustration was important in clarifying the concept of the lead mining phases, and the lead mining cycle.

ACKNOWLEDGEMENTS

I must thank Richard Smith for taking my hand-drawn OHP pictures and converting them to computer format for publishing, a difficult job which he does so well. One day perhaps they can appear in their original colours.

Alan Blackburn, Rookhope Nurseries, Rookhope, Weardale, Co. Durham DL13 2DD, UK

NOTES

[1] For a more detailed description of the practices of the Weardale Moormaster, see Blackburn 1994a.

[2] For the state of the mines at the end of the Entrepreneurial phase, see the early account books and chief agent's letter book of the W. B. Co., Northumberland Record Office Deposits; Letter Book NRO673/2, Cash book NRO672/2/1, Journal NRO672/2/19, Ledger book NRO672/2/27.

[3] For details of the mines in the 18th and 19th centuries, see in general Northumberland Record Office deposits NRO, 672 and 673; also the Weardale Lead Company deposit in Durham County Record Office at D/WL.

[4] For details of the Rookhope Valley Mining Company and other mines on the Dean and Chapter lands in Rookhope, see Blackburn 1994b.

BIBLIOGRAPHY

Blackburn, A. 1994a, 'Mining Adventurers in the Rookhope Valley', *The Bonny Moor Hen*, Journal of the Weardale Field Study Society 7, 41–53.

Blackburn, A. 1994b, 'Mining without Laws: Weardale under the Moormasters', in Ford, T. D. & Willies, L. (eds), *Mining before Powder*, Historical Metallurgy Society special publication, 69–75.

British Geological Survey 1990, *Geology of the North Pennine Orefield, Vol. 1*, 2nd edition, London: HMSO.

Crosby, J. 1989, *Weardale in Old Photographs*, Gloucester: Alan Sutton.

Crosby, J. 1993, *Weardale in Old Photographs: a second edition*, Gloucester: Alan Sutton.

Hunt, C. J. 1970, *The Lead miners of the Northern Pennines in the Eighteenth and Nineteenth Centuries*, Manchester: Manchester University Press.

Raistrick, A. & Jennings, B. 1965, *A History of Lead Mining in the Pennines*, London: Longman.

METAL MINING AND VEGETATIONAL HISTORY OF THE UPPER ROOKHOPE VALLEY, WEARDALE, NORTHERN PENNINES

By TIM M. MIGHALL, LISA DUMAYNE-PEATY *and* STUART FREETH

INTRODUCTION

Deposits of peat and lake sediments contain a valuable store of fossil material (e.g. pollen, macrofossils, particulate material, charcoal and geochemical aerosols). These products accumulate and become preserved in sediments through time, providing scientists with a chronological record of data. The collection, analysis and application of that data has given rise to the discipline of palaeoecology. Palaeoecologists have analysed the pollen content of sediments to reconstruct past vegetational environments and discuss any changes in vegetation in the context of factors such as climate change or human activity.[1] Combined with the analysis of charcoal, pollen analysis has afforded palaeoecologists the opportunity to consider the impact of humans on the landscape. In particular, a plethora of pollen diagrams have been produced from sites scattered throughout the British Isles which have provided evidence that prehistoric peoples have disturbed or altered the landscape with varying intensity since the Mesolithic period.[2] The discovery and identification of pollen grains released from the anthers of cereals, grasses and weeds that are commonly associated with agricultural activity has shown that the introduction of arable and pastoral farming into the British Isles and Europe has made a significant contribution to changing the landscape by clearing large tracts of woodland.[3]

Following the recent upsurge in interest in prehistoric mining and metal-working in the British Isles and Ireland, a small number of studies have been conducted to investigate the impact of these industrial activities on the landscape. For example, it has been demonstrated that the impact of early mining on woodlands at Copa Hill, Cwmystwyth and Mount Gabriel, Co. Cork, Ireland, was probably not as severe as first presumed.[4] Findings from a pollen-analytical study of iron-working sites at Bryn y Castell and Crawcwellt Common in north-west Wales suggest that such activities also did not have a dramatic impact on the landscape. The duration and scale of mining, allied with possible woodland management or a low demand for wood, seem to have reduced the level of woodland clearance during the known tenancy of these sites.[5] Studies of this kind demonstrate that the application of palaeoecological techniques can be extremely useful for testing hypotheses concerning the environmental impact of mining and metal-working activities.

Surprisingly, even less consideration has been given to assessing the impact of mining and metal-working from the Roman period onwards. The application of palaeoecological techniques would be useful in order to provide further supporting evidence concerning the exploitation of woodlands for wood fuel by the metal mining and metal-working industries. In certain areas the demand for wood fuel appears to have been substantial. For example, one estimate suggests that the six main centres of iron-working in the Weald used 792,000 tonnes of charcoal and that without woodland management this demand could have resulted in the clearance of 15km.^{2} of woodland.^{6} Darby has suggested that metal mining and metal-working industries were responsible for the destruction of woodlands throughout north-west Europe.^{7} However, others have argued that woodlands were managed rather than destroyed.^{8} Pollen analysis of sediments can be used to reconstruct the vegetation history of the area surrounding such sites and any changes in percentages of tree taxa could be related to changes in the amount of woodland or woodland composition.

Moreover, sediments such as peat also store geochemical aerosols. Analysis of chemicals contained within a sediment can provide circumstantial evidence for atmospheric pollution as a result of mining and/or metal-working. Several studies, both of prehistoric and historic industrial sites, have shown that chemical records reconstructed from peat and lake sediment can be correlated with metal mining and smelting.^{9} Geochemical analyses of sediments from Loch Dee, Galloway revealed increased levels of lead and copper deposition within the catchment since AD 1500, probably as a result of mining and smelting activities.^{10} Measurements of lead and zinc in peats located within the Gordano Valley, Avon, and lead in peats from the Snake Pass in Derbyshire have been attributed to Roman metal mining.^{11} Chemical analysis of floodplain deposits within the River South Tyne, just south of Garrigill, has shown that levels of lead, copper and zinc peak in sediments dated to the mid to late 19th century. These peaks have been attributed to metal mining activities.^{12} Thus, the chemical analyses of sediments can provide a valuable record of pollution that could be related to industrial activities from the Bronze Age onwards. Furthermore, studies of this kind could be useful to provide circumstantial evidence in areas devoid of other forms of evidence such as archaeological finds.

Pollen analytical studies have shown that the landscape of the northern Pennines and north-east Yorkshire has been subjected to human disturbance since prehistoric times and this activity has contributed to shaping the landscape in to its present form.^{13} However, it is noteworthy that within the northern Pennines there has been much discussion as to the extent of Roman and medieval metal mining in the absence of firm archaeological evidence. A different, but possibly fruitful, approach might be to conduct geochemical analyses of sediments within the area to ascertain whether higher concentrations of chemicals, such as lead, can be correlated with the Roman or medieval period. Because there is little evidence to confirm that metal mining took place before medieval times, the northern Pennines is an ideal study area to test the applicability of using palaeoenvironmental techniques to accrue supporting or circumstantial evidence (particularly where archaeological evidence is absent). So far, only the discovery of traces of lead found in bronze tools and the increasing relative abundance of lead objects at Iron Age sites suggests that these cultures possibly exploited lead deposits.[14] As yet there is little archaeological or documentary evidence to support the claim that lead mining occurred during Roman times in the Pennines.[15] Most of the evidence for Roman lead mining consists of artefact evidence such as the discovery of pigs of lead. For example, remains of lead smelting have been found at a site on Wolsingham South Moor in Weardale. Wooler has suggested that the origins of these lead workings date back to the Roman period.[16] There is some circumstantial evidence to support this claim, as a putative Roman settlement lies less than 3km. away at Hamsterley.[17] Further north, in the south Tyne valley, the discovery of metal objects including smelted lead and ore at Corbridge and at the Roman camp or fort on the Maiden Way also point to a lead mining industry during Roman times.[18] Thus, there is still some controversy and debate to the extent and scale of metal mining during pre-Roman, Roman and medieval times.

The evidence for metal mining in the northern Pennines is more forthcoming from the medieval period onwards and it has resulted in the publication of numerous volumes and research papers.[19] Documentary records, archaeological surveys and excavation work have provided detailed evidence about the structure and processes of metal mining in post-medieval times.[20] Under these circumstances, palaeoenvironmental studies can provide evidence in order to understand the environmental effects of metal mining in terms of vegetation change, pollution and landscape change.

This paper presents the preliminary findings of an ongoing study within the upper Rookhope Valley, Weardale, that aims to investigate the extent to which historical metal mining has influenced the local environment. Particular emphasis has been given to establishing whether metal mining has influenced the processes of vegetational change and to determine the levels of local pollution as recorded by chemical aerosols deposited in blanket peat deposits which surround the mines. The results will illustrate the role that palaeoenvironmental studies can play in contributing to our understanding of the metal mining landscape.

SITE DETAILS

The Rookhope Valley is a tributary of the River Wear, located to the north-west of the village of Stanhope in Weardale, approximately 25km. north-west of Bishop Auckland (Fig. 1a and b). A series of metal mines are located in the upper reaches of the valley which extend back to the 17th century and possibly earlier.[21] A mining complex known as Fraser's Grove mine, Fraser's Quarry and Fraser's Hush is located at the head of the valley, an area known as Rookhope Head (grid reference NY 882 445). In this area a number of interesting features exist including a group of bellpits or shaft mounds. Several small prospecting hushes fed by small dams and a possible small ore-dressing area, that are thought to date to the 17th century, have been identified by the Cranstone Consultancy. Two monoliths of peat were extracted from freshly cut exposures of blanket peat approximately 75m. west of remnants of Frasers Quarry at an altitude of approximately 1550m. OD (Fig. 1c). The blanket peat covers a large proportion of the upper Rookhope Valley floor, sides and top, forming part of

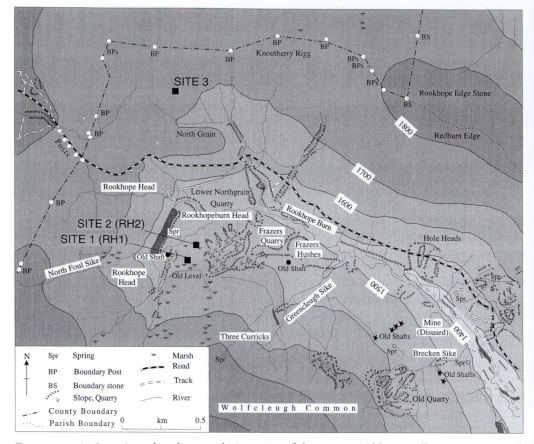

FIGURE 1. (a) Location of study area; (b) Location of the upper Rookhope Valley; (c) Location of the sampling sites, RH1 and RH2.

Stanhope Moor to the north and Middlehope Moor to the south. The exposures from which the samples were taken in November 1992 and September 1993 were later destroyed by fluorspar extraction and reclamation work by Weardale Minerals Ltd.

METHOD

Sub-samples of peat 0.5cm. thick and 2g. wet weight were prepared for pollen analysis using the procedure described by Barber.[22] One *Lycopodium clavatum* tablet was added to each sub-sample[23] in order to calculate charcoal and pollen concentrations. At least 500 land pollen grains were counted for each sub-sample. Pollen identification was made using the pollen identification keys from Faegri *et al.* (1989) and Moore *et al.* (1991) and a pollen type slide collection housed in the Geography Subject Area at Coventry University. Charcoal was analysed using the point-count estimation method described by Clark.[24]

Samples 1cm. thick were cut from the RH2 monolith at 4cm. intervals and prepared for chemical analysis by acid digestion (HNO_3, $HClO_4$ and H_2SO_4) and atomic absorption spectrophotometry (AAS) following the procedure outlined in detail by Foster *et al.* (1987). Elements (Pb, Zn and Fe) were measured using a Varian model 1472 atomic absorption spectrophotometer.

RESULTS

Pollen analysis

Percentage pollen diagrams of selected taxa for sampling sites RH1 and RH2 are presented in Figures 2 and 3. The pollen data are expressed as percentages of total land pollen (TLP), excluding spores and aquatics. Spores and aquatics are also expressed as percentages of total land pollen. A cross denotes one pollen grain. The application of the computer programme CONISS to the data assisted in the delineation of local pollen assemblage zones. The pollen diagrams were drawn using the computer programme TILIA and TILIA.GRAPH.[25] A brief description of the main characteristics of each zone for sampling sites RH1 and RH2 are presented in Tables 1 and 2. Plant nomenclature follows Stace (1991) and Bennett *et al.* (1994). *Corylus avellana*-type refers to *Corylus* and/or *Myrica*.

TABLE 1
CHARACTERISTICS OF THE ZONES FOR SITE RH1

Zone	Depth (cm)	Characteristics	Human activity
RH1f	0–16	Falling AP percentages, increasing NAP representation, especially Poaceae. High *Calluna*. Regular cereal-type and *Plantago lanceolata*. High *Sphagnum*.	Lead mining & agriculture
RH1e	16–39	High AP percentages. High *Calluna*. Low NAP. *Corylus avellana*-type decreases from 36–28cm. Cereal-type and *Plantago lanceolata* are recorded as total AP% fall between 22–18cm.	Lead mining & agriculture
RH1d	39–70	High total AP percentages that fall during this zone, characterized by *Betula*, *Alnus*, *Corylus avellana*-type and *Quercus*. Rising *Calluna*. Erratic *Sphagnum* percentages.	Pastoral agriculture?
RH1c	70–92	High total AP percentages suffer a short-lived decrease between 96 and 90cm. *Betula* values remains low thereafter. *Corylus avellana*-type decrease sharply at 72cm. High *Calluna* and Cyperaceae except in mid-zone. *Plantago lanceolata* percentage increases at 90cm. Erratic *Sphagnum* percentages.	Pastoral agriculture?
RH1b	92–108	High *Betula* and *Corylus avellana*-type pollen. *Ulmus* and *Pinus* decrease mid zone. Low *Calluna* and NAP characterized by Poaceae and Cyperaceae. *Potentilla-type* and *Melampyrum* pollen percentages decrease.	Pastoral agriculture?
RH1a	108–122	High AP, especially *Betula* and *Corylus avellana*-type pollen. Noticeable *Quercus* and *Alnus*. Low NAP but *Potentilla*-type and *Melampyrum* are well represented.	Little/no evidence

AP = arboreal pollen percentages; NAP = non-arboreal pollen

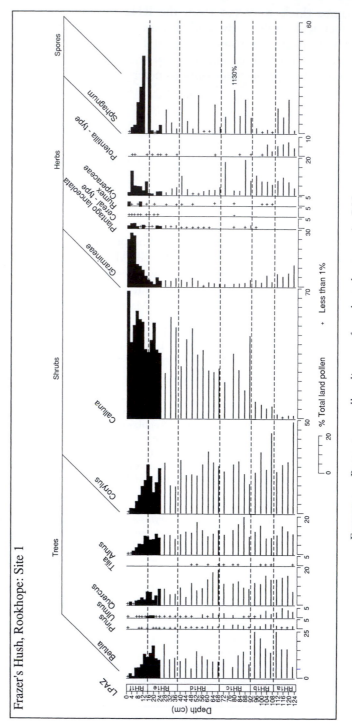

FIGURE 2.　Percentage pollen diagram for selected taxa at site RH1.

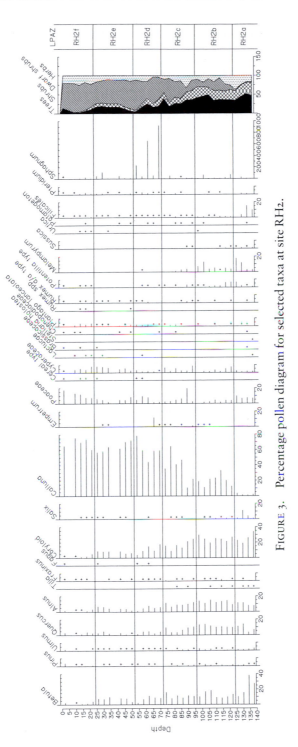

FIGURE 3. Percentage pollen diagram for selected taxa at site RH2.

TABLE 2
CHARACTERISTICS OF THE ZONES FOR SITE RH2

RH2f	0–24	Decreasing AP. High *Calluna*. Increasing NAP, especially Poaceae and *Plantago lanceolata* percentages. Cereal-type and *Rumex, Artemisia*-type, *Urtica* and Pteropsida are recorded. Charcoal peaks mid-zone.	Lead mining & agriculture
RH2e	24–51	Slight increase in total AP percentages. High *Calluna* but percentages decline throughout the zone. Increasing Cyperaceae; low *Spaghnum* percentages. Low percentages of *Plantago lanceolata*, Cereal-type, *Rumex* and Pteropsida are recorded regularly.	Lead mining & agriculture
RH2d	51–71	Total AP percentages decrease throughout the zone. Increasing *Calluna*. Poaceae, Cyperaceae and *Plantago lanceolata* percentages are noticeable. Cereal-type pollen recorded at the top of the zone. High but erratic *Sphagnum* percentages.	Grazing and arable agriculture.
RH2c	71–95	*Quercus, Alnus* and *Corylus avellana*-type pollen all decrease until the end of the zone. Increasing *Calluna*, Poaceae and Cyperaceae. Small peaks in *Rumex* and *Plantago lanceolata* percentages. Lower *Melampyrum*. Charcoal peaks in mid-zone.	Woodland clearance grazing?
RH2b	95–123	Total AP percentages exceed 35% TLP. *Calluna* pollen peaks mid-zone. Poaceae Cyperaceae and *Potentilla*-type percentages fall. *Melampyrum* pollen is well represented.	Grazing?
RH2a	123–140	*Betula* and *Corylus avellana*-type pollen decrease in the first part of the zone. *Salix* peaks mid-zone whilst *Quercus* pollen percentages increase. Pteropsida is well represented. *Melampyrum* and *Potentilla*-type pollen increase.	Little evidence

Chemical analysis

Profiles for lead, zinc and iron are shown in Figure 4. Lead concentrations peak in the basal 20cm. and from 34 to 2cm., achieving a maximum concentration of 194.44 μg g^{-1}. Zinc concentrations peak at 514.7 μg g^{-1} at 110cm. but remain low, or below the limit of detection until 30cm. when they rise gradually to the mire surface. Iron concentrations between 1400 and 2800 μg g^{-1} are recorded in the basal 80cm., decline from 42 to 6cm., before peaking at 2cm.

Radiocarbon dates

The results of the radiocarbon assay are shown in Table 3. The radiocarbon dates are calibrated using CALIB 4.1 radiocarbon calibration program and IntCal98[26] and the calibration age ranges to two sigma are shown in Table 3.

INTERPRETATION AND DISCUSSION

A chronology of vegetation change in the upper Rookhope Valley

An uncalibrated radiocarbon date of 4440 ± 50 years BP at the base of site RH2 confirms that peat started to accumulate in the upper Rookhope Valley during the

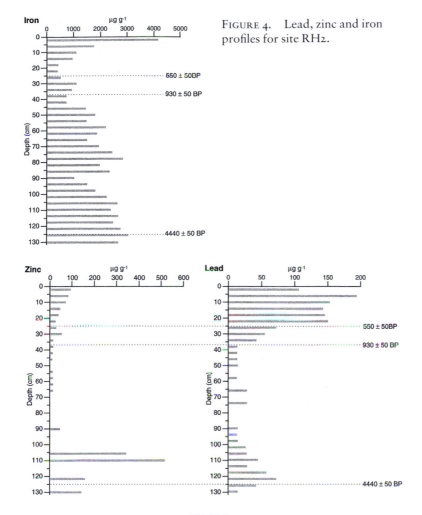

FIGURE 4. Lead, zinc and iron profiles for site RH2.

TABLE 3
RADIOCARBON DATES FOR SITE RH2

Lab code	Sample description	Depth (cm)	uncalibrated age	calibrated age range (2σ)
SRR-6470	*Sphagnum* peat	23–25	550 ± 50	cal AD 1300–73 cal AD 1378–1441
SRR-6471	*Sphagnum* peat	35–37	930 ± 50	cal AD 1002–11 cal AD 1016–1219
SRR-6473	*Sphagnum-Eriophorum* peat	125–30	4440 ± 50	cal BC 3346–2917

Neolithic period. Without the application of an absolute dating technique to monolith RH1 it is not possible to establish a firm chronology for the pollen data from this site. Because of the close proximity between the two sampling sites, it is more than likely that peat accumulation commenced at a similar time at RH1 to RH2, although the timing of peat initiation can vary over short distances.[27] The suggestion that peat accumulation began at a similar time at both sites is also supported by similarities in their pollen records and the identification of changes in the RH1 pollen record that have been recorded and dated as relatively contemporaneous throughout large areas of the British Isles. One such feature is the mid-Holocene elm decline that is recorded in pollen diagrams throughout north-west Europe. Radiocarbon dating of sediments suggests that the elm decline occurred within several hundred years either side of 5,000 years BP and the decline of elm pollen values at the end of zone RH1a and during RH1b may represent this decline although a prominent elm decline is not observed at site RH2. The relatively large increase in *Calluna* (heather) pollen at both sites (zones RH1c and RH2b) may also be contemporaneous. Furthermore, *Tilia* pollen is not recorded after the end of zones RH1d and RH2c. Huntley and Birks suggest that *Tilia* (lime) started to retreat from its northern limit in the British Isles (northern England) as a result of a deterioration in climate around 3,000 years BP.[28] It is possible, therefore, that the disappearance of *Tilia* from the pollen records at Rookhope equates to the retreat of *Tilia c.* 3,000 years BP. It is likely, therefore, that both pollen records extend back into the mid Holocene. The pollen record appears to extend up to the present day as *Pinus* (pine) percentages increase at the top of zone RH2f representing the planting of conifers during recent times.

Vegetational history with particular reference to human disturbance

Zones RH1a and RH2a are characterized by high frequencies of *Betula* (birch), *Quercus* (oak), *Corylus avellana*-type (hazel and/or *Myrica*) and *Alnus* (alder) pollen. Combined with the presence of other tree pollen, such as *Pinus*, *Ulmus*, *Tilia*, *Salix* (willow) and *Fraxinus* (ash), it appears that some mixed deciduous woodland was present in the pollen catchment. More open areas also existed at this time in the upper Rookhope Valley, characterized by the presence of Poaceae (grasses), Cyperaceae (sedges), *Potentilla*-type (tormentils), *Melampyrum* pollen (cow-wheat) and *Sphagnum* spores (clubmosses) (Figs 2 and 3).

A summary of the palaeoecological evidence for human disturbance is presented in Tables 1 and 2. Evidence for human activity is circumstantial, as indicated by small decreases in certain arboreal (trees and shrubs) pollen curves and the sparse occurrence and low percentages of non-arboreal taxa (herbs) with cultural-affinities, during zones at RH1a and b and RH2a and b. Neolithic cultures may have contributed to the prominent decline of *Betula* and *Corylus avellana*-type pollen, and a small gradual decline in *Ulmus* during the early part of zone RH2a. The decline of these tree taxa suggests that some woodland cover may have been lost. This reduction correlates with the presence of a suite of non-arboreal taxa that are collectively considered to be 'cultural indicators' (including *Plantago lanceolata* (ribwort plantain), *Rumex* spp (docks and sorrels), Brassicaceae (cabbage family), Lactucae (dandelions) and Chenopodiaceae (goosefoot family), and consistent recording of Poaceae (grass family).

By the beginning of zones RH1c and RH2b, *Calluna* (heather) pollen values rise dramatically, coinciding with a fall in the representation of *Betula*, *Corylus avellana*-type, Cyperaceae and Poaceae pollen. This suggests that open woodland, characterized by birch and hazel, was replaced by a heather-dominated community. The expansion of *Calluna* may have been facilitated by the development of organic, acidic soils locally. As *Calluna* pollen values rise, the percentages of *Melampyrum* and *Potentilla*-type fall midway through zone RH1b. A similar pattern can also be observed as *Calluna* values increase to over 35% TLP across the RH2b/c zone boundary. The transition from woodland and grassland to *Calluna*-dominated vegetation is characterized by the sparse occurrence and low values of non-arboreal taxa usually associated with human activity (as described in the previous paragraph). The presence of *Melampyrum* and *Potentilla*-type pollen during first two zones in both pollen diagrams could also be related to human disturbance. Certain species of *Melampyrum* are arable weeds, whilst relatively high values of *Potentilla*-type could be the result of grazing, although species of both taxa grow naturally in a variety of habitats.[29] Thus, it is difficult to assert, with any degree of confidence, that human disturbance contributed to the initiation of *Calluna*-dominated blanket peats as suggested for numerous other sites throughout the British Isles.[30]

Several other changes in the pollen records for sites RH1 and RH2 could be due in part to some form of prehistoric human disturbance. A noticeable decline in several tree taxa occurs between 92 and 84cm. at site RH1 (Table 3). Moreover, the percentages of *Betula* and *Corylus avellana*-type do not return to their former values, suggesting that a decrease in birch and hazel woodland cover had taken place. Human activity may have contributed to the reduction in woodland cover as pollen taxa thought to be indicative of pastoral agriculture, such as *Plantago lanceolata* and *Rumex*, are recorded at these levels. Another drop in the total arboreal curve occurs, characterized by a reduction in *Betula* and *Alnus* pollen, which follows after a more gradual and prolonged fall in *Quercus* from possibly its mid-Holocene maxima, and *Corylus avellana*-type values from 60cm. to 54cm. at site RH1. *Tilia* is also recorded for the last time at 48cm. This reduction in woodland cover corresponds to the point in the diagram where cereal-type pollen is recorded for the first time. Combined with the presence of a suite of non-arboreal pollen taxa with anthropogenic affinities, the detection of cereal pollen indicates that agricultural activity has resulted in a limited amount of woodland clearance. A similar pattern can be discerned from the pollen record during zone RH2d (between 62 and 54cm.) at site RH2 (Table 4). The total percentage of arboreal pollen does not recover to its former level suggesting that a permanent reduction in woodland cover has occurred. In contrast, the percentages of arboreal taxa generally recover after the episodes of human disturbance outlined at site RH1 (Table 3).

Metal mining and its impact on the landscape

Metal mining in Weardale can be traced back to at least the 1100s when King Stephen confirmed the rights of Bishop Hugh Puiset to extract silver and lead.[31] Historical documents also provide evidence that lead and iron mining and smelting was common practice between the 14th and 16th centuries.[32] However, survey and inventory work conducted by the Cranstone Consultancy at Frasers Grove mine has not revealed any evidence to ascertain whether mining took place in the upper Rookhope Valley before the 17th century.[33] The discovery of some fine wooden pipes during this survey is the only evidence for the exploitation of wood by the miners. As the mining took place underground, it is probable that some wood was used during the construction of the mining shafts, but it is not possible to quantity or estimate accurately how much wood would have been required for these purposes.[34] Regionally, a supply of wood was clearly imperative for metal mining. Historical documents describe the destruction of woodlands as early as 1306 and, according to the Parliamentary survey of 1647, timber was scarce in the Weardale area forcing miners to exploit peat for fire-setting fuel.[35]

The radiocarbon date of 930 ± 50 years BP at 37 to 35cm. at site RH2 dates the upper part of zone RH2e from the 11th to early 13th centuries AD (see Table 3 for calibrated age ranges). The arboreal pollen record at RH2 is below 25% TLP: a reflection of the permanent loss of woodland clearance during prehistoric times. There are no further reductions in arboreal pollen percentages at RH2 to coincide with the initial rise in lead concentrations (Fig. 4). Higher arboreal percentages are recorded at site RH1 in zone RH1e (considered to be chronological equivalent with zone RH2e). During this zone there are temporary drops in *Quercus* and *Corylus avellana*-type pollen percentages between 40 and 32cm. and from 22cm. to 20cm. suggesting that these trees have been cleared, possibly by miners or for charcoal production. The recovery of arboreal pollen suggests that any mining or smelting that took place in the vicinity of the upper Rookhope Valley before 550 ± 50 years BP did not permanently remove any remaining woodland.

In contrast, the pollen data presented in this paper is in close agreement with the evidence described in historical documents for woodland loss from AD 1300 onwards. Both zones RH1f and RH2f are marked by a permanent loss of woodland cover; values for the total tree and shrub pollen percentages fall to below 10% of TLP, indicating that virtually all of the woodland present in the upper Rookhope Valley was lost during this zone. This corresponds with a sharp rise in the percentages of Poaceae, Cyperaceae and *Calluna* pollen at both sites, and *Sphagnum* spores at site RH1. High *Calluna* values, associated with the presence of taxa such as *Empetrum* (crowberry), indicate that a further expansion of a *Calluna*-dominated heath on local acidic soils and peat coincided with the loss of woodland cover. Raistrick suggests that the smelting of lead ores occurred away from the mines from the 15th century onwards.[36] Lead smelting required a substantial amount of timber therefore the ore was transferred from Upper Weardale to more wooded areas such as Wolsingham.[37] The pollen data presented in this paper is consistent with this scenario as arboreal pollen percentages gradually decline from just before 550 ± 50 years BP at RH2 suggesting that the area became treeless.

Documentary evidence also informs us that land in valley bottoms was set aside for agricultural purposes whilst hill grazing was common on higher ground during the summer months in the mining areas of Weardale.[38] Evidence for agriculture, coincides with the decline in woodland cover between the eleventh and present century. The recording of cereal-type pollen from 24cm. at site RH1 suggests that arable farming was being practised in the pollen catchment. Grazing is also suggested by the presence of taxa such as *Plantago lanceolata*, *Potentilla*-type and *Rumex acetosa/acetosella* (Rumex a/a in Fig. 3). A similar pattern can be discerned from the pollen record at site RH2. Cereal-type pollen is recorded during the end of zone RH2e and throughout RH2f as arboreal pollen percentages decrease. Thus, the evidence presented here strongly suggests that the upper Rookhope Valley became virtually treeless as a result of both agriculture and metal mining.

Moreover, the link between metal mining and woodland clearance is strengthened by the chemical data: lead concentrations rise as arboreal pollen falls in the upper Rookhope Valley. Results from the chemical analyses of the peat monolith at site RH2 are presented in Figure 4. It is noteworthy that lead concentrations rise dramatically from below 20 μg g^{-1} at 38cm. to peak at c. 200 μg g^{-1} at 6cm. Natural background values for lead average 30 μg g^{-1} for soils in England and Wales[39] suggesting that the rise in lead concentrations at RH2 represent the accumulation of atmospheric lead pollution produced by mining in the upper Rookhope Valley. These concentrations are slightly higher than those recorded by Martin *et al.* (1979) in the Gordano Valley, but may be simply a result of the distance between the source of lead and the sampling site. Wild and Eastwood state that lead concentrations around industrial sites can range between 30.0 and 16460 μg g^{-1}.[40] The movement of lead ores to more wooded areas for smelting from the 15th century AD is possibly the most likely explanation for the relatively low lead concentrations recorded in the upper Rookhope Valley compared with the figures presented by Wild and Eastwood.

Notwithstanding the potential errors in the radiocarbon dating method, the chronology of lead pollution and woodland clearance at site RH2 site is in close agreement with the historical documentary evidence for mining in Weardale. A radiocarbon date of 930 $\pm$ 50 years BP at 34cm. suggests that mining and smelting is first recorded in the RH2 peat profile between the 11th and 13th centuries. The dramatic rise in lead concentrations between 26 and 22cm. is radiocarbon dated to 550 $\pm$ 50 years BP providing evidence that lead mining and smelting intensified during the 14th and 15th centuries AD in Weardale. At least one mine, known as Bashamere is known to have been working in 1457/8, whilst four mines are also known in the Rookhope Valley between 1600 and 1800: a period when up to 120 lead mines were leased by the Moormaster in Weardale.[41] The peak in lead concentrations at 6cm. probably reflects the lead pollution generated during the 18th century when lead mining was most prosperous in the British Isles.[42] Alternatively, if the lead was crushed, washed and smelted at a place close to the mine, as suggested by Raistrick and Jennings for parts of the Pennine lead mining industry,[43] the amount of atmospheric pollution would increase. Lead concentrations fall in the uppermost level to nearer 100 μg/g^{-1} and this signals the cessation of mining and trial workings in the local area during World War II.

Zinc is commonly associated with lead mineralization[44] and the rise in concentrations from 30cm. upwards could be linked with either lead mining or the increased deposition of heavy metals from long distance transport from the 18th century onwards.[45] Data for iron is also presented in Figure 4 as iron smelting was common throughout County Durham from the 1300s[46] and there is evidence of ironstone quarrying in the Rookhope Valley. The removal of ironstone probably took place during the 1860s to the 1890s when the Weardale Iron Company opened a quarry.[47] The rise in iron concentrations from 18cm. onwards may reflect, in part, the atmospheric pollution associated with the ironstone industry and subsequent fossil fuel combustion culminating in a peak at the peat surface.[48] Below this, the distribution of iron is difficult to interpret solely as a result of mining and smelting activities. In contrast to lead, iron concentrations are low between 42 and 10cm. A possible explanation for this is discussed below.

Heavy metals in peat can be influenced by a number of factors besides mining pollution. The movement and leaching of cations, the degree of peat humification, the position of the water table, redox conditions, pH and other natural causes can re-distribute or remove metals from the peat and distort the stratigraphic integrity of the geochemical record.[49] Shotyk (1988), Urban et al. (1990) and Shotyk et al. (1992) have suggested that lead, zinc and iron may be prone to post-depositional transformation once incorporated into peat. Lead peaks have been attributed to the movement of the water table and differences in peat micro-topography.[50] However, Shotyk et al. (1997) suggest that recent evidence is clearly in favour of lead retention and a consistent relationship between the stratigraphic record of Pb and the time of deposition. Stewart and Fergusson suggest that in a reducing environment of high organic content, low pH and Eh, lead (II) can be immobilized as long as there is sufficient sulphur to form sulphides in the peat.[51] Therefore the record of lead in the peat at site RH2 should be representative of the pollution history of mining in the area.

According to Rastrick zinc was not smelted in this country before 1720[52] so there are no early zinc works, although the carbonate ore of zinc was used in brass making and mined in the 1500s. The chemical curve for zinc is, however, difficult to interpret with no evidence for zinc mining in the Rookhope area. Like lead, zinc concentrations are relatively high in the basal 20cm. of the RH2 profile. Zinc could have accumulated here and at the present surface via bio-accumulation in plants. Weathering of the parent material or the presence of enriched groundwaters may also account for these basal concentrations. Iron is soluble in anaerobic, acidic peats and can be lost to drainage waters or it can accumulate with depth especially when the basal part of the peat profile is minerotrophic rather than ombrotrophic.[53]

It is important to realize, therefore, that 'early' peaks in metals in peat and lake sediments may not necessarily represent contamination from mining and smelting activities but can be the result of natural processes operating in these systems. Until the effect of all these factors are better understood it is more difficult to interpret zinc and iron profiles.[54] Fortunately, elements such as copper and lead are more immobile and are *less likely* to suffer from remobilization. Clearly replication of the chemical data and a reliable chronology would be two ways of detecting anomalous concentrations. Those studies that provide archives of metal deposition without a radiocarbon or another reliable chronology[55] must be viewed circumspectly.

SUMMARY

Pollen and chemical data, analysed from a radiocarbon-dated blanket peat that covers an extensive area of the upper Rookhope Valley, provides evidence that the present landscape has been influenced by human actions over the past four millennia. The most dramatic and permanent changes in vegetation were initiated in the 13th century when woodland was cleared permanently from the upper Rookhope Valley. The data presented in this paper suggests strongly that woodland was cleared to create agricultural land and to supply timber for the lead mining industry. The reconstruction of a chronological record of atmospheric lead pollution accords well with archaeological and documentary evidence of lead mining in Weardale. The close agreement between these two datasets suggests that lead has not suffered from post-depositional translocation. Lead pollution is first recorded during medieval times and appears to have intensified from the 14th century. The drop in lead concentrations at the top of the RH2 profile most probably records the cessation of mining during the 20th century. The profiles of zinc and iron are more problematic and cannot be fully accounted for by mining and smelting; this demonstrates the dangers in interpreting chemical profiles in former metal mining regions without some consideration of other parameters.

ACKNOWLEDGEMENTS

Thanks are due to David Cranstone for alerting TM to the site, and to Ros Nichol and Tom Gledhill for collecting the RH1 peat monolith. Dr J. J. Blackford helped to collect the RH2 peat monolith. David Cranstone and Alan Blackburn kindly allowed us access to their unpublished data. Laboratory analyses were conducted in the Geography Subject Area at Coventry University. Mrs S. E. Turner provided valuable assistance with the chemical analysis. Erica Milwain and Joanne Beverley helped reproduce the figures. Support for radiocarbon dates, provided by NERC (application number 744.0798), is gratefully acknowledged.

Tim M. Mighall & Stuart Freeth, Geography, School of Science and the Environment, Coventry University, Priory Street, Coventry CVL 5FB, UK
Lisa Dumayne-Peaty, School of Geography and Environmental Sciences, University of Birmingham, Edgbaston, Birmingham B15 2TT, UK

NOTES

[1] Faegri *et al.* 1989; Moore *et al.* 1991.
[2] For example Behre 1981; Birks *et al.*, 1988; Chambers 1993.
[3] Behre 1981.
[4] Mighall & Chambers 1993a, 1993b; Mighall *et al.* 2000a.
[5] Chambers & Lageard 1993; Mighall & Chambers 1997.
[6] Cleere 1974, 1976.
[7] Darby 1951, 1956.
[8] Flinn 1959; Lindsay 1975.
[9] For example Mighall *et al.* 2000b.
[10] Williams 1991.
[11] Lee & Tallis 1973; Martin *et al.* 1979.
[12] Aspinall *et al.* 1986.

[13] See, for example, Roberts *et al.* 1973; Simmons & Cundill 1974; Bartley *et al.* 1976; Davies & Turner 1979; Simmons 1993; Spratt 1993.
[14] Raistrick & Jennings 1965.
[15] Ibid.
[16] Wooler 1928.
[17] Raistrick & Jennings 1965
[18] Ibid.
[19] For example Raistrick & Jennings 1965; Willies & Cranstone 1992; Ford & Willies 1994.
[20] For example Drury 1992; Blackburn 1994.
[21] Pers. comm., David Cranstone.
[22] Barber 1976.
[23] Stockmarr 1971.
[24] Clark 1982.

[25] Grimm 1991.
[26] Stuiver & Reimer 1993; Stuiver et al. 1998.
[27] Moore 1993.
[28] Huntley & Birks 1983.
[29] See Moore, Evans & Chater 1986.
[30] Moore 1988; 1993.
[31] Blackburn 1994.
[32] Drury 1992.
[33] Cranstone 1992.
[34] Ibid.
[35] Blackburn 1994.
[36] Raistrick 1972.
[37] Ibid.
[38] Blackburn 1994.
[39] Reaves & Berrow 1984.

[40] Wild and Eastwood 1992.
[41] A. Blackburn, unpublished data.
[42] Livett 1988.
[43] Raistrick & Jennings 1965.
[44] Rastrick 1972.
[45] Livett 1988.
[46] Drury 1992.
[47] Cranstone 1992.
[48] Shotyk 1988.
[49] Shotyk 1988, 1996; Van Geel et al. 1989.
[50] Damman 1978; Shotyk 1988.
[51] Stewart and Fergusson 1994.
[52] Rastrick 1972.
[53] Shotyk 1988.
[54] Shotyk 1988, 1996.
[55] For example Lee & Tallis 1973; Martin et al. 1979.

BIBLIOGRAPHY

Aspinall, R., Macklin, M. G. & Brevis, T. 1986, 'Metal mining and floodplain sedimentation at Garrigill and their influence on terrace and floodplain soil development', in Macklin, M. G. & Rose, J. (eds), *Quaternary River Landforms and Sediments in the Northern Pennines, England*, Field Guide. British Geomorphological Research Group/Quaternary Research Association, 35–45.

Barber, K. E. 1976, 'History of vegetation', in Chapman, S. B. (ed.), *Methods in Plant Ecology*, Oxford: Blackwell, 5–83.

Bartley, D. D., Chambers, C. & Hart-Jones, B. 1976, 'The vegetational history of parts of south and east Durham', *New Phytologist* 77, 437–68.

Behre, K.-E. 1981, 'The interpretation of anthropogenic indicators in pollen diagrams', *Pollen et Spores* 23, 225–45.

Bennett, K. D., Whittington, G. & Edwards, K. J. 1994, 'Recent plant nomenclatural changes and pollen morphology in the British Isles', *Quaternary Newsletter* 73, 1–6.

Birks, H. H., Birks, H. J. B., Kaland, P. E. & Moe, D. (eds) 1988, *The Cultural Landscape — Past, Present and Future*, Cambridge: Cambridge University Press.

Blackburn, A. 1994, 'Mining without laws: Weardale under the Moormasters', in Ford & Willies (eds) 1994, 69–75.

Chambers, F. M. (ed.) 1993, *Climate Change and Human Impact on the Landscape*, London: Chapman and Hall.

Chambers, F. M. & Lageard, J. G. A. 1993, 'Vegetational history and environmental setting of Crawcwellt, Gwynedd', *Archaeology in Wales* 33, 23–25.

Clark, R. L. 1982, 'Point count estimation of charcoal in pollen preparations and thin sections of sediments', *Pollen et Spores* 24, 523–35.

Cleere, H. 1974, 'The Roman iron industry of the Weald and its connexions with the *Classis Britannica*', *Archaeological Journal* 131, 171–99.

Cleere, H. 1976, 'Some operating parameters for Roman ironworks', *Bulletin of the Institute of Archaeology* 13, 233–46.

Cranstone, D. 1992, 'Frasers Grove Interim Report', Cranstone Consultancy, unpublished report.

Damman, A. W. H. 1978, 'Distribution and movement of elements in ombrotrophic peat bogs', *Oikos* 30, 480–95.

Davies, G. & Turner, J. 1979, 'Pollen diagrams from Northumberland', *New Phytologist* 82, 783–804.

Darby, H. C. 1951, 'The clearing of the English woodlands', *Geography* 36, 71–83.

Darby, H. C. 1956, 'The clearing of woodland in Europe', in Thomas, W. L. (ed.), *Man's Role in Changing the Face of the Earth*, Chicago: University of Chicago Press.

Drury, J. L. 1992, 'Medieval smelting in County Durham: an archivists point of view', in Willies, L. & Cranstone, D. (eds), *Boles and Smeltmills*, Matlock Bath: Historical Metallurgy Society Ltd, 22–24.

Faegri, K., Kaland, P. E. & Krzywinski, K. 1989, *Textbook of Pollen Analysis*, 4th edition, Chichester: John Wiley and Sons.

Flinn, M. W. 1959, 'Timber and the advance of technology: a reconsideration', *Annals of Science* 15, 109–20.

Ford, T. D. & Willies, L. (eds) 1994, *Mining Before Powder*, Peak District Mines Historical Society 12:3 and Historical Metallurgy Society Special Publication.

Foster, I. D. L., Dearing, J. D., Charlesworth, S. M. & Kelly, I. A. 1987, 'Paired lake catchment studies: a framework for investigating chemical fluxes in small drainage basins', *Applied Geography* 7, 115–33.

Grimm, E. 1991, *TILIA and TILIA.GRAPH*, Illinois: Illinois State Museum.

Huntley, B. & Birks, H. J. B. 1983, *An Atlas of Past and Present Pollen Maps for Europe 0–13,000 years ago*, Cambridge: Cambridge University Press.

Lee, J. A. & Tallis, J. H. 1973, 'Regional and historical aspects of lead pollution in Britain', *Nature* 245, 216–18.

Lindsay, J. M. 1975, 'Charcoal iron smelting and its fuel supply; the example of Lorn furnace, Argyllshire, 1753–1876', *Journal of Historical Geography* 1:3, 283–98.

Livett, E. A. 1988, 'Geochemical monitoring of atmospheric heavy metal pollution: theory and application', *Advances in Ecological Research* 18, 65–177.

Martin, M. N., Coughtrey, P. J. & Ward, P. 1979, 'Historical aspects of heavy metal pollution in the Gordano Valley', *Proceedings of the Bristol Naturalists Society* 37, 91–97.

Mighall, T. M. & Chambers, F. M. 1993a, 'The environmental impact of prehistoric mining at Copa Hill, Cwmystwyth, Wales', *The Holocene* 3:3, 260–64.

Mighall, T. M. & Chambers, F. M. 1993b, 'Early mining and metalworking: its impact on the environment', *Historical Metallurgy* 27:2, 71–83.

Mighall, T. M. & Chambers, F. M. 1997, 'Early ironworking and its impact on the environment: palaeoecological evidence from Bryn y Castell hillfort, Snowdonia, north Wales', *Proceedings of the Prehistoric Society* 63, 199–219.

Mighall, T. M., Chambers, F. M., Lanting, J. & O'Brien, W. F. 2000a, 'Prehistoric copper mining and its impact on vegetation: palaeoecological data from Mount Gabriel, Co. Cork, south-west Ireland', in O'Connor, T. P. & Nicholson, R. (eds), *People as Agents of Environmental Change*, Oxford: Oxbow, in press.

Mighall, T. M., Timberlake, S., Grattan, J. P. & Forsyth, S. 2000b, 'Bronze Age lead mining at Copa Hill, Cwmystwyth — fact or fantasy?' *Historical Metallurgy* 34:1, 1–12.

Moore, P. D. 1988, 'The development of moorlands and upland mires', in Jones, M. (ed.) *Archaeology and the Flora of the British Isles*, Oxford: Oxford University Committee for Archaeology Monograph No. 14, 116–22.

Moore, P. D. 1993, 'The origin of blanket mire, revisited', in Chambers (ed.) 1993, 217–24.

Moore, P. D., Evans, A.T. & Chater, M. 1986, 'Palynological and stratigraphic evidence for hydrological changes in mires associated with human activity', in Behre, K.-E. (ed.), *Anthropogenic Indicators in Pollen Diagrams*, Rotterdam: A. A. Balkema.

Moore, P. D., Webb, J. A. & Collinson, M. E. 1991, *Pollen Analysis*, 2nd edition, London: Blackwell Scientific Publications.

Raistrick, A. 1972, *Industrial Archaeology: an historical survey*, London: Eyre Methuen.

Raistrick, A. & Jennings, B. 1965, *A History of Lead Mining in the Pennines*, London: Longmans.

Reaves, G. A. & Berrow, M. L. 1984, 'Total lead concentrations in Scottish soils', *Geoderma* 32, 1–8.

Roberts, B. K., Turner, J. & Ward, P. F. 1973, 'Recent forest history in Weardale, northern England', in Birks, H. J. B. and West, R. G. (eds), *Quaternary Plant Ecology*, London: Blackwell, 207–20.

Shotyk, W. 1988, 'Review of the inorganic geochemistry of peats and peatland waters', *Earth Science Reviews* 25, 95–176.

Shotyk, W. 1996, 'Peat bog archives of atmospheric metal deposition: geochemical evaluation of peat profiles, natural variations in metal concentrations, and metal enrichment factors', *Environmental Reviews* 4, 149–83.

Shotyk, W. Norton, S. A. & Farmer, J. G. 1997, 'Summary of the workshop on peat bog archives of atmospheric metal deposition', *Water, Air and Soil Pollution* 100, 213–19.

Simmons, I. G. 1993, 'Vegetation change during the Mesolithic in the British Isles: some amplifications', in Chambers (ed.) 1993, 109–18.

Simmons, I. G. & Cundill, P. R. 1974, 'Late Quaternary vegetational history of the North York Moors 1. Pollen analyses of blanket peats', *Journal of Biogeography* 1, 159–69.

Spratt, D. (ed.) 1993, *Prehistoric and Roman Archaeology of North-East Yorkshire*, London: Council for British Archaeology Research Report 87.

Stace, C. 1991, *New Flora of the British Isles*, Cambridge: Cambridge University Press.

Stewart, C. & Fergusson, J. E. 1994, 'The use of peat in the historical monitoring of trace metals in the atmosphere', *Environmental Pollution* 86, 243–49.

Stockmarr, J. 1971, 'Tablets with spores used in absolute pollen analysis', *Pollen et Spores* 13, 615–21.

Stuiver, M. & Reimer, P. J. 1993, 'A computer program for radiocarbon age calibration', *Radiocarbon* 35, 215–30.

Stuvier, M., Reimer, P. J., Bard, E., Beck, J. W., Burr, G. S., Hughen, K. A., Kromer, B., McCormac, F. G., v. d. Plicht, J. & Spurk, M. 1998, 'INTCAL98 radiocarbon age calibration 24,000–0 cal BP', *Radiocarbon* 40, 1041–83.

Urban, N. R., Eisenreich, S. J., Grigal, D. F. & Schurr, K. T. 1990, 'Mobility and diagenesis of Pb and ^{210}Pb in peat', *Geochimica et Cosmochimica Acta* 54, 3329–46.

Van Geel, B., Bregman, R., Van der Molen, P. C., Dupont, L. M. & Van Driel-Murray, C. 1989, 'Holocene raised bog deposits in the Netherlands as geochemical archives of prehistoric aerosols', *Acta Botanica Neerlandica* 38:4, 467–76.

Wild, M. & Eastwood, I. 1992, 'Soil contamination and smelting sites', in Willies, L. & Cranstone, D. (eds) 1992, 54–57.

Williams, T. M. 1991, 'A sedimentary record of the deposition of heavy metals and magnetic oxides in the Loch Dee basin, Galloway, Scotland, since *c.* AD 1500', *The Holocene* 1:2, 142–50.

Willies, L. & Cranstone, D. (eds) 1992, *Boles and Smeltmills*, Matlock Bath: Historical Metallurgy Society Ltd.

Wooler, E. 1924, 'Roman lead mining in Weardale', *Yorkshire Archaeological Journal* 28, 93–100.

SOCIAL ARCHAEOLOGY: A POSSIBLE METHODOLOGY OF THE STUDY OF WORKERS' SETTLEMENTS BASED ON THE 18TH- AND 19TH-CENTURY COPPER INDUSTRY OF SWANSEA

By STEPHEN HUGHES

In many ways the Industrial Revolution produced a whole new system of living and with it a range of both social as well as functional structures. The policy document produced by the Association for Industrial Archaeology in 1991 made the case for all the buildings of the modern Industrial Period to be worthy of inclusion in the study of Industrial Archaeology.[1] There is much need for this integrated social/industrial approach but it was not immediately apparent how, for example, a 19th-century Anglican church might be studied using methodologies employed by, and relevant to, 'industrial archaeologists', rather than those methods well established by art and architectural historical practitioners. The basis of this paper concerns an initial study in which a sole concern with the usual fodder of industrial archaeological studies — conventional process techniques and functional structures and architecture — was transformed into a study of all types of material evidence remaining from the 18th- and 19th-century international centre of copper smelting in Swansea.[2] This extends in scope some of the more focused studies already done in social archaeology in which, for example, an analysis of housing types has been undertaken to quantify and characterize those elements of apparently domestic structures that have a functional origin and purpose. Such research aspirations aimed at elucidating, for example, the functional origins of the textile industry are not generally applicable to the study of primary extractive and smelting industries where functional and domestic structures did not overlap, but where the latter depend on the success and ownership of the former for their own forms and elaboration.

The larger part of the text of the Royal Commission's newly published study of the archaeology and architecture of the industrial period at Swansea is devoted to social rather than functional archaeology and this approach was directly prompted by two factors. Firstly, the local community (as represented by Swansea City Council, who gave a substantial grant towards publication) was concerned that the social side of industrialization should not be ignored in any study. This view of a wider study of the archaeology of the industrial period was also reinforced by a paper given at one of the first professional study days (held in Leicester in 1994) for those involved professionally in industrial archaeology. This lamented the neglect of *social* archaeological evidence that could be provided by an examination of the fabric and relationship between elements of the new industrial landscape – that is, the relationship between the spacing and design of industrial works and owners' and workers' dwellings.[3]

The financial resources unlocked by the Industrial Revolution provided both industrialists and their workers with the ability to meet the needs of, and endow the new industrial communities with new types of buildings. The major elements of the material manifestation of industrial society in Britain in 1750–1850 included workers', managers' and employers' housing; the development of workers' settlements and employers' estates; workers' Nonconformist chapels and employers' Anglican churches; works and schools. How all these elements related socially, economically, in the form of structures constructed, and spatially to each other and to the works that provided employment and attracted people to each industrial area, is of some considerable interest. Some of these types of structures were not necessarily confined to industrial areas but certainly tended to occur in a particularly concentrated form within them, this concentration providing the economic and institutional form for structures which might then be provided in more rural areas. However, workers' settlements, works schools and institutes were structure types that were definitely specific to industrial districts.

How much the nature of each of these elements examined in the Swansea study is particularly Welsh rather than British, or generally European, in character is open to discussion. Certainly in the world's first industrial revolution many of these elements were found throughout Britain, but the density of some types, such as workers' Nonconformist chapels, works schools and institutes, was particularly concentrated in the international centres of the metals-smelting industries in south Wales and did evolve some particular architectural traits. However, similar institutions evolved in every industrial area of Britain, some more generally in Europe and internationally, and the inter-relationships of these need further study. As the industrial revolution expanded, many of these social institutions spread with it, but with varying combinations of elements.

In and around Swansea there still remain substantial workers' houses, settlements and former industrialists' mansions from the period when the city was the copper-smelting capital of the world. In common with many of the metals-smelting works of the late 18th and early 19th centuries the twelve main copper-smelting works founded in the lower Swansea Valley were located away from pre-existing urban centres and sited in relatively isolated areas. In addition two of the copperworks, and many collieries, were built to the west of the River Tawe on the locally abundant common land with the sanction of the Duke of Beaufort, who had charge of the Seignory of Gower (exercising the long-held traditional rights of a Marcher Lord). Interestingly, further cartographic study has shown that most of the hundreds of workers' cottages built in the early 19th century were not squatter occupation on the numerous commons, but were instead built in ever-increasing groups on small roadside plots enclosed from farmland and must have been viewed as a useful new source of income by the land-owning gentry.

Immediately the works were founded, they needed two sets of social architecture to function. One was a substantial dwelling for the resident 'agent' or manager, mostly newly built, although on two occasions an old gentry house standing alongside the old works site was initially adapted for this purpose. The other was a terrace of dwellings for key workmen and foremen, often located on or alongside the works site. The rest of the workforce could either travel from Swansea town or build thatched single-storey cottages with sleeping-lofts in traditional style, as many did in the 19th and early 20th centuries on the plots already mentioned. Such cottages had already been built by local landowners in the 17th and 18th centuries for their colliery workers. Again, some of the first workers' houses, such as the multi-storey colliers' apartment block called Morris Castle (1773) and six semi-detached foremen's houses for the Forest Copperworks (1775), were also built on common land.

WORKERS' HOUSING

The large-scale provision of workers' housing in the lower Swansea Valley had already been pioneered before Swansea became a centre of the copper industry, with housing being provided for colliers in the lower eastern valley. Both self-built and employer-provided housing was prompted by the presence of the underlying coastal coal deposits attracting works which needed operating by workers in what was a sparsely populated rural area.

Contemporary maps indicate that over a period of 150 years some factors seem to have remained surprisingly constant when coppermasters provided housing for their workforce. From the cartographic, structural, documentary and Census evidence it has been possible to calculate that all copper-smelting concerns accommodated about a third of their workforce in purpose-built housing in the later 18th and the 19th centuries. The housing that the copper-smelting concerns constructed generally compared well with the insanitary courts and dwellings built for workers in the northern part of Swansea town. Most rentals were lower and map evidence and surviving remains indicate that substantial gardens were provided in most copper industry housing constructed before the later 19th century. By comparison, little housing was provided for the dispersed, shorter-lived and smaller-scale centres of employment provided by later 18th- and early 19th-century collieries.

The coppermasters did take advantage of their capital resources, and even more the large amounts of capital generated by the industry in its heyday, to provide a substantial amount of housing which is still good enough to be occupied. As far as is known, nothing was produced which was as small, or as short-lived as the timber houses built, for example, for the early workforce employed on the Severn Tunnel at Sudbrook in Monmouthshire, which was built of temporary materials. Similarly inferior to the houses provided by the coppermasters were the timber houses built by local under-capitalized entrepreneurs in the early days of the Rhondda coal industry (for Fernhill and Dunraven Collieries, Blaenrhondda and the 22 wooden dwellings at Baptist Square and Mountain Row, Blaenllechau, by the innovative entrepreneur

David Davies and his partners) and the turf-walled houses for workers employed on the early railways of the Brecon Forest at the head of the Swansea Valley in the late 1820s.[4] Similarly, the archaeological studies already carried out on the surviving housing-stock of the international centre of contemporary iron production in the heads of the Valleys region around Merthyr Tydfil and Blaenavon have shown how much smaller and less elaborate were the houses that were built there. These were produced for a larger extent of the workforce than at Swansea in what was then a much more remote area, with the building carried out by relatively under-capitalized entrepreneurs in the early days of their involvement in large-scale industry.[5]

There were identifiable types of Swansea houses built by the coppermasters. By contrast the detailed recording already undertaken at the Heads of the east Glamorgan and west Monmouthshire valleys has shown that a primary determinant of the type of housing built there was the policy of the (smelting) company concerned in undertaking the building, and not usually the building type predominant in the locality before industrialization.[6] The examination of housing built at Swansea shows that different factors were important in the industrial settlements in that location, related instead both to the existing local building traditions of the semi-rural workforce and to those of the adjacent town. The early and mid 18th-century single-storeyed colliers' houses built by the landowner/industrialist Thomas Price and the Lockwood, Morris & Company partnership were obvious derivatives from the west Wales *crogloft* cottages (i.e. single-storeyed with partial sleeping-lofts) already being used by the local collier builders on roadside verges and by squatters on the plentiful commonland.

Later, the original 48 catslide-roofed (i.e. built with a large roof slope covering extra rooms) houses built by the Vivians (owners of the large Hafod Copperworks) in *c.* 1837 were modelled on pre-existing housing types in the town. Even so, copper-smelting concerns almost immediately developed distinctive housing types of their own.

However, the development of workers' housing in the lower Swansea Valley was not entirely a consistent evolution in type. There were many types of accommodation existing at any one time, including isolated single-storey cottages (with sleeping-lofts), single-storey terraces, detached two-storey houses, two storey terraces, and three-to-four-storey apartment blocks. The surviving evidence shows that there were also diverse approaches that Swansea industrial entrepreneurs might adopt in providing houses for their workforces. A works owner could convert existing structures to provide habitations for his workforce, build houses for a varying core of his workforce directly, or else provide land for his workers themselves to build on.

PLANNED WORKERS' SETTLEMENTS

What has been considered so far have been the individual workers' dwellings and terraces and not the assemblages of some planned and partly planned settlements, of which they formed a part. The earlier coal industry in the lower Swansea Valley was organized on a smaller dispersed scale than the later copper-smelting industry, except perhaps for the landowner Bussy Mansel's collieries at Llansamlet in the eastern

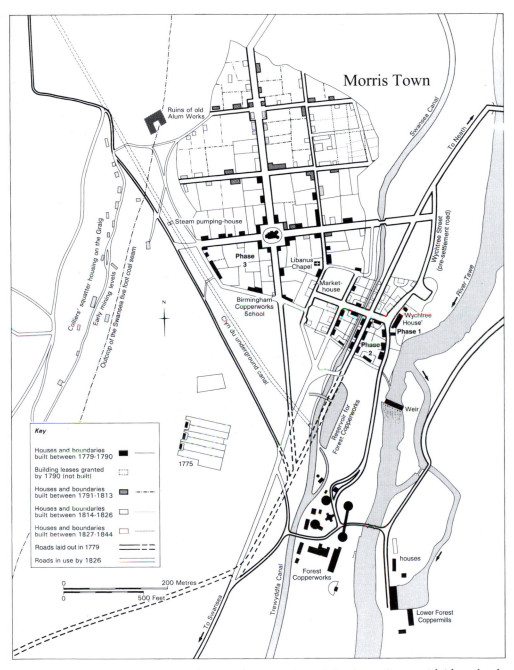

FIGURE 1. Plan of the workers' settlement of Morris Town (Morriston, Swansea) laid out by the coppermaster John Morris I in 1779 with two grids of streets on which workers could build their own houses to an approved design; the Anglican church built by the coppermaster dominated the central square. (Crown copyright: RCAHMW)

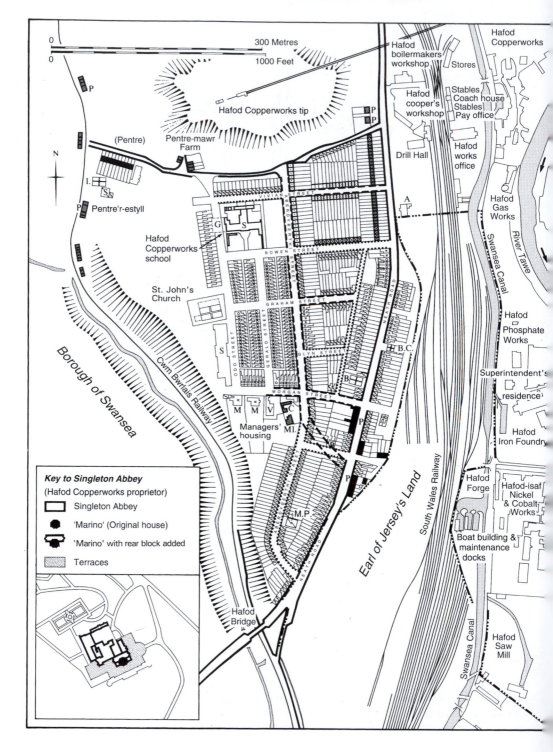

Key to Trevivian Map

Existing pre-settlement roads

'Trevivian' roads laid out by 1844

Roads added 1845-1867

Roads added 1868-1897

Boundary of Vivian land in 1844

M   Managers' houses   M1. Main manager's house

S   Schools   G   Original garden

Chapel buildings

Anglican church building   Planned extensions

V   Vicarage

A   Possible temporary school 1844-1846

P   Public house

B   Philadelphia Baptist Chapel (seats for 800)

I.   Siloam Independent Chapel

B.C.   Bible Christian Chapel

C   Coach house (main manager)

Pre-1837: Buildings on the Vivian's Hafod Estate pre-dating Trevivian.

1837: First workers' houses built by Vivian

Hafod Copperworks schools 1846-1847 & 3 teachers houses.

Built 1838-1844

Built 1845-1848   M.P. Missionary Chapel/Sunday school of Mount Pleaseant Baptist Chapel

Built 1849

Built 1850-1867

Built 1868-78

Built 1879-1896

Built 1897-1914

Built 1914

FIGURE 2. Plan of the workers' settlement of Trevivian (Vivian's Town) at Hafod, Swansea, laid out and built by John Henry Vivian in *c.* 1837 with a very large school (1,114 pupils by 1893) for the children of his workers at the centre of the settlement. The only structures built by the workers themselves were the several Nonconformist chapels. (Crown copyright: RCAHMW)

lower Swansea Valley. However, the houses that Mansel built for his workers consisted, as far it is possible to tell, of cottages sited in fairly irregular plots enclosed from adjacent farmland and sited along winding pre-existing roadsides at Bon-y-maen (Mansel and Cefn Roads), rather than in the regular grids found later in the copper-workers' settlements at Morriston ('Morristown') built in 1779 (Fig. 1) and Trevivian ('Vivian's Town'), built in c. 1837 (Fig. 2).

The founding of the Forest Copperworks, some two miles to the north of Swansea, prompted the development of Morriston on an altogether more ambitious scale than the earlier colliers' layouts, with the laying-out of a completely new settlement, arranged on two adjacent grids of streets and provided with a church and market. Morriston may be one of the earliest metalworkers' settlements founded in the world's first Industrial Revolution. The workers from two other adjacent late 18th-century copperworks (Rose and Birmingham) for the most part also lived in the same town, and one of the works provided a school (1815) for the children of employees of the three nearby works.

Another full-scale workers' settlement with a grid of streets was not laid out for another 60 years, with the construction of Trevivian (c. 1837). This was in open country nearer the town and its construction may have been prompted by concerns that sub-standard housing, built by speculators during a time of cholera fears, would have produced circumstances severely damaging to coppermasters who were also MPs.

During the RCAHMW's 'Copperopolis Project' it was possible to evaluate the considerable amount of available information concerning the communities surrounding the twelve main copper-smelting works in operation in Swansea between 1717 and 1860. The noxious nature of the industry meant that from the very beginning attempts were made to keep the works away from the existing urban core of Swansea. The larger settlements, laid out on a large grid-plan and provided with churches, were only established by second generation resident managing-partners of copper concerns at Morriston and Trevivian. Three other simpler settlements were built, two with a high degree of worker design and settlement.

There is no evidence at Swansea that company-provided housing and settlements were built to enforce social control of the workforce. Rather, evidence from the Rhondda points to the employer-provision of rented housing as being a liberator in that workers involved in a strike were able more easily to leave the area without prior notice or complication.[7]

The involvement of the entrepreneurs with the local communities socially and politically, as well as economically, was a vital ingredient in making sure that their philanthropy was dispensed locally rather than elsewhere. Local political involvement was in their interest, and once they were involved they had to be seen to be responsive to the needs of the local community: this was enlightened self-interest.

This process is very apparent in the contrasting housing and social provision made by the owners of the two large-scale and neighbouring Hafod and Morfa Copperworks founded in the early 19th century. The Cornishman Michael Williams, owner of the Morfa Copperworks, with his partners provided some housing for key workers but never a large settlement with educational and religious facilities or large-scale culverted drainage. He reserved most of his philanthropy and enlightened self-interest for the West Country, where he was MP for north Devon, and supported charitable causes both there and around his Cornish home — Caerhays Castle, the coastal mansion designed by John Nash.

This was in stark contrast to his Swansea-based, originally Cornish compatriots, the Vivians, at the neighbouring Hafod Copperworks, who constructed the large settlement of Trevivian for their workforce (which at times was smaller than that for the huge adjoining Morfa Works of the absentee Williams). A subsidiary residence could be enough to stimulate considerable local philanthropy, as with the Grenfell coppermasters' Maesteg House on Kilvey Hill. However, if the primary residence of a coppermasters' dynasty was elsewhere, that is where much of the family profits would go. In the Grenfells' case it went to maintain and develop the main family mansion (near their copper-rolling mills) at Taplow in Buckinghamshire which still dominates the landscape. There, the resident family, involved in local public life, felt obliged to build workers' housing and fund the construction of local churches. Principal family members might have lived in Swansea for a substantial part of the year, but the family gathered at Taplow and the vault where they lay in death was alongside the River Thames and not the Tawe or Tamar (for this was a third copper-smelting family originating from Cornwall).

Economic forces, to some extent, determined that copper-manufacturing entrepreneurs would live near their main markets rather than, or as well as, at the centre of their copper-smelting activities; the Morrises had also had London houses and used part of their wealth to found the first purpose-built art gallery in Britain, at Dulwich rather than in Swansea. The Grenfells were merely following Thomas Williams, the outstanding 'Copper King' of Anglesey, to political and economic eminence at Marlow, alongside the mills that rolled Swansea copper for the London market and which had earlier been used by the Swansea and London entrepreneur, Chauncey Townsend.

CONTRASTING CAPITALISTS' AND WORKERS' HOUSES

Three distinct and widely differing types of copperworks housing have been examined in detail in the Swansea study: those for resident managing partners, for agents or managers, and for the mass of workers. Yet there were some common traits: all the copper-smelting concerns were primarily concerned to see that their activities were a commercial success and that all available capital should initially reserved for the productive process. This explains why three out of four of the resident dynasties of copper-smelters first moved into existing small gentry houses and either enlarged them as the money became available or left them much as they were. Only when the works were successful and producing enough profit were these relatively modest mansions enlarged or, more rarely, completely new houses constructed as for example the Morrises' Palladian home (Clasemont) overlooking their works in the lower Swansea Valley in c. 1775. A third generation of the Morris family of industrialists subsequently moved away from the area of smelting in the Swansea Valley but not away from the potentialities of additional industrial wealth in the form of the collieries that were established in the proximity of their new west Swansea regency mansion at Sketty Park.

A similar picture of the re-use of existing buildings emerges with the management housing. Two of the four copperworks agents' houses were conversions of former local gentry houses, at the White Rock Copperworks and the Upper Forest Coppermills. Only later, when the works were more successful, were these replaced by newly-built large houses. With the large works, a couple of large houses might also be built for under-managers, as happened at the Hafod Copperworks when the works were at the height of their prosperity, 50 years after their original construction.

The situation with regard to the general mass of the workers was rather similar. There was an initial concern to house only those workers essential to the productive process, while all available capital was used in the building up of the core business. However, the remoteness of the works from Swansea town meant that substantial accommodation needed to be provided for a greater number of workers as the works expanded. Sometimes this could be provided in accommodation adapted from existing buildings, as in the 24 dwellings made available at the White Rock Copperworks in a former gentry house or in the first collier's house provided by the Morrises at Tirdeunaw Colliery. New housing on a large scale was often provided some 30 years after the construction of a works. They were generally made with sufficient living space to attract workers but did not usually have what the works owners might consider unnecessary ornamentation unless they were visible from an industrialist's mansion (as at Morris Castle and Haynes Buildings). There is evidence that workers' houses at both Trevivian and Grenfelltown were enlarged as general standards of housing improved and profits became available.

THE INSTITUTIONAL BUILDINGS OF THE INDUSTRIAL TOWNSHIPS

The industrial settlements of Swansea had rows of workers' housing interrupted by three types of larger institutional buildings: schools, churches and chapels. All three were generally present in the townships built by the workers themselves and also in those completely, or mostly, constructed by the coppermaster employers.

It has been possible to begin to understand the issues that concerned these early industrial communities, and their influential employers, by examining institutional buildings. There may also have been a need to ensure social control and to ensure the docility of a large workforce by providing educational and religious buildings; but, with the provision of workers' housing settlements, it could be that there were more altruistic motives of philanthropy and paternalism at work. All of these factors may have manifested themselves in the provision of institutional buildings that were, in effect, material displays of enlightened self-interest.

WORKS SCHOOLS

It is difficult to assess how statute affected the building of schools for the children of workers by works managements. The Factory Act of 1833 probably had little influence

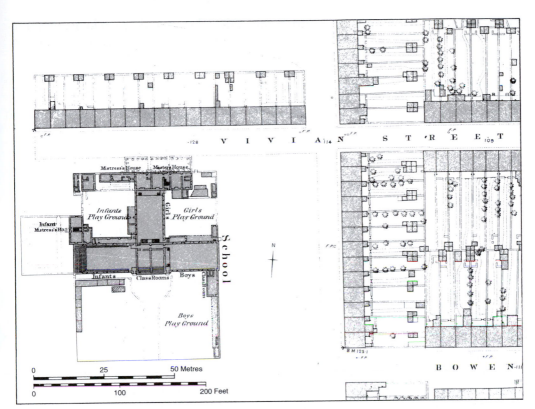

FIGURE 3. Plan of the centre of the surviving Hafod Works Schools at Trevivian showing the simple girls' school and teachers' houses which can be interpreted as the original building of 1847 with a large Gothic range added in 1848 to accommodate large boys' and infants' schools. The multiple outhouses in the larger house gardens (of *c.* 1837) to the right include pigsties, representing ideas of worker self-sufficiency which were not provided for in the late 19th-century house-yards visible at the top of the picture. (Crown copyright: RCAHMW)

on the provision of education for the children of workers in the Swansea copperworks as it was concerned with the much smaller number of (usually older) children who were employed in the works themselves and this legislation post-dated the foundation of the two earliest works schools. These were the schools at Kilvey (1806) and Morriston (1815) which seem to have catered for all the children of parents employed at the three copperworks nearest to each building.

The development of the Swansea works schools was similar, in general terms, to that known elsewhere in industrial south Wales. Most of the earlier schools in the metal-smelting centres of the coalfield had more than one phase of development, whilst the largest, that at Dowlais, went through at least three or four phases of expansion. In Swansea, the Birmingham Copperworks School at Morriston had three recorded phases of development, the Kilvey Copperworks Schools four phases, and the Hafod Copperworks School five phases. The first phase of development of the south Wales works schools was usually humble; the school would be held in any spare room attached to the works or in disused buildings near them — even in the lofts of stables. The second phase, after about 1840, saw the provision of proper and substantial accommodation. By the mid 19th century works schools had some basic Gothic ornamentation which became more elaborate as the century progressed.

RELIGIOUS BUILDINGS

The most numerous class of communal structure comprised the Nonconformist chapels. It is worth asking how central these were to the workers' social and economic lives; how they were funded and what factors determined which architects built them.

There was a distinct division of religious opinion between the largely Anglican coppermasters and their mostly Nonconformist workforces. Perhaps this is visually most apparent in Morriston, where the unfinished Anglican church occupies a focal point in the street layout but where the later 'Cathedral of Nonconformity', complete with towering spire, dominates the main street. All of the most influential locally resident coppermaster dynasties in Swansea were Anglican: the Morrises, Vivians and Grenfells. In fact, this was not a great change from the domination which the established Church had had amongst influential local families who had also started the large-scale coal-mining that underpinned the later copper industry.

Even when the coppermasters did not meet the whole cost of a church, it has been possible to show that they still determined its style, ornamentation and, consequently, the price of building it. The Vivian family, owners of the large Hafod Copperworks, came from the copper-mining area of Cornwall and determined that the large Perpendicular Gothic church planned for their worker township of Trevivian, or 'Vivian's Town', should be closely based on St Mary's Church in Truro where many of their family were buried. The initially-projected eight bay, triple-aisled structure with elaborate tower and large areas of cut Bath-stone ashlar work would have cost at least £10,000. That cost was five to ten times the average cost of building a much plainer Nonconformist chapel erected by poorer workforce congregations. However, an indication of the religious allegiance of the workers at Trevivian is given by the fact that only fourteen out of 779 (0.02%) children attending the Hafod Copperworks Schools in the settlement belonged to the Established Anglican Church.[8] The Vivians were only prepared to provide about a quarter of the cost of building the church design they had chosen (£2,000: £1,500 from the company and £500 from the managing director personally). Therefore the small number of workers who attended the Anglican Church could only afford to contribute towards a much reduced budget of £5,000, used in 1878–80 to construct a less elaborate finished version of the original design.

A comparison of the architectural drawings with the present remains of the church shows four major ways in which the design was simplified to take account of the lack of worker support. Firstly, a third aisle had been allowed for, but was omitted at the drawing stage. Second, the original church design was nine bays long, but the drawing was modified to a modest six bays, before a compromise design of seven bays was built. Then, the grand pinnacled tower was omitted and a humble bellcote for a

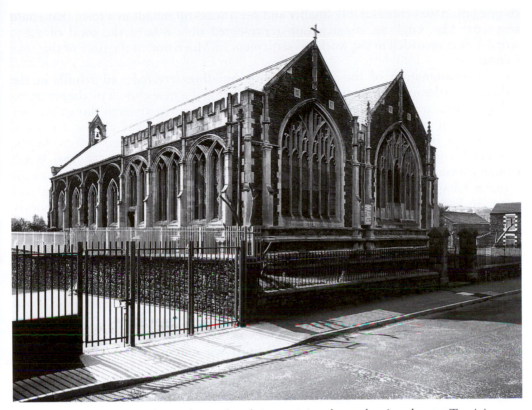

FIGURE 4. The design of the Anglican Church (1879–80) at the workers' settlement Trevivian was chosen by the coppermasters, the Vivians, in imitation of their original parish church at Truro, but lack of worker support meant that only half the original design was realized with only three out of fourteen bays receiving crenellated parapets and large traceried windows and with the church lacking the intended elaborate tower. (Crown copyright: RCAHMW)

single bell (not shown on the surviving design drawings) was added to one gable. Finally, the intended large traceried windows and ashlar work castellated parapets were only completed on the south-eastern three bays of the church, while the other eleven side bays were finished with simple, and cheaper, chapel-like lancet windows, and lack any parapet elaboration.

The other later 19th-century coppermaster's church added to a copperworkers' settlement at Swansea also shows structural evidence of a lack of worker support for the Established Anglican Church. The second church built in the middle of the central square at Morriston ('Morris Town') in 1859–62, remains with its west (liturgical north) aisle unbuilt. Both churches retain structural arches in their outside walls to allow for a future elaboration and aggrandisement that was never attainable with their lack of worker support. The 1851 religious Census in Wales reveals that the tiny 108-seat original church of Morriston was only about half-full with its English-language congregation of 43 adults and fifteen scholars while its Welsh-language congregation was considerably smaller and yet it was still rebuilt in a form that could seat 350. The Anglican congregation represented only 6% of the total of 1,839 worshippers recorded in the workers' settlement of Morriston at the time of the 1851 Census.[9]

An examination of the many religious buildings erected and rebuilt in the industrial settlements has indicated that the building of a new church or chapel seems to have roused a sense of obligation in neighbouring congregations to show that they had an equal commitment to their faith. As a result there was almost a cyclical competition in building between the various denominations and causes in the industrial communities. For example, in 1839–40 the members of the Welsh Congregational cause at Foxhole dug a shelf on the hillside and laid foundations for Canaan Chapel after working their shifts at the copperworks (self-building was common in Nonconformist chapels but was probably unknown in contemporary Anglican churches),[10] and the 342-seat chapel was erected at a cost of £702 6s. 0d.; three years later the Grenfell family of coppermasters were persuaded to fund the first Anglican church in the community with a capacity of 346 for the sum of £1,350.[11]

The average cost of building a new workers chapel was between £1,000 and £2,000.[12] However, the influence of both works managers and of new industrialists arising from the local Nonconformist population radically altered matters in a few notable examples that became the centrepieces of two of the worker settlements. The late 19th-century entrepreneurs of the newly emergent tinplate industry at Morriston were local men, originally with little capital, who were able to cheaply re-use redundant water-powered copper rolling mills. They supported a Nonconformist congregation at Tabernacl in Morriston that was able to afford a building cost of £8,000–£15,000 in 1873.[13] The congregation at the next workers' settlement at Landore included the managers of one of the largest copperworks (Hafod) and came closest to matching the expenditure on the Nonconformist 'cathedral' when nearly £7,000 was spent on the next Welsh Independent chapel down the valley at Landore.[14] This high level of spending on Nonconformist places of worship was not possible elsewhere in Wales. The Swansea area was becoming the world centre of two metals industries, copper and then tinplate. Between 1843 and 1890 the greatest sums recorded in *The Builder* for chapel building outside Swansea were £6,000 at both Colwyn Bay (1882) and Wrexham.

The fairly frenzied building work left all the worker congregations with large debts. The small Anglican congregation of St John's Trevivian did not pay off even its reduced cost of building until the early years of the 20th century. However, such large and long-continuing debts were not confined to larger spending Anglican congregations supported by works owners: the enthusiastic Welsh Baptists at the neighbouring Philadelphia Chapel had spent £1,850 on their elaborately façaded chapel fourteen years earlier in 1866 and the last of the £1,200 debt was not cleared until 1906, whilst the huge cost of Tabernacl, Morriston was not cleared until 1914.

The architects building the chapels in the industrial settlements were not from the professional architectural classes in the adjacent city of Swansea but were artisan carpenters and builders who became deacons and ministers in their respective Nonconformist denominations. The architectural vocabulary they employed was generally that of the Italian Romanesque and Renaissance: pointing back to the early Christian classical world where the *word* had originated and not towards the elaborate rituals of the 19th-century religious establishment. Documentary evidence of this fast-disappearing Nonconformist worker heritage is slight and understandably preoccupied with the spiritual rather than the temporal. The once profuse buildings are disappearing at an alarming rate and yet it is the surviving architectural features of what some regard as the 'primitive architecture' of the worker folk that yield the clues in the shape of date plaques, groupings of doorways and windows, and in the use of the affordable architectural device of a giant blind arch breaking through a classical cornice into the pediment of the many gables that provided the architectural, spiritual and social focus of many industrial communities.

CONCLUSION

What did the Swansea industrial landscape mean in historical terms? What can a study of a complex social and functional infrastructure belonging to the world's first Industrial Revolution tell us that we do not already know from documentary sources? Two elements that can distort conventional historical synthesis are the patchiness and uneven nature of the surviving documentary record and the selectiveness with which this is studied, and an ignorance of the related archaeological and architectural evidence which often survives in abundance even in apparently largely reclaimed and redeveloped landscapes. A historical landscape analysed in totality should advance objective historical analysis.

One significant example is that of the quantification of entrepreneurial philanthropy. One historical text by W. O. Henderson, on the industrialization of Europe, in a standard popular series, offers the following generalization:

> But for one enlightened employer like Robert Owen [of New Lanark textile mills] or Titus Salt [founder of the model textile mill community at Saltaire, near Bradford, *c.* 1853] there were a hundred who ignored the plight of their workers.[15]

The accuracy of this statement in relation to other industries, such as that of copper-smelting, can be assessed from the fairly comprehensive topographical and archaeological evidence that has been studied at Swansea.

There were twelve main copper-smelting works in operation in Swansea between 1717 and 1860. The nature of the industry meant that attempts were made from the very first to keep the foundation of large new works away from the existing urban core of Swansea. Therefore, all the works needed to make provision for some of their key workers. However, no less than six of the works made provision for housing a substantially greater number, starting with the White Rock Works in 1737.

Five of these settlements were also provided with large gardens for the employees to keep pigs and grow vegetables. Beyond this, schooling provision started in 1806 and at least four of the works owners are known to have made provision for the schooling of their workforce. Four of the works owners provided, in full or in part, Anglican churches, and one provided a Nonconformist place of worship. One also built a secular meeting hall for the use of the employees of three of the local works and one provided a poorhouse.

Henderson, and many other historians besides, have assumed that the few very famous philanthropists were the exception and that only very few employers made provision for the welfare of their workforce. By contrast, the Swansea evidence suggests that some 50% of employers made substantial provision for the housing of their workforce and that 33% provided schooling for employees' children and places of worship. Indications from published works on Welsh workers' housing and works schools suggest that this level of provision in industrial communities may not have been exceptional.

It is hoped that some of the historical conclusions of this archaeological and architectural study will help to clarify perceptions of what was one of the most significant landscapes of the world's first Industrial Revolution. They also provide a pointer to what information might be derived from similar studies in social archaeology elsewhere, in Britain, in Europe and on a wider scale internationally, as a new social order spread inevitably with global industrialization.

ACKNOWLEDGEMENTS

This article is based on material in a new RCAHMW volume which includes social archaeology as a substantial part of its content: Hughes, S. R. 2000, *Copperopolis: Landscapes of the Early Industrial Period in Swansea*, Aberystwyth: RCAHMW. A database of buildings and sites is available on the RCAHMW website at www.rcahmw.org.uk. Charles Green produced the plans of worker settlements. The text and illustrations are Crown copyright and are reproduced by permission of the Royal Commission on the Ancient and Historical Monuments of Wales; copies are available through the National Monuments Record of Wales (the Royal Commission's public archive).

Stephen Hughes, Royal Commission on the Ancient and Historical Monuments of Wales, Crown Building, Plas Crug, Aberystwyth, Ceredigion SY23 1NJ, UK

NOTES

[1] Palmer 1991, 2.
[2] Hughes 2000.
[3] Gould 1995, 51.
[4] Fisk 1996, 24; Hughes 1990, 204–05.
[5] Lowe 1994, 59–88; Hughes 2000, 190–92.
[6] Lowe 1994, 63.
[7] Fisk 1996, 47.
[8] Evans 1971, 312.

[9] Jones & Williams 1976; Hughes 2000, 254.
[10] Rees & Thomas 1872, 83.
[11] Royal Commission 1911.
[12] Hughes & Seaborne 1993–94.
[13] Hughes n.d.
[14] Thomas, 1969, 53.
[15] Henderson 1969, 138.

BIBLIOGRAPHY

Evans, L. W. 1971, *Education in Industrial Wales, 1700–1900; A Study of the Works School System*, Cardiff: Avalon Books.

Fisk, M. J. 1996, *Housing in the Rhondda 1800–1940*, Cardiff, Merton Priory Press.

Gould, S. 1995, 'Industrial archaeology and the neglect of humanity', in Palmer & Neaverson (eds), 49–54.

Henderson, W. O. 1969, *The Industrialization of Europe: 1780–1914*, London: Thames & Hudson.

Hughes, S. R. 1990, *The Archaeology of an Early Railway System: The Brecon Forest Tramroads*, Aberystwyth: RCAHMW.

Hughes, S. R. 2000, *Copperopolis: Landscapes of the Early Industrial Period in Swansea*, Aberystwyth: RCAHMW.

Hughes, V. n.d., MS in National Monuments Record of Wales of references to buildings in Wales contained in *The Builder*.

Hughes, V. & Seaborne, M. 1993/94, 'Welsh Chapel Architects', *Capel Newsletter* 27 (Winter 1993/94), 13.

Jones, I. G. & Williams, D. (eds) 1976, *The Religious Census of 1851–A Calendar of the Returns Relating to Wales, Volume 1 — South Wales*, Cardiff: University of Wales Press.

Lowe, J. P. 1994, 'Survey for Thematic-Based Research: An Industrial "Housing Stock"', in Wood (ed.), 59–88.

Palmer, M. 1991, *Industrial Archaeology: Working for the Future*, Ironbridge: Association for Industrial Archaeology.

Palmer, M. & Neaverson, P. 1995, *Managing the Industrial Heritage*, Leicester Archaeology Monographs No. 2, Leicester: University of Leicester.

Report of the Royal Commission on the Church of England and Other Religious Bodies in Wales and Monmouthshire, 1911, London: HMSO.

Rees, T. & Thomas, J. 1872, *Hanes Eglwysi Annibynol Cymru*, Cyfrol (Vol. 2), Liverpool: Tyst Cymreig.

Thomas, N. L. 1969, *The Story of Swansea's Districts & Villages*, Swansea: Qualprint.

Wood, J. (ed.) 1994, *Buildings Archaeology: Applications in Practice*, Oxford: Oxbow.

THE ATLANTIC WORLD AND INDUSTRIALIZATION: CONTEXTS FOR THE STRUCTURES OF EVERYDAY LIFE IN EARLY MODERN BRISTOL

By ROGER H. LEECH

The interval between presenting a paper at a conference and submitting it to the editors allows for some changes to be made. When I first read this paper in October 1999 I had little idea that excavations in Charlestown on the Caribbean island of Nevis, planned for April 2000 as part of Southampton University's Nevis Heritage Project, would contribute so directly to a change of focus.

Our venue for the conference was Clifton Hill House, one of the grandest earlier 18th-century mansions in the wealthy Bristol suburb of Clifton. It was built by Paul Fisher, a linen draper and ship owner, in 1747. It is a romantic house; the initials of Paul and his wife are entwined within the pedimented façade to what was formerly Clifton Green. It is also a distinguished house, probably the first house built in Bristol, or more correctly its 18th-century suburb of Clifton, to have been published in plan and elevation by a London architect. Isaac Ware's illustration of the house, in his *Complete Body of Architecture* of 1756, has attracted much attention from architectural historians. Clifton Hill House is also a dwelling of notoriety. It was associated with the trade in human cargo, the trade in slaves for which Bristol's past is now infamous and on which the Fisher fortune was in part made.[1]

Clifton Hill House is one of a number of larger houses in the suburbs of 18th-century Bristol which one can associate anecdotally with the slave trade that now dominates our thinking about the Atlantic world in that period. Paul Fisher traded in slaves. The house demonstrates what wealth this trade created for him. Similar associations can be drawn from a few surviving large houses of the 18th century in the centre of the city. The guide to the slave trail around central Bristol takes us to Prince Street. On the left hand side of the street, we are told, is the 'Shakespeare', originally one of three houses built for Bristol merchants who invested in slaving vessels. We can continue to Queen Square, a reminder we are told of the genteel lifestyle made possible by the wealth of the Atlantic trade, much of which was in slaves or commodities produced by slaves. In total the published slave trail would take us to 42 venues, and a further fourteen sites of interest outside central Bristol.[2]

FIGURE 1. Nos 38–41 Old Market, built for Llewelyn Evans, clay tobacco pipe-maker, probably by William Barrett house carpenter, between 1684–88.

Excavations in Charlestown on Nevis during April 2000 have reinforced my belief that trails of merchant houses and related locales give us only half the story. It is very easy to understate the degree to which the trade in slaves and slave-produced commodities underpinned prosperity and change at virtually every level of society in Bristol in the later 17th and 18th centuries. Our excavation site in Main Street Charlestown is a waterfront plot, on the opposite side of the Atlantic to its counterparts on Narrow Quay in Bristol. Thus far the archaeology has many resonances of Bristol, in the glass, the ceramics and in the clay pipes. Amongst the last was a pipe stem with the initials 'LE'; similar stems have been found in the abandoned island town of Jamestown. 'LE' are the initials of Llewellyn Evans, well documented as active in clay pipe manufacture until his death in 1688. The archaeology tells us that Evans's commercial ventures extended to trade with the Caribbean.

From the discovery of Evans's pipes in Charlestown, it was an immediate leap to Evans's role as an investor and developer of property or real estate in Bristol during the 1680s. These too had been the subject of an archaeological investigation, in 1979. The author has vivid memories of this, crawling through half-blocked-up windows and doorways with the architectural historian Eric Mercer to record nos 38–41 Old Market (Fig. 1), part of a row of late 17th-century houses, then decaying but now restored.[3] Evans was responsible for the rebuilding of nos 40 and 41, two adjacent houses, built with economy and very much in the medieval style, gable-end-on to the

FIGURE 2. Nos 33–34 King Street, built by Thomas Wickham, c. 1650.

street with timber-framed façades and overhanging jetties at the first floors. In the search for grand merchant houses to symbolize Bristol's links with slavery these might have continued to be overlooked, but for the clay pipe stems from Nevis.

Evans was not the only property developer in 17th-century Bristol whom we can link with the Caribbean trade. Thirty years earlier in June 1654, Thomas Wickham, carpenter, had sent three of his men to Nevis to work as carpenters for John Knight, a planter and a member of a Bristol family deeply involved in sugar production on both sides of the Atlantic.[4] In time we may discover Knight's Nevis plantation and some evidence of 17th-century Bristol carpentry. Wickham's own housebuilding activities in Bristol can be viewed alongside those of Llewellyn Evans. One of Wickham's houses survives (Fig. 2), in a street the wealth of which has indeed been associated with the Caribbean trade.[5] The house is the oldest one in King Street, nos 33–34 on the north side, its association with trade reinforced by its combining domestic quarters and warehousing on a single plot.[6]

It is in these contexts that I would like to propose several ways in which we might study the housing being built in late 17th- and early 18th-century Bristol. First, we need to look at the late 17th and early 18th centuries as a continuum. Why this is particularly pressing for any study of housing in relation to the Atlantic trade should now be evident, but it is worth highlighting that studies of the economy of Bristol, of the mentality of its inhabitants, and of its architecture have tended to see 1700 as a magic date, one at which to finish, as in the case of Patrick McGrath's study of merchants and merchandise[7] or David Sacks's *Widening Gate*,[8] or at which to start, as has been the case with Kenneth Morgan's study of the Atlantic trade[9] and the works of Walter Ison[10] and Timothy Mowl on the 18th-century architecture.[11]

Secondly, we need to venture beyond the anecdotal in studying the expansion of the city's housing stock. We need to know how many houses were being built and then occupied for the first time in successive decades, whose wealth made it possible for new houses to be built and then sold or let, from whence such wealth came; we need to know the occupations and status of those living in different parts of the city, the extent to which and how closely the inhabitants of these new houses were linked to the Atlantic trade.

We could also look at the changing, or not so changing designs and plans of houses, as a means of identifying and understanding the ways in which people lived and how this has changed through time. We need to see housing as one facet of consumption — in which the influences of global awareness played an increasingly important part. But these last questions are beyond the scope of this short paper.

The new streets laid out in 17th-century Bristol were the first developments of new housing to be embarked upon since the 13th century. In the 1650s Castle Street and Castle Green were laid out on the site of the castle and King Street was laid out in the Marsh immediately to the south of the city wall; the first houses here were built by Thomas Wickham. These three new streets accounted for *c.* 160 new houses, largely completed and occupied by *c.* 1670.

A few more new streets were laid out in the remaining part of the 17th century. The streets with the greatest number of new houses were Narrow Quay and its side streets. The grand 18th-century thoroughfare of Prince Street originated in the later 17th century as the back lane to these quayside houses. In Host Street a row of ten new houses was first occupied in the late 1690s. The row on the south side of Broad Plain was commenced by *c.* 1700. The next major development was in 1700, when Queen Square was laid out, to be followed by St James's Square. By 1710 most of the new houses in Queen Square were occupied; three quarters of those in St James's Square were occupied by 1713. Those living through this first decade of the new century would have seen building activity on a considerable scale, not only here but also in St James Barton, on St Michael's Hill, in Trenchard Street and in at least five other new streets. Rocque's map of 1742 gives a rapid guide to the new built streets of the intervening three decades — at least 40 new streets can be identified as having been developed between *c.* 1710 and 1742. By 1773 at least a further 20 streets had been added — and so on. In brief, the scale of building activity from the late 1690s far outstripped anything which had happened earlier in the 17th century.[12]

It is easier to talk about new streets than new houses. Identifying the numbers of new houses is more difficult. Larger plots were sometimes subsequently subdivided. Older houses were rebuilt, as happened in much of Old Market. Only if we understand the micromorphology that makes up the larger picture, does the latter then have validity.

It remains to be asked why developments of new housing took place first from the 1650s onwards, and on a greater scale from the late 1690s onwards. What was happening in or by the 1650s, and on a much greater scale from the late 1690s, to create such optimism amongst building promoters, and from whence came the wealth which continued to fuel such optimism throughout most of the 18th century?

Bristol's expansion in the later 17th century was intimately bound up with the Atlantic trade. By the end of the century Bristol's dependence upon trade with North America and the Caribbean was as great as that with France had been some two centuries earlier.[13] The population of the city rose markedly in this period, but rose even more steeply from the last decades of the century.[14]

The rise in the rate of rebuilding and of new building from the 1690s can be linked most convincingly to the much increased involvement of the city in the trade in slaves. From 1689 the Royal African Company lost its hold on the monopoly of the slave trade; in 1698 Parliament formally allowed private slave ships to participate in the African trade. These events opened up the slave trade to Bristol merchants and ship-owners. Patrick Mcgrath concluded that it was doubtful if 'the trade was of any great importance until after 1698' and understood that no Bristol ships appeared in the register kept by the Royal African Company of ships seized while trading illegally.[15] Richardson's volumes on Bristol, Africa and the slave trade show that this was certainly not the case from 1698 onwards.[16]

To identify more closely the links between the Atlantic trade and the scale on which new housing was provided from the late 1690s, we need to look at whole streets of new houses and identify the background of the first occupants. This is hard grind but rewarding. It demands that one looks at the records of property ownership, essential for the framework of which house was where, but also at the records of occupancy, principally tax and rate assessments. Wealth might permit the ownership of a house which was then let for income. Wealth might permit also the occupation of a house. We need therefore to identify both owners and occupiers. In practice the latter can be identified with near 100% coverage, the former only intermittently in some streets. With an awareness of the character of the housing may come further insights.

Queen Square was an obvious block of housing for which to attempt such an exercise; its houses have frequently been variously ascribed to the wealthy wishing to escape the stifling city and to merchants wishing to have suitable accommodation and warehousing together close to the quaysides.

Identifying the first occupants of the east side of the square, including Queen Charlotte Street the first side to be started, has provided a complex picture. In the twenty houses occupied by 1711 only three persons, two masters and one merchant, are recorded as by that date being involved in the slave trade. At least five sea captains occupied other houses but without any proven involvement in the trade. At no. 22 was George Stephens, a linen draper who had been mayor four years earlier. Comparing the accommodation provided by different houses in this east row, some narrow, some wide, and correlating this data with that from probate inventories shows a varied mix of wealth and lifestyle. The overall analysis of Queen Square in its first decades is likely to show a similarly complex picture of wealth, social status and occupational background. Many of the individuals living within the square may have derived wealth from the Atlantic trade, but indirectly. We are left therefore with

FIGURE 3. Old Park Hill, a row of ten houses built from 1714 onwards; by c. 1730 the individuals living here had been directly concerned with the shipment of upwards of 15,000 slaves.

simply the association between many more new houses being built and the rapid increase in the Atlantic trade.[17]

A much more direct relationship between the individuals involved in the slave trade and the building of many more new houses is evident in the data for the new streets and rows on and close to St Michael's Hill. Old Park Hill was demolished to enable the construction of new building for Bristol University in the 1960s. The street was developed as a row of ten houses from 1714 onwards, all completed and occupied by 1722 (Fig. 3). If we run through the first occupants they include John Brickdale, a shipowner responsible for shipping 220 slaves in 1728, Mrs Kennah the widow of Capt. William — who had shipped over 1,300 by 1719, Capt. Skinner, 1,400 by 1727, and Capt. Barry over 1,200 by 1729. The ships' captains occupying the remaining houses in the row were similarly involved in the slave trade, and only two houses in the row were not occupied by ships' captains. Here then we see a direct correlation between the wealth generated by the slave trade and the occupancy of new houses. By c. 1730 the individuals living here had been directly concerned with the shipment of upwards of 15,000 slaves — this could well have been called slavers' row.[18]

More distant from the waterfront than Queen Square, this was from the evidence of occupancy a more attractive place of residence for those nevertheless deeply involved with the sea. The shell hoods that sheltered some of the entrance doorways were possibly more than simply the use of a fairly archaic ornament for houses being built from 1714 onwards. They could be seen as deeply symbolic for occupiers whose lives were so bound up with the sea. This line of reasoning would provide a context for the shell hood over the entrance doorway of no. 65 St Michael's Hill, built c. 1725 by Capt. Joseph Barnes, as one of two houses which completed a row of six dwellings in total. There is no evidence that Barnes himself was involved in the Atlantic trade, but his two neighbours in the houses higher up the hill were both directly concerned, Capt. John Constant with three voyages and Capt. Francis Pitts with seven. The house below Barnes's was a occupied by a widow, Mrs Hollister. By 1716 Lawrence Hollister had been involved in nine slave voyages.[19]

Thus far we have walked in what were well-heeled neighbourhoods in early 18th-century Bristol. Nearly a mile to the north-east of St Michael's Hill was a very different suburb, visited in the 1710s by Daniel Defoe. He called it a remarkable part of the city, an area where it had been possible to expand beyond the limits of the city boundaries. This was the area now known as St Jude's, an estate with a regular grid of streets, promoted by Nathaniel Wade. This was a development populated by families of artisans and craftsmen. Four houses survive, of an altogether lesser scale than those of Queen Square, Old Park Hill or St Michael's Hill. No. 17 Wade Street is an extremely rare survival of a house built in the early 17th century with the accommodation restricted to one room on each floor.[20]

We might see Wade's development in St Jude's as industrial housing, as housing developed speculatively but used predominantly by those involved in cottage or domestic industry. This may be so, and in this respect Wade's development was similar in its occupancy to parts of the Castle Street development of the 1650s. Here exceptionally complete documentation for the 1650s and 1660s enables us to pinpoint the locations of various trades — John Meredith glazier at no. 58, Flower Hunt tobacco pipe-maker at no. 59, Thomas Bason distiller at no. 61, Robert Jones card-maker at no. 62; on this side of the street almost every house occupied by a different trade.[21]

In quantitative terms, though, the Castle Street and St Jude's developments were exceptions rather than the rule in 17th- and 18th-century Bristol. Most new housing was entirely residential in character, increasingly so by restrictive covenants. The majority of new housing developments were also for the more prosperous, the middling sort and the affluent. New housing for the families of artisans and craftsmen was almost entirely confined to the low-lying areas adjacent to St Jude's, northwards to what is now the line of the M32 motorway. Here we know almost nothing of the material culture of the small narrow houses and plots set out in such thoroughfares as Callowhill, Hollister, Penn and Philadelphia Streets. Some houses here were as narrow as 12ft (0.3m.). The names, intimately bound up with Quaker and North American associations, provide pointers to a historical context yet to be fully explored.

The provision of purpose-built housing for industrial workers was on an even smaller scale. Purpose-built housing is recorded only in the context of industries where housing was essential to attract workers, in the 17th century sugar-refining, and in the 18th century brass-making — both were intimately connected with the Atlantic trade.

The sugar house on St Augustine's Back was the second such enterprise in the city. Thirteen workmen's houses were built at a cost of £1,200 for its proprietor John Knight in 1661 (Fig. 4). Disposed around two sides of a courtyard to the west of the Great House, the houses were each of three storeys with one room on each floor and

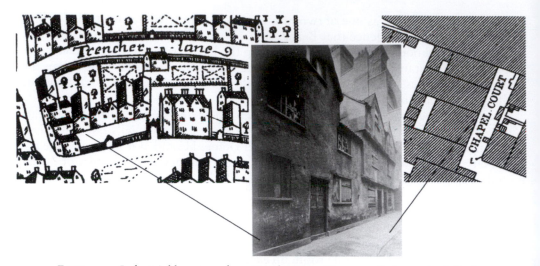

FIGURE 4. Industrial housing of *c.* 1661, the Sugar House on St Augustine's Back.

a small yard to the rear.[22] In a similar context three houses were built in *c.* 1666 at the Whitson Court sugar house at the instigation of its proprietor Thomas Ellis for his works manager and foreman. Watercolours of the 1820s show one of these houses. This was Ellis's own house, part of which survives.[23] Beyond the city at Baptist Mills, William Champion's brassworks possessed 25 houses for key workers by 1761. Even with a few additions this quantity of purpose built industrial housing would account for a minute proportion of Bristol's expansion from the 1690s onwards.[24]

The rapid expansion of the city from the 1650s raises some interesting questions for archaeology. The archaeological resource can provide data not simply for occupations and industry, but also for the changes in society wrought by the provision of new housing, in turn enabled by the Atlantic trade. Developments such as Queen Square and the host of residential streets that followed heralded a much more residentially differentiated city, a city in which ever more marked differences in wealth and place of residence culminated in the Bristol riots of 1831 and the burning of a good part of Queen Square, arguably the closest which Britain has come to revolution. Such changes will be evident especially in the material record, the very subject matter of archaeology. Richard Dunn concluded that the (Caribbean) island colonies evolved a more extreme version of social stratification than in England. The trade with the colonies also heightened social stratification in England.[25] In seeking to better understand these areas, housing and the detritus of the household are prime areas for archaeological consideration. Our North American colleagues, so active in the investigation of the 17th- and 18th-century city and its suburbs, might be surprised that we know so little of the archaeology of Defoe's suburb of St Jude's, or for that matter of the gardens, archaeology and conspicuous consumption of the 18th-century inhabitants of Clifton, not least those of Clifton Hill House.

Roger H. Leech, Department of Archaeology, University of Southampton, Highfield, Southampton SO17 1BJ, UK

NOTES

[1] Ison 1952, 177–81.
[2] Dresser *et al.* 1998.
[3] NMR Building Records.
[4] Nott & Ralph (eds) 1948, 160.
[5] Dresser *et al.* 1998, 12.
[6] Leech forthcoming for this and other references to specific houses.
[7] McGrath (ed.) 1968.
[8] Sacks 1985 and 1991.
[9] Morgan 1993.
[10] Ison 1952.
[11] Mowl 1991.
[12] Chalklin 1989 charts some of the 17th-century promotions.
[13] Sacks 1991, 332.
[14] Sacks 1985, 207, Fig. 1.
[15] McGrath (ed.) 1968, xii.
[16] Richardson 1986 and subsequent volumes.
[17] Bristol Record Office, rate assessments; Leech forthcoming.
[18] Leech 2000.
[19] Ibid.
[20] Leech 1999, 25–27.
[21] Ibid.
[22] Hall 1949, 141, 156.
[23] Hall 1944.
[24] Buchanan & Cossons 1969, 119.
[25] Dunn 1972.

BIBLIOGRAPHY

Buchanan, R. A. & Cossons, N. 1969, *The Industrial Archaeology of the Bristol Region*, Newton Abbot: David and Charles.

Chalklin, C. W. 1989, 'Estate Development in Bristol, Birmingham and Liverpool, 1660–1720', in Chalklin, C. W. & Wordie, J. R. (eds) *Town and Countryside: The English Landowner in the National Economy 1660–1860*, London: Unwin Hyman, 102–15.

Dresser, M. *et al.* 1998, *Slave Trade Trail around central Bristol*, Bristol: Bristol Museums and Art Gallery.

Dunn, R. S. 1972, *Sugar and Slaves. The Rise of the Planter Class in the English West Indies, 1624–1713*, Chapel Hill: University of North Carolina Press.

Hall, I. V. 1944, 'Whitson Court Sugar House, Bristol, 1665–1824', *Trans. Bristol and Gloucestershire Archaeol. Soc.* 65, 1–97.

Hall, I. V. 1949, 'John Knight, junior, sugar refiner at the great house on St Augustine's Back (1654–1679)', *Trans. Bristol and Gloucestershire Archaeol. Soc.* 68, 110–64.

Ison., W. 1952, *The Georgian Buildings of Bristol*, London: Faber and Faber.

Leech, R. H. 1999, 'The processional city: some issues for historical archaeology', in Tarlow, S. & West, S. (eds) *The Familiar Past? Archaeologies of later historical Britain*, London: Routledge, 19–34.

Leech, R. H. 2000, 'The St Michael's Hill precinct of the University of Bristol. The topography of medieval and early modern Bristol, Part 2', *Bristol Record Society* 52, 1–133.

Leech, R. H. forthcoming, *House and Household in Medieval and Early Modern Bristol*, in preparation for RCHME/English Heritage.

McGrath, P. V. (ed.) 1968, 'Merchants and merchandise in seventeenth century Bristol', *Bristol Record Society* 19, 2nd edition.

Morgan, K. 1993, *Bristol and the Atlantic Trade in the eighteenth century*, Cambridge: Cambridge University Press.

Mowl, T. 1991, *To build the second city, architects and craftsmen of Georgian Bristol*, Bristol: Redcliffe Press.

Nott, H. E. & Ralph, E. 1948, 'The Deposition Books of Bristol, Vol. II, 1650–1654', *Bristol Record Society* 13.

Richardson, D. (ed.) 1986, 'Bristol, Africa and the eighteenth-century slave trade to America, Vol. 1 The years of expansion', *Bristol Record Society* 38.

Sacks, D. H. 1985, *Trade, Society and Politics in Bristol, 1500–1640*, 2 vols, New York: Garland Publishing.

Sacks, D. H. 1991, *The Widening Gate, Bristol and the Atlantic Economy*, Berkeley: University of California Press.

URBAN INDUSTRIAL LANDSCAPES: PROBLEMS OF PERCEPTION AND PROTECTION[*]

By Paul Belford

INTRODUCTION

One of the most important aspects of industrial development in England in the 18th and 19th centuries was the development of new urban centres. Indeed, the development of large industrial conurbations was one of the defining characteristics of the period of rapid large-scale industrialization which took place from the 1750s onwards. However, the discipline of 'industrial archaeology' has tended to de-emphasize the role of the city in the development of an industrial society. Instead, there has been a tendency to concentrate on the more picturesque and monumental manifestations of industrial development — such as the cotton mills, blast furnaces and porcelain factories. Even where industry is considered in an urban setting attention is usually only paid to those particular schemes where the urban environment was strictly controlled — places such as Saltaire, for example. However, for the majority of people in late 18th-century England the experience of industrialization took place in an apparently more poorly defined setting — streets on the edges of the new cities which had grown from empty fields, filling with workshops, warehouses, shops, stables, pubs, houses and furnaces, seemingly without order or organization.

This perception of the industrial city as a place of overcrowded, disorganized, filthy chaos is a 19th-century one, but it is also one that persisted throughout the 20th century and up to the present day. The middle-class image of inner cities as slums — breeding grounds for disease, dishonesty and disreputable behaviour — was based on its essential fear of the working class. This fear led ultimately to the slum clearances which took place in most English cities from the 1890s until the 1950s. The so-called slums were replaced by planned, ordered, 'garden' estates on the suburban fringe, and later by architects' visions of 'streets in the sky'. The original inner cities became derelict and abandoned in the later 20th century, places where few people lived, but places still strong in the minds of those outside them as centres of social, moral and physical decay. Today the term 'inner city' is seen as a synonym for unemployment, racial division and poverty — certainly not as the engine of enterprise and the busy hive of industry that it was in the 18th and 19th centuries.

In order fully to explore the notions of perception and protection for urban industrial landscapes, this paper examines a typical area of 18th-century expansion,

19th-century consolidation and 20th-century decay. The case study is from Sheffield, and considers an area to the north-west of the medieval core of the town — an area known as the 'crofts' (Fig. 1). Most people in Sheffield today are largely unaware of the 'crofts' as an area with a distinct identity. It is rarely a destination in itself, and it is bypassed by the arteries of the modern city (Fig. 2). Instead, the place is defined by an older identity as a slum — an identity which has been used to characterize the 'crofts' since the 19th century. However, the earlier history of the crofts — as investigated by the author during research on early steel-making[1] — has found that this area of Sheffield was in fact the first industrial suburb of the city. Indeed the 18th-century 'crofts' contained some of the most innovative enterprises within the Sheffield trades, including the first urban steel furnaces and the earliest integrated steelworks, as well as large precision tool-making concerns. Moreover, the people behind these industries — many of them pillars of early 19th-century society — actually chose to live in the 'crofts'.

VIEWS, PERCEPTIONS AND MISCONCEPTIONS

The story of the 'crofts' began in the 17th century, when Sheffield (population 3,500) was still very much a market town in a medieval townscape which was dominated by the castle, church and corn mill.[2] The main industry of Sheffield and its hinterland was the manufacture of blades and edge tools, including knives, scythes, razors, sickles and forks. These activities took place in rural or semi-rural locations, principally on the Rivers Sheaf and Don and their tributaries the Porter, the Rivelin and Loxley.[3] This trade grew considerably in the first quarter of the 17th century, a development which led to the establishment of a regulatory body — the Cutlers' Company — in 1624. This body oversaw apprenticeships, trademarks and the use of materials.[4] This was one of a series of events which saw a modern industrial town emerge from the ruins of the medieval one. The feudal castle, which had dominated the physical architecture of the town and symbolized the social architecture of its people, was torn down after the Civil War. The manorial deer park to the east of the town was turned over to farming, charcoal-burning and, later, coal mining.

In the following century industry relocated from the rural fringes into the centre of the town — altering both the overall urban design and the character of the places within it. This movement was first depicted on Ralph Gosling's map of 1736, the first accurate plan of Sheffield. Although the medieval core was still evident — the urban focus remained the former site of the castle — there was a new development to the north and west of the town. The built area had encroached beyond the old township boundary and onto the Town Fields, formerly open fields or 'crofts' (Fig. 3). Gosling noted that the population at the time of his survey was just under 10,000; by the end of the century this had more than tripled to over 30,000 and the 'crofts' had emerged as a densely populated area in its own right. The 'crofts' were the setting for a wide range of industrial activities – steel-making and cutlery manufacture perhaps the most prevalent. Such industries helped to create the distinct character of the 'crofts', where 'shops, warehouses and factories, and mean houses, run zig-zagging up and down the slopes'.[5] The physical appearance of this scene changed little over the next hundred

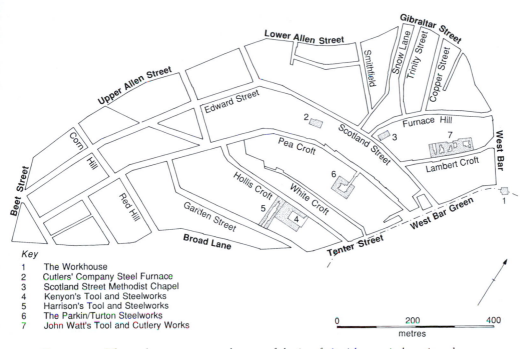

Key
1 The Workhouse
2 Cutlers' Company Steel Furnace
3 Scotland Street Methodist Chapel
4 Kenyon's Tool and Steelworks
5 Harrison's Tool and Steelworks
6 The Parkin/Turton Steelworks
7 John Watt's Tool and Cutlery Works

FIGURE 1. The 19th-century street layout of the 'crofts' with certain key sites shown.
(Drawing: Author)

FIGURE 2. The landscape of the northern part of the 'crofts' today. (Photo: Author)

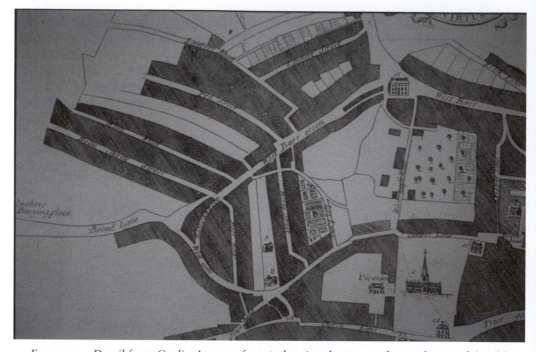

FIGURE 3. Detail from Gosling's map of 1736, showing the area to the north-east of the old medieval town. Note the parish church, workhouse and emerging street of the 'crofts' to the left of the map.

years. A visitor to the 'crofts' in the 1830s used almost the same words to describe what he saw — it was a place with 'numerous streets, which . . . are narrow and inconvenient: the houses, chiefly of brick, have obtained from the works a sombre appearance'.[6]

However, the later visitor's perception of the scene before him was completely different from that of his 18th-century predecessors. The 'crofts' was no longer perceived as a setting for industrious activities, representative of the Malthusian 'productive body'.[7] Instead, this apparently haphazard mixture of working, living and meeting places was — by implication, if not direct observation — morally filthy, chaotic and rotten. By the 1850s, Frederich Engels was able to say that 'immorality amongst young people seems to be more prevalent in Sheffield than anywhere else'.[8] Such views were typical of those who read the reports of the various Royal Commissions into housing, sanitation and working conditions which were published at around that time.[9] Areas like the 'crofts' acted as a blank page for the projection of Victorian middle-class perceptions of immorality, vice and poverty. The 'crofts' image — a place where 'early, unbridled sexual intercourse [and] youthful prostitution . . . [was] extraordinarily frequent' and 'crimes of a savage and desperate sort [were] a common occurrence' — reflected the perceived anarchy which was the result of this disordered and polluted environment.[10] Similar remarks have been made in more recent times about English inner cities, and from the similar perspective of the seemingly permanently outraged 'middle England'. This has its origins in the 19th-century comments, which were repeated again and again. Thus in the 1860s the 'crofts' was seen as being 'as devoid of the decencies of civilization as it was in the Dark Ages'.[11] The 'crofts' consequently became an easy target for middle-class reformers keen to identify slum areas ripe for improvement.

DESIGNING AN URBAN INDUSTRIAL LANDSCAPE

The explicit identification of the 'repugnant' landscape with social and moral problems relied on an understanding of the landscape as chaotic (i.e. unplanned and meaningless). However, the landscape of the 'crofts' was far from meaningless — it was the product of more than two hundred years of human activities and interactions within the landscape. Landowners, industrialists, workers, builders and tenants were all engaged in a process of defining who was being controlled and who was controlling. The urban landscape itself was the crucible of Bourdieu's 'alchemy' of personal action, reaction and interaction, which transformed 'the distribution of capital, the balance sheet of a power relation, into a system of perceived differences, distinctive properties'.[12] Moreover, the physical shape of that crucible was dynamic, for, as Anthony Giddens has suggested, shifts in social practices and structures were reflected in the material construction that was the urban landscape.[13] At each turn the landscape was modified, the creation and manipulation of space a necessary evolution of an arena in which social differences were displayed.

One of the most important factors in the ability of the various interests to manipulate its form and meaning was its location. For this land represented neither the town nor the country; it was a liminal place, both a physical space between the old town and its hinterland, and also a mental space within which the new industrial town could flourish beyond the confines of the medieval one. This liminality had already been made explicit by the Town Trustees, for the Sheffield Workhouse — an institution for those who were simultaneously 'parasites and victims'[14] — was, between 1733 and 1829, located on the very edge on the town boundary at the bottom of West Bar Green. The name West Bar simply means 'western boundary'. The otherness of the 'crofts' was further reinforced by developments such as the innovative steel furnace erected by the Cutlers' Company in 1763 (the first and only time that organization undertook a commercial venture), and the influx of Irish immigrants to Sims Croft and Tenter Street half a century later. The liminal status of the area was thus always apparent, enabling the 'crofts' continually to generate new identities and new social relations, which in turn fuelled perceptions of it as a place apart.

Such an analysis might imply that the landscape was tending toward the chaotic; however, this reforging of identities was not haphazard. Everything within the 'crofts', from the basic street plan to the arrangement of individual plots, was planned. However, the level of planning involved escaped the Victorians, who presumably associated the concept of planning with the landowners and the new middle-class professional surveyors, architects and others; they could not conceive that ordinary people could influence the design of the landscape. Certainly the surveyors who laid out the streets would have been aware of the liminality of the place.[15] The streets of the 'crofts' are not quite straight, the lines a little too irregular to suggest confidence in the identity of the landscape. Older social practices had established 'locales' within the rural landscape which had a strong influence on the character of the new urban one.[16]

Initially, the enclosed fields (themselves fossilizing the outlines of parcels of earlier open-field strips) which ran up and down the slope opposite the town guided the surveyors in the layout of new streets; later, new elements of the built environment had an impact. Christopher Tilley has argued that the memory of events, people and practices associated with such 'locales' were reinforced through the act of naming them.[17] The first phase of development in the 'crofts' included Lambert Croft, White Croft, Hawley Croft, Scargill Croft and Sims Croft — all named after the tenants of the fields in which they were created. Later streets were named for the land use at the time of survey (Pea Croft, Corn Hill and Garden Croft); others for structures that had become landmarks in the new urban setting (School Croft, Workhouse Croft and Furnace Hill); and yet others apparently for fun (Scotland Street was so named for its length). Only one — Hollis Croft — was named for the landowner.

This is not to say that the original design of the 'crofts' did not attempt to order the landscape; indeed the original design of the 'crofts' had been much more regular than 19th-century writers liked to admit. However, the approach to the landscape within the 'crofts' was to evolve an organic street plan, based around earlier landscape elements — rather than to impose a new landscape without reference to the previous one, and to the 'locales' within it, as happened in later developments in Sheffield and elsewhere.

This development of an urban industrial landscape reflected and complemented the emergence of an industrial urban society in Sheffield. This new urban society had little to do with its antecedents, for the main impetus behind the growth of the 'crofts' in the second half of the 18th century was an increase in migration to the town. Amos Rapoport has argued that the spaces, or 'locales', within the urban landscape form a system of settings, within which the system of activities that is human action takes place. These systems were based within the physical landscape, but they were not dependent upon it; consequently the intended plan of the landscape could be subverted.[18] Thus, the design of the (urban) landscape was modified by the (rural) experience of those who moved into it. Hence the boundaries in the spaces between streets in the 'crofts' shifted over time as properties expanded and contracted. Similarly, the streets themselves, which had been intended as thoroughfares, became extensions of the house and workshop. The people who spent 'the whole of Sunday lying in the street tossing coins or dog-fighting'[19] were creating locales of their own; streets were also used for negotiation between employers and employees, and for more formalized activities such as funerals, meetings and riots.[20] This role as public open space was critical, and it seems to have gained a greater meaning from the late 18th century as the relationship between the street and the buildings on either side of it began to change.

FIGURE 4. An open landscape in Hollis Croft: early 19th-century houses on the street frontage, and workshops behind. (Photo: Author)

MEANINGS OF BUILDINGS AND SPACES

In another context, Matthew Johnson has talked about the process of 'closure' as housing forms changed to reflect a greater desire for privacy from the medieval to the post-medieval periods.[21] A similar process occurred in the Sheffield 'crofts' — and indeed elsewhere in the country — during the 18th and 19th centuries. During the 18th century each property generally comprised an open yard. The principal buildings ran down the sides, gable-end facing the street; buildings were also constructed across the back of the yard. The basic functions of any one group of buildings could therefore generally be observed from the street. Some of the wider blocks may have had a low brick wall or fence, but the overall character of the landscape was open (Fig. 4). The entrance onto the main street was the only one, for no back lanes were consciously incorporated into the design of the 'crofts'. From the 1790s these open-fronted yards began to disappear as leaseholders added an additional range of buildings along the street frontage. This would incorporate a through passage (locally called a 'ginnel') giving access to the yard, but the inhabitants were now separated visually from the street. An opportunity was therefore created for landlords formally to differentiate between different street frontages; moreover, it became easier to ensure what Stefan Muthesius has termed the 'inspectibility of the working classes'.[22] This process of 'closure' was not only defined by the desires of the landlords and builders; it reflected ongoing changes in the nature of society. For the inhabitants, the creation of new spaces provided new settings for activities other than those which took place on the street.

The almost universal use of the yard as the key component in the arrangement of space attracted the attention of later observers. Yards formed the basic core of the ground plan of both industrial and domestic properties, and although in some cases the two functions were mixed on one site, the adoption of this layout enabled them to be separated. The use of the yard (or 'court') in the domestic context was the particular focus of those who saw the enclosed space as a contributor to poor health, and consequently a major factor in the moral decline of the population. Thus in 1848 it was found that the houses on the slopes to the west of West Bar, 'especially those erected in the yards . . . are ill constructed, badly lighted and ventilated; being built back-to-back, and generally of three storeys high, which of itself is an impediment to the free access of light and air . . . in many places the evil [smoke] is so extensive that the inhabitants find the greatest difficulty in maintaining personal or domestic cleanliness'.[23] Documentary sources suggest that the dislike of smoke was unheard of before the 1840s; whereas fifty years earlier very much the opposite feeling had prevailed. 'It has often been remarked', wrote the Sheffield *Iris* in 1794, 'that infectious distempers are not apt to spread in this place . . . the smoke, produced by the manufactories, is thought by many persons to be serviceable in this view'.[24] Perhaps because of this attitude by no means all of the residents of the 'crofts' were the working-class poor. A number of manufacturers built their own residences adjacent to or on the same property as their works. The saw-maker John Harrison, for example, constructed an impressive three-storey four-bayed brick mansion at the Hollis Croft end of his works in the 1780s. The family lived there until the early 19th century.[25] Likewise the steel-maker Thomas Turton lived in a new house within sight of his furnaces on Pea Croft in the early part of the 19th century; as did Daniel Doncaster, who owned a house and orchards on the fringes of the 'crofts'.

The Sheffield 'court' conformed to Roderick Lawrence's model of a 'transition space', which 'simultaneously linked and separated the private and public domains, and the interior from the exterior'.[26] The enclosed 'court' was separated from the street by the 'ginnel' and the street frontage. It therefore became a semi-private space, in which private activities such as going to the toilet and doing the laundry were undertaken alongside more public activities such as arguments and children's games. Later, the yard area also acted as what Oscar Newman has termed a 'defensible space'.[27] It was overlooked by all the tenants, and consequently a stranger in the yard could be instantly detected and treated appropriately. This may explain why much of Sims Croft came to be 'inhabited principally by the Irish'; as an immigrant community subject to racist attacks and official harassment, they chose places to live in which there was a relatively safe communal space.[28] Many social groups, therefore, continued to see the 'crofts' as a desirable place to live.

Indeed, the use of the yard and the ginnel continued to be a factor in the design of Sheffield houses design well into the 20th century, long after the abandonment of the 'back-to-back' house type and the development of the through house. All of the surviving 19th- and early 20th-century terraced housing stock in Sheffield are built in groups of four arranged around a central ginnel (Fig. 5). Until relatively recently the back yards were universally open, paved areas shared between the four houses. Custom means that even today access to these terraced houses is always by the back door, which means that visitors must walk up the ginnel and be subject to observation by any or all of the residents. Title deeds specify that no extensions can be built which impede access across the backs of the inner houses to the outer ones. This social architecture is only now being modified by the rise in owner-occupation and a consequent desire to 'privatize' formerly communal spaces — a continuation of .. ' earlier process.

The yard space, and the conventions of domestic architectural spatial usage, were adopted by industrial concerns for their premises (Fig. 6). The principal difference for industrial sites was that a greater area was given over to a wider variety of buildings, and the entrance archway, or 'ginnel', was wide enough to admit wheeled traffic. Otherwise, the general level of architectural craftsmanship was much the same as for domestic buildings. The buildings in the yard, unseen from the street, continued to be constructed in a vernacular style appropriate to their use. Such styles changed little (except in detail of materials) from the mid 18th century to the end of the 19th. Until the mid 19th century the design of industrial premises was still very much 'the builders' domain'.[29]

The layout of sites was often a reflection of the character of the industries that took place within them. As in the Birmingham Jewellery Quarter, the relatively small scale of the Sheffield cutlery industries strongly influenced the layout of their sites in the 19th century. Property was frequently shared by more than one firm, and in such cases the relatively ornate street frontage provided a communal veneer of respectability. Thus the saw manufacturers Grayson and Cocker shared part of their frontage with the workshops of Thomas Makin, file-maker. The yard behind not only accommodated both firms, but also had room for Samuel Tingle's steel furnace.[30] Not all sites were shared by related businesses. The file-makers Jepson and Company, for example, shared a block of workshops on Furnace Hill with W. and H. Guest, bone button-makers.[31] At the other extreme, many yards could be occupied by a single firm. Firms which had expanded into adjacent properties often retained the mixed identity of the original buildings. John Watts' cutlery firm, for example, founded in 1765 in Lambert Croft, had expanded by the mid 19th century to occupy ten adjoining properties[32] (Fig. 7).

For larger sites, such as those of the steel-makers, an architectural treatment of form and layout was more overt. The components of a steel-making site varied according to the processes undertaken there; moreover, because of the relative permanence of steel-making structures they were able to be treated more expensively than their counterparts in the lighter trades.[33] Sites came in a wide range of shapes and sizes: some steelworks contained either cementation or crucible furnaces, some contained both, and some tool-making sites added steel furnaces at a later date. Sites of all categories shared a common framework, again based around the enclosed yard. The mysterious glowing furnaces were potent symbols; the tall cementation cones in particular denoted the prosperity of the firm and industrial progress generally, and were therefore displayed prominently. In sites where steel-making was the primary

FIGURE 5. Later survival of the ginnel form in through houses: Olive Grove Road, 1904. (Photo: Author)

FIGURE 6. Typical industrial yard of small-scale premises in the 'crofts' with multi-owner occupation: Edward Street. (Photo: Author)

FIGURE 7. Mixed identities behind a united façade: Lambert Croft — John Watts and Company. (Photo: Author)

concern, cementation furnaces were typically used as a focal point, situated on the opposite side of the yard to the entrance; firms with only crucible furnaces used them in the same way. Even on sites where steel-making was not the primary activity, the prestige of having furnaces was emphasized by their placement in dominant positions. The steel-makers therefore appear to have arranged their sites so that, simultaneously, visitors could be mystified and impressed and employees observed and controlled.

TOWARDS THE PROTECTION OF URBAN INDUSTRIAL LANDSCAPES

It is clear from this case study that the 'crofts' was not the random collection of filthy houses and crowded industries; it was a planned, ordered and controlled space — or rather a collection of such spaces — with a complex series of interactions between them. The obscuring of these facts by later Victorian (and indeed 20th-century) prejudice has been a decisive factor in the way that this landscape is valued and protected. The 'crofts' is only a small part of the mosaic of developments that produced the modern city; however the archaeology of urban Sheffield is poorly understood. No excavation work has been carried out in the 'crofts' themselves — although it is to the credit of local archaeologists that archaeological exploration of the urban industrial landscape has taken place increasingly since this paper was originally presented three years ago. Nevertheless focus still tends to remain on impressive industrial features in isolation, rather than looking at the context of the urban landscape in which they were situated.

As Dell Upton has remarked, the built environment was 'only the shell of the urban artifact'.[34] It is likely that the meanings intended by the designers of industrial premises were not always adopted by those who used them; however, the actuality of people's working lives has been obscured by the often contradictory perspectives of later observers. Therefore, a true understanding of the reality of life in 18th- and 19th-century cities such as Sheffield can only be obtained through archaeological excavation and recording. However, a programme of such works can only be devised once the resource itself has been recognized. Hopefully this paper and other research can pave the way for this to occur, but many planners still view such areas through the foggy spectacles of Victorian disapproval. Our industrial cities — Sheffield amongst them — have not valued their archaeological heritage generally; industrial sites which have been conserved and protected are usually atypical examples.

The story of the 'crofts' represents in microcosm the development of the industrial city. Starting with the idealized landscape, in which owners and planners were still a little unsure of its identity, the 'crofts' today is remembered only as a slum. This characterization of the area has led to its archaeological and indeed social neglect; it is regarded as unsuitable for study, it is a 'dead' space within the modern city. This is unfortunate, for there is a great deal to be learned in places like the 'crofts' about the development of English industrial society. Investigations of shifting property boundaries and the occupations of local residents are a start — hopefully this brief investigation has shown just how much innovation and excitement has been masked by Victorian perceptions.

Work in other environments has shown that a detailed investigation of the material culture produces yet further insight into slum lives. The pioneering excavation in the 'Rocks' in Sydney, for example, which drew together historical, anecdotal and physical evidence, provided a rare and special glimpse into the lives of people outside the establishment history of Australian settlement.[35] As Grace Karskens points out '. . . much of the earliest European settlement was focused here, and most of the occupants were convicts and ex-convicts who created an "unofficial" town . . . the Rocks had always excited the fears and fascination of outsiders, and by the 1880s and 1890s it was the kind of area which the advocates of slum clearance held up as a blight on the city . . .'.[36] Likewise, the more recent explorations in the Little Lon area of Melbourne have shed new light on another slum area (Fig. 8). As the Melbourne *Age* reported in 2002, the area 'had been known historically as a working-class slum with no sewerage or lighting. Cottages were small and narrow, cramped together off dark laneways . . . [yet] artefacts such as Chinese coins, imported English ceramics, cosmetic cases and champagne bottles suggested a more material and diverse community than previously thought'.[37] The discovery of contraceptives which had been ordered by catalogue from the United States provided a particularly interesting insight into life in this former slum area. There is also hope in the extent of public interest generated by these Australian excavations, which suggests that this relatively new area of archaeological exploration touches a deep nerve in wider society.

In many ways both the Rocks and Little Lon areas can compare with the 'crofts' and similar parts of other European cities. There can be no doubt that the story of the

FIGURE 8. Archaeological excavations in Little Lon, Melbourne. (Photo: R. K. Belford)

'crofts' embodies the whole essence of the modern English experience — first a distinct place of exciting experimentation, then a place whose true value was stifled and suppressed by Victorian snobbery, before finally becoming a forgotten place on the edge of world consciousness. But the idealism, innovation, industriousness and interconnections of the 'crofts' are still obscured by the Victorian and later misconceptions of the place as a slum. Only by turning our backs on Victorian and 20th-century perceptions, and by looking afresh at all the evidence — documentary, archaeological and oral — can we look beyond the slum and 'instead of the pale, anonymous . . . hapless inhabitants of slumland, we can substitute real people with real names, family and neighbourhood bonds, and the webs of social aspiration and cultural practice, in all their vanished complexity'.[38] Hopefully the wide-ranging and forward-looking approaches of our Australian colleagues can be adopted by us in this less fortunate climate; for without correcting the perceptions of our urban industrial landscapes we will never be able to protect them adequately and learn from them about our past.

ACKNOWLEDGEMENTS

Thanks to David Cranstone and David Barker for their support during the completion of this paper. The original research was greatly assisted by staff in the Sheffield Archives and Local Studies Library; and the subsequent gestation of ideas was given essential input and support by David

Crossley, James Symonds and Alan Mayne. Many thanks also for various reasons to Austin Ainsworth, Anna Badcock, Derek Bayliss, Glyn Davies, Graham Hague, Ken Hawley, Tim Murray and John Powell. Special thanks to Bob and Linda, the people of Horsham (Vic) and Dunsborough (WA), and of course to Annsofie Witkin. This paper is dedicated to the memory of George, who departed this life 12 March 2002.

Paul Belford, Ironbridge Archaeology, Ironbridge Gorge Museum Trust, Ironbridge, Telford TF8 7AW, UK

NOTES

* The present paper was originally presented in a slightly different form in 1999, at which time it was largely based on research undertaken tangentially to an MA dissertation in 1997; it has subsequently been slightly modified.

[1] Summarized in Belford 1998; see also Belford forthcoming.

[2] Scurfield 1986, 168.

[3] Crossley (ed.) 1989.

[4] Leader 1905–06, 8–39.

[5] Sidney 1851, 130.

[6] Lewis 1835, 267.

[7] Gallagher 1987.

[8] Engels 1844, 216.

[9] Haywood & Lee 1848, 77–78.

[10] Engels 1844, 216.

[11] 'The Condition of Our Chief Towns — Sheffield', *The Builder*, 21 September 1861.

[12] Bourdieu 1989, 172.

[13] Giddens 1984, 17.

[14] Lucas 1999, 135.

[15] Leader 1903, 2–4.

[16] Giddens 1984, 20–21.

[17] Tilley 1994, 18–19.

[18] Rapoport 1990, 16–19.

[19] Engels 1844, 216.

[20] Donelly & Baxter 1976, 103–10.

[21] Johnson 1993.

[22] Muthesius 1982, 114–15.

[23] Haywood & Lee 1848, 80.

[24] Sheffield *Iris*, 1794.

[25] Olive (ed.) 1994, 119.

[26] Lawrence 1990, 89.

[27] Newman 1982, 3–66.

[28] Haywood & Lee 1848, 82–83; Pollard 1959, 91–93.

[29] Beauchamp 1996, 149.

[30] Sheffield Archives, Fairbank Collection, M.B.392.

[31] Smith 1997, 98.

[32] Tweedale 1996, 289.

[33] Belford forthcoming.

[34] Upton 1992, 59.

[35] Karskens 1999.

[36] Ibid., 18.

[37] Tomazin 2002.

[38] Karskens 1999, 23.

BIBLIOGRAPHY

Beauchamp, V. A. 1996, *The Workshops of the Cutlery Industry in Hallamshire 1750–1900*, University of Sheffield PhD Thesis.

Belford, P. 1998, 'Converters and Refiners: the archaeology of Sheffield steelmaking', *South Yorkshire Industrial History Society Journal* 1, 21–37.

Belford, P. forthcoming, *Art, Trade, Mystery and Business: The Archaeology of Steelmaking Technology in eighteenth century Sheffield*, Ironbridge Archaeology Monograph No. 1 (BAR British Series).

Bourdieu, P. 1989, *Distinction: A Social Critique of the Judgement of Taste*, trans. by R. Nice, London: Routledge.

Crossley, D. (ed.) 1989, *Water Power on the Sheffield Rivers*, Sheffield: Sheffield Trades Historical Society/University of Sheffield Division of Continuing Education.

Donelly, F. K. & Baxter, J. L. 1976, 'Sheffield and the English Revolutionary Tradition', in Pollard, S. (ed.), *Economic and Social History of South Yorkshire*, Sheffield: South Yorkshire County Council, 90–117.

Engels, F. 1844, *The Condition of the Working Class in England*, London: Penguin Books (1987 reprint), 216.

Gallagher, C. 1987, 'The body versus the social body in the works of Thomas Malthus and Henry Mayhew', in Gallagher, C. & Laquer, T. (eds), *The Making of the Modern Body*, Berkeley: University of California Press, 83–106.

Giddens, A. 1984, *The Constitution of Society: Outline of a Theory of Structuration*, London: Polity Press.

Haywood, J.& Lee, W. 1848, *Report on the Sanatory Condition of the Borough of Sheffield*, 2nd edition, Sheffield.

Johnson, M. 1993, *Housing Culture: Traditional Architecture in an English Landscape*, Washington: Smithsonian Institution Press.

Karskens, G. 1999, *Inside the Rocks: The Archaeology of a Neighbourhood*, Sydney: Hale and Iremonger Pty Ltd.

Lawrence, R. J. 1990, 'Public collective and private space: a study of urban housing in Switzerland', in Kent, S. (ed.), *Domestic Architecture and the Use of Space*, Cambridge: Cambridge University Press, 73–91.

Leader, R. E. 1903, *Surveyors of Eighteenth Century Sheffield*, Sheffield: privately published lecture transcript.

Leader, R. E. 1905–06, *History of the Company of Cutlers in Hallamshire* 1, Sheffield: J. W. Northend Ltd.

Lewis, S. 1835, *A Topographical Dictionary of England,* London: Macmillan.

Lucas, G. 1999, 'The Archaeology of the Workhouse: the changing uses of the workhouse buildings at St. Mary's, Southampton', in Tarlow, S. & West, S. (eds), *The Familiar Past: archaeologies of later historical Britain*, London: Routledge, 125–39.

Muthesius, S. 1982, *The English Terraced House*, New Haven and London: Yale University Press.

Newman, O. 1982, *Defensible space: people and design in the violent city*, London: Architectural Press.

Olive, M. (ed.), 1994, *Central Sheffield*, Stroud: Chalford Publishing.

Pollard, S. 1959, *History of Labour in Sheffield*, Liverpool: Liverpool University Press.

Rapoport, A. 1990, 'Systems of activities and systems of settings', in Kent, S. (ed.), *Domestic Architecture and the Use of Space*, Cambridge: Cambridge University Press, 9–20.

Scurfield, G. 1986, 'Seventeenth century Sheffield and its environs', *Yorkshire Archaeological Journal* 58, 168.

Sidney, S. 1851, *Rides on Railways, leading to the Lake and Mountain Districts of Cumberland, North Wales, and the Dales of Derbyshire*, London.

Smith, D. 1997, 'The Buttonmaking Industry in Sheffield', in Jones, M. (ed.), *Aspects of Sheffield 1*, Barnsley: Wharncliffe Publishing, 84–101.

Tilley, C. 1994, *A Phenomenology of Landscape*, Oxford: Berg Publishing.

Tomazin, F. 2002, 'Little Lon underworld surrenders its riches', *The Age*, 19 July, Melbourne.

Tweedale, G. 1996, *The Sheffield Knife Book: a history and collectors guide*, Sheffield: Hallamshire Press.

Upton, D. 1992, 'The City as Material Culture', in Yentsch, A. E. & Beaudry, M. C. (eds), *The Art and Mystery of Historical Archaeology*, Boston: CRC Press, 3–59.

PATHWAYS OF CHANGE: TOWARDS A LONG-TERM ANALYSIS OF THE CERAMIC INDUSTRY

By PAUL COURTNEY

Capitalism with a capital 'C', what date shall we assign to its appearance? The twelfth century in Italy? The thirteenth in Flanders? At the time of the Fuggers and the Exchange at Antwerp? The eighteenth century, or even the nineteenth? There are as many birth certificates as there are historians.

(Marc Bloch, *The Historian's Craft*)

SOME CONCEPTS

Capitalism and industrialization are not one and the same, but Bloch's statement reminds us of the long-standing nature of the debate: when do economic and technological change constitute a Revolution?[1] In the 1980s new calculations of economic growth rate showed much more gradual expansion in the 18th century than had been previously calculated. This led some economic historians to question whether a revolution had taken place at all in Britain's economy. Furthermore, Crafts and Harley argued that the technological revolution was limited to just three sectors (iron, cotton and transport) while the rest of the economy stagnated with little technological advance.[2] A spirited defence was mounted by Maxine Berg and Pat Hudson in their 1992 article in the *Economic History Review*.[3] They argued, convincingly in the opinion of the current writer, that the Industrial Revolution comprised a series of distinct transformations in different industrial and economic sectors at different times, but still cumulatively amounting to an overall revolution in British economy and society.

Industrial Archaeologists have not questioned the validity of the Industrial Revolution. However, in recent years they have tried both to contextualize their subject and lay claims to the wider remit of studying the archaeology of the industrial period.[4] One means of doing this has been by stressing the notion of industrialization as a process as reflected in the title of this volume. However, industrialization was only one facet, albeit an important one, in the modernization of Western Europe and North America. It was very clearly a regional phenomenon which barely affected some countries or regions.[5] The Netherlands stands out as country which in the 16th and 17th centuries achieved the status of becoming the 'world's first modern economy', in the words of de Vries and van der Woude's recent book title. It did so without ever having undergone a process of industrialization let alone an Industrial Revolution.[6] If we are to understand the emergence of modern Europe we also need to understand the impact of change on Pennine and Frisian farmers, and the fishermen of Brittany and Hull, as well as the capitalists and cotton workers of Manchester and Lyon.

Even the broader concept of modernization has its problems if one accepts the Marxist position that capitalist progress was at the expense of the poor and the Third World.[7] A reaction to the prevalence of the notion of progress in modernization theory, especially as developed by American social scientists, led German historians in the 1970s to develop *alltagsgeschicte* (the history of everyday life). This was an attempt to examine change through the experiences and struggles of everyday people rather than by studying large scale economic and social structures.[8] Furthermore, as Funari, Hall and Jones have recently reminded us, even such a broad and currently fashionable project as the 'archaeology of capitalism' is woefully inadequate in dealing with the experiences of a substantial part of the world's population over the last two centuries.[9]

A further perspective is that gained by studying economic and social structures over long periods of time. The long-term has been occasionally tackled by 20th-century historians, notably the French *Annales* school, in regard to regional economies and such variables as climate, grain production and prices. The *Annales* historian, Fernand Braudel gave the term the *longue durée* to the study of the long-term, especially the re-occurring cycles or wave patterns of history.[10] Some economists and historians prefer to refer to waves for irregular repeating patterns and restrict the use of cycles to regular patterns, for example of 30 years.[11] Prices, wages, productivity and population all show linked phases of growth and expansion, though scholars have varied from seeing demography to prices as prime movers behind change.[12] Certainly we should be cautious about seeing all technological and economic change as being necessarily linear.

One recent historian who has tackled long-term change is Joel Mokyr in his 1990 book, *The Lever of Riches: technological creativity and economic progress*. In this important work, he addressed the problem of why different societies have had radically different levels of technological creativity.[13] Mokyr has produced a number of interesting concepts derived from modern evolutionary biology. In particular, he makes an important distinction between macro-inventions and micro-inventions. The former are the product of individual genius and occur without precedents while the latter result from the intentional search for solutions to specific problems. Like Marc Bloch, in his classic study of medieval mills, Mokyr also stresses that the willingness of different societies to implement inventions is a crucial factor.[14] In regard to the classic Industrial Revolution, Mokyr has argued that England was notable for both its inventiveness and willingness to implement innovation which he ascribes to its social and political characteristics. By contrast, the autocratic *ancien régime* of France is seen as stifling creativity and entrepreneurship in the 18th century. Indeed, Louis XV invested in, and later purchased, France's premier porcelain manufactory at Sèvres, but the institution was plagued by financial losses, despite its great artistic and technical suceess.[15]

CERAMICS AND LONG-TERM CHANGE

Archaeologists have in pottery and coinage two potentially extremely interesting indicators of long-term economic change. Few synthetic or theoretical studies have crossed period boundaries, but one can point to Chris Going's study of economic waves and ceramic supply within Roman Britain, papers by Jean Le Patourel and Hugo Blake on medieval ceramic change and the late Stuart Rigold's study of loss rates of medieval coins. John Allan's monograph on the excavated ceramics from post-Roman Exeter is a masterly integration of both archaeology and documentary research, while Jan Baart has produced a survey of the ceramic supply to Amsterdam from the 13th to 19th centuries.[16] One advantage of long-term history is that it allows us to identify recurring patterns. Another is that it allows an opportunity to re-examine and re-evaluate continuity and change from a different and broader perspective.

Within such a short paper, one can only hint at the potential of studying long-term change within ceramic production, and this essay will focus on a loosely defined Midlands (especially Leicestershire and Staffordshire) at least for the earlier period. Discussion of the post-1700 period will be limited as David Barker deals with this elsewhere in this volume but our papers are intended to be complementary. Regional and local variation will be found in every period, but nevertheless one can still identify general trends.

After the collapse of Roman potting industries an aceramic hiatus was ended by the spread of the Anglo-Saxons westward across the Midlands, bringing with them coil-made pottery probably fired in clamps or bonfires. In addition to the well-known material from pagan cemeteries, ceramics of this period have been increasingly recognized on domestic sites in such counties as Northamptonshire and Leicestershire.[17] One major discovery made by David Williams and Alan Vince has been the widespread diffusion of pottery with granodiorite inclusions, originating in the Charnwood area of Leicestershire, as far away as Southampton and the Humber.[18] Such long-distance movement can be paralleled in other kin-based tribal societies without coinage, such as the exchange networks of the native North Americans. In such societies the exchange of goods usually takes the form of reciprocal gift giving.[19]

In the middle Saxon period funerary use of pottery ends with the arrival of Christianity. Domestic ceramic use continues in Northamptonshire and over much of Lincolnshire, but appears to cease in the Leicestershire/Rutland area, unless the Middle Saxon production is identical to that in the pagan period. Possibly domestic production did not survive because in this area it was only an adjunct of the production and distribution of funerary vessels. If ceramic usage did indeed cease it suggests that domestic ceramic usage was not an essential element of contemporary life-style. However, it should be remembered that much of the West Midlands and Wales remained aceramic throughout this period. Ipswich-type ware has a regional distribution in eastern England. It was wheel-made and fired in single-flue kilns such as those excavated in Ipswich.[20] The occasional occurrence of Ipswich ware north of the River Welland, on the periphery of its distribution, may be a guide to high-status estate centres which acted as nodes in local redistributive networks.[21] The importance of Ipswich as the main international trade centre of the East Anglian kingdom parallels that of *Aldwic* (London) in Mercia and *Hamwic* (Southampton) in Wessex. Influences from both Frisia and Flanders have been suggested as influencing Ipswich ware, leading Hurst to suggest a movement of ideas rather than potters.[22] Whatever the process of transmission, this kind of cultural hybridization bears a strong resemblance to the process which American historical archaeologists term 'creolization', a process to which sea-trading ports, with their tendency to have ethnically-mixed populations, may have been especially predisposed. The theory of 'creolization' suggests that individuals or groups in cultures of mixed origins often choose to select or discard what is pleasing or useful from the full range of cultural traits to hand, creating new hybrid cultural forms.[23]

A major turning point came with the Viking influence of the late 9th century and 10th centuries. The first traces of true urban life in towns like Leicester, Lincoln and Northampton appear to date to this period and all have evidence for urban production of wheel-thrown ceramics. One of the most important industries to emerge was that at Stamford with its wheel-thrown and lead-glazed wares. As well as being found in urban contexts it is one of the ceramic type-fossils of the newly-created villages of the East Midlands.[24] Its distribution therefore suggests a developed trading network at the very least between urban markets. A mixture of influences from northern France and the Meuse valley can be seen in Stamford ware, perhaps representing the movement of potters by the Vikings in the late 9th century.[25] However, the specific role of the Vikings in encouraging urban development in the Danelaw needs to be placed in a larger context. The penetration of urban pottery to widespread rural consumption sites is just one indication of the so-called 'commercial revolution' that extended across western Europe in the 10th century.[26] For example, the same period has also been seen as a period of key transition in the organization of both settlements and the pottery industry of central Italy.[27]

By contrast the rural West Midlands and Wales appear to have remained aceramic apart from the Cotswolds/Mendip region. Both production and consumption of wheel-thrown Chester and Stafford wares appear to have been restricted to the burhs, many of whose origins arose from the Viking threat.[28] Lack of ceramic use in the countryside may partly reflect cultural conservatism, but may also partly relate to the less intensive and less commercialized economies of the west Midlands, a state which prevailed across much of the high Middle Ages. Staffordshire, like many areas which underwent industrialization, lay outside the core zone of intensive agrarian production.[29] At Monmouth on the Welsh border ceramics were introduced soon after the founding of the borough in the late 11th century. However, Welsh settlements in its vicinity appear not to have used ceramics in any quantity until the second half of the 13th century.[30] Increasing involvement in a market economy may have helped wear down cultural resistance.

The Norman Conquest does not appear to have had much direct impact on English pottery production, though immigrant French potters appear to have worked at or near Castle Neroche (Somerset) in the late 11th and at Canterbury in the third quarter of the 12th century.[31] The most marked features of the 12th and 13th century are the spread of pottery production sites into the countryside, increasingly serving very localized markets. One new production centre of the 12th century was Potters Marston in Leicestershire, initially using coil-made technology and clamp bonfires to produce glazed and unglazed wares rather than the more sophisticated technology of the Saxo-Norman urban potters.[32] However, wheel-throwing and the use of kilns had become the norm in both the west and east Midlands by the end of the 13th century.[33] High medieval kilns were mostly semi-permanent structures which might have single, double or multiple flues but their history seems to reflect adaptation rather than large-scale innovation.[34]

From the 12th century, potters tended to concentrate on glazed jugs and large cooking pots/jars as opposed to the smaller cook pots and pitchers of the Saxo-Norman potters. They also tended to have less diverse ranges of products.[35] It is unclear whether this change reflects changes in food consumption, such as a move to the cooking of communal stews as suggested by John Hurst. It is unclear why such a change in cooking habits should occur at this time, a change apparently not paralleled across the Channel.[36] One alternative explanation is that these changes partly reflect the changing structural relationship between the industry and its market. It is possible that the difficulties less skilled potters had initially in meeting growing rural and urban demand may have led to a more simplified range in order to maximize output. Not only was pottery use becoming more widespread but the population was expanding rapidly. Perhaps we are seeing the relatively expensive, custom-made products of urban producers being undercut by the more 'pile it high and sell it cheap' philosophy of rural potters with lower overheads. This explanation does not entirely explain the move to a larger cooking pot though it may partly represent the production of a more general purpose vessel. One missing factor is our poor knowledge of the changing role of metal vessels.[37]

As supply cyclically caught up with demand one might expect competition to increase and more diversification. A modern analogy would be Henry Ford's 'any colour as long as it is black' marketing approach in the affluent post World War I years which contrasted with Ford's marketing of the Mustang in the more competitive 1960s, offering a bewildering array of options on specifications. Certainly by the 13th century pottery was being widely used by rural and urban populations to an extent not seen since the Roman period. An Oxford market ordinance of 1318 even indicates where the specialist sellers of earthen pots should set their stalls.[38] One aspect of increased diversification is the emergence by the 13th century of highly decorated wares across north-west Europe. Frans Verhaeghe has interpreted this phenomenon as an indication of market segmentation as potters, under increasing competitive pressures, tried to fill the gap below the more expensive metal vessels with a decorative, consumer product.[39] This may have been encouraged by the increasing gap between slow moving industrial prices and rapid inflation in agricultural commodities, making manufactured items more affordable.

All pottery was considerably lower in price than metal vessels. Few pottery vessels cost more than a penny or two, to judge from documents, while brass vessels were several shillings. Several high medieval industries took advantage of the closeness of suitable clays to ports with international trade connections to develop international markets. Notable examples include the Saintonge potters of western France who piggy-backed on the Gascon wine trade, and eastern English potteries, such as Stamford and Scarborough, who shipped pots to Norway.[40] The indications are that water transport costs were very low and that imported wares were often cheaply priced, at least in the ports. One can point to such finds as the polychrome Saintonge and Rouen jugs associated with a cob (mud) building in a poor Exeter suburb or the finds of polychrome and green Saintonge jugs from fishermen's cottages in the Scilly Isles.[41] Unlike the Mediterranean with its tin-glazed pottery, ceramics have not proved to be a very sensitive indicator of status in northern Europe, though urban, monastic and manorial sites often produce more diversity of sources and higher percentages of jugs than rural peasant assemblages. Only a very few imported ceramics specifically made for the luxury market, notably Mediterranean tin-glazed wares, were probably unequivocal symbols of high status and even these were used by a wider social group by the 15th century.[42]

The 14th century saw the loss of about a third of the population. Recent work on late medieval ceramic change has tended to concentrate on social changes such as improved standards of living, increased social drinking and a filtering down of courtly behaviour.[43] The prices of agrarian commodities fell, but rising wage costs led to higher prices for manufactured goods. Certainly ceramic prices rise significantly after the Black Death perhaps from an average of a half-penny to a penny or more, though there are considerable difficulties of comparison due to the vagaries of medieval terminology and changing sources of documentation.[44] As Chris Dyer has pointed out, supply-side changes as well changing demand are also evident in the late Middle Ages. One reaction to a shrunken market and rising wage costs is to attempt to reduce the unit cost of production and expand market areas.[45] In the iron industry the spread of the blast furnace achieved this through technological innovation and implementation.[46] Other industries such as ceramics probably saw adjustment through organizational rather than technical advances. There is evidence that late 14th- and 15th-century metal-workers in London turned to the production of 'populuxe' goods, cheap luxury items which could be cheaply produced in large numbers.[47] The well-dated London ceramic sequence sees the highly decorated jugs being replaced in the mid 14th century by plainer forms, an example of a much wider trend.[48]

The main technological innovation in the late medieval ceramic industry seems to be a tendency, at least in the Midlands, for higher-fired wares. At Chilvers Coton in Warwickshire it has been argued that there is some evidence for the use of larger kilns in the 14th and 15th centuries.[49] However, this does not seem to have been a universal pattern and the dating assumptions of this site have been questioned.[50] One certainly sees a reduction in the number of late-medieval potting centres and evidence for wider land-based trade networks, though it is generally unclear whether potters, pedlars, merchants or a combination thereof were distributing pottery. Unfortunately many of the 15th- to 16th-century Midland wares (Midland Purple, Midland Yellow and Cistercian-type wares) are difficult to provenance. However, around 1500 one could have travelled the entire length of the Welsh border and encountered a mere three wares dominating local markets: Malvernian oxidized ware in the south, West Midlands orange ware/Midland Purple (a higher-fired variant) in the centre and Ewloe-type whitewares in the north.[51] The late 15th and 16th centuries saw the end of local production across much of Wales, a gap partially filled by English, French and Iberian imports. However, pottery appears to have been scarce even on many high status sites and assemblages are dominated by drinking vessels.[52] Again this is a reminder that pottery supply or usage was not a constant, especially on the periphery.

In Paris, excavations on the site of the Carrousel garden at the Louvre have uncovered suburban tileries dating from the 13th to 16th centuries. The sequence points to considerable capitalistic investment in the tilery buildings of the late 15th and 16th centuries. By the late 15th century documents also point to a division of labour between those who prepared the earth, the tilers and those who constructed and repaired the kilns.[53] This may suggest an evolution from household to workshop production in the late Middle Ages. In Brittany, the surviving documentary sources have allowed historians to make a detailed study of the late medieval ceramic industry in several communities.[54] Organizational changes are apparent in the 15th century with the emergence of potters' guilds, which controlled the activities and number of workers. One might expect to see ceramic industries adapting to the new circumstances of the late Middle Ages across Europe. However, local and regional differences are likely to be apparent in their responses, reflecting variations in demography, political structures and economy.

In the Rhineland the stoneware industries captured a wide market, initially selling small, plain drinking vessels in huge numbers utilizing ready access to the cheap water transport of the Rhine and North sea. By the 16th century urban production is evident at centres like Cologne, though a significant sector of the industry continued to be rural, household-based and linked to an agrarian economy.[55] The success of Rhenish stoneware was at least partly due to its competitive price even after shipment.[56] The massive production and shipment of simple, low-price mugs, beakers and jugs was facilitated through the organization of merchants who took full advantage of cheap water transport to expand the market.[57] This presumably allowed individual potteries (the number of which also presumably expanded) to work at a level nearer their full potential, producing economies of scale in both production and transport. In the 16th century the Rhenish industry diversified, probably due to increasing competition and rising costs, by also producing more decorative wares, paralleling Verhaeghe's highly decorated medieval phase. Again this phase is marked by clear evidence for the copying of metal forms.

Late 15th- and 16th-century England saw a new variety of continental-influenced forms such as cups, chafing dishes and chamber pots, a change frequently termed the 'ceramic revolution'.[58] However, as Verhaeghe has recently pointed out this is a purely English phenomenon with Flanders showing a much longer and more evolutionary time-scale to ceramic form change.[59] This may perhaps be a reflection of the more urbanized and prosperous nature of the Low Countries at the heart of the European economy. David Gaimster has suggested that colonies of alien merchants may have played a role in changing tastes. The 15th century was also notable for the impact of Burgundian courtly fashions on England, to be replaced by the influence of the French court in the following century.[60] One major change in the early-modern period was the introduction of tin-glaze technology to northern Europe. This happened around three centuries years after it had reached southern France, suggesting that fundamental socio-economic or cultural differences persisted between the Mediterranean and northern Europe.[61] The use of saggars (coarse vessels used to contain pots during firing) and double (biscuit and glaze) firing also spread to the earthenware industries of northern Europe. Saggars were used for producing Cistercian ware cups at Wrenthorpe (Potovens) in Yorkshire in the 16th century.[62] Double firing was also used for some 16th- to 17th-century slipwares, notably in the industries of north Devon, the Beauvaisis in northern France, Holland and the Weser area of north Germany.[63] Double firing, saggars and spacers were used to produce the luxurious Saint Porchaire ware in the late 16th century, possibly in both the Paris and Loire areas of France.[64] The movement of Italian maiolica (tin-glaze) potters into the Spanish Netherlands at the end of the 15th century suggests one possible route for the northward movement of this ultimately eastern technology.[65] However, maiolica production was also established from the 13th century in Provence, an area with a long history of Italian immigrant potters and Mediterranean influences.[66] It should be noted that the movement of craftsmen, artists and ideas in the Renaissance was often complex and via multiple channels.

The north Devon industry of the 17th century has particularly strong evidence of continental influences.[67] Three double-flued, updraught kilns excavated in Barnstaple are similar to earthenware kilns excavated in the Rhineland.[68] The use of double firing and sgraffito decoration (in which a slip coating was cut away to create a design), is also clearly imported.[69] Nevertheless the forms and decorative schemes are not closely paralleled by any other industry. The technology could have been transferred by the emigration of a single potter or even perhaps by a potter travelling to the Continent. English pipe-making was introduced to the Netherlands by the emigration of English craftsmen.[70] However, what is noticeable is that, whatever the source of the technology transfer, the adoption of new techniques, and especially styles, is selective. This sort of selective absorption is typical of the previously mentioned process of 'creolization'.

More generally this phenomenon of technology transference can be partly related to wider events, notably the Renaissance, the spread of craftsmen between royal courts and bourgeois emulation of court culture. The emergence of the expansionist absolutist state, in this case Spain, is also significant in explaining the movement of craftsmen into its north European colony of Flanders. The religious persecutions of the late 16th and 17th centuries also helped promote the movement of craftsmen across Europe while greater literacy and the printing press also helped technology transfer.[71]

By the end of the 16th century tin-glazed wares were being made in England and by the late 17th century stoneware as well, both utilizing specialist kiln types.[72] However, it should be noted that neither were new technologies. Tin-glaze technology appears to have been invented in the area of modern Iraq in the early 9th century AD, almost certainly in imitation of Chinese porcelain. Rhenish potters were producing some true-stonewares by around 1300, over a millennium after their first production in China.[73] Tin-glazed wares were double-fired using protective saggars or coarse pottery containers. These wares in particular marked a major innovation in industrial organization as they tended to be capitalized by entrepreneurs and utilized a range of specialist craftsmen.[74] The late 16th and early 17th centuries saw rising prices and a growing inland trade. The re-emergence of localized production on the woods and wastes of the Welsh borders providing simple glazed wares for a very localized market reflected a growing landless population and the breakdown of 'feudal' controls. Such potters were probably often squatters and rarely turn up in probate inventories.[75]

By the late 17th century earthenwares were being produced at Ticknall in south Derbyshire and in north Staffordshire for regional markets. The Staffordshire potteries were also using their access to the Severn to exploit the emerging Atlantic trade. Their production was still likely to be seasonal and household-based but many of these yeoman-potters were rich enough to produce inventories.[76] Several brick-built, multi-flued kilns, using coal as fuel and saggars, have been excavated in the Stoke area dating to around 1700. However, they are no larger, at least in diameter, than the pair of five-flued kiln bases of the medieval period dug at Sneyd Green in Stoke.[77] The period is marked by both a growing population and increased evidence for consumer spending. De Vries has suggested that the period after 1650 saw a demand-led spurt of economic growth. Women and children were increasingly drawn into wage labour enticed by the lure of buying the new consumer goods, many a by-product of colonial trade and exploitation.[78] Like earlier successful potteries, effective marketing networks, especially access to water navigation, allowed the Staffordshire industry to maximize production, cutting prices and undercutting rivals even when goods where shipped some distance overland. At the beginning of the 18th century, the Northamptonshire antiquary, John Morton, noted that the potters of Potterspury in south-west Northamptonshire were being undercut by the Derbyshire and Staffordshire because 'the way of living here is more expensive'.[79] Early-modern documents in the Midlands indicate pots being carried on the backs of 'crate-men', by 'little horses or asses' and by 'pot wains' (wagons). Both urban merchants and rural pedlars, often from squatter settlements, appear to have filled different niches in the transportation system.[80]

However, as in the medieval period, most early-modern potteries which captured more than a local market were still dependent on access to water transport and piggy-backed on existing trade routes for other commodities. In Elizabethan England, though the long-distance carriage of goods was widespread, recorded costs per ton per mile for land transport ranged from $4d.$ to $12d.$, compared to a cost of $1d.$ or less per ton per mile for inland water transport.[81] Not surprisingly penetration of imports inland is uneven in this period. Both 16th- to 17th-century German stonewares and Martincamp flasks from N. France are found in small quantities in Leicester, 20 miles (32km.) from the nearest navigable river. However, imports are extremely rare in Staffordshire probably reflecting both its relatively isolated position and local production.[82] Tin-glazed wares and stonewares were produced largely in towns and probably all the year round for their regionally-scaled niche markets. Imported porcelain started off as a luxury ware but mass importation meant it increasingly went down-market. Its blue and white decorative schemes also totally changed European sensibilities, replacing at the quality end of the market, the brown, greens and yellows which had for so long dominated ceramic colour palates. European-produced porcelains in particular as the price scale (Table 2) for Amsterdam shows,

TABLE 1
HIERARCHY OF CERAMIC
TECHNOLOGIES AND DECORATIVE
STYLES (AFTER BLAKE 1980)

Coating	Decoration
Porcelain	Lustre
	Painting quality
Tin-opacified	Colours — exotic
	local
	Plain
Slip	Decorated
	Plain
Lead glazed	Decorated
	Plain

TABLE 2
PRICE IN STUIVERS OF A BOWL IN
AMSTERDAM PROBATE
INVENTORIES (AFTER BAART ET AL.
1986)

Amstel porcelain	40
Local/regional pewter	10
Chinese porcelain	8
Decorated delft	3–4
White delft	3
English earthenware	3
Maiolica	3
Local/regional redware	1–2
Lower Rhine redware	1

followed earlier wares such as the exotic earthenwares produced by the French Saint-Porchaire and Palissy schools in the 16th century in limiting themselves to an exclusive luxury market.[83]

Blake has produced a generalized hierarchy of ceramic technologies which can be compared with the league table produced by Baart for Amsterdam using valuations in probate inventories (Tables 1 and 2). However, interpreting social status in the early-modern period is not quite as easy as producing hierarchies of pottery types. One must distinguish between kitchen wares used in houses of every status and luxury goods. Unfortunately, most of the real status items such as silver, and to a lesser extent pewter, rarely survive archaeologically, while tin-glazed ware appears to have been affordable by a large segment of the population. In Amsterdam, Chinese porcelain was clearly affordable only by a few in the 17th century but in the 18th century, as prices fell, it is found in 40% of excavated households including the dwellings of wage workers. Only Amstel porcelain, rare in excavations, is an unequivocal sign of high status across both centuries.[84] Inter-site analysis of the proportions of decorated and undecorated redwares in Sweden have demonstrated that this was not a useful indicator of wealth with, for example, more decorated wares occurring in rural contexts than in urban contexts. This probably reflects the low price differentials and cultural differences between towns and countryside.[85]

Before 1650 ceramic innovation in Britain was slow and mostly the result of introducing old technologies developed elsewhere. The capitalized nature of the new urban potteries made experimentation more economically feasible than in a household-based industry. John Dwight's experiments at Fulham in the second half of the 17th century marked the rise of the scientifically educated capitalist in the pottery industry.[86] However, the early-modern period was marked by growing diversity and complexity not just of technology but also of economic organization. A marked feature of the early-modern period was the wide range of technologies and levels of industrial organization operating alongside each other. Potters, varying from squatters to capitalist-owners, produced a wide range of fabrics, forms and finishes to fit niches in local, regional or international markets though the true-national market was probably some way off. The increased technical and decorative range of early modern pottery allowed ceramics to become increasingly a fashion as well as a functional item. The transport revolution of, first, canals and, then, railways had yet to happen, but a growing population, rising standards of living and demand-led competition for markets, especially after 1650, was producing some of the conditions for a supply-led revolution – that is, led by technological and organizational innovation.

CONCLUSION

The long-term study of particular industries and economic waves deserves greater study. Understanding long-term patterns of change, and comparing other so-called 'revolutions' or periods of rapid transformation, will shed further light on the uniqueness or otherwise of the Industrial Revolution. The new study of consumption has added a new dimension to our understanding of ceramic use and change. However, the currently less fashionable areas of technology, industrial and marketing organization, prices and competition are also vital to understanding the history of ceramic production and use. The Industrial Revolution still remains a valid concept but is clearly a much more diverse phenomenon than was once thought. Many industries and sectors of the economy were transformed without the impact of macro-inventions.[87] Adaptation, micro-invention and organizational change also played significant roles in the modernization of the economy.

Like earlier successful pottery industries, Staffordshire's success was initially achieved by maximizing kiln output, allowing reduced prices to compensate for transport costs and still undercut rivals. This was generally made possible either through easy access to large urban markets or via an effective rural marketing network but above all by access to water transport. Certainly, Stoke had the last two of these advantages and increasingly all three. Expansion of the number of production units may have also fed both competition and co-operation, for instance, facilitating the growth of informal marketing, skill and credit networks. The number of potters in north Staffordshire rose from around 67 to 150 between the decades of 1710–19 and 1750–59, while the Westerwald potters' guild in the Rhineland had about 600 members at the beginning of the 18th century.[88] However, in the Staffordshire industry, unlike other medieval and early-modern success-stories, cost cutting and diversification was extended for a sustained period through micro-technological innovation and adaptation, a process whose origins clearly pre-date the opening of Wedgwood's Burslem works in 1759.[89] This story is described in detail by David Barker in his accompanying paper. The 18th-century Staffordshire industry was also able to take advantage of improved communications and marketing infra-structures to create a truly global market. It did not break the competitive cycle, but transformed its rhythm and character through its ability to produce ceramics at competitive prices for multiple, niche-markets, responding to diverse global consumer needs and the increasing dictates of fashion. The expansion of the 18th- and 19th-century Staffordshire industry, though not without precursors, thus represented a truly revolutionary transformation.

ACKNOWLEDGEMENTS

I am grateful to Nick Cooper, Debbie Sawday, Neil Finn, Steve Clark, Debbie Ford, Philomena Goodall, Oliver Kent, Frans Verhaeghe and George L. Miller for information or discussion, and especially Yolanda Courtney and David Barker for reading and commenting on the text. I would also like to thank David for many stimulating discussions on the meaning of post-medieval ceramics in locations ranging from Stoke curry houses to Québecois museums.

Paul Courtney, 20 Lytton Road, Clarendon Park, Leicester LE2 1WJ, UK

NOTES

[1] Courtney 1997a.

[2] Crafts 1985; Crafts & Harley 1992.

[3] Berg & Hudson 1992; see also Hudson 1992.

[4] Palmer 1990.

[5] Pollard 1981; Hudson 1999.

[6] de Vries & van der Woude 1997.

[7] Gunder Frank 1972; Wallerstein 1974–89; Wolf 1982.

[8] Braun 1990; Lüdtke 1995.

[9] Funari, Jones & Hall 1999.

[10] Braudel 1980.

[11] See Kondratieff 1975 for the classic statement on long waves. Rostow 1975, Going 1992 and Hackett Fisher 1996 offer useful summaries of work on economic and business waves/cycles.

[12] Postan (1966) and Le Roy Ladurie (1974) are examples of historians who have seen demography as the prime mover while Hackett Fisher (1996) has stressed price curves.

[13] Mokyr 1990. I have avoided a discussion of the controversial concept of proto-industrialization due to lack of space, but see Elizabeth Musgrave's 1998 article on the pottery industry of the Saintonge, while Duplessis (1997, 206–15) provides a useful recent summary of the broad debate.

[14] Bloch 1967.

[15] Eriksen & De Bellaigue 1987.

[16] Going 1992; Le Patourel 1979; Blake 1978 and 1980; Rigold 1977; Allan 1984; Baart 1990.

[17] Foard 1978; Cooper 1996 and 2000; Parry 1994 and forthcoming.

[18] Williams & Vince 1997.

[19] Cleland 1999. See Mauss 1954 and Sahlins 1972 on the theory of redistribution systems.

[20] Hurst 1976, 299–308; Cooper 1996; Liddle 1996.

[21] Rare finds of Ipswich ware from villages west of the Lincolnshire peat fens probably pre-date the phase of village formation in the late 9th and 10th centuries, rather than indicating a middle Saxon date for nucleation as is sometimes suggested.

[22] Hurst 1976, 314–46. A major work on Ipswich wares by Paul Blinkhorn is to be published shortly by the Medieval Pottery Research Group.

[23] Mouer 1993.

[24] Kilmurry 1980; Vince 1994.

[25] Kilmurry 1980, 180–84; Gierz 1996, 51–52.

[26] Lopez 1971.

[27] Patterson 1985, 105; Hodges 1985, 269.

[28] Cane *et al.* 1983; Rutter 1988; Ford 1995, 29–31.

[29] Campbell 1990, 89–92.

[30] Courtney 1994, 126; S. Clark, pers. comm.

[31] Davison 1972; Cotter 1997.

[32] Sawday 1990. See McCarthy & Brooks 1988, 139–207, for a general survey.

[33] See McCarthy & Brooks 1988, 352–69.

[34] Musty 1974; Hurst 1976, 343–46; Moorhouse 1981; McCarthy & Brooks 1988, 40–54.

[35] Hurst 1976, 342–43.

[36] Cotter 1997, 71–72.

[37] Egan 1997.

[38] Hinton 1973, no. 13.

[39] Verhaeghe 1991 and 1996.

[40] Davey & Hodges 1983; Reed 1990; Vince 1995.

[41] Allan 1984, 67–70, and 1994, 47–48.

[42] Courtney 1997b, 98–102; Brown 1997; Gutiérrez 1997 and 2000. Compare with Mannoni & Mannoni 1975 for the situation in Italy with social stratification is more evident in ceramic assemblages. The latter paper is summarized in English in Blake 1978 and 1980.

[43] Dyer 1989; Courtney 1997a and 1997b; Gaimster 1997, 115–41.

[44] Courtney 1997b, 103–04. In addition to the prices cited in Courtney 1997 note the following additions: 'And for 2 earthenware jars purchased for carrying milk from Stainer this year 3d' bought for the Selby Abbey, Yorkshire, kitchen in 1416–17 (Tillotson 1988, 168); 'And for 2 earthen pots for watering the plants in both the cellarer's and kitchen garden 2d', bought in 1464–65 by the Battle Abbey, Sussex, cellarer (Searle and Ross 1967, 146) (Latin terminology not given). However, please note that the 8s. paid for 20 dozen stone pots in 1467 by the Duke of Norfolk (ibid., 98–99) should have been cited as the price of hire, not sale (Crawford 1992, 1, 400).

[45] Dyer 1982.

[46] See Bellhoste *et al.* 1991, 37–46, for a brief summary of the spread of the blast furnace in 15th-century Wallonia and northern/eastern France, and the Swedish and German evidence for its European origins in the 13th and 14th centuries. However, similar technology was already in use in China by 200 BC. See Mokyr 1990, 210–12.

[47] G. Egan, pers. comm. Also Egan 1996; Keene 1996.

[48] Pearce & Vince 1988, 82–91.

[49] Mayes & Scott 1984, 23–25; Musty 1984, 26–48.

[50] See Moorhouse 1985 for criticism of the Chilvers Coton kiln sequence. The parallel-flued 13th-century kiln at Lyvedon (Northants) in the 13th century, for example, is comparable in size with the large multi-flued kins at Chilvers Coton Musty 1974, fig. 1.

[51] Vince 1977 and 1985; Ford 1995, 35–37; Knight 1991; Harrison & Davey 1977.

[52] For instance, Courtney 1994b and the recently excavated 16th-century assemblages from the George Hotel, Brecon, and Aberglasney in Carmarthenshire, sites directed by S. Clark and Blockley respectively.

[53] Dufaÿ 1998.

[54] Fichet de Clairfontaine & Beuchet 1996.

[55] See Gaimster 1997. It should be noted that the medieval Siegburg potters, despite having an early urban guild, were still located in specialist villages beyond the walls, notably Aulgasse (Körte-Boger & Salies 1991).

[56] Elizabethan Books of Rates (in a period of price inflation) valued stone cups without covers at 5s. per 100 for customs purposes (Allan 1994, 119).

[57] Vandenbulke and Groeneweg 1988; Allan 1984, 117–26 and 1994; Haselgrove & van Loo 1998.

[58] Dawson 1979, microfiche; Barton 1992; Gaimster & Nenk 1997.

[59] Verhaeghe 1997, 29–32.

[60] Gaimster 1993; Courtney 1997a, 17; Keene 1996, 100–01.

[61] See Marchesi *et al.* 1997 and Marseilles 1995 for the Mediterranean tin-glaze potteries and the papers in Gaimster 1999 for the movement of the technology into the north. However, it should be noted that tin-glazed tiles were occasionally made in northern France and the Low Countries, for use in great noble houses or ecclesiastical sites in the 14th and 15th centuries. French nobles are recorded as specially importing craftsmen, including Saracens and Spaniards, for their building projects (Rosen 1995, 79–82).

[62] See Moorhouse & Slowikowski 1992 on Wrenthorpe.

[63] For the continental slipware industries see Hurst *et al.* 1986 and Stephan 1987.

[64] Tite 1996; Ecouen 1998, 29–41 (Saintes 1990, 62–63). Palissy referred to saggars (*caisses protectices*) as 'lanternes de terre'.

[65] Brears 1971, 27–30.

[66] Marseilles 1995.

[67] Malcolm Watkins 1960; Grant 1983; Allan 1984.

[68] Barnstaple n.d.; Lovatt n.d.; Dawson & Kent 1999. Note the close parallels with the excavated 19th-century earthenware kilns at Frechen (Jürgens & Kleine 1988; Jürgens 1988). For their medieval prototypes see Jansenn 1987.

[69] Sgraffito, long established in the Islamic world, appears in the Beauvaisis region of northern France in the 16th century. See Hurst *et al.* 1986 and Stephan 1987 for sgraffito in the Beauvaisis, Low Countries and Werra industries, and see Abel & Amouric 1993 and Pannequin 1999 for Provence.

[70] Duco 1981.

[71] Cipolla 1972.

[72] Crossley 1990, 267–74.

[73] Crowe 1975–77; Gaimster 1997, 165.

[74] See Carel *et al.* 1997 for excavations on 17th- and 18th-century tin-glazed workshop complexes in Rouen. See also Britton 1986 on the London industry.

[75] See Courtney 1986–87 on the industry on Gwehelog common in Gwent.

[76] Weatherill 1971. The documentary history of the Ticknall industry is currently being studied by Janet Spavold and Sue Brown.

[77] For the Sneyd Green kilns see Middleton 1984. Compare with the Old Hall Street (Kelly & Greaves 1974) and Albion Square kilns (Celoria & Kelly 1973) excavated in Hanley, Stoke-on-Trent. The latter pair are respectively about 2.25 m and 2 m diameter internally and the depressed floors of the Sneyd Green kilns 2.1 m and 2.4 m in diameter.

[78] De Vries 1994.

[79] Brears 1971, 196.

[80] Weatherill 1971, 66–95; Brears 1971, 40–54; Spufford 1984. Pot wains are recorded at Hemington (Leics) in 1539, presumably carrying pots from nearby Ticknall: see Public Record Office SC6/Hen 8/1827 and Courtney forthcoming.

[81] Willan 1976, 4–8.

[82] See Woodland 1981 and Sawday 1994 for Leicester. Also D. Sawday, D. Ford and D. Barker, pers. comm. For the national distribution of Martincamp flasks see Ickowicz 1993, fig. 5. Icowicz suggests the flasks were specially made for export to Britain. This niche marketing took advantage of the growth of the English-Normandy trade in the 16th and early 17th centuries but did not exploit the major Rouen-Antwerp trade route (Brunelle 1991, 9–29; Mendenhall 1953, passim).

[83] Amico 1996; Barbour & Sturman 1996.

[84] Baart *et al.* 1986, 94; Baart 1990, 80.

[85] Hållans & Andersson 1992; Rosén 1995.

[86] Green 1999.

[87] See Berg 1993, Behagg 1998 and Y. Courtney 2000 (and this volume) on organizational transformation within workshop-based industries.

[88] Weatherill 1971, 4–6; Gaimster 1997, 251–52.

[89] Weatherill 1970; Barker & Halfpenny 1990; Barker 1999.

BIBLIOGRAPHY

Abel, V. & Amouric, H. 1993, *Un gout d'Italie: céramiques et céramistes italiens en Provence du Moyen Age au XXe siècle*, Aubagne: Narration.

Allan, J. P. 1984, *Medieval and Post-Medieval Finds from Exeter, 1971–1980*, Exeter: Exeter City Council.

Allan. J. P. 1994, 'Imported pottery in south-west England, c. 1350–1550', *Medieval Ceramics* 18, 45–50.

Amico, L. N. 1996, *Bernard Palissy: In Search of Earthly Pleasures*, Paris: Flammarion.

Baart, J. 1990, 'Ceramic consumption and supply in early modern Amsterdam: local production and long-distance trade', in Corfield, P. J. & Keene, D. (eds), *Work in Towns: 850–1850*, Leicester: Leicester University Press, 74–85.

Baart, J. M., Krook, W. & Lagerweij, A. C. 1986, 'Opgravingen aan de Oostenburger-Middenstraat', in Kist, J. B. (ed.), *Van VOC tot Werkspoor: Het Amsterdamse Industrieterrein Oostenburg*, Utrecht: Matrijs, 83–142.

Barbour, D. & Sturman, S. (eds) 1996, *Saint-Porchaire Ceramics*, Washington DC: National Gallery of Art.

Barker, D. 1999, 'The ceramic revolution 1650–1850', in Egan & Michael (eds), 226–34.

Barker, D. & Halfpenny, P. 1990, *Unearthing Staffordshire: towards a new understanding of 18th century ceramics*, Stoke-on-Trent: City Museum & Art Gallery, Stoke-on-Trent.

Barnstaple, n.d., *An Excavation at the North Devon Area Library Site, Tuly Street, Barnstaple. Summary Report*, Barnstaple: North Devon Archaeological Unit.

Barton, K. 1992, 'Ceramic changes in the western European littoral at the end of the Middle Ages: a personal view', in Gaimster, D. R. M & Redknap, M. (eds), *Everyday and Exotic Pottery from Europe c. 650–1900: Studies in Honour of John G. Hurst*, Oxford: Oxbow, 246–55.

Behagg, C. 1998, 'Mass Production without the Factory: craft producers, guns and small firm innovation 1790–1815', *Business History* 40:3, 1–15.

Bellhoste, J.-P. *et al.* 1991, *La métallurgie normande XIIe-XVIIe siècles: la révolution du haut forneau*, Cahiers de l'inventoire 14, Caen: Association histoire et patrimoine industriel de Basse-Normandie.

Berg, M. 1993, 'Small producer capitalism in eighteenth-century England', *Business History* 35:1, 17–39.

Berg, M. & Hudson, P. 1992, 'Rehabilitating the Industrial Revolution', *Econ. Hist. Rev.* 45:1, 24–50.

Blake, H. 1978, 'Medieval pottery: technological innovation or economic change?', in Mc K. Blake, H., Potter, T. W. & Whitehouse, D. B. (eds), *Papers in Italian Archaeology* 2, British Archaeological Reports Supp. Ser. 41:2, Oxford, 435–73.

Blake, H. 1980, 'Technology, supply or demand?', *Medieval Ceramics* 4, 3–12.

Bloch, M. 1967, 'The advent and triumph of the watermill', in Bloch, M., *Land and Work in Medieval Europe: Selected Papers by Marc Bloch*, London: Routledge & Kegan Paul, 136–68 (Original French article, 1935).

Bourne, J. (ed.) 1996, *Anglo-Saxon Landscapes in the East Midlands*, Leicester: Leicestershire Museums.

Braudel, F. 1980, 'History and the social sciences: the longue durée', in Braudel, F., *On History*, Chicago: University of Chicago Press, 25–54 (Original French article, 1958).

Braun, R. 1990, *Industrialization and Everyday Life*, Cambridge: Cambridge University Press (Original German edn 1979).

Brears, P. 1971, *The English Country Pottery: its History and Techniques*, Newton Abbot: David & Charles.

Britton, F. 1986, *London Delftware*, London: Jonathan Horne.

Brown, D. 1997, 'Pots from houses', *Medieval Ceramics* 21, 83–94.

Brunelle, G. K. 1991, *The New World Merchants of Rouen 1559–1630*, Kirksville: Sixteenth Century Journal Publishers Inc.

Campbell, B. M. S. 1990, 'People and land in the Middle Ages, 1066–1500', in Dodgshon, R. A. &. Butlin, R. A (eds), *An Historical Geography of England*, 2nd edition, London: Academic, 69–121.

Cane, C., Cane, J. & Carver, M. O. H. 1983, 'Saxon and medieval Stafford, new results and theories 1983', *West Midlands Archaeology* 26, 49–65.

Carel, P. *et al.* 1997, *Saint Sever: le temps des manufactures de faïence*, Rouen: Archéologie et histoire en Seine-Maritime.

Celoria, F. S. C. & Kelly, J. H. 1973, 'A Post-Medieval Pottery Site with a Kiln Base found off Albion Square, Hanley, Stoke-on-Trent, Staffordshire, England, Stoke-on-Trent', *City of Stoke-on-Trent Museum Archaeological Society Report* 4.

Cipolla, C. 1972, 'The diffusion of innovations in early modern Europe', *Comparative Studies in Society and History* 14, 46–52.

Cleland, C. 1999, 'Traders, Indians and middlemen: the foundations of the British north American fur trade', in Egan & Michael (eds), 322–41.

Cooper, N. J. 1996, 'Anglo-Saxon Settlement in the Gwash Valley, Rutland', in Bourne 1996, 165–77.

Cooper, N. J. 2000, 'Settlement in the Gwash valley to the Norman Conquest', in Cooper, N. J. (ed.), *The Archaeology of Rutland Water: Excavations at Empingham in the Gwash Valley, Rutland, 1967–73 and 1990*, Leicester Archaeology Monograph 6, Leicester: School of Archaeological Studies, Leicester University, 142–55.

Cotter, J. 1997, *A Twelfth-Century Pottery Kiln at Pound Lane, Canterbury: Evidence for an Immigrant Potter in the Late Norman Period*, Canterbury: Canterbury Archaeological Trust.

Courtney, P. 1986–87, 'Documentary evidence for the Gwehelog pottery industry', *Medieval and Later Pottery in Wales* 9, 71–73.

Courtney, P. 1994a, *Medieval and Later Usk*, Cardiff: University of Wales Press.

Courtney, P. 1994b, 'The Pottery', in Blockley, K., 'Langstone Castle motte: excavations by L. Alcock in 1964', *Archaeology in Wales* 34, 21–22.

Courtney, P. 1997a, 'The tyranny of concepts: some thoughts on periodisation and culture change', in Stamper & Gaimster (eds), 9–23.

Courtney, P. 1997b, 'Ceramics and the history of consumption: pitfalls and prospects', *Medieval Ceramics* 21, 95–108.

Courtney, P. forthcoming, 'The bridges in historical and regional context', in Cooper, L. & Ripper, S. (eds), *Excavation of the Medieval Bridges on the River Trent at Hemington, Leicestershire*, Leicester Archaeology Monographs, Leicester: School of Archaeological Studies, Leicester University.

Courtney, Y. C. S. 2000, 'Pub Tokens: material culture and regional marketing patterns in Victorian England and Wales', *International Journal of Historical Archaeology* 4:2, 159–90.

Crafts, N. F. R. 1985, *British Economic Growth during the Industrial Revolution*, Oxford: Clarendon Press.

Crafts, N. F. R. & Harley, C. K. 1992, 'Output growth and the Industrial Revolution: a restatement of the Crafts-Harley view', *Economic History Review* 45:4, 703–30.

Crawford, A. (ed.), 1992, *The Household Books of John Howard, Duke of Norfolk 1462–71, 1481–83*, Stroud: Sutton.

Crossley, D. 1990, *Post-medieval Archaeology in Britain*, Leicester: Leicester University Press.

Crowe, Y. 1975–77, 'Early Islamic pottery and China, *Transactions of the Oriental Ceramic Society* 41, 263–65.

Davey, P. & Hodges, R. (eds) 1985, *Ceramics and Trade: Production and Distribution of Later Medieval Pottery in North-West Europe*, Sheffield: Department of Prehistory and Archaeology, University of Sheffield.

Davison, B. K. 1972, 'Castle Neroche: an abandoned Norman fortress in south Somerset', *Somerset Archaeological and Natural History Society* 116, 189–208.

Dawson, G. J. 1979, 'Excavations at Guy's Hospital 1967', *Research Volume of the Surrey Archaeological Society* 7, 27–65 (and microfiche).

Dawson, D. & Kent, O. 1999, 'Reduction-fired lower temperature ceramics', *Post-Medieval Archaeology* 39, 164–78.

de Vries, J. 1994, 'The industrial revolution and the industrious revolution', *Journal of Economic History* 54, 249–70.

de Vries, J. & van der Woude, A. 1997, *The First Modern Economy: Success, Failure, and Perserverance of the Dutch Economy, 1500–1815*, Cambridge: Cambridge University Press.

Duco, D. H. 1981, 'De kleipijp in de zeventiende eeuwse Nederlanden', in Davey, P. J. (ed.), *The Archaeology of the Clay Tobacco Pipe*, v, Europe 2, pt ii, British Archaeological Reports Int. Ser. 106:2, Oxford, 11–468.

Dufaÿ, B. 1998, 'La Croissance d'une ville: les tuileries parisiennes du fabourg Saint-Honoré', in Van Ossel, P., *Les jardins du Carrousel (Paris)*, Documents d'Archéologie Française 73, Paris: Éditions de la maison des sciences de l'homme, 261–310.

Duplessis, R. S. 1997, *Transitions to Capitalism in Early Modern Europe*, Cambridge: Cambridge University Press.

Dyer, C. C. 1982, 'The social and economic changes of the later Middle Ages and the pottery of the period', *Medieval Ceramics* 6, 33–42.

Dyer, C. C. 1989, *Standards of Living in the Later Middle Ages: social change in England c. 1200–1520*, Cambridge: Cambridge University Press.

Ecouen 1991, *Une orfèvrerie de terre: Bernard Palissy et la céramique de Saint-Porchaire*, Exhibition catalogue, Château d'Ecouen, Paris: Réunion des Musées Nationaux.

Egan, G. 1996, 'Some archaeological evidence for metalworking in London, c. 1050 to c. 1700 A.D.', *Historical Metallurgy* 30:2, 83–94.

Egan, G. 1997, 'Medieval vessels of other materials — a non ceramic view', *Medieval Ceramics* 21, 109–14.

Eriksen, S. & De Bellaigue, G. 1987, *Sèvres Porcelain. Vincennes and Sèvres 1740–1800*, London: Faber.

Fichet de Clairfontaine, F. & Beuchet, L. 1996, 'L'artisanat céramique breton au XVe siècle: potiers et tuiliers', in Fichet de Clairefontaine, F. (ed.), *Ateliers de potiers médiévaux en Bretagne*, Documents d'Archéologie Française 55, Paris: Éditions de la maison des sciences de l'homme, 29–40.

Foard, G. 1978, 'Systematic fieldwalking and the investigation of Saxon settlement at Northampton-shire', *World Archaeology* 9, 357–74.

Ford, D. A. 1995, 'Medieval Pottery in Staffordshire, AD800–1600: A Review', *Staffordshire Archaeological Studies* 7.

Funari, P. P. A., Jones, S. & Hall, M. 1999, 'Introduction: archaeology in history', in Funari, P. P. A., Hall, M. & Jones, S. (eds), *Historical Archaeology: Back from the Edge*, London: Routledge, 1–20.

Gaimster, D. R. M. 1993, 'Cross-channel ceramic trade in the late Middle Ages: archaeological evidence for the spread of Hanseatic culture to Britain', in Gläser, M. (ed.), *Archäologie des*

Mittelalters und Bauforschung im Hanseraum: eine Festschrift für Günter P. Fehring, Rostock: K. Reich, 251–60.

Gaimster, D. R. M. 1997, *German Stoneware 1200–1900: Archaeology and Cultural History*, London: British Museum Press.

Gaimster, D. R. M. (ed.) 1999, *Maiolica in the North: the Archaeology of Tin-glazed Earthenware in North-West Europe c. 1500–1600*, British Museum Occasional Paper 122, London: British Museum Press.

Gaimster, D. R. M., Redknap, M. & Wegner, H.-H. (eds) 1988, *Zur Keramik des Mittelalters und der beginnenden Neuzeit im Rheinland*, British Archaeological Reports Int. Ser. 440, Oxford.

Gaimster, D. R. M. & Nenk, B. 1997, 'English households in transition 1450–1550: the ceramic evidence', in Gaimster & Stamper (eds), 171–95.

Gaimster, D. R. M. & Stamper, P. (eds) 1997, *The Age of Transition: the Archaeology of English Culture 1400–1600*, Oxford: Oxbow.

Gierz, W. 1996, 'Middle Meuse valley ceramics of Huy-type: a preliminary analysis', *Medieval Ceramics* 20, 33–64.

Going, C. J. 1992, 'Economic "long waves" in the Romano-British period? a reconnaissance of the Romano-British ceramic evidence', *Oxford Journal of Archaeology* 11:1, 93–117.

Grant, A. 1983, *North Devon Pottery: the Seventeenth Century*, Exeter: Exeter University Press.

Green, C. 1999, *John Dwight's Fulham Pottery: Excavations 1971–79*, English Heritage Archaeological Reports 6, London: HMSO.

Gunder Frank, A. 1978, *Dependent Accumulation and Underdevelopment*, London.

Gutiérrez, A. 1997, 'Cheapish and Spanish. Meaning and design on imported Spanish pottery', *Medieval Ceramics* 21, 73–82.

Gutiérrez, A. 2000, *Mediterranean pottery in Wessex households (13th to 17th centuries)*, British Archaeological Reports 306, Oxford.

Hackett Fischer, D. 1996, *The Great Wave: Price Revolutions and the Rhythm of History*, Oxford.

Hållans, A-M. & Andersson, C. 1992, 'Acquiring, using and discarding — consumption patterns in the 18th century town of Nyköping', in Ersgärd, L., Holmström, M. & Lamm, K. (eds), *Rescue and Research, Reflections of Society in Sweden 700–1700 A.D.*, Stockholm: Riksantikvarieämbetet, 101–206.

Harrison, H. M. & Davey, P. 1977, 'Ewloe kiln', in Davey, P. J. (ed.), *Medieval Pottery from Excavations in the North West*, Liverpool: University of Liverpool, 92–99.

Haselgrove, D. & van Loo, J. 1998, 'Pieter van den Ancker and imports of Frechen stoneware bottles and drinking pots in Restoration London c. 1660–67', *Post-Medieval Archaeology* 32, 33–44.

Hinton, D. A. 1973, *Medieval Pottery of the Oxford Region*, Oxford: Oxfordshire Museums.

Hodges, R. 1985, 'San Vincenzo al Volturno and its region between the 5th and 11th centuries', in Hodges & Mitchell (eds), 259–71.

Hodges, R. & Mitchell, J. (eds) 1985, *San Vincenzo al Volturno: the Archaeology, Art and Territory of an Early Medieval Monastery*, British Archaeological Reports Int. Ser. 252, Oxford.

Hudson, P. 1992, *The Industrial Revolution*, London: Edward Arnold.

Hudson, P. 1999, 'Regional and local history: globalism, postmodernism and the future', *Journal of Regional and Local Studies* 20:1, 5–24.

Hurst, J. G. 1976, 'The pottery', in Wilson, D. M. (ed.), *The Archaeology of Anglo-Saxon England*, London: Methuen, 283–348.

Hurst, J. G., Neal, D. & van Beuningen, H. J. E. 1986, *Pottery Produced and Traded in North-West Europe 1350–1650*, Rotterdam Papers 6, Rotterdam: Museum Boymans-van Beuningen.

Ickowicz, P. 1993, 'Martincamp Ware: a problem of attribution', *Medieval Ceramics* 17, 51–60.

Jannsen, W. 1987, 'Der technische Wandel der Töpferöfen von der Karolingerzeit zum Hochmitteralter, dargestellt anhand rheinischer Beispeile', in Chapelot, J., Galinié, H. & Pilet-Leemière, J. (eds), *La ceramique (Ve-XIXe s.): fabrication — commercilaisation — utilisation*, Caen: Centre de recherches archéologiques médiévales de l'université de Caen, 107–19.

Jürgens, A. 1988, 'Langerwehe-Brühl-Frechen: neue Grabungen und Erkenntnisse in Rheinischen Topfereizentren', in Gaimster *et al.* 1988, 125–49.

Jürgens, A. & Kleine, D. 1988, 'Werkstatt-funde aus Frechen. Brennöfen und Irdenware', in Naumann, J. (ed.), *Keramik vom Niederrhein*, Cologne: Kölnisches Stadtmuseum, 101–15.

Keene, D. 1996, 'Metalworking in medieval London: a survey', *Historical Metallurgy* 30:2, 95–102.

Kilmurry, K. 1980, *The Pottery Industry of Stamford, Lincolnshire, AD 850–1250*, British Archaeological Reports 54, Oxford.

Kelly, J. H. & Greaves, S. J. 1974, 'The Excavation of a Kiln Base in Old Hall Street, Hanley, Stoke-on-Trent, Staffs.', *City of Stoke-on-Trent Museum Archaeological Society Report 6.*

Knight, J. K. 1991, 'The pottery from Montgomery Castle', *Medieval and Later Pottery in Wales* 12, 1–100.

Kondratieff, N. D. 1979, 'The long waves in economic life', *Review* 2, 519–62 (Original Russian article 1925).

Körte-Boger, A. & Salies, G. H.(eds) 1991, *Eine Siegburger Töpferwerkstatt der Familie Knütgen: Neue archäologische und historische Forschungen zur Unteren Aulgasse*, Cologne and Bonn: Rheinland Verlag.

Le Patourel, H. E. J. 1979, 'Pottery as evidence for social and economic change', in. Sawyer, P. H. (ed.), *English Medieval Settlement*, London: Edward Arnold, 86–96.

Le Roy Ladurie, E. 1974, *The Peasants of Languedoc*, Urbana: University of Illinois Press (Original French edn 1966).

Lewis, C., Mitchell-Fox, P. & Dyer, C. C. 1997, *Village, Hamlet and Field: Changing Medieval Settlements in Central England*, Manchester: Manchester University Press.

Liddle, P. 1996, 'The archaeology of Anglo-Saxon Leicestershire', in Bourne 1996, 1–10.

Lopcz, R. S. 1971, *The Commercial Revolution of the Middle Ages 950–1350*, Eaglewood Cliffs, NJ: Prentice Hall.

Lovatt, A. n.d., 'The N.D.D.C./D.C.C. Site — Potters Lane, Barnstaple', in Blanchard, L. (ed.), *Archaeology in North Devon 1987–8*, Barnstaple: North Devon Archaeological Unit, 5–15.

Lüdtke, A. 1995, 'Introduction: what is the history of everyday life and who are its practitioners?', in Lüdtke, A. (ed.), *History of Everyday Life: Reconstructing Historical Experiences and Ways of Life*, Princeton, NJ: Princeton University Press, 3–40 (Original German edn 1989).

Malcolm Watkins, C. 1960, 'North Devon pottery and its export to America in the 17th century', *United States National Museum Bulletin* 225, 17–59.

Mannoni, L. & Mannoni, T. 1975, 'La ceramica dal medioevo all'età moderna nell'archeologia di superficie della Liguria centrale e orientale', *Abisola* 8, 121–36.

Marchesi, H., Thiriot, J. & Vallauri, L. 1997, *Marseilles, les ateliers de potiers de XIIIe s. et la quartier Sainte-Barbe (Ve-XVIIe s.)*, Documents d'Archéologie Française 65, Paris: Éditions de la maison des sciences de l'homme.

Marseilles 1995, *Le vert et le brun de Kairouan à Avignon céramiques du Xe au XVe siècle*, exhibition catalogue, Marseilles, Paris: Réunion des musées nationaux.

Mauss, M. 1954, *The Gift: Forms and Functions of Exchange in Archaic Societies*, London: Cohen and West (Original French edn 1925).

Mayes, P. & Scott, K. 1984, *Pottery Kilns at Chilvers Coton, Nuneaton*, Society for Medieval Archaeology Monograph 10, London.

McCarthy, M. R. & Brooks, C. 1988, *Medieval Pottery in Britain AD 900–1600*, Leicester: Leicester University Press.

Mendenhall, T. C. 1953, *The Shrewsbury Drapers and the Welsh Wool Trade in the XVI and XVII Centuries*, Oxford: Oxford University Press.

Middleton, S. 1984, 'The Sneyd Green medieval kilns: a review', *Staffordshire Archaeological Studies* 1, 41–48.

Mokyr, J. 1990, *The Lever of Riches: Technological Creativity and Economic Progress*, Oxford: Oxford University Press.

Moorhouse, S. 1981, 'The medieval pottery industry and its markets', in Crossley, D. W. (ed.), *Medieval Industry*, CBA Res. Reports 40, London, 96–125.

Moorhouse, S. 1985, 'Review of P. Mayes & K. Scott, *Pottery Kilns at Chilvers Coton, Nuneaton*', *Medieval Ceramics* 9, 87–96.

Moorhouse, S. & Slowikowski, A. M. 1992, 'The pottery', 89–142 in S. Moorhouse & I. Roberts, *Wrenthorpe Potteries: Excavations of 16th- and 17th-Century Potting Tenements near Wakefield*, Wakefield: West Yorkshire Archaeology Service.

Mouer, L. D. 1993, 'Chesapeake Creoles: the creation of folk culture in colonial Virginia', in Reinhart, T. R. & Pogue, D. J. (eds), *The Archaeology of 17th-Century Virginia*, Charlottesville: Archaeological Society of Virginia, 105–65.

Musgrave, E. 1998, 'Pottery production and proto-industrialisation: continuity and change in the rural ceramics industries of the Saintonge region, France, 1250–1800', *Rural History* 9:1, 1–18.

Musty, J. 1974, 'Medieval pottery kilns', in Evison, V. I., Hodges, H. & Hurst, J. G. (eds), *Medieval Pottery from Excavations*, London: J. Baker, 41–65.

Musty, J. 1984, 'Technology and affinities of the Chilvers Coton kilns', in Mayes & Scott 1984, 26–38.

Palmer, M. 1990, 'Industrial archaeology: a thematic or a period discipline?', *Antiquity* 64, 275–82.

Pannequin, B. 1999, 'De l'Italie à la Provence, le décor gravé', in *L'art de la terre vernissée du Moyen Âge à l'an 2000*, exhibition catalogue, Sèvres and Arras: Réunion des Musées Nationaux, 114–17.

Parry, S. 1994, 'The Raunds area project survey', in Parker Pearson, M. & Schadla-Hall, R. T. (eds), *Looking at the Land: Archaeological Landscapes in Eastern England*, Leicester: Leicestershire Museums, 36–42.

Parry, S. forthcoming, *The Raunds Area Project Survey*, English Heritage Archaeological Reports, London: HMSO.

Patterson, H. 1985, 'The late Roman and early medieval pottery from Molise', in Hodges & Mitchell 1985, 83–110.

Pearce, J. & Vince, A. G. 1988, *A Dated Type-Series of London Medieval Pottery, Part 4: Surrey Whitewares*, London: HMSO.

Pollard, S. 1981, *Peaceful Conquest: The Industrialization of Europe, 1760–1970*, Oxford: Oxford University Press.

Postan, M. M. 1966, 'Medieval agrarian society in its prime: England', in Postan, M. M. (ed.), *The Cambridge Economic History of Europe, I: the Agrarian Life of the Middle Ages*, 2nd edn, Cambridge: Cambridge University Press, 548–632.

Reed, I. W. 1990, *1000 Years of Pottery: An Analysis of Pottery Trade and Use*, Trondheim: NIKU.

Rigold, S. E. 1977, 'Small change in the light of medieval site-finds', in Mayhew, N. J. (ed.), *Edwardian Monetary Affairs (1279–1344)*, British Archaeological Report 36, Oxford, 59–80.

Rosen, J. 1995, *La faïence en France du XIVe au XIXe siècle: histoire et technique*, Paris: Errance.

Rosén, C. 1995, 'Keramik som kulturell spegel. Yngre rödgods I olika milljöer ca 1550–1850', *Meta* 3, 25–38.

Rostow, W. W. 1975, 'Kondratieff, Schumpeter and Kusnets: trend periods revisited', *Journal of Economic History* 35:4, 719–73.

Rutter, J. A. 1988, 'Saxon pottery', in Ward, S., *Excavations at Chester: 12 Watergate Street 1985*, Grosvenor Museum archaeological excavations and survey reports no. 5, Chester: Grosvenor Museum, 29–31.

Sahlins, M. 1972, *Stone Age Economics*, Chicago: Aldine-Atherton.

Saintes 1990, *Bernard Palissy mythe et réalité*, exhibition catalogue, Museums of Saintes, Niort and Agen.

Sawday, D. 1991, 'Potters Marston Ware', *Transactions Leicestershire Archaeological and Historical Society* 65, 34–37.

Sawday, D. 1994, 'The post-Roman pottery', in Clay, P. & Pollard, P., *Iron Age and Roman Occupation in the West Bridge Area, Leicester: Excavations 1962–71*, Leicester: Leicestershire Museums, 115–29.

Searle, E. & Ross, B. 1967, *The Cellarer's Rolls of Battle Abbey 1275–1513*, Sussex Record Society 65.

Spufford, M. 1984, *The Great Reclothing of Rural England: Petty Chapmen and their Wares in the Seventeenth Century*, London: Hambledon.

Stephan, H.-G. 1987, *Die bemalte Irdenware der Renaissance in Miteleuropa*, München: Deutscher Kunstverlag.

Tillotson, J. H. 1988, *Monastery and Society in the Late Middle Ages: Selected Account Rolls from Selby Abbey, Yorkshire 1398–1537*, Woodbridge: Boydell.

Tite, M. S. 1996, 'Comparative study of the production technology of "Saint-Porchaire" ware and related European ceramics', in Barbour & Sturman 1996, 99–106.

Vandenbulke, L. V. & Groeneweg, G. 1988, 'The stoneware stock of Jan-Peters and Cornelius-de-Kanneman: two merchants of Rhenish pottery at Bergen-op-Zoom (NL.) during the 2nd quarter of the 16th century', in Gaimster *et al.* 1988, 343–57.

Verhaeghe, F. 1991, 'An aquamanile and some thoughts about ceramic competition with quality medieval goods in the Middle Ages', in Lewis, E. (ed.), *Custom and Ceramics: essays presented to Kenneth Barton*, Wickham: APE, 25–61.

Verhaeghe, F. 1996, 'Aspects sociaux et économiques de la céramique très décorée. Quelque réflexions', in Dilly, G. (ed.), *La céramique très decorée dans l'Europe du nord-ouest (Xème-XIVème siècle)*, Berck-sur-Mer: Groupe de recherches et d'études sur la céramique dans le Nord-Pas-de-Calais, 233–48.

Verhaeghe, F. 1997, 'The archaeology of transition: a Continental view', in Gaimster & Stamper (eds), 25–44.

Vince, A. G. 1977, 'The medieval and post-medieval ceramic industry of the Malvern region: the study of a ware and its distribution', in Peacock, D. P. S. (ed.), *Pottery and Early Commerce*, London: Academic, 257–305.

Vince, A. G. 1985, 'The ceramic finds', in Shoesmith, R. (ed.), *Hereford City Excavations, vol. 3, The Finds*, Council for British Archaeology Research Report 56, London, 34–82.

Vince, A. G. 1994, 'Saxo-Norman urban economics', in Rackham, J. (ed.), *Environment and Economy in Anglo-Saxon England: A Review of Recent Work on the Environmental Archaeology of Anglo-Saxon Settlements In England*, Council for British Archaeology Research Report 89, York, 108–19.

Vince, A. G. 1995, 'Trade in pottery around the North Sea: the 11th Gerald Dunning memorial lecture', *Medieval Ceramics* 19, 3–9.

Wallerstein, I. M. 1974–89, *The Modern World System*, New York: Academic.

Weatherill, L. 1970, 'Technical change and potters' probate inventories 1660–1760', *Journal of Ceramic History* 3, 3–12.

Weatherill, L. 1971, *The Pottery Trade and North Staffordshire 1660–1760*, Manchester: Manchester University Press.

Willan, T. S. 1976, *The Inland Trade: Studies in English Internal Trade in the Sixteenth and Seventeenth Centuries*, Manchester: Manchester University Press.

Williams, D. F. & Vince, A. G., 1997, 'The characterization and interpretation of early to middle Saxon granite tempered pottery in England', *Medieval Archaeology* 41, 214–20.

Wolf, E. 1982, *Europe and the People without History*, Berkeley: University of California Press.

Woodland, R. R. 1980, 'The pottery', in Mellor, J. E. & Pearce, T. (eds), *The Austin Friars, Leicester*, Council for British Archaeology Research Report 35, York, 81–129.

THE INDUSTRIALIZATION OF THE STAFFORDSHIRE POTTERIES

By David Barker

The 18th and 19th centuries saw a tremendous expansion of ceramic manufacture in Britain, accompanied by an equally dramatic increase in ceramic consumption. McKendrick's view that a 'consumer revolution' in the mid 18th century stimulated growth in pottery manufacture and other sectors of industry has been challenged in recent years.[1] There were, however, sufficient significant developments within both the manufacture and the consumption of ceramics at this time to constitute a 'ceramic revolution' of sorts whose effects were far reaching.[2] The 'ceramic revolution' of the 16th century[3] resulted in the growth of regional industries producing new wares and vessel forms which were modelled on continental prototypes, and which shared some basic, but significant, ceramic processes which had hitherto been unknown in this country.[4] The 18th-century 'ceramic revolution' was also one of scale — of production, in the number of factories and workers employed, and in the volume and diversity of output. There were indeed many new types of ware and new vessel forms but, unlike its 16th-century precursor, this 'ceramic revolution' had a major impact beyond the shores of the British Isles and, as a result of the prevailing economic and cultural climate, upon consumers across a large part of the globe.

The developments within the ceramics industry have generally been studied from the narrow perspectives of specific ware types and individual manufacturers, while the investigation of the manufacturing processes and of the factories in which manufacture took place lags behind.[5] Narrowly-focused studies of this kind, while useful in many respects, have limitations and overlook the reality of the situation — that developments within the ceramics industry were not merely a series of improvements and innovations in processes which facilitated, increased, or speeded up manufacture and made possible the introduction of new wares. They were a response to, and were dependent upon, a range of inter-related economic, social and technological factors, which came to shape both production throughout Britain and consumption world-wide.

At the beginning of the 18th century, ceramic production in Britain was dominated by lead-glazed earthenwares — slipwares, mottled wares and blackwares, for example, together with all the regional variations — which were mostly once-fired. These 'unrefined' wares (many can hardly be called 'coarse', as they are often well-made, with well-prepared clay bodies) were made in small workshops, which were concentrated in manufacturing centres such as north Staffordshire, Ticknall in

Derbyshire, Harlow in Essex, Donyatt in Somerset, or Barnstaple in north Devon, or operated in comparative isolation away from their competitors. These workshops' markets were as diverse as their wares; some flourished and achieved a substantial share of the regional and national market, while others remained purely local concerns. Between them their products supplied the bulk of the ceramic needs of the population at large, as drinking vessels for the home or the tavern, as food storage and food preparation vessels, and as dairy wares. The scale of manufacture varied in size and complexity, and potters were as likely as not to carry on their trade on a part-time basis, combining this with farming in some form. Raw materials for production were usually available locally, workshops may simply have been converted dwellings, and capital costs for the establishment of a business were low.

The scale of the early manufacture of refined earthenware — delftware — was, however, different. From the outset, this country's delftware manufacture — centred on London — demanded a greater degree of organization than was necessary in the contemporary coarseware sector of the industry. This was partly a result of its reliance upon raw materials — fuel and clay — which were not available locally. Investment was required and partnerships between potters and financial backers were commonplace.[6] Larger, more specialized workforces, which included painters, also distinguished delftware manufacture from coarseware production from an early date.

The 17th century had seen an expansion of pottery-making in north Staffordshire, with good quality clays and coals providing the basis for this, and with lead and salt for glazing being available in the neighbouring counties. By the second half of that century a significant skills base was developing. Archaeological excavations within the Staffordshire Potteries[7] provide tangible evidence for greatly-increased production, of very fine quality earthenwares from c. 1660 onwards,[8] and of salt-glazed stonewares from the 1680s.[9] Archaeological finds from elsewhere in England, the Caribbean and North America show that the market for these wares was also steadily growing from this time, although small quantities of Staffordshire wares have been found in Virginia from as early as the 1610s.[10]

However, in the period 1720–30 developments in manufacturing in north Staffordshire transformed the local industry, exerting an influence which was to change the course of ceramic production throughout Britain. The stimulus for change was largely the growing popularity of the new beverages, tea, coffee and chocolate, bringing a swift response from Staffordshire potters. Recognizing the need for suitable, affordable wares from which to consume the new drinks, they refocused their manufacture, introduced new vessel forms and new types of ware, and adopted new processes for their production. These new wares were to form the basis for the growing success of the Staffordshire manufacturers at home and abroad. Staffordshire wares soon became, in effect, the industry standard, exerting a great influence upon home production generally and hastening the decline and ultimate demise of some sectors of the British industry, notably delftware manufacture.

The transformation of the north Staffordshire industry was complete by the 1740s, by which time the manufacture of new tea and coffee wares was widespread. Many traditional practices were supplanted; new wares required new processes, new raw materials and improved preparation. Perhaps the most significant change was the

FIGURE 1. A white salt-glazed stoneware teapot, made from white-firing ball clay. This vessel exhibits turned and cut decoration, carried out on the lathe, as well as applied moulded reliefs formed in brass dies. Probably 1720s.

diminishing reliance upon local raw materials, and a growing need for white firing clays. The fine white salt-glazed stonewares, introduced by 1720,[11] were made entirely from white 'ball clays' which are found only in Dorset and Devon, with calcined flint added to the clay bodies to enable them to withstand high firing temperatures of 1250°C (Fig. 1). Flint was brought in from the south-east and east coasts but was calcined and crushed in the vicinity of the potteries in north Staffordshire.[12] A very large sector of the industry consequently became dependent upon imported raw materials and was sustained by a whole new network of contacts, carriers and middlemen, and increased traffic on the sea and the rivers, and on the roads.

New refined red earthenwares (redwares) were also introduced around 1720, with multi-coloured agate wares following later in the decade, and although they continued to use local red-firing clays, they belong in every respect to the new era of ceramic development. Significantly, these wares were twice-fired, with separate biscuit and glost firings giving greater control over the final product (Fig. 2). Twice-firing made possible the production of consistently high quality earthenwares and seems to have accompanied the introduction of refined earthenware manufacture. Saggars,[13] already standard in single earthenware and stoneware firings, were now required for both stages of the firing process and are common finds on excavations of factory and factory waste sites. The culmination of refined earthenware production was the development of cream-coloured earthenware, or creamware, during the 1740s.

By the 1730s these new refined wares had benefited from the movement of clay preparation from outdoors, where drying took place in sun kilns, to indoor mixing tanks with the appropriate sieving of slips and heated 'slip kilns'.[14] The introduction of the great wheel freed the thrower from the need to power his wheel, for this was done by another — usually a child (Fig. 3). The innovation which improved the

FIGURE 2.   Redwares, biscuit and glost, illustrating the introduction of twice firing for refined wares. Probably 1720s.

First process of potting is Throwing: forming round pieces of ware with the Hands and Machine.

FIGURE 3.   Throwing. The great wheel was a significant innovation in the early 18th-century pottery industry, speeding up the thrower's work and increasing control over the wheel. The power was provided by children. (Source: *A Representation of the Manufacturing of Earthenware*, Anon. 1827)

appearance of all thrown wares was lathe-turning by 1720, by which the leather-hard bodies of thrown wares were pared down to a thinness rarely achieved previously by throwing alone. Lathe turning also opened up a range of decorative possibilities for the wares.

These changes had an impact upon the size and organization of the unit of production which began to be transformed from a small workshop which could have been operated by few multi-skilled operatives, to a larger unit in which a degree of specialization necessitated discrete areas for different processes. The potworks which emerged during the second quarter of the 18th century came to comprise small groups of specialized workshops, each housing workers with definable specialist 'craft' skills. In writing about early production, Simeon Shaw states that 'Up to 1740, in each manufactory, all the persons employed were, the slip-maker, thrower, two turners, handler (*stouker*), fireman, warehouseman, and a few children, and, to be really useful to the master and secure sufficient employment, a good workman could *throw*, *turn* and *stouk* [i.e. apply handles]'.[15] After 1740, however,

> The increase of workmen, the subdivision of labour in every process; and the dexterity and quickness consequent on separate persons confining themselves solely to one branch of the Art, with the time saved in the change of implements and articles, instead of retarding, greatly promoted the manufacture, by increasing its excellence and elegance.[16]

What little evidence there is suggests that workshops in the early 18th century were small, often modified from other uses — perhaps domestic — frequently thatched and typically having just one oven.[17] Weatherill's examination of potters' probate inventories has shown how the number of workshops increased in the second quarter of the 18th century to provide the additional accommodation required for the greater number of processes which were carried out by a growing workforce.[18] New shops became necessary for the turner's lathe, for slip-making and clay preparation, for throwing, for handling, for glazing, for saggar-making and for warehousing. The increase in the number of workshops with discrete functions almost certainly reflects the wider division of labour within factories, while the increase in the number of ovens in a factory reflects an increase in either the scale or the diversity of production. The manufacture of twice-fired refined earthenwares required separate ovens for biscuit and glost firings, and a further, separate oven was necessary for salt-glazed stoneware. Those factories which made both lead-glazed earthenwares and salt-glazed stonewares — and there were many of these — would therefore have accommodated a minimum of three ovens. Significantly, from 1720 all references to ovens in wills are in the plural,[19] but it would be wrong to assume that the number of ovens necessarily increased in all factories during the later 18th and 19th centuries. Increased output demanded a larger capacity for firing, and some of the largest 19th-century factories had as many as ten or more ovens. Nevertheless, these are exceptional and many small 'potbanks' pursued profitable businesses well into the 19th century with just one biscuit and one glost oven.[20]

The well-documented partnership of 1719/20, between north Staffordshire businessman John Fenton and his potter nephew Thomas Hill,[21] typifies developments at the beginning of the ceramic revolution, and highlights the new role of the non-potter entrepreneur. Fenton — described as 'gentleman' of Newcastle-under-Lyme — put money into a new pottery-making venture in Shelton to produce new-style fine earthenwares and stonewares, erected workshops and ovens, and allowed buildings held by him to be used by the business, for which he received rent and interest on money spent on the buildings. The partnership relied heavily upon imported ball clay, for there are references to clays from Bridgnorth and Liverpool, and in November 1721 Fenton paid for 66 clodds [sic] of clay which, at around 35 lb for each ball, is the equivalent to eleven packhorses or a little over one ton,[22] and both the documentary and archaeological evidence show that the factory processed its own flint. At the dissolution of the partnership in 1721, the factory's workforce is recorded at ten, although precise roles are not specified. This number roughly coincides with Josiah Wedgwood's estimate that in the period 1710–15 it took six men and four boys to fire one oven-full of once-fired lead-glazed black and mottled wares per week,[23] an operation which involved far fewer processes than the manufacture of fine wares.

The progress towards a more rigid division of labour in pottery manufacture, suggested by the inventory evidence, is illustrated in the records of Thomas Whieldon, a successful manufacturer of Fenton, Stoke-on-Trent. By 1747 Whieldon occupied a new factory comprising 'pot ovens, houses, buildings, warehouses, work houses, throwing houses . . .'.[24] His success was such that, by 1780, he was able to join a growing number of manufacturers who, having made fortunes, were able to retire from the business, to lead the lives of gentlemen.[25] He produced white salt-glazed stoneware, creamware and the full range of contemporary ceramic types. His workforce in 1750–55 varied between 16 and 25, including children. Thomas Whieldon's *Account and Memorandum Book* lists the following named workers during this period:

> Slip maker from Lane End; Little Bet Blour to learn to flower [i.e. to decorate 'scratch blue']; John Austin for placing white; Thomas Dutton for vining [i.e. sprigging]; William Keeling for handling; Wm. Cope for handling, vining & cast ware; John Barker for the hovel; George Bagnall for firing; Elijah Simpson for turning; Samuel Jackson for throwing saggars & firing; & a boy of Bet Bloor for treading the lathe.[26]

The range of processes involved in the manufacture of ceramics at the time of Whieldon can easily be determined. Archaeological evidence provides clues that are not immediately apparent when examining extant wares, but the extent to which these processes are performed by different workers cannot be understood without reference to contemporary documentary sources, such as apprenticeship agreements. Here the trend involves a definite move away from the old-fashioned all-embracing training in the 'Art & Mystery of the Potter' to apprenticeships which exclude certain of the manufacturing processes. In 1731, for example, Aaron Wood was apprenticed 'the art, trade, mystery, and occupation of a potter to learn, that is to say, turning in the lathe, handling, and trimming (throwing on the wheel being out of this indenture excepted)',[27] while by contrast Josiah Wedgwood was apprenticed, in 1744, to learn the 'Art of Throwing and Handleing'.[28]

The Staffordshire ceramics industry continued to expand and, by the mid 18th century, a second wave of innovations was shaping the nature of production. These included the greater use of moulding from the 1740s, permitting the mass production of identical forms; coloured glazes from the late 1750s; painted decoration, both over glaze (1750s) and under-glaze (1760s); and the introduction of the engine lathe in the mid 1760s which brought about a range of new decorative possibilities for the bodies of wares. However none of these can be said to have revolutionized manufacture:

they merely added to, or improved upon what was already an increasingly sophisticated but standardized set of processes. Indeed, the most significant technical developments within the industry had already taken place by the 1740s. Only the development of transfer printing, during the 1780s, had a profound and lasting impact upon the appearance of ceramics. Using tissue paper as the medium for transferring images from engraved copper plates to the bodies of pots, transfer printing set the scene for an explosion in the quantity and range of decorated wares in the 19th century, and increased the potential for standardization of output.

Each development necessitated new specialist workers with clearly-defined roles, such as the mould-maker, the presser (for making moulded flat and hollow wares), the slip caster, the painter, and the printer and his team (Fig. 2) which comprised a cutter — usually a young girl — a transferer, a washer, and another to prepare the colour. The larger factories are more likely to have employed staff on the design side, such as engravers who worked on the copper plates used in transfer-printing, or more exceptionally, a modeller to provide the original models from which moulds would be made.

The mid to late 18th century also saw the introduction of many new bodies, of which creamware was arguably the most important and influential. This was first introduced in the 1740s, to be improved in the early 1760s. Technically it was not a significant development — it was simply a white bodied, lead-glazed earthenware made from ball clay — but through its marketing, such as Josiah Wedgwood's well-documented promotion of it amongst the gentry, nobility and royalty,[29] it was to become *the* fashionable ware of the later 1760s and 1770s, replacing Chinese porcelain as the table ware of choice at the dinner tables of the upper classes.

The search for porcelain had only a limited impact upon production in Britain. The prospect of the rewards which would follow success inspired a number of English entrepreneurs to back ventures to seek out its secret. There were some successes, the most notable being the factories at Worcester and Derby which managed to find workable 'soft paste' recipes suitable for high quality, costly wares for an affluent clientele, thereby ensuring the factories' long-term future. All too frequently, however, porcelain-making ventures were short-lived: the manufacture of porcelain required considerable capital as a period of experimentation was frequently required to find a body which would be stable during firing. Commercial success eluded most, and the attempts of English manufacturers to produce an acceptable white, translucent body are well known. Even the discovery of true, 'hard paste' porcelain did not transform the industry, for its protection by patent from 1768 until 1796, ensured that its manufacture was limited. Thereafter there was an explosion in the manufacture of hard paste bodies by Staffordshire factories, but this was short-lived for around 1800, a new porcelain body, bone china, was developed. Although itself not true porcelain, bone china was a reliable body, fine, very white and very translucent, ensuring its success as the dominant British porcelain of the 19th century.

In contrast to what had preceded, however, the technical innovations and new wares of the later 18th century were simply part of an on-going process of development. What really marked the period was not so much the technical developments, but considerable growth — in the numbers of factories, in employment within the industry, in the ancillary trades, in the volume of production, in the distribution networks, and in the increasing confidence of manufacturers. There was also at this time a significant increase in investment in the industry which changed the nature of many of the larger businesses. Partnerships between practical potters and financial backers had been a feature of the delftware sector of the industry from the mid 17th century,[30] while the nature of porcelain manufacture necessitated substantial financial backing from non-potter partners from the very beginning.[31] Such partnerships are unknown in north Staffordshire before the 18th century, although their appearance coincides with the introduction of new types of ware and development within the industry around 1720. The partnership between John Fenton and Thomas Hill in 1719/20, referred to above, is one of the first in north Staffordshire.

The businesses of the *majority* of potters were very different and involved comparatively little capital investment. They operated from leased premises (the normal lease being for seven years) owned either by other successful potters who had perhaps outgrown their premises and moved on (such as John and Thomas Wedgwood who rented out the Ivy House Works in Burslem), or from businessmen with no direct involvement in the trade. Speculative building of factories to provide an income was commonplace. Factories were frequently taken on with the necessary equipment of wheels, lathes, printing presses and boards, and with sufficient stocks of clay, coal, moulds and other necessaries to enable new tenants to commence production immediately. Most of the tools, such as ribs used in throwing or profiles used in pressing, would have been provided by the workmen themselves.[32] Start-up costs were therefore low. Throughout both the 18th and 19th centuries, the majority of pottery-making businesses were small in scale, modest in outlook and often short-lived. Most trod a fine line between success and failure and bankruptcy was a constant threat. The vicissitudes of international trade — especially in times of war — and a reliance upon credit left potters extremely vulnerable.

The growth in the size of the industry during the 18th century was rapid. Josiah Wedgwood estimated that in 1710–15 there were about 50 potteries operating in north Staffordshire, and employment is thought to have been in the region of 500.[33] In 1762 local manufacturers claimed that:

> In Burslem and its neighbourhood, are near 150 separate Potteries, for making various kinds of Stone and Earthen Ware; which together find constant Employment and Support for near 7,000 People.[34]

In 1769, Arthur Young visited the area and perhaps over-estimated the number of factories:

> Viewed the Staffordshire Potteries at Burslem and the neighbouring villages, which have of late been carried on with such amazing success. There are 300 houses, which are calculated to employ on an average 20 hands each or 6,000 on the whole, but if all the variety of people that work in what may be called the preparation for the employment of the immediate manufactories, the total number cannot be much short of 10,000 and it is increasing every day.[35]

A realistic figure for direct employment in the factories at the end of the 18th century is thought to be around 15,000.[36]

The key to success of the industry was marketing. McKendrick's view that 'in 1730, the Staffordshire potters sold their wares almost solely in Staffordshire. Their goods found their sale in the local market towns . . . To sell in London in any quantity was rare, to sell in Europe virtually unknown',[37] can no longer be substantiated. It is abundantly clear that Staffordshire was by no means isolated, despite its geographical disadvantages and the distance to river and coastal ports. The largest and smallest manufacturers alike were dependent upon marketing their wares beyond their immediate locality, and the means by which raw materials were brought into the district also served as a convenient route for the distribution of wares. The improved navigation of rivers by the 1730s facilitated the movement both of raw materials and of goods. Clay from Poole and from Devon, and flint from the south-east and east coasts, were brought in by sea, by river and then by packhorse for the remaining 30 miles of the journey from the river ports of Chester (Dee), Winsford (Weaver), Bridgnorth (Severn) and Willington (Trent), and finished goods were moved out by the same routes. Figures for the movement of goods down the Weaver, opened to river traffic in 1733, show a steady rise from around 50 tons (almost 1,000 crates) of ware, taken out down the Weaver in 1734, to more than 600 tons in 1760.[38]

Potters aiming to sell their wares further afield were served by a distribution network which was well-established and spanned the greatest part of the country, and which involved specialist dealers, general retailers, and hawkers or itinerant dealers. In London, there were the chinamen, who were dealers specializing predominantly in imported oriental porcelain, although many also dealt in earthen-wares and glass. Some of the larger manufacturers established and maintained warehouses in London, giving themselves and their wares a highly visible presence before their most well-to-do customers.[39] The whole system, however, was under-pinned by a great number of carriers, large and small, who maintained thousands of packhorses and horses for wagons for the movement of raw materials and finished goods.

Again, the records of John Fenton of Shelton are useful. Here in the very early years of the development of the north Staffordshire industry there is clear evidence for his network of contacts. The names of Fenton's customers — many whom are clearly dealers — and carriers are recorded, and there is one clear reference from 1721 to £13 9s. worth of ware being taken to London.[40] Wares were packed in crates and hogsheads and were transported by packhorse and wagon. Archaeology confirms the increasingly widespread occurrence of Staffordshire wares throughout Britain, and finds from the Caribbean and North America highlight the growing importance of exports by this date.

The benefits of an improved transport network were not lost upon pottery manufacturers, and they actively sought and promoted such improvements. The first road to be turnpiked in the area, in 1759, was that from Newcastle-under-Lyme, through Stoke, Fenton and Lane End, to Derby. This was strongly supported by local manufacturers, with the trustees including the potters Thomas Whieldon of Fenton, John Harrison of Stoke, Thomas Wedgwood of Burslem, John Bourne and William Adams.

Then in 1762 Burslem potters petitioned Parliament for a new turnpike from Burslem to Lawton (Cheshire), claiming that:

> The Ware of these Potteries is exported in vast Quantities from London, Bristol, Liverpool, Hull, and other Sea Ports, to our several Colonies in America and the West Indies, as well as to almost every Port in Europe . . . And the Trade flourishes so much, as to have encreased [sic] Two-thirds, within the last fourteen years.[41]

This was achieved in 1763 with the active support of Josiah Wedgwood, and by 1765 the local turnpike road network was completed.

Even more significantly, Josiah Wedgwood was a leading promoter of, and investor in the Grand Trunk, or Trent and Mersey canal, which was to link the Staffordshire pottery towns to the ports of Hull and Liverpool. Wedgwood was treasurer of a scheme which was backed by local gentry, landowners, merchants and pottery manufacturers. In 1766 he purchased an estate through which the canal was to pass and set about building his new Etruria factory, supremely sited on the canal side to enjoy all the advantages of easy movement of goods and materials.

The argument in favour of the canal was well-made:

> The town of Burslem, and the villages of Stoke, Hanley-Green, Lane-delf and Lane-End, are employed in the manufacturing of various kinds of stone and Earthenwares, which are carried, at great expense, to all parts of the Kingdom, and exported to our islands and colonies in America, and to almost every part of Europe; but the ware which is sent to Hull is now carried by land upwards of thirty miles to Willington; and that for Liverpool twenty miles to Winsford. The burthen of so expensive a land carriage to Winsford and Willington, and the uncertainty of the navigations from those places to Frodsham in Cheshire and Wilden in Derbyshire, occasioned by the floods in winter and the numerous shallows in summer, are more than these low-priced manufactures can bear; and without some relief as this under consideration, must concur, with their newly established competitors in France, and our American colonies, to bring these potteries to a speedy decay and ruin.[42]

The benefits were very real, for in 1777 the cost of transportation by canal was stated to be around one-quarter of carriage by road.[43]

Many of the large manufacturers had business interests beyond pottery production. John Baddeley of Shelton, for example, was heavily involved in the milling of flint, which was sold to local factories.[44] John and Thomas Wedgwood of Burslem are, however, typical of a new breed of pottery-capitalists. Next to their younger second cousin Josiah Wedgwood, John and Thomas Wedgwood (1743–70s) are the best-documented 18th-century manufacturers in north Staffordshire, as a result of the survival of their sales account books.[45] They quickly became the wealthiest potters in Burslem, building a new factory with three (later five) ovens, and the largest brick-built Georgian house in the town (Fig. 4). They invested widely, bought and let land, buildings and factories, and became the leading money-lenders of the town. They had interests in coal mines and in a flint mill (until they built their own windmill in 1751), and invested considerable sums in local turnpike roads. Between 1766–70 they invested £2,000 in the Trent and Mersey Canal, which was destined to improve the business of all north Staffordshire manufacturers, and they

FIGURE 4. The business success and local influence of the Wedgwood brothers, John and Thomas, are powerfully advertised by their substantial Georgian house, the Big House, in Burslem, which was built in 1751.

were major shareholders in the Caldon Canal Company. The minutiae of their business are recorded, and consequently they are an excellent case study of the progress of industrialization in the mid 18th century.

A very good record of the brothers' manufactured output is preserved. More than 260 different vessel types are listed in their account book. These were mostly of white salt-glazed stoneware, but there were also dipped and mottled wares, and they began to manufacture creamware as the demand for it increased around 1760. The brothers traded widely within the Potteries, buying wares from more than 20 local potters while supplying wares to 50 manufacturers.[46] This was not exceptional — the buying-in of wares to meet orders has always been standard practice for manufacturers.

The Wedgwoods' wares were distributed widely to customers — private individuals and dealers — in most major towns and cities, as well as in minor towns, with concentrations in London (37), Bristol (22), Newcastle upon Tyne (8), Sunderland (8), Manchester (6), and Liverpool and Gloucester each with four. They supplied all sectors of the market, from taverns to the houses of the nobility, many of whom are listed amongst their customers.

Ironically, John and Thomas Wedgwood's records also shed light on business at the opposite end of the scale. Their brother-in-law, Jonah Malkin, was a small-scale manufacturer of jugs, porringers, mugs and bowls in dipped salt-glazed stoneware. In

1748 he employed just three men and two boys in his works.[47] Even so, Malkin sold his wares far afield — in Bristol, Exeter, London, Plymouth, Gloucester, Liverpool and Ireland. In 1749, a consignment of two crates of ware, containing 26 dozen pint mugs marked 'T. Pope', was delivered to a Gloucester huckster, who in turn seems to have supplied a Cheltenham innkeeper, Thomas Pope. There is also evidence that Malkin was exporting his wares through Bristol.[48]

As pottery became the consumer's material of choice — at the tea table, at the dining table, and in the tavern — during the second half of the 18th century, so the share of the world market occupied by the British ceramics industry increased. The home market remained important, but by the end of the 18th century the Staffordshire industry and other home producers were dependent upon a growing export trade. In 1785 the Staffordshire potters Committee of Commerce claimed that 'Not less than five-sixths of earthenware manufactured in Staffordshire is exported'.[49] At that time Europe was the major market: between 1760 and 1780 Josiah Wedgwood, for example, was selling to Russia, Spain, Portugal, the Netherlands, France, Italy, Germany, Sweden and Turkey.[50] Surprisingly, with the exception of a few isolated studies, the vast and important European market for British ceramics has received little attention from scholars.

Other markets were also developing during the late 18th and early 19th centuries, significantly in Africa and Asia and the West Indies,[51] but it is the North American market which has received most attention. Exports to the USA increased from 1.2 million pieces in 1770 to almost 14 million pieces in 1830, although with major slumps at the time of the War of Independence, the 1807 trade embargo, and the War of 1812. Despite these setbacks the market continued to grow, but it was not until 1835 that the USA overtook Europe as the main consumer of English ceramics, taking 17.5 million pieces to Europe's 10.8 million.[52] The North American trade was well organized and sophisticated, with dealers acting as middle-men for the majority of the factories which were unable, themselves, to become directly involved in the marketing of their wares abroad. The various mechanisms of the trade, and the manner in which manufacturers learned of customer preferences, have been examined by Neil Ewins.[53]

During the 19th century British manufacturers became increasingly dependent upon their exports to North America for their survival. A number of factories came to rely solely upon the American trade, leaving them extremely vulnerable to events beyond their control. Major difficulties were experienced in north Staffordshire after the War of 1812 and one of the significant outcomes was a lowering of prices to re-establish the volume of trade at the end of the conflict.[54]

Nevertheless, the late 18th and 19th centuries were in the main a period of unparalleled growth for the British ceramics industry. This growth was achieved without major technological innovation within the pottery factories. Rather the resources and technology that were available to the factory owners were more efficiently harnessed. Growth was achieved by the employment of ever greater numbers of workers within larger factories,[55] by more rigid divisions of labour, by the rationalization of complex processes, by reducing costs and by not investing in new machinery, new buildings or comforts for the workers. Manufacture depended upon

Printing on thin paper, impressions transferred to the fired ware, and paper washed off.

FIGURE 5. Transfer printing (hot printing) with tissue paper was introduced around 1780 and remained important until the introduction of lithography in the 1880s. The process is simple, repetitive and labour intensive. Once again the importance of children in the factory is evident. (Source: *A Representation of the Manufacturing of Earthenware*, Anon. 1827)

a mixture of individuals' skills as throwers, turners, pressers, painters, transferers, placers and firemen, and upon a mass of unskilled labour, with little mechanized assistance. Machinery was virtually unknown before the mid 19th century, except in the preparation of clay bodies in the mill house. Machines to replace hand-pressing and throwing (the jigger and the jolley) were not developed until the 1840s, and even then were only slowly adopted. The main reason for this was simply that labour was both plentiful and cheap. Even in those larger factories which had introduced steam engines in their mills, the power for throwing wheels and turners' lathes continued to be provided by children and women.[56] In most factories the motive power for wheels and lathes was provided by children.

Children were employed in many areas of the factories, as jiggers and wheel turners, in mould running, dipping, balling, handle making, stilt-making, treading the lathe, painting and cutting transfers (the latter being girls' work), as well as in clay carrying and other manual duties. Many of these jobs were the heaviest and hardest in the factories, and most were injurious to health. The 1841 *Report on the Staffordshire Potteries by the Commission on the Employment of Children and Young Persons in Trades and Manufacturers* presents a clear picture of the work undertaken by children and of the conditions in which they worked.[57] By 1861 Staffordshire pottery factories employed 4,605 children under the age of ten (14% of the workforce), and of these 593 were five years old.[58] This situation continued until after 1864, when the Factory Extension Act restricted the maximum working hours to ten; no child under eight could be employed, and for those of eight to thirteen, a half-day had to be spent at school for every half-day at work. By 1871, the number of children under thirteen had fallen to 2,971.[59] Their unskilled labour was slowly replaced by the more widespread harnessing of steam power. Even so, the pottery industry remained highly labour intensive into the 20th century, as can be seen in the illustrated 1908 publication *Cup & Saucer Land*.[60]

Even by the end of the 18th century, a number of the leading factories each employed several hundreds of workers. In 1841 Scriven stated that the most numerous of the pottery factories were those employing from 50 to 800 workers: 'most of them have been erected many years, and as trade has increased, so the rooms appear to have increased in corresponding ratio. Some here and there, upon, around, and about the premises, so that there is neither order nor regularity, nor proportion'.[61] However, there were also many smaller factories, and as late as 1851 over 60% of factories employed fewer than 20 workers,[62] a level comparable with early to mid 18th-century workforces.

A dominant feature of the pottery trade from the mid 18th century has been a gradual fall in prices. Prices fall when output begins to exceed the market's capacity to consume, and there is evidence for this as early as 1759 when Josiah Wedgwood, complaining of the declining state of trade, wrote that white salt-glazed stoneware:

> . . . was the principal article of our manufacture; but this had been made a long time, and the prices were now reduced so low that the potters could not afford to bestow much expense upon it, or make it so good in any respect as the ware would otherwise admit of; and with regard to elegance of form, that was an object very little attended to.
>
> The article next in consequence to stoneware was an imitation of tortoise-shell, but as no improvement had been made in this branch of manufacture for several years, the consumer had grown nearly tired of it; and though the price had been lowered from time to time in order to increase the sale, the expedient did not answer . . .[63]

George Miller's pioneering work has shown how, from as early as 1770, manufacturers were attempting to counter falling prices by price fixing.[64] By agreeing to fixed price lists, leading potters determined the level below which the prices of wares would not fall. However, their general lack of success in preventing falling prices can be seen in the frequent revisions which were made to the lists,[65] with prices falling for all classes of wares from the 1796 onwards,[66] and the widespread practice of potters discounting their wares to wholesalers and retailers, especially when trade was bad.[67]

As prices fell, so economies in production were effected. Labour costs were reduced by the use of faster, cheaper methods of decoration.[68] These included, for example, more simple painted designs, such as 'sprig' patterns, which could be quickly produced by semi-skilled workers, often children, and the use of decoration applied by sponges cut to predetermined designs. Elsewhere, corners were cut and quality was compromised. The use of worn or re-engraved copper plates brought down costs but resulted in poorer quality printed designs. The size variations of printed patterns were reduced, with one print frequently being used to fit several sizes of vessel, and gaps being filled by splicing-in pieces of the design from elsewhere.

Miller has argued convincingly that prices fell as a result of production exceeding the capacity of the market to consume.[69] While falling prices might have played a part in encouraging the market to consume more ceramics, they also had a significant

FIGURE 6. Pearlware plate with transfer-printed 'willow pattern' in blue. 'Willow' quickly became the most popular printed pattern for table wares, a popularity which has endured to the present. Date, *c.* 1820.

impact upon the types of ceramics consumed. Declining prices were most marked for decorated ceramics — especially printed wares — with the differential between these and undecorated wares being greatly reduced (Fig. 6). So, with the cost of decorated ceramics of all types falling during the first half of the 19th century, they were more likely to be purchased by the less well-to-do customer, for whom they might once have been too expensive.

Any broadening of the ceramics market benefited the Staffordshire manufacturers. Their great success during the 19th century was to capture the vast middle and lower sections of the market, by mass-producing ever greater quantities of wares that could be sold ever more cheaply. Contemporary accounts of the industry[70] emphasize the 'common earthenware', the 'ordinary classes of earthenware', 'the usual classes of useful articles', and so on, which constituted the main production of most factories in north Staffordshire for home and foreign markets.

However, most recent works on ceramics have been blind to the true nature of the industry and its market, and have ignored the reasons for its very existence. They have emphasized the importance of style and fashion, the tastes of the wealthy and influential, and the high-class products of a few exceptional factories. The result is that our view of consumption is dominated by the material culture of the middle class, and the achievements of a small number of well-documented and well-researched factories overshadow the contribution of their numerous yet little-known neighbours.

A more holistic view of the pottery industry in north Staffordshire, and in Great Britain as a whole, is clearly needed. The work of individual manufacturers is, of course, important, but without contextualization can be misleading. The context must extend to the dynamics within the industry and the relationships between factories, and it must embrace the range of social and economic factors which spurred the industry's development, and which determined its relationship with consumers. Indeed, many of the factors which influenced consumption had their roots in the industrial process — significantly the cost of manufacture and, following on from this, the cost of the product to the consumer.

The industrialization of ceramic manufacture was a complex process, involving new processes and new wares, and increases in the scale of production, the number of factories and workers employed, and in the volume of output. These were not accompanied by the extensive use of machinery, and the industry remained labour-intensive to the end of the 19th century. The availability of cheap labour kept costs low and contributed to the industry's success. It is clear that the home market was well organized by the beginning of the 18th century, but that exports were also important by this time. By the early 19th century the substantial European and north American trades sustained the industry. Clearly, the industry did not develop in isolation, and it can only be properly understood in the context of its markets and its consumers. Once this has been recognized, the interdependence of production and consumption becomes clear.

ACKNOWLEDGEMENTS

I extend my thanks to colleagues at the Potteries Museum & Art Gallery, Stoke-on-Trent, and particularly to Miranda Goodby; their support and patience have made this paper a reality. I acknowledge particularly the work of George Miller; his many stimulating presentations have been a source of great inspiration.

David Barker, The Potteries Museum & Art Gallery, Bethesda Street, Hanley, Stoke-on-Trent ST1 3DE, UK

NOTES

[1] Hudson 1992, 175–80; Weatherill 1996, 20–21.
[2] Barker 1999.
[3] Courtney 1997, 98–99.
[4] Courtney, this volume.
[5] But see Baker 1991, Celoria 1973, Barker 1991 and 1998.
[6] Weatherill 1986, 138–39.
[7] The collective name adopted for the districts around the six towns of Stoke-upon-Trent, Hanley, Burslem, Tunstall, Fenton and Longton.
[8] For example, Celoria & Kelly 1973; Kelly 1968; Mountford 1975a & b; Kelly & Greaves 1974.
[9] Kelly 1973, 17–18; Kelly 1974, 19.
[10] At, for example, Jamestown where butter pots occur in contexts of the 1610s, and at the Maine site

where butter pots have been found in a context of 1620–30.
[11] The earliest dated piece of white salt-glazed stoneware, in the Burnap Collection at the William Rockhill Nelson Gallery in Kansas City, bears the date 1720.
[12] Copeland 1972.
[13] Saggars are containers made of heavily grogged marl in which vessels were placed for protection during both firings. Their use in Britain goes back to the 16th century at least.
[14] Weatherill 1971, 20.
[15] Shaw 1829, 166.
[16] Ibid.
[17] Baker 1991, 8.
[18] Weatherill 1971, 59–72.
[19] Ibid., 38.

[20] The so-called Ivy House Works, Josiah Wedgwood's first factory in Burslem, still had just two ovens at the time of its demolition in 1835. This is by no means unusual even later into the century.

[21] Rodney Hampson, unpublished manuscript 'Shelton Farm Potworks — The Documentary Evidence'.

[22] Grant 1983, 39.

[23] Meteyard 1965, 190.

[24] Mountford 1972b, 176. Such descriptions of pottery-making premises have the feel of the 'generic' about them, but even the general inclusion of terms such as warehouses, throwing houses, etc., is significant.

[25] Halfpenny 1997, 247.

[26] Thomas Whieldon's Account and Memorandum Book (The Potteries Museum & Art Gallery, unpublished).

[27] Shaw 1829, 151.

[28] Reilly 1992, 3.

[29] McKendrick 1982.

[30] Weatherill 1986, 138–39.

[31] At Bow, for example. See Adams & Redstone 1981, 21–22.

[32] Surviving examples of these are usually initialled and dated, and frequently signed.

[33] Meteyard 1865, 191–92.

[34] Potters' petition to Parliament, 1762, in Mountford 1971, 11.

[35] Young 1769.

[36] Thomas 1971, 13.

[37] McKendrick 1982, 103.

[38] Weatherill 1971, 80–81.

[39] Weatherill 1986, 206–14.

[40] Hampson 1996.

[41] Staffordshire County Record Office d/4842, quoted in Mountford 1971, 11.

[42] *A View of the Advantages of Inland Navigations* (1765), quoted in Hawke-Smith 1985, 28.

[43] *Williamson's Liverpool Advertiser* (8 August 1777).

[44] Weatherill 1971, 65–66.

[45] Mountford 1972a.

[46] Ibid., 77.

[47] Ibid., 55, 67.

[48] Ibid., 82–83.

[49] Resolution in the Committee's minute book of 22 February 1785, quoted in Thomas 1971, 116.

[50] Thomas 1971, 116.

[51] Ibid.

[52] Ewins 1997, 6.

[53] Ewins 1997.

[54] Miller 1991, 2; Miller 1996, 6.

[55] Burchill & Ross 1977, 27. Employment in the 19th-century north Staffordshire industry rose from 20,000 in 1835, to 25,000 in 1850, 30,000 in 1861 and 34,651 in 1987.

[56] The Spode factory was one of the first to use steam power and remained one of the largest users. Even here, apart from the mill, steam was used only for two wheels and ten lathes.

[57] Scriven 1843.

[58] Baker 1991, 66.

[59] Ibid., 67.

[60] Graham 1908.

[61] Scriven 1843, 13.

[62] Burchill & Ross 1977, 25.

[63] Wedgwood's Experiment Book, quoted in Mankowitz 1966, 27.

[64] Miller 1980; Miller 1991; Miller 1994.

[65] Miller 1980, 20–21; Miller 1994, 7.

[66] Miller 1994, 17.

[67] Miller 1991, 1–4.

[68] Miller 1994, 28–30.

[69] Ibid., 7–8.

[70] Such as Jewitt 1878.

BIBLIOGRAPHY

Adams, E. & Redstone, D. 1981, *Bow Porcelain*, London: Faber.

Baker, D. 1991, *Potworks*, London: RCHME.

Barker, D. 1991, *William Greatbatch — a Staffordshire Potter*, London: Jonathan Horne.

Barker, D. 1998, 'Bits and Bobs — the development of kiln furniture in the 18th-century Staffordshire Pottery Industry', *English Ceramic Circle Transactions* 16:3, 318–41.

Barker, D. 1999, 'The Ceramic Revolution 1650–1850', in Egan, G. & Michael, R. L. (eds), *Old and New Worlds*, Oxford: Oxbow, 226–34.

Burchill, F. & Ross, R. 1977, *A History of the Potters' Union*, Stoke-on-Trent: CATU.

Celoria, F. 1973, 'Ceramic machinery of the 19th century in the Potteries and other parts of Britain', *Staffordshire Archaeology* 2, 11–48.

Celoria, F. A. S. & Kelly, J. H. 1973, *A Post-medieval pottery site with a kiln base found off Albion Square, Hanley, Stoke-on-Trent*, City of Stoke-on-Trent Museum Archaeological Society Report 4.

Copeland, R. 1972, *A Short History of pottery raw materials and the Cheddleton Flint Mill*, Hanley: Cheddleton Flint Mill Industrial Heritage Trust.

Courtney, P. 1997, 'Ceramics and the History of Consumption: Pitfalls and Prospects', *Medieval Ceramics* 21, 95–108.

Ewins, N. 1997, '*Supplying the Present Wants of Our Yankee Cousins . . .': Staffordshire Ceramics and the American Market 1775–1880*, Journal of Ceramic History 15.

Graham, Revd M. 1908, *Cup and Saucer Land*, London: Madgwick, Houlston & Co.

Grant, A. 1983, *North Devon Pottery: The Seventeenth Century*, Exeter: University of Exeter.

Greaves, S. J. 1976, 'A Post-medieval excavation in Woodbank Street, Burslem, Stoke-on-Trent', *City of Stoke-on-Trent Museum Arch. Soc. Report* 10.

Halfpenny, P. A. 1997, 'Thomas Whieldon: his life and work', *English Ceramic Circle Transactions* 16:2, 237–54.

Hampson, R. 1996, 'Shelton Farm Potworks: the documentary evidence' (unpublished paper).

Hawke-Smith, C. 1985, *The Making of the Six Towns*, Stoke-on-Trent: City Museum & Art Gallery.

Hudson, P. 1992, *The Industrial Revolution*, London: Arnold.

Jewitt, L. 1878, *The Ceramic Art of Great Britain*, London: Virtue & Co.

Kelly, J. H. 1969, 'The Hill Top site, Burslem', *City of Stoke-on-Trent Museum Arch. Soc. Report* 3.

Kelly, J. H. 1973, 'A rescue excavation on the site of Swan Bank Methodist Church, Burslem, Stoke-on-Trent', *City of Stoke-on-Trent Museum Arch. Soc. Report* 5.

Kelly, J. H. & Greaves, S. J. 1974, 'The excavation of a kiln base in Old Hall Street, Hanley, Stoke-on-Trent', *City of Stoke-on-Trent Museum Arch. Soc. Report* 6.

McKendrick, N. 1982, 'Josiah Wedgwood and the Commercialization of the Potteries', in McKendrick, N., Brewer, J. & Plumb, J. H. (eds), *The Birth of a Consumer Society: The Commercialization of Eighteenth-Century England*, London: Europa Books, 100–45.

Mankowitz, W. 1966, *Wedgwood*, London: Spring Books.

Meteyard, E. 1865, *The Life of Josiah Wedgwood*, London: Hunt & Blackett.

Miller, G. L. 1980, 'Classification and Economic Scaling of 19th Century Ceramics', *Historical Archaeology* 14, 1–40.

Miller, G. L. 1991, 'A Revised Set of CC Index Values for Classification and Economic Scaling of English Ceramics from 1787 to 1880', *Historical Archaeology* 25:1, 1–25.

Miller, G. L. 1994, 'Demand Entropy as a Byproduct of Price Competition: a Case Study from Staffordshire' (unpublished paper for the School of American Research seminar The Historical Archaeology of Capitalism, August 1994).

Miller, G. L. 1996, 'War and Pots: The impact of wars on ceramic consumption patterns' (unpublished paper).

Miller, G. L., Martin A. Smart, & Dickinson, N. S. 1994, 'Changing Consumption Patterns. English Ceramics and the American Market from 1770 to 1840', in Hutchins, C. E. (ed.), *Everyday Life in the Early Republic*, Winterthur: Henry Francis du Pont Winterthur Museum, 219–48.

Mountford, A. R. 1971, *The Illustrated Guide to Staffordshire Salt-Glazed Stoneware*, London: Barrie & Jenkins.

Mountford, A. R. 1972a, 'John Wedgwood, Thomas Wedgwood and Jonah Malkin, Potters of Burslem' (unpublished MA thesis, University of Keele).

Mountford, A. R. 1972b, 'Thomas Whieldon's Manufactory at Fenton Vivian', *English Ceramic Circle Transactions* 8:2, 164–82.

Mountford, A. R. 1975a, 'The Sadler teapot manufactory site, Burslem, Stoke-on-Trent, Staffs', *City of Stoke-on-Trent Museum Arch. Soc. Report* 7, 1–20.

Mountford, A. R. 1975b, 'The Marquis of Granby Hotel site, Burslem, Stoke-on-Trent', *City of Stoke-on-Trent Museum Arch. Soc. Report 7*, 21–27.

Reilly, R. 1992, *Josiah Wedgwood*, London: Macmillan.

Scriven, S. 1843, *Report by Samuel Scriven, Esq., on the Employment of Children and Young Persons in the District of the STAFFORDSHIRE POTTERIES; and on the actual State, Condition, and Treatment of such Children and Young Persons*, Commission on the Employment of Children and Young Persons in Trades and Manufactures, 1841; reprinted as *Children in the Potteries* (parts 1 & 2), Staffordshire Study Books 3 and 4, 1975, Stafford: Staffordshire County Council.

Shaw, S. 1829, *The History of the Staffordshire Potteries*, Hanley: Simeon Shaw.

Thomas, J. 1971, *The Rise of the Staffordshire Potteries*, Bath: Adams & Dart.

Weatherill, L. 1971, *The Pottery Trade and North Staffordshire 1660 — 1760*, Manchester: Manchester University Press.

Weatherill, L. 1986, *The Growth of the Pottery Industry in England 1660–1815*, New York: Garland Publishing.

Weatherill, L. 1996, *Consumer Behaviour & Material Culture in Britain 1660–1760*, 2nd edn, London: Routledge.

Young, A. 1769, *A Six Months Tour through the North of England*, London.

RURAL BURIAL AND REMEMBRANCE: CHANGING LANDSCAPES OF COMMEMORATION

By HAROLD MYTUM

INTRODUCTION

The rural graveyard is a category of evidence that might, at first sight, seem to have little to do with industry. This is, however, far from the case. Gravestones were produced within craft traditions progressively influenced by industrial methods, and they were increasingly consumed by those who worked in rural industries, or provisioned them. Rural churchyards and burial grounds offer rich opportunities for examining social, economic and technological change as well as shifts in ideology.[1] The monuments are relatively well-dated items of material culture, though not always as closely as some have assumed.[2] Moreover, most memorials have not moved much if at all from their place of erection, and they are linked to named individuals for whom much contextual information can be derived from the stones themselves and other sources. Thus, subtle patterns of variability and change can be identified, and the effects of industrialization can be considered and explained.

Three themes have been selected for brief treatment to illustrate the quality of evidence and some aspects of interpretation that can be gained from rural graveyards and their memorials.

1. Gravestone manufacture changed from folk art to standardized craft production.
2. Increased gravestone consumption dramatically affected the appearance of churchyards.
3. New types of landscape were added to the repertoire of burial areas.

No technological or economic determinist model for cultural change is applied here, but rather a recognition that individual and group conscious and unconscious motivations play a part in the construction of the material culture under study. These need to be set within local, regional, national and indeed international forces which included economic, technological, artistic and religious aspects. At the level of analysis offered here, the larger scale forces are identified, though the phenomena can be examined at a small scale level to see how variation within the trends were played out by individuals and groups and formed parts of their strategies of allegiance or differentiation. Each theme can only be briefly outlined here using a small region or a single graveyard, but it will illustrate the relevance and potential of mortuary evidence.

CHANGES IN MEMORIAL PRODUCTION

Gravestone manufacture can be seen to change during the 18th and early 19th century from one expressed through elements of folk art to one where standardization played a greater role. This trend has been frequently stated in both Britain and North America[3] though surprisingly little has been published documenting it in detail, or considering the mechanisms by which it came about. Too often, a romantic art-historical attitude has bemoaned the loss of the carver's skill and personalized contribution, and the factors behind this change have not been considered. Most scholars have therefore concentrated their efforts on the earlier craftsmen.[4] In Britain in particular, only a few have examined later products in any detail, and then often only the more elaborate of the standard memorials.[5] The change from one style of production to another has, surprisingly, been little investigated.

James Deetz saw the change from death's heads to cherubs in New England as part of the package of material culture changes which accompanied the Enlightenment, the move exemplified later still to urn and willow motifs within a more symmetrical design and no longer a folk art tradition.[6] Whilst there is much in support of ideological changes affecting material culture, other factors regarding the changes in production methods, sources of raw materials available, and other aspects of attitudes and expectations of consumers should also be considered. Many examples of the change from cherubs to urns (sometimes with willows) can be seen in Britain, but the shift from folk art to more uniform craft products is not coincident with this shift in motifs, and deserves more attention.

The change in production away from folk art headstones in Leicestershire and Nottinghamshire has been briefly studied in seminal papers by Herbert and Barley,[7] and has also been noted by that doyen of gravestone studies, Burgess.[8] A recent limited programme of fieldwork by the author allows these classic and visually stunning memorials to be used as an example of a folk art tradition which was replaced by a craft tradition with an increasing emphasis on standardization and participation in national, if not international, trends in memorial design and production.

In the East Midlands there is an excellent, widespread survival of slate headstones, but it is possible to demonstrate the three phases of changes in local production through just one graveyard, that of Hickling, Nottinghamshire. The earliest external memorials in any numbers were immediately high quality folk art, then moved onto more sophisticated craft production with much individual flair, and then to a phase of local production where standardization was dominant. The craftsmen remained competent but worked within a very much more constrained framework, even though memorials tended to become larger.

FIGURE 1. Slate headstones of phase one, Hickling, Nottinghamshire. Thomas Hardy (d. 1720); John Smith (no date given but early 18th century).

The first phase of the East Midlands tradition was a rustic folk art with cherubs, but often with a remembrance of mortality in the associated text and in minor symbols (Fig. 1). The stone of Thomas Hardy is an example of this type. The text 'MENTO MORI' was placed above the cherub, and an hourglass and cross bones were carved in the top corners. Beneath were panels containing text. One common arrangement was a panel containing the biographical details of the deceased in false relief lettering, and then a further panel with an epitaph in incised lettering, as with John Smith's stone. Despite the clear quality of the carving and a plan for the overall design, with several types of lettering produced for each of the panels, there was little detailed anticipation in the laying out of text within each panel. Letters had to be squeezed in at the end of lines, sometimes above or below; the year of death is missing. The text itself is an instructive one regarding the deceased's view of the world: 'The world's a city full of crooked streets, Death is ye market place where all men meets. If life were merchandise yt men cold buy, The rich would often live and poor men die.' Often these headstones were quite small, well under a metre high.

The second phase, during the middle of the 18th century, was one where some of the calligraphic skills already exemplified in earlier work were taken on to new heights of elaboration (Fig. 2). Headstones now had cartouches of varying shapes, and elaborate lettering, a change described by Burgess as from 'austere to exuberant'.[9] Most elaboration was now by incision, and the calligraphy was very complex and

FIGURE 2. Slate headstones of phase two, Hickling, Nottinghamshire. John Collishaw (d. 1756); Elizabeth Butler (d. 1766); William Mann (d. 1759); Robert Collishaw (d. 1798).

varied throughout the inscription, though often only incised with very shallow lines, as exemplified by the headstone to John Collishaw (d. 1756). The lettering was now carefully planned out, and symmetrical. Other design elements also reinforced this balanced effect, as with the skull and cross bones on each side of Elizabeth Butler's stone. The headstones were now taller, allowing room for the calligraphic flourishes, but also making a bigger impact within the graveyard. Some, such as that of William Mann (d. 1759), were carved with shapes other than a flat top, again attracting attention. Another way in which individuality was achieved by the late 18th century was by the use of small classical figures carved in deep false relief, often in oval panels, as with the monument to Robert Collishaw (d. 1798). There was still considerable individuality, but aspects of the lettering and layout were losing their earlier creativity.

In the third phase, headstones increased still further in size, and by the early 19th century the impact of printed lettering styles was apparent (Fig. 3). In the case of the headstone to Joseph Davis, died 1819, the introductory 'ERECTED' was derived from typography, and the margins to the rectangular panel no longer displayed the calligraphic flourishes of earlier borders but again designs familiar from the printed media. Another example of edging akin to printed material frames is the memorial to Sarah Davis (d. 1841). The local features still lived on in some aspects of the incised lettering, such as the introduction 'Sacred' in this case, but the stones were much more within a national style. Simple lettering and the appearance of foliage on the slate headstone of Elizabeth Featherstone (d. 1862) were comparable to numerous occurrences on sandstone and limestone elsewhere at the same time. There was no longer any need to cover all parts of the surface of the headstone with pattern; text could stand out clearly from the smooth surface of the slate as text is legible against the plain page. Some of the memorials had no trace of the local traditions at all; Joseph Wild (d. 1857) was no longer identified with a local cultural tradition through death. He was part of a national, indeed imperial, culture; stones with designs like his could be seen from Australia to Scotland. The production of such memorials now followed a workshop practice that was more akin to that in a factory, with blanks for some types prepared at the quarry, and details of the designs chosen from pattern books.[10]

The first generations of clients for stone memorials were happy with small headstones, as they were the only memorials in the graveyard apart from the chest tombs of the more wealthy, and they could be easily seen. As time went by, memorials became taller, not really to allow for more text (a lot of words had been packed onto the early stones) but for greater visibility (Fig. 4). In the middle phase this space was filled with calligraphic flourishes, but in the last phase it was mere bulk that was being emphasized with the most substantial headstones. Individual creativity was made subservient to a more basic form of consumerism and display. As the graveyard filled with monuments, size was the most obvious way to attract attention.

At a later date still, other materials in a range of forms became widely available. They provided yet another strategy by which the late Victorian and Edwardian family could signal their identity through perhaps a locally distinctive (though in a wider sense, ubiquitous) monument form and material. Marilyn Palmer and Peter Neaverson have noted how the Dukes of Rutland kept the domestic hosiery industry out of the

FIGURE 3.   Slate headstones of phase three, Hickling, Nottinghamshire. Joseph Davis (d. 1819);
Sarah Davis (d. 1841); Elizabeth Featherstone (d. 1862); Joseph Wild (d. 1857).

FIGURE 4. View of the Gill family plot, Hickling, Nottinghamshire. Small phase one stones can be seen with a larger phase two stone. Some headstones belonging to phase three, larger still, can be seen in the row behind.

Vale of Belvoir;[11] they could not stop the effects of industrialization on the memorials of their tenants.

INCREASED CONSUMPTION

The second theme involves increased patterns of consumption which raised the proportion of the population that had memorials erected, and so dramatically affected the appearance of churchyards.

During the late 18th century, memorials begin to appear in some numbers in graveyards in many parts of the country, and the numbers steadily increase throughout the 19th century. This pattern of growth was impressive everywhere, and can be seen in Britain, Ireland, North America and Australia. Undoubtedly in some areas there was significant population expansion, but most of the increase can be linked to the greater proportion of the population having lasting memorials. This raises two issues: was the increase due to a change in demand (more people wanted stones), or supply (stones were available for the first time)? Just as supply and demand are intimately linked, so is the answer. Changes in production methods made stones more readily available, but also the increased level of materiality within people's lives led to an expectation of a more permanent memorial.

Sarah Tarlow has studied the growth in the popularity of gravestones in Orkney, but set within a wider context.[12] She suggests that the late 18th-century boom in gravestones was due to developing middle-class feelings concerning grief, and the relationship between the living and the dead. She does not consider that early stones in Orkney reflected any emulation of the aristocracy with their existing internal memorials. This may have been so in Orkney and also was the case in parts of Ireland,[13] where the early stones were very simple if not crude. In some other areas such as the Cotswolds, however, many stones were decorated with cartouches and designs closely linked to those of internal memorials and emulation may have been an important factor. Complex dynamics were clearly operating in different regions, and we have hardly begun even to define these yet alone explain them.

Whilst Tarlow correctly emphasizes client demand, factors other than emotion played a part in creating and moulding that demand. Moreover, supply must have been effective (and usually not by home-made means), otherwise the stones would not survive in such numbers. The issue of supply still needs much more detailed analysis, as do the changes in form of memorials which must be linked to this increased scale of production. These new forms, in their turn, were clearly acceptable to the clients, and suggest a changing expectation of what memorials could and should look like. Regional tastes and expectations were clearly important in the early phases where the folk art traditions can be seen to vary from one area to another.

The extent of the gravestone boom can be most clearly identified by comparing the numbers of people recorded on stones from a surveyed graveyard with the numbers interred as recorded in the parish burial registers. In this way the proportion of deaths that become commemorated in a physical way in the burial ground can be calculated. The impact this increased memorialization has on the landscape of commemoration varies, depending on the average number of people recorded on a stone, and what sort of memorial is chosen. Three interconnected variables, changing over time, affected the appearance of the burial ground:

1. Proportion of people commemorated on memorials;
2. Number of new memorials (and their types);
3. Average number of people commemorated on a memorial.

These trends can be examined using the example a large rural parish in north Pembrokeshire, that of Nevern. There is a large graveyard and full surviving burial registers for the 18th, 19th and 20th centuries, considered here from the 1700s to the end of the 1970s to give a good perspective of long term trends.

Burials follow a series of peaks and troughs throughout the 18th century, then level off at around 150 per decade until a long period of decline in burials begins in the 1870s.[14] This reflects the gradual decline in rural population due to increased efficiency in farming practice which included the introduction of machinery,[15] and also the decline in the maritime importance of the nearby small town of Newport.[16] Most of the people buried at Nevern were from the parish, but we know from the gravestone inscriptions that quite a number styled themselves as of Newport, or of other nearby parishes. The reasons for this small-scale migration between burial ground and parochial place of residence has yet to be explored, but for the trends examined here it can be ignored.

Against the pattern of burials can be compared the number of individuals commemorated on the memorials and for which there is a date of death. Other deceased were commemorated on the stones, particularly the young, but before the 20th century children were often only recorded by name; sometimes just the number of family members who died in infancy is mentioned, often after the commemoration to the mother. Because there are no dates of death, they cannot be placed on any graphs or tables. Also, some individuals will be remembered on stones, but are not necessarily buried in that graveyard. The most obvious cases of this in north Pembrokeshire (though less so at Nevern) are mariners lost at sea far away, but it can also apply to other deaths.

There is another caveat regarding the origins of the graveyard memorial boom in that just over 100 of the 575 memorials could not be read with a date when the graveyard was recorded. Many of these were overgrown, others badly eroded. Since the survey of Nevern there has also been considerable clearance of undergrowth in the graveyard by the parish, and new techniques to recover inscriptions are being applied, so the number of illegible stones is gradually being reduced. However, it is possible that erosion, and any loss of memorials by tidying up the churchyard and lying them flat or burying them, may have disproportionately reduced the number of early stones incorporated in the data used here.

Clear patterns have emerged despite the various potential difficulties with the data.[17] The cumulative graph of currently dated memorials suggests that the trends identified are likely to represent past reality, not just factors of survival and legibility.

For most of the 18th century almost no one had a permanent memorial in the graveyard. The small numbers from the 1770s shows the beginnings of a trend, but this took a generation to take hold. The numbers commemorated began to rise sharply from the 1790s and apart from a dip in the 1840s, continued to a peak in the 1860s. This shows that over the whole of the first half of the 19th century an increasing proportion of the burials were being commemorated. After the 1860s, the number of commemorations fell, but the number of burials fell even faster, so that higher proportions of burials were commemorated until about the turn of the century. Thereafter, the proportion of burials to memorials remained roughly constant, with around two thirds of burials commemorated.

The number of new memorials closely mirrored the trends in commemoration. This shows that the average number of people commemorated on a memorial did not change greatly over time, with about two people for whom we have dates of death being remembered on each. Only in the 1970s do we have the numbers of deaths commemorated and memorials coming together. This is due to the tendency to list husband and wife at most on a stone, and the increased numbers of cremations for which individual plaques set flush with the ground are used at Nevern.

It is thus possible to observe at Nevern a pattern of gravestone accumulation which led to the filling up of the graveyard. An extension was opened in 1930,[18] though burials did continue in family graves, and now cremations can be placed in the old graveyard. The most dramatic changes in the landscape of commemoration would have happened during the first half of the 19th century, though the demand for new monuments continued to be strong, hence the need for the extension. The historic graveyard is now quite full, and will not fill further with obtrusive memorials because of the extension. But clearly the graveyard is now a very different landscape from that of the mid 19th century, and vastly different from that of the late 18th century.

The social and economic range of people having memorials was broad by the late 19th century. By examining some of the deceased as they were described in the census prior to their deaths, the range of occupations can be noted. These are given here merely as examples to show the range of people who could afford stones, and also chose to have them; insufficient research has yet been conducted to give any statistical insight into this matter. Thus, from the 1851 Census four farmers, three agricultural labourers, two millers, a carpenter, cabinet maker, shopkeeper, stone mason, vicar and magistrate in the parish all acquire gravestones after their deaths which have been identified in the survey. By the 1881 Census the range is even greater, with thirteen farmers, seven agricultural labourers, four mariners, two farm bailiffs, two stone masons, two carpenters, two tailors, two corn millers, and a clog maker, innkeeper, blacksmith, saddler and woolage manufacturer.

It should also be noted that monumental forms shifted from family chest tombs for major families, to a wider range of the population (including those families) having headstones. Not only was the graveyard visibly filling up, but monument styles were changing. The zones of the churchyard used for burial also shifted over time, but the implications of increased popularity of memorialization, and the rise of different burial settings, is the subject of the third theme.

NEW LANDSCAPES

New types of rural landscapes of commemoration were developed during the 19th century. Whilst the development of urban cemeteries has attracted much attention, particularly from architectural and landscape historians,[19] the ways in which it has been linked to issues of health[20] are of less relevance in the countryside. The matter of Nonconformist burial beyond the control of Anglican clergy was also a concern in urban cemetery foundation,[21] but the development of Nonconformist burial grounds in a rural context has only just begun to be considered.[22]

The new locales for rural burial altered the wider geography of remembrance, and provided more potential choices for interment. They thus took away some of the demand from the traditional churchyards, but this was still insufficient to stem the requirements of further grave spaces. With the increased proportion of the population having durable grave markers, churchyards gradually became full. The response in the case of the established church was to be more effective in utilizing existing space, and often the addition of extensions to existing graveyards, and a fine example of this can be seen at Kellington, North Yorkshire (Fig. 5).

Kellington church stands on a low hillock a few hundred metres beyond the present village, and is sited in this low lying landscape in a position which is both relatively visible and above the flood level. Survey of the surface topography and monuments in the churchyard has allowed the history of burial to be elucidated over

FIGURE 5.   Kellington church and graveyard, North Yorkshire.

the whole curtilage of the existing graveyard. This has been enhanced by a GIS system which has allowed the changes to be plotted decade by decade.[23]

The medieval burials have been found by excavation to concentrate on the southern side of the church, with many also at the east end, and quite a few to the west.[24] Here, very considerable inter-cutting can be seen in the most popular burial areas. In the early modern period, many of the more wealthy were buried inside the church, particularly down the nave and north aisles. Some parts of the churchyard were also used by major families: to the south, by the path leading to the porch, and also at the east end of the church. It is in these areas that the earliest exterior memorials can be found (Fig. 6). Grouped by family, these stones are now set flat in the ground as ledgers. However, from the profiles of the slabs and the presence of fragments of tomb panels by the churchyard walls, it is likely that many if not all were elaborate upstanding chest tombs. Thus, the approach to the church in the late 18th century would have been made by walking between several groups of tombs, each representing a local successful farming dynasty. Headstones do occur in the late 18th century, but they tend to be on the periphery of the distribution of memorials, suggesting that those who could only afford such stones were placed at the edges of the core area; the vast majority of burials lay unmarked.

The period of memorial expansion at Kellington occurred at the beginning of the 19th century, with a significant peak between 1860 and 1880 (Fig. 7). This was mirrored closely by the numbers of burials recorded on the stones, suggesting little

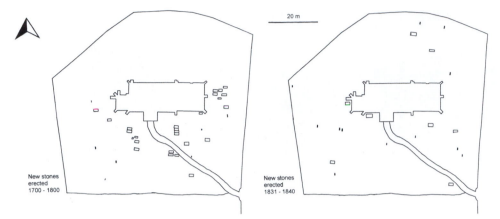

FIGURE 6. Kellington, North Yorkshire, graveyard plan. Left: stones first erected 1700–1800; Right: stones first erected 1831–40.

change over time in the average number of people (under two) recorded on each stone at this site. From the 1820s there was an average of at least two commemorations a year, and by the 1870s this had risen to five a year, and reached ten in the 1950s.

As soon as burial monuments were erected, plots were perceived as reserved, and only further members of the same family might be interred in that place. This led to an accelerating need for graveyard space which can be examined over the decades at Kellington. From the 1830s the previously neglected north side of the church was at last used for some marked burials, whilst infilling continued elsewhere (Fig. 6). Those plots used only for unmarked graves were, after sufficient time for the location to be forgotten, given over to a further cycle of burial which could then be marked by a stone. However, this was a strategy which could only last for a certain amount of time.

By the 1870s a graveyard extension to the south was opened, and a peak in gravestone erection occurred (Fig. 8) at a level which was not to be exceeded again until the 1940s. The extension was, unlike the original graveyard, a regular rectangular shape, designed to be divided up into plots in regular rows. Although this efficiency model was applied to the burial ground, it is clear from the distribution of memorials that, as with a public cemetery at that time, all plots were available for reservation or choice at time of need. In a single decade, monuments were placed in almost every single row of the extension. There was still the opportunity for families to have groups of plots in the rows. Many of the graves were marked not only by headstones but also kerbs; these were not decorative, but indicated the extent of the plot. Many kerbs are now overgrown, as their purpose has faded and the grounds management strategies hide them, but they emphasized the uniformity of plots, and the desire to mark off what was owned, to be used only by those entitled to burial there.

Access to the extension was directly west from the churchyard gate, but also from a path which can still be seen as a small depression running from the main

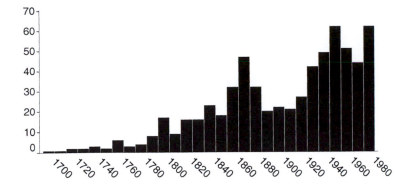

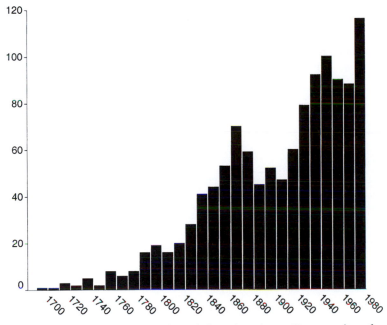

FIGURE 7. Kellington, North Yorkshire, bar charts. Top: number of memorials, by decade; bottom: number of deaths recorded on memorials, by decade.

church path a little south of the porch. This was the most direct route between the new area for graves and the church. The association between the church and burial ground was weaker because of the increased distance, but this path provided an important link to the church. The infilling of the extension continued for the next half century, with opportunistic use of the old graveyard also.

As the process of graveyard evolution continued, further land was required. A second extension, similar in size and shape, was added to the south of the first (Fig. 9).

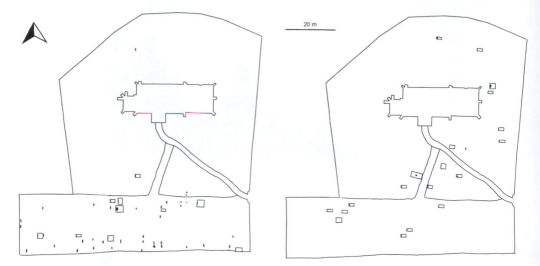

FIGURE 8.   Kellington, North Yorkshire, graveyard plan with first extension. Left: stones first erected 1871–80; Right: stones first erected 1911–20.

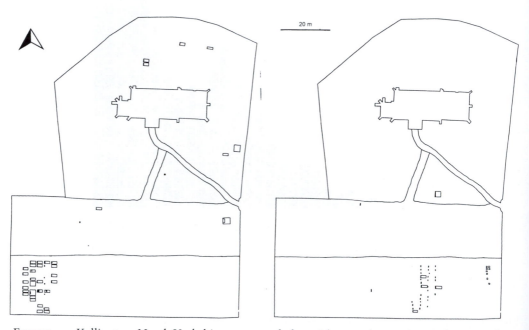

FIGURE 9.   Kellington, North Yorkshire, graveyard plan with second extension. Left: stones first erected 1931–40; Right: stones first erected 1971–80.

Access to the rows of graves was provided by a path along the north edge of the new extension, next to the line of the now removed boundary which had marked the southern edge of the graveyard following the first extension. Once again the new ground was measured out into rows of plots, but unlike the previous management strategy, plots were now allocated in chronological order, the memorials showing the concentration of burials in new plots for each decade (Fig. 8). Within the sight of the Eggborough power station in one direction and Ferrybridge in another, both using coal mined nearby, the 20th-century inhabitants of Kellington were buried according to a pattern extolled in industrial management. Just as the coal beneath the graveyard itself is mined away on mechanized faces that work in long straight lines, so the burials follow the same logic. Gone are the organic family groupings of the old graveyard, gone also are concepts of the organic community affirmed through reuse of burial ground.

The link between church and graveyard was further attenuated with the second extension, and with the placing of a separate gate at the southern end of the east wall by the road and parking space, those visiting graves do not have to go anywhere near the church. Indeed, in the case of cremations, which have been placed starting at the eastern end of the extension and are spreading west, the whole process of funeral and mourning need not involve any visit to the church at all. This third part of the graveyard is like that of a municipal cemetery in its management, appearance, and attitude to commemoration and mourning. The sense of community is in yet another way broken down to that of the individual — the spouse, parent or child.

Within the new burial locales of the 19th century, a different attitude to space was taken compared with earlier approaches to graveyard management. This can be noted in the vast majority of newly-established Nonconformist burial grounds and rural cemeteries as well as churchyard extensions. The overwhelming attitude within these additions to the repertoire of burial areas was one of efficiency, an attitude to space engendered by the maxims of industry. Plots were carefully laid out in numbered rows, like rows of workers' housing. By the 20th century, concerns over familial association over generations were overridden in many cases by the perceived need to organize space. Serried ranks of grave plots advanced across the new areas, an army standing to attention, wave after wave added as the decades passed. This is an attitude which persists to this day, for inhumations and cremations alike, in many though not all forms of burial ground.

Changes in attitude by the church authorities during the 20th century to burial space and the types of monuments allowed has been a major factor in the changes exemplified here by Kellington.[25] However, the individual clients had plenty of choice which was not exercised within the rules; indeed there are systems in place to allow for atypical monuments to be approved, yet few have considered this opportunity. Clearly the population has for over a century accepted and even welcomed the structuring principles imposed upon them.

Alternative burial modes are developing in some parts of Britain, such as woodland burial, which at least give the impression of a less regimented and more natural context for interment and remembrance, though they have to be commercially viable. This is an example, perhaps, of post-industrial reaction to death. For most, however, the existing alternatives are acceptable.

CONCLUSIONS

The landscape of commemoration can be seen to have changed as vividly as workers' housing or settlement layout as the processes of industrialization and that concomitant, increased consumerism, took hold through the later 18th and 19th centuries. Every community, however remote and rural, was caught up in these trends of industrialization and consumerism. They are archaeologically manifested not only in changes in the domestic architecture and ceramic assemblages in even poor households, but in their places of worship and their final resting places after their lives of toil. Many were still not represented by memorials, but a much larger proportion were. Changes in production and selection of memorials have been identified, increased memorialization has been quantified, and new arenas for burial and remembrance have been plotted. Through burial grounds a link can be made to many named workers, as well as landowners and capitalists, with their hopes for remembrance living on through their gravestones. Within this research they are remembered in a manner which they would never have dreamt of, and their lives can be appreciated in new and refreshing ways.

ACKNOWLEDGEMENTS

I would like to thank all who helped in the survey of the burial grounds reported here, especially the Center for Field Research volunteers and their supervisors Jackie Chester and Caroline Mytum at Nevern, and students from the Department of Archaeology, University of York, at Kellington. Computing work on the Kellington data was undertaken by Helen Fenwick and Robert Evans.

Harold Mytum, Department of Archaeology, University of York, Kings Manor, York yo1 7ep, UK

NOTES

[1] Mytum 2000.
[2] Mytum 2000a.
[3] Burgess 1963; Deetz & Dethlefsen 1967.
[4] Classic studies include Benes 1977, Ludwig 1966, and Slater 1996 in New England, and Chater 1976, 1977, Elliott 1978, Willsher & Hunter 1978, and Willsher 1992, 1996 in Britain.
[5] Buckham 1999; Mytum 1999.
[6] Deetz 1977.
[7] Herbert 1944; Barley 1948.
[8] Burgess 1963.
[9] Burgess 1963, pl. 4.
[10] Buckham 1999; Burgess 1963, 124–26.
[11] Palmer & Neaverson 1998, 19.

[12] Tarlow 1998.
[13] Mytum forthcoming b.
[14] Mytum 2002b.
[15] Jenkins 1971.
[16] Kilminster & Mytum 1987; Miles 1995, 79.
[17] Mytum 2002b.
[18] Miles 1998, 35.
[19] Brooks 1989; Curl 1972; Sloane 1991.
[20] Mytum 1989.
[21] Rugg 1998.
[22] Mytum 2002b.
[23] Mytum 1996.
[24] Mytum 1993.
[25] Stapleton & Burman 1976.

BIBLIOGRAPHY

Barley, M. W. 1948, 'Slate headstones in Nottinghamshire', *Thoroton Society Transactions* 52, 69–86.

Benes, P. 1977, *The Masks of Orthodoxy: Folk Gravestone Carving in Plymouth County, Massachusetts, 1689–1805*, Amherst: University of Massachusetts Press.

Brooks, C. 1989, *Mortal Remains: the history and present state of the Victorian and Edwardian cemetery*, Exeter: Wheaton Publishers.

Buckham, S. 1999, ' "The Men that Worked for England They Have Their Graves at Home": consumerist issues within the production and purchase of gravestones in Victorian York', in Tarlow, S. & West, S. (eds) *The Familiar Past? Archaeologies of Later Historical Britain 1550–1950*, London: Routledge, 199–214.

Burgess, F. 1963, *English Churchyard Memorials*, London: Lutterworth Press.

Chater, A. O. 1976, 'Early Cardiganshire Gravestones', *Archaeologia Cambrensis* 125, 140–61.

Chater, A. O. 1977, 'Early Cardiganshire Gravestones', *Archaeologia Cambrensis* 126, 116–38.

Curl, J. 972, *The Victorian Celebration of Death*, Newton Abbot: David and Charles.

Deetz, J. F. 1977, *In Small Things Forgotten: The Archaeology of Early American Life*, Garden City: Anchor Books.

Deetz, J. & Dethlefsen, E. 1967, 'Death's Head, Cherub, Urn and Willow', *Natural History* 76:3, 29–37.

Elliott, W. R. 1978, ' "Chest tombs" and "tea-caddies" by Cotswold and Severn', *Transactions of the Bristol and Gloucestershire Archaeological Society* 95, 68–85.

Herbert, A. 1944, 'Swithland slate headstones', *Transactions of the Leicestershire Archaeological Society* 22:3, 215–40.

Jenkins, D. 1971, *The Agricultural Community in South-West Wales at the Turn of the Twentieth Century*, Cardiff: University of Wales Press.

Kilminster, G. & Mytum, H. 1987, 'Mariners at Newport, Pembrokeshire: The Evidence from Gravestones', *Maritime Wales* 11, 7–27.

Ludwig, A. I. 1966, *Graven Images: New England Stonecarving and its Symbols, 1650–1815*, Middletown: Wesleyan University Press.

Miles, D. 1995, *The Ancient Borough of Newport in Pembrokeshire*, Haverfordwest: Cemais Publications.

Miles, D. 1998, *A Book on Nevern*, Llandysul: Gomer Press.

Mytum, H. 1989, 'Public health and private sentiment: the development of cemetery architecture and funerary monuments from the eighteenth century onwards', *World Archaeology* 21:2, 283–97.

Mytum, H. 1993, 'Kellington Church', *Current Archaeology* 133, 15–17.

Mytum, H. 1996, 'Intrasite Patterning and the Temporal Dimension using GIS: the example of Kellington Churchyard', in Kamermans. H. & Fennema, K. (eds) *Interfacing the Past. Computer applications and quantitative methods in archaeology CAA 95. Annalecta Praehistorica Leidensia* 28, Leiden, Institute of Prehistory, University of Leiden, 363–67.

Mytum, H. 1999, 'Welsh Cultural Identity in Nineteenth-century Pembrokeshire: the pedimented headstone as a graveyard monument', in Tarlow, S. & West, S. (eds) *The familiar past? Archaeologies of later historical Britain 1550–1950*, London: Routledge, 215–30.

Mytum, H. 2000, *Recording and Analysing Graveyards*, York: Council for British Archaeology Practical Handbook 15.

Mytum, H. 2002a, 'The Dating of Graveyard Memorials: evidence from the stones', *Post-medieval Archaeology*, 36, 1–38.

Mytum, H. 2002b, 'A comparison of nineteenth- and twentieth-century Anglican and Nonconformist memorials in North Pembrokeshire', *The Archaeological Journal*, 159, 194–241.

Mytum, H. forthcoming, 'Local traditions in early eighteenth-century commemoration: the headstone memorials from Balrothery, County Dublin, and their place in the evolution of Irish and British commemorative practice', *Proceedings of the Royal Irish Academy, Section C*.

Palmer, M. & Neaverson, P. 1998, *Industrial Archaeology: principles and practice*, London: Routledge.

Rugg, J. 1998, 'A new burial form and its meanings: cemetery establishment in the first half of the 19th century', in Cox, M. (ed.), *Grave concerns: death and burial in England 1700 to 1850*, York: Council for British Archaeology Research Report 113, 44–53.

Slater, J. A. 1996, *The Colonial Burying Grounds of Eastern Connecticut and the Men Who Made Them*, North Haven, Memoirs of the Connecticut Academy of Arts and Sciences 21, revised edition.

Sloane, D .S. 1991, *The Last Great Necessity. Cemeteries in American History*, Baltimore: Johns Hopkins University Press.

Stapleton, H. & Burman, P. 1976, *The Churchyards Handbook. Advice on their Care and Maintenance*, London: CIO Publishing.

Tarlow, S. 1998, 'Romancing the stones: the graveyard boom of the later 18th century', in Cox, M. (ed.) *Grave Concerns: death and burial in England 1700 to 1850*, 33–43, York: Council for British Archaeology Research Report 113.

Willsher, B. & Hunter, D. 1978, *Stones: eighteenth century Scottish gravestones*, Edinburgh: Cannongate.

Willsher, B. 1992, 'Adam and Eve scenes on kirkyard monuments in the Scottish lowlands', *Proceedings of the Society of Antiquaries of Scotland 124*, 413–51.

Willsher, B. 1996 *Scottish Epitaphs. Epitaphs and Images from Scottish Graveyards*, Edinburgh: Cannongate.

'FOR THEIR OWN CONVENIENCE': THE ARCHAEOLOGY OF 19TH-CENTURY PUB TOKENS

By YOLANDA COURTNEY

INTRODUCTION

A coherent series of tokens, mainly made in Birmingham, were used in pubs in England and Wales *c.* 1830–*c.* 1920. Pub tokens have been collected since they were issued. The main sources for the present study were museum and private collections and publications by collectors, usually based on pre-1974 counties, comprising a database of over 10,000 examples.[1] Typical pub tokens (Fig. 1) are brass, around an inch (25 mm) in diameter and show combinations of pub name, landlord's name, town name, maker's name and advertisement, references to pub facilities and other information.

At a time when other Birmingham hardware was reaching every town and village in Britain, the overall national distribution of pub tokens is extremely uneven. Figure 2 shows pub token totals for each county with separate totals (in circles) for the largest urban centres. Highest numbers (indicated by stippling) were issued along a 'corridor' running from Birmingham through Worcestershire and Gloucestershire into south-east Wales. North of Birmingham incidence of high pub token issue runs through Staffordshire and, with a gap in Cheshire and Derbyshire, concentrates on densely populated areas of southern Lancashire and the West Riding of Yorkshire. There are also substantial numbers in rural Devon and Somerset. However, to the east and south, including a swathe of counties around London, there is a sharp drop to very low numbers of pub tokens.

This paper examines contrasting 19th-century documentary accounts and 20th-century anecdotal evidence for pub token usage. It argues that, although pub tokens

FIGURE 1.   Typical Birmingham-made pub tokens.

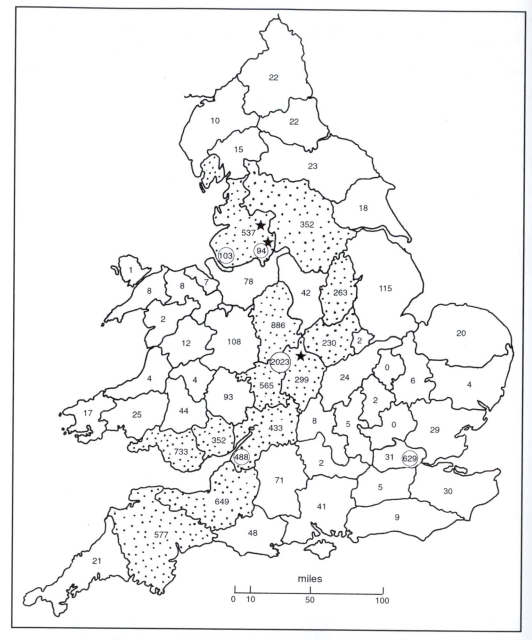

FIGURE 2. Distribution of pub tokens: England and Wales.

reflect stresses in the licensed trade, the uneven national distribution of the tokens and other factors strongly suggest that standard pub tokens were a primarily supply-led phenomenon. Explanations for the spatial patterning of pub tokens are rooted in the organization of the hardware trade and its regional marketing infrastructure.

TOKEN USAGE BEFORE $c.$ 1830–$c.$ 1920

Documentary evidence shows use of metal tokens and paper tickets in 'wet admission' and 'wet rent' practices from the mid 18th century, long before the $c.$ 1830–$c.$ 1920 series of tokens. 'Wet admission' tickets gave admission to a show and also entitled the buyer to a drink. The earliest known reference to this was in 1744 when an advertisement appeared for a theatrical performance in Mayfair: 'Each person to be admitted for Sixpence at the door, which entitles them to a Pint of Ale, upon delivering the ticket to the waiter.'[2] Wet admission arrangements for London and Bath pleasure gardens are documented from the mid 18th century. A charge was made for entrance and the visitor was presented with a metal token which also entitled him/ her to refreshment. London gardens with these arrangements included the Mulberry Garden, Clerkenwell (1752), Finch's Grotto Gardens (1764) and Marylebone Gardens (1770s). At the Spring Gardens, Bath (1769): 'Every person . . . pays Sixpence for Admittance into the Gardens, for which a Ticket is given that entitles you to any Thing at the Bar to that Value.' In Bath, King James's Palace Gardens had a sixpenny brass ticket, which, counter-stamped with the initials 'RT' may refer to 1791 when Robert Tanner opened 'a Subscription Book for Ladies and Gentlemen walking in the garden . . . Non-subscribers at 6d each, for which they are entitled to any refreshment to that amount'.[3]

In 'wet rent' arrangements friendly societies did not pay cash rents for pub meeting rooms, but instead purchased a fixed quantity of liquor. In 1762 the articles of a Beaminster (Dorset) society state: 'Every member at each club meeting who shall attend, shall have a two-penny ticket out of the club-box, to spend at the club-house . . . if any member shall call for more liquor than the value of his two-penny ticket, he shall pay for it out of his own pocket.' Article six of the 1806 articles of the Society of Journeymen Brush-makers who met monthly at the *Craven Head*, Drury Lane (London), states that 'on every meeting night each member shall receive a pot ticket at eight o'clock, a pint at ten, and no more'.[4]

In addition, the concept of tokens as metal trade cards or advertising pieces also considerably predates $c.$ 1830–$c.$ 1920 pub tokens. Lowe's Grand Hotel, Covent Garden issued a copper advertising token bearing the legend 'FOR THE RECEPTION OF NOBLEMEN AND GENTLEMEN' in 1774. Writing in 1834, Sharp associates late 18th-century tokens with 'a desire on the part of shop-keepers to obtain local notoriety by the issue of tokens, which became a sort of metallic cards of address'.[5]

USES OF $c.$ 1830–$c.$ 1920 TOKENS: DOCUMENTARY EVIDENCE

Despite their relatively recent date, there are proportionally very few pub tokens whose precise use is or can be known. Documentary sources exist for only a very few pieces and the evidence of legends and motifs on the pub tokens needs careful interpretation. Excluding liquor advertisements, an average of only 14% of pub tokens in a sample of five high issue counties have additional information of possible relevance to uses of the tokens.[6] Even when a legend or motif does refer to a possible use-context such as a pub game it does not necessarily follow that the token was actually used in that context. Instead the legend may be merely advertising the facility mentioned. Moreover usage could change during a landlord's tenure. It is important to dispose of the suggestion, still occasionally made, that pub tokens were used as general small change. Pub tokens were few before the 1840s, and a general lack of small change after 1821 is not demonstrated by mintage records.[7] Moreover it is inconceivable that a general lack of small change in early Victorian England would have escaped contemporary comment, though it is possible that shortages continued in remote areas for a while. However, in the particular circumstances of long pay periods in industrial areas, for example South Wales, alternative 'currencies' such as company notes and tobacco emerged.[8] Only in this and similar 'in-house' situations, controlled by the issuing pub itself, were pub tokens used as change.

In the 1830s organized music in pubs was becoming more frequent and pub music saloons were becoming more elaborate. The 1843 Theatres Act required that saloons either become licensed theatres which meant that they could not sell drink in the auditorium, or remain as tavern concert rooms with drink, but without the right to produce stage plays.[9] Music Hall emerged from pub concert rooms as some enterprising publicans moved into purpose-built halls.[10] More modest entertainments in concert rooms and long rooms continued however, often in breach of the law. Use of tokens as 'wet' admission tickets in Victorian music halls and pub concert rooms is well documented. For example, a newspaper advertisement in the *Bolton Advertiser* (1847) announced that, at the Star Inn and Concert Room 'in order to keep the establishment select and orderly the visitors are required to take tickets but the full amount will be returned in refreshments'.[11] Some tokens state this purpose unambiguously: 'REFRESHMENTS 6D', 'REFRESHMENT TICKET' and 'TO BE SPENT THE SAME EVENING AS RECEIVED'.

Sale of liquor was an important element in the economy of early music hall and the pub concert rooms from which it emerged. The likely profits to be made can be seen from the numbers of customers — 25,000 at three beerhouse music saloons in Manchester in 1853.[12] A Birmingham pub had room for a thousand customers who were charged the huge sum of $3s.\ 6d.$ 'the same amount being returned in beer, spirits and tobacco'.[13] The method facilitated increasing profits from groups of people who had no tradition of paying extra for their entertainment.[14] Use of tokens for other refreshments as well as liquor, a feature of 18th-century pleasure gardens, is also noted in the more modest pleasure gardens of the later 19th century. 'NOTTS GARDEN 1872' on a $3d.$ token refers to George Nott's pleasure garden near Swansea, where 'all classes' could drink tea or liquor, and up to 1,500 people might be there on one day. A $3d.$ token was sold at the entrance, and for this the bearer was entitled to 'a game of skittles, dancing on the green, as many strawberries as he could eat or some other form of refreshment'.[15]

Benefit societies, including burial societies, building societies, dividing societies and investment societies, were important users of pub facilities. These were an attractive means of practical self-help due to the inadequacies of public alleviation for the miseries of sickness and unemployment. Membership was approaching three-quarters of a million in Britain in 1801.[16] The earliest societies were independent and local, but especially after about 1830 there was a trend towards affiliation and larger organizations such as the Oddfellows groupings emerged. Benefits were paid out to subscribers in times of need, but there was also a strong element of conviviality at meetings, for which regular sums were contributed. 'Wet rent' or 'lodge liquor' was a familiar custom, well-documented for friendly societies, burial, building and trade societies. A fixed quantity of beer would be purchased in exchange for use of the meeting room, a system which could be operated using paper or metal tickets.[17]

Friendly societies and clubs of all kinds were common in Birmingham. A manager of a Birmingham friendly society, estimated in 1849 that 'there are about 1,700 public houses and beershops . . . two out of every three have one of these societies, and some have five or six'.[18] In addition to rent arrangements, friendly and burial societies gave liquor tokens to committee members as an allowance for attending meetings. An Oldham solicitor who acted for 22 societies reported in 1871 that it was the invariable rule that members paid $3d.$ each at meetings for refreshments 'and that money is spent in the house. The committee have part of it, and the members have the remainder'.[19] Societies dispensing funeral or burial benefits often worked arrangements whereby those who attended funerals of fellow members were recompensed with liquor tokens. A token issued from the Childers Inn, Macclesfield, reads 'BURIAL TICKET'.[20]

Another element in the efforts of pubs to attract long-stay custom was facilities for playing games. A small number of pub tokens unequivocally declare their use in this context, for instance two Birmingham tokens dating prior to 1865: 'COMMERCIAL INN, 3D . . . RECEIVED SUBJECT TO THE RULES OF KNOCK 'EM DOWN', 'DIAL INN, A. CORLETT, $2\frac{1}{2}$D, SKITTLE CHECK'.[21] In 1855 Epaphras Seage advertised in the *Exeter Western Times*, 'Yellow metal cheques for skittle alleys, bagatelle &c.', and H. S. Gill, writing in 1873, describes a token issued from the Windmill Inn, Exeter, as 'a specimen of the ordinary check frequently used in billiard rooms, bowling greens, skittle-alleys etc., entitling the bearer to have the value of threepence, or other sums impressed on the token, in ale, cider or spirits'.[22] Grant Francis, in South Wales, refers to tokens used 'nearly always at small taverns where games are played, to enable the customer . . . to call in at any subsequent time and have his refreshment to the value indicated'.[23] Also, French states that in 1860s Dublin, customers who used the gaming table were expected to buy a round of drinks as payment for the facilities. The losers, by custom, bought drinks for the winners, but a habitual winner could be given a token for a drink on another night.[24] The same practice, operating in Chepstow (South Wales) in the early 20th century, is described by Ivor Waters: tokens were 'purchased by losing players and given to the winner, so that there was no need for a highly successful player to drink all his winnings on the spot'.[25]

The best evidence for pub token use in the industrial context comes from South Wales. The 1870 parliamentary investigation into the operation of the Truck Act collected testimony which includes evidence for use of pub tokens as change for beer notes as part of truck arrangements and also as straight beer allowances. In both cases it is likely that landlords issued tokens for use as in-house change. W. Coppin, a blast-furnaceman at Nantyglo, said:

Sometimes I get a one shilling note for beer. If I do not take it all out in beer at once they give me at the public a cheque or dib for the change, with which I can get the balance in beer at another time . . . The only place I can take the beer note is the *Bush*.[26]

USES OF *c*. 1830–*c*. 1920 TOKENS: ORAL AND ANECDOTAL EVIDENCE

From the early 20th century, different sources for pub token usage become available. Oral and anecdotal evidence shows a wider range of uses, indicating that earlier usage was probably more diverse than the surviving classes of documentary evidence suggest.

In a newspaper interview in 1978, an 84-year-old retired wholesale fruit merchant from Hull said

they were brass tokens issued chiefly in the dock area . . . you could buy 5 for 1/- at various pubs and present one of them for a drink when you liked. Working men's wages were 30/- or less . . . this arrangement made sure they could get a glass of beer on other days besides pay day. It removed the temptation to part with the money to the bookie's runner.[27]

The possibility that standard pub tokens were used to issue beer allowances directly rather than as change for paper notes is suggested by Mrs N. Darke, landlady of the Papermakers Inn and later of the Sawyers Arms in Exeter, writing in 1964: 'I was told this token entitled employees of a nearby papermills to two pints of beer valued at 5d. The boss would then collect the tokens at the end of each week.' J. Samper, also writing in 1964, contributes a similar account from another part of the country: 'In the north-east foundries the furnace men worked in teams and a boy was employed to "run the cutter" to the inn [i.e. collect ale in jug or can]. The men would buy tokens at the inn for use the following week.' The practice of making beer allowances to workers was not confined to heavy industry. Wilfred E. Court, writing in 1964, regarding tokens of the Mulberry Tree Inn, Stratford on Avon, said that 'they were given to cattle drovers, porters on the market and were exchanged for a drink at the house which bore the name on the token'.[28]

A kind of prepayment system, in effect a simple mechanism for keeping account of drinks paid for, but not served to customers, was operating in a Cardiff pub in the later 1960s/early 1970s.[29] The barmaid of the Cow & Snuffers, Llandaff North, Cardiff, used iron washers stamped 'CS' to keep account of 'drinks in' — that is, paid for in advance of requirements. The purchaser of a 'round' might pay for drinks for everyone in the round, despite the fact that some people were not ready for another drink. A skittles or darts team might win a match, but they would already have drinks and so would be given tokens for a drink later. Uniface aluminium tokens stamped with the pub name, made by a Padstow engineering firm, were used in this way in Cornwall after World War II, as were discs stamped 'KHSC 1 PINT' at the King's Head Skittle Club, Ross (Herefordshire).[30] Mr and Mrs Ward of the Naval & Military in Taunton discovered metal tokens previously issued by the pub when they took it over in the 1970s. They promptly put them to use to record buying in of drinks on busy nights such as skittles or stag nights.[31]

Pub tokens also appear to have been quite widely used in skittle games after World War I, though in different ways from games uses noted from documentary sources for the peak period of token use. For instance, W. J. Morgan says that

> In the years 1918–25 I was a keen picker up, and sometimes runner of the checks. At the *Seven Sisters Hotel*, Seven Sisters, Neath, 'the runner' collected names for a game, at 6d a game per person, put the names up on a blackboard and kept score. He would have been given, by the landlord, a pile of 4d brass tokens which could only be exchanged for beer. The winners would be given tokens as prizes, and the picker up would be given two or three for his trouble . . . Many of us youngsters, not being big beer drinkers used to sell them or give them away to fathers etc. [32]

THE TRADE CONTEXT

The evidence for 'wet rent' and 'wet entrance' arrangements prior to the emergence of *c.* 1830–*c.* 1920 pub tokens suggests that a low-level, customer-led demand existed for discs for these purposes in the half century or so before 1820. The post-1820 upsurge in token types may have been a reaction by Birmingham die-sinkers under pressure to develop new products after the early 19th-century series of copper tokens were outlawed, with a few named exceptions, in 1817.[33] Manufacturers of the early 19th-century token series were primarily button-makers.[34] Changes in fashion led to a decline in the market for buttons by the 1830s;[35] this appears to correlate with a further surge in production of general checks, tickets and passes from the 1830s onward.

Demand would have been stimulated by increased competition within the licensed trade. Passage of the 1830 Beer Act led to a short-lived 50% increase in numbers of liquor sellers.[36] The growth of temperance feeling, progressive urbanization, the growing railway network and the leisure needs of a concentrated workforce, had a significant effect on competition for custom within the licensed trade. Expansion of facilities for entertainment, club meetings and pub games was a reflection of this situation. The 1830s and 1840s saw the emergence of music hall from pub concert rooms and expansion of non-traditional games such as bagatelle.[37] The bulk of landlords' profits came from liquor sales since licensed premises seldom sold much except liquor. Provision of additional facilities in pubs had a clear profit motive, encouraging customers to stay longer and drink more or to return on another night. Tokens used in the context of new games and for 'wet admission' and 'wet rent' appear to have been part of the landlord's arrangements to organize and profit from use of games equipment, musical entertainment and club meeting rooms.

The earliest pub tokens date to the 1830s and early 1840s. These have a limited distribution, comprising the West Country (including Bath), the Manchester area and London. These have stylistic affinities with the general advertising tokens of the post-1820 period.[38] It may be significant that 'wet entrance' to pleasure gardens is a factor common to three of the early issuing areas, Bath, London and Manchester. From the mid 1840s pub tokens became more standardized. Against the background of increased competition in the licensed trade and existing customer-led demand, it is likely that Birmingham die-sinkers conceived the idea of a specialized token series aimed specifically at pubs. The Hiron workshop at 52 St Paul's Square, Birmingham, may have been the first to recognize the potential of pub tokens as a specialized series. Hiron's pub tokens, produced from 1846, were larger than most post-1820 general trade tokens and bore pub-related motifs and advertising. The die-sinking workshop at 52 St Paul's Square, was occupied successively by Hiron, Pope and Cottrill, and it dominated the market until the mid 1860s.[39]

MARKETS

Token manufacture and related stamping and piercing trades were low capital enterprises carried on in the workshops of Birmingham's jewellery quarter. Pub tokens were customized objects and they could not be carried in shops or by salesmen for ready sale. Detailed study of pub tokens shows how die-sinking workshops and their customer records were acquired by successive individuals.[40] However, the numbers ordered at any one time were limited, apparently not exceeding a few thousands and sometimes much less. Profit margins were not high, so producers needed to reach their customers cost-effectively, and the question must be asked what made it worthwhile to produce pub tokens?

If the national pub token distribution is examined in more detail, five different types of distribution can be identified. *Dense* urban distributions are characterized by close clustering with high numbers of tokens between clusters: these include Birmingham and the Black Country (Fig. 3), the Potteries, south-east Lancashire, the West Riding of Yorkshire and the South Wales valleys. *Discrete* distributions have separated clusters of pub tokens in and near larger population centres, for instance much of Nottinghamshire and Leicestershire and parts of Worcestershire and Gloucestershire (Fig. 3). *Dispersed* distributions with strong rural elements are found mainly in east Somerset/north Dorset, east and south Devon and west Gloucestershire. *Sparse* distributions have low numbers of tokens, for example Derbyshire, southern Cheshire. In *rare* distributions, incidence of pub tokens is very low or non-existent, for instance including east Gloucestershire. Most southern counties have *sparse* or *rare* distributions.[41]

Examination of Birmingham newspapers over a period from the end of the 1840s until the 1890s shows die stampers advertising businesses for sale and changes of business address. Straight advertisements for die-sinkers' wares appear only rarely, probably reflecting the low capital nature of the trade and the expense of advertising relative to results. Trades directory advertisements were cheaper than newspaper advertising and longer lasting. However the incidence of pub tokens beyond Birmingham implies additional marketing mechanisms. The earliest evidence for travelling salesmen working regular circuits out of the Birmingham area dates from the early 18th century. In 1719–20, Tobias Bellaers was buying metal goods from local makers and marketing them to dealers in the East Midlands.[42] Thomas English set out in 1791 with 'samples and stock, lists of customers and outstanding accounts, and a route book detailing the principal stopping places and distances between them'.[43] The English firm found that acting as both hardware merchants and manufacturers was uneconomic due to difficulties with monitoring the work and

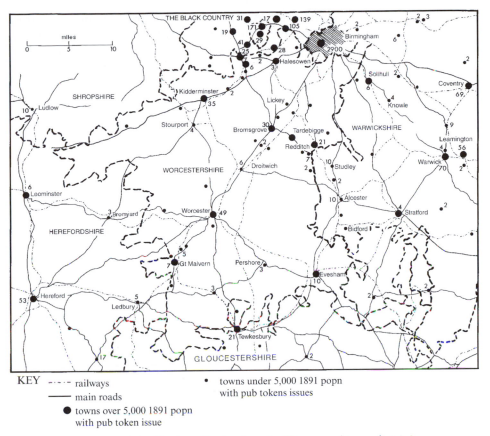

KEY ----- railways ● towns under 5,000 1891 popn
with pub tokens issues
——— main roads
● towns over 5,000 1891 popn
with pub token issue

FIGURE 3. Distribution of pub tokens in Worcestershire and vicinity.

reaching a sufficiently large market. Reasons of economics thus ensured the existence of a large body of commission agents or factors, who could handle marketing for a number of firms. These established links with retailers in population centres on a regional basis using salesmen who travelled country routes selling to country dealers and urban shopkeepers. Even larger firms such as Kenrick & Sons the West Bromwich hardware manufacturers were allowing commission agents to handle the bulk of their trade in the 19th century.[44]

Commission agents or factors continued to exist throughout the 19th century, especially in trades where small units survived.[45] Commercial agents and factors are listed in trades directories dating to the boom period of pub token production. In 1861 123 factors are listed in Cornish's Birmingham directory including specialists in jewellery, tobacconist's goods and hardware. There are also 116 merchants, and some individuals are listed under both factor and merchant. Free-lance salesmen advertised their services in Birmingham newspapers. Typical examples in 1849 included: 'Commercial traveller, calling upon ironmongers and iron-founders twice a year through the West of England and South Wales is desirous of one or two heavy commissions'; 'A traveller of many years experience in the Birmingham trades . . . .'.[46]

Small die-sinking firms almost certainly keyed into the existing agent/retailer infrastructure by establishing working arrangements with salesmen. Once a link with a retail agency such as an ironmonger or stationer was established, further transactions could be carried out using the cheap and reliable postal system from 1840. Tokens and dies were delivered by rail and then by the carrier network. Bath Industrial Heritage Museum holds the archives of J. B. Bowler, mineral water manufacturer, ironmonger and retail agent for Birmingham die-sinkers. Bowler's correspondence includes orders with rough sketches of pub tokens, quotations and payments.[47]

Rankings of 1891 population figures against numbers of pub tokens issued in key locations show a range of anomalies. There are sizeable towns with low numbers of token issues or none at all, for instance Grimsby, Worksop, Mansfield, Chesterfield and Crewe. In Warwickshire, Warwick, Leamington and Coventry have the highest numbers of tokens per head of 1891 population. However Nuneaton and Rugby, with populations of similar size to that of Warwick, have among the lowest. The highest numbers of pub tokens per head of 1891 population nationally are found at Birmingham, Exeter and the Dudley area, all production centres.[48]

Strong clustering of pub tokens around population centres (Fig. 3)[49] suggests that makers acquired agents there. Absence of issues in some neighbouring towns suggests that when retail agencies were set up, salesmen were following routes which excluded some towns (or that some retail agency arrangements failed). The clusters may be on regular sales routes. Only one actual call was necessary during which a salesman established an initial link with an appropriate retail agent. Retail agents would stock then manufacturers' catalogues and submit orders from customers. Examples of main roads and rail routes with clusters of pub token issues include the main road from Birmingham through Worcestershire and Gloucestershire (Fig. 3). In South Wales there are high numbers of pub tokens along the valleys ribbon developments. Corridors of high incidence of pub tokens seem to link areas in which density of population made salesmanship worthwhile. This includes routes north into Staffordshire, Lancashire and the West Riding of Yorkshire, routes that pick up major towns in the East Midlands such as Leicester, Nottingham and Newark and the traditional Severn marketing route between Birmingham and Bristol and into South Wales. The power of London's own marketing arrangements, with large warehouses, would lead to exclusion of London and surrounding counties from such routes and explain the low numbers of tokens there.

Discrete token clusters can be interpreted as resulting from the market function of the town where the agent is based, servicing the immediate rural hinterland. A cluster of eight pub tokens at Beeston (Nottinghamshire), could be related to the presence of a retail agent in Nottingham, the nearby market centre for Beeston. *Dispersed* rural distributions might result when retail agents supplied other items to pubs or operated a delivery route for items other than tokens. These agents would show a catalogue or samples to customers, especially those buying relevant merchandise such as pub games equipment. The cluster of pub tokens in Bath and vicinity area in itself suggests the existence of an agency. The Bowler firm delivered and attended jobs in a number of horse-drawn carts known as 'lurries'. There were five daily mineral water rounds covering Bath itself, two villages on the outskirts and the Radstock mining area and Bowler had a delivery radius which extended 'throughout the city and for a radius of 20 miles around'.[50] A retail agent like Bowler, with a distribution network and transport for delivering other merchandise, would create a different pattern of token distribution compared with a more static retail agent. *Sparse* distributions with low figures of tokens, but some clustering suggest some agent activity. Low-level, *rare* distributions suggest a lack of retail agents with a connection to a die-sinker producing pub tokens.

The surprisingly low numbers of pub tokens relative to population in some large urban centres, notably London and surrounding counties, Liverpool and Manchester can be explained by the operation of economic cut-out mechanisms. The existence of 'Birmingham and Sheffield' hardware warehouses in these large cities may have effectively removed them from regional trading routes, thus excluding smaller manufacturers. London directories (e.g. Kelly's for 1870) list 'Birmingham and Sheffield warehouses', nearly all with addresses in the East Central postal district. Gore's Liverpool directory for 1870 lists warehouse keepers and hardware merchants including the Birmingham Hardware Company. Warehouses for Birmingham and Sheffield hardware also existed in Manchester (38 in Slater's 1876 directory). These warehouses presumably dealt directly with the largest hardware manufacturers and supplied local hardware stockists. The salesmen who acted for the Birmingham token-makers presumably saw such large towns as having less potential for either direct sales or setting up retail agencies. The customized nature of pub tokens meant that they were an unsuitable product line for the large warehouses of the national and international network.

Comparison of pub token dating analyses establishes a broad chronology of pub token usage. These show expected first use nearest the Birmingham workshops, then a delay further away, for example in the East Midlands and South Wales. Later chronology is far less predictable. The Birmingham analysis (Fig. 4) peaks in the mid 1860s, followed by swift decline from the end of the 1860s. Apart from the phase of levelling out, the Birmingham analysis is virtually a textbook example of the classic product life cycle. This postulates phases of introduction, growth, maturity, saturation and decline of a product, though when the rate of growth slows down, 'corrective action' such as market development, can take the product into additional stages of growth.[51]

In contrast with Birmingham, token usage in the East Midlands continued to thrive, in Nottingham surviving until after 1900. Nottingham and Newark and some other places including Exeter and the Rhondda Valleys (Glamorgan) have secondary peaks around 1900.[52]

Temperance feeling was undermining liquor customs even before the pub token series began. Provision of beer allowances became less common; wet entrance and wet rent arrangements had become rarer by the end of the century.[53] However, these factors do not explain the wide variation in the regional pattern of pub token decline. Using the classic product life cycle model, it can be suggested that a market saturation factor was operating. Pub tokens may have matured and ceased to be a novelty in the Birmingham area, prompting producers to take corrective action in seeking markets

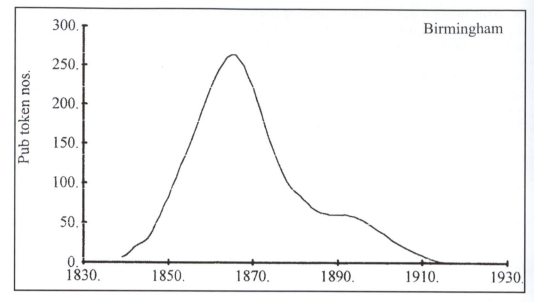

FIGURE 4. Dating analysis of pub tokens issued in Birmingham.

further afield. Birmingham's early decline could be because the novelty of pub tokens wore off soonest in the area where they were most familiar. The market for pub tokens was less likely to be exhausted further away from Birmingham and more susceptible to subsequent marketing drives. It is possible that the phase of pub building that accompanied the scramble for licensed property in the 1890s inspired die-sinkers to seek to refresh their markets for pub tokens.[54]

CONCLUSIONS

Pub tokens and other post-1820 metal discs were in the Birmingham tradition of 'toy' or novelty-makers who were driven by a perpetual need to develop new products. 'Toy' manufacture has been defined as 'any portable article . . . having the common characteristic that the pattern changes with even greater frequency than in buttons . . . novelty alone sold the object'.[55] Pub tokens were 'novelties', certainly not essential items, since paper and card could be used to fulfil the same purposes. The ability of the Birmingham die-sinkers to identify potentially profitable new product lines and swiftly market them, is also shown by other groups of artefacts, for example loyal medalets produced to mark each stage of George III's provincial journeys in 1788–89.[56] Once established as a product line, however, pub tokens were used for whatever purpose a landlord chose rather than the limited range of uses suggested by documentary evidence, and usage could vary through time. As Hiley, manager of shop at the Nantylgo ironworks, put it in 1871, 'It is for their own convenience that the people at the *Bush* give those dibs'.[57]

Yolanda Courtney, 20 Lytton Road, Clarendon Park, Leicester LE2 1WJ, UK

NOTES

[1] Courtney 1996, vol. 3, 43–169, *Catalogue*; Courtney 2000.

[2] Wager 1987.

[3] Wroth 1896, 8, 41, 107, 231–32, 242; Davis & Waters 1922, 45, nos 14–15; Sydenham 1907, 90, 97, 104; Minnitt & Young 1990, nos 64–65.

[4] Hine 1928, 116; Fuller 1964, 59; Kiddier 1931, 37 and author's note opposite title-page.

[5] Neumann 1865, vol. 4, no. 27600; Sharp 1834, i.

[6] Courtney 1996, vol. 3, fig. 146.

[7] Challis 1992, 490.

[8] *Parliamentary Papers* 1871 (c.327), liv.

[9] 1843 *Theatres Act* (6 & 7 Victoria, c.68).

[10] Walton & Walvin 1983, 54; Harrison 1971, 48.

[11] Stockton 1996, 346; see also Poole 1982, 61, n.3.

[12] Harrison 1971, 324.

[13] Hopkins 1998, 168.

[14] Bailey 1978, 29–30.

[15] *Royal Institution of South Wales*, 6–7; *Cambrian Daily Leader*, 1910.

[16] Gosden 1961, 4–5.

[17] Gosden 1961, 11, 117; Fuller 1964, 58–59; Thompson & Wager 1982, 221–23.

[18] *Parliamentary Papers* 1849, Q1263.

[19] *Parliamentary Papers* 1871 (c.452), QQ6427–51.

[20] British Museum, Freudenthal collection.

[21] Neumann 1865, nos 26774, 26781.

[22] Andrews 1986; Gill 1873, 168.

[23] Grant Francis 1867, 116.

[24] French 1918, 165.

[25] Waters 1976, 47; Waters *in lit.*, 6 September 1984.

[26] *Parliamentary Papers* 1871 (c.327), Q27,812.

[27] Durnell Papers: *Somerset County Gazette*, 27 January 1978.

[28] Monckton papers: Mrs N. Darke in lit. 26 February 1964; J. Samper *in lit.* 13 March 1964; Wilfred E. Court *in lit.*, 13 March 1964.

[29] Stanton (Courtney), 1983.

[30] L. McCarthy, pers. comm. 1989; L. Bennett, pers.comm. 1989.

[31] Minnitt *et al.*, 1985, 12.

[32] Todd 1980, 235–36.

[33] 57 Geo.III, c.46.

[34] Withers & Withers, 1998.

[35] White 1977, 70–71.

[36] Gourvish & Wilson, 1994, 16–18, Table 1.2.

[37] Spiller 1973, 104; Hawkins 1975, 35.

[38] Courtney 1996, vol. 3, fig. 4.

[39] Ibid., vol. 1, 342–49.

[40] Ibid.; Hawkins 1989, 181–85, 416–17.

[41] Ibid., vol. 3, figs 17–20, 42–45, 60–63, 86–89, 95–96.

[42] Wise 1949–50.

[43] Jones 1984, 28–29, 39–40.

[44] Hawkes Smith 1836, 21; Jones 1984, 24, 41, n. 1, 3.

[45] Allen 1929, 345.

[46] *Birmingham & General Advertiser*, 7 June 1849, 14 June 1849.

[47] Bath Industrial Heritage Museum collections; Bath Industrial Heritage Museum, 10–11; Minnitt *et al.* 1985, 17–19; Minnitt & Young 1990, 102–03, 111–12.

[48] Courtney 1996, vol. 3, fig. 109.

[49] Ibid., figs 17–20, 42–45, 60–63, 86–89, 95–96.

[50] Anon. 1893, 252; Hudson 1978.

[51] McDonald 1995, 135–38.

[52] Dating analyses in Courtney 1996, vol. 3, figs 52–53, 72, 102.

[53] Webbs 1920, 113; Hackwood 1909, 203; Courtney 1996, vol. 1, 525–28.

[54] Vaizey 1960, 8–12; Gourvish and Wilson 1994, 250, 267–73.

[55] Eversley 1964, 103; Hopkins 1998, 48.

[56] Hawkins 1989, xii, 3.

[57] *Parliamentary Papers* 1871 (c.327), Q29,408.

BIBLIOGRAPHY

Allen, G. C. 1929, *The Industrial Development of Birmingham and the Black Country 1860–1927*, London: Allen & Unwin.

Andrews, J. 1986, 'An early Exeter "cheque" maker: a new discovery about Epaphras Seage', *Token Corresponding Society Bulletin* 4/5, 14–15.

Anon. 1893, *Ports of the Bristol Channel*, London: London Printing & Engraving Co.

Bailey, P. 1978, *Leisure and Class in Victorian England: Rational recreation and the contest for control 1830–1885*, London: Routledge & Kegan Paul.

Bath Industrial Heritage Museum 1992, *Kegs & Ale*, Bath: Millstream Books.

Challis, C. E. (ed.) 1992, *A New History of the Royal Mint*, Cambridge: Cambridge University Press.

Courtney, Y. C. 1996, *British Public House Tokens c. 1830–c. 1920: Material culture in the industrial age*, University of Wales PhD thesis.

Courtney, Y. C. 2000, 'Pub tokens: Material culture and regional marketing patterns in Victorian England & Wales', *International Journal of Historical Archaeology* 4:2, 59–90.

Davis, W. J. & Waters, A. W. 1922, *Tickets and Passes of Great Britain and Ireland*, Leamington Spa: Courier Press.

Durnell Papers, notes (1982) by John Durnell of conversations with people remembering pub tokens in use in the Bristol area.

Eversley, D. E. C. 1964, 'Industry and trade, 1500–1880', in *Victoria County History for Warwickshire* VII, Oxford: Oxford University Press, 81–139.

French, E. J. 1918, 'Tavern tokens', *Journal of the Royal Society of Antiquaries of Ireland* 48, 164–73.

Fuller, M. D. 1964, *West Country Friendly Societies*, Reading: Oakwood Press for the Museum of Rural Life.

Gill, H. S. 1873, 'On Devonshire tokens, Part I', *Transactions of the Devonshire Association* 5, 159–71.

Gosden, P. H. G. H. 1961, *The Friendly Societies in England 1815–1875*, Manchester: Manchester University Press.

Gourvish, T. R. & Wilson, R. G. 1994, *The British Brewing Industry 1830–1980*, Cambridge: Cambridge University Press.

Grant Francis, G. 1867, *The Smelting of Copper in the Swansea District of South Wales from the time of Elizabeth to the present day*, Swansea: privately printed.

Hackwood, F. W. 1909, *Inns, Ales and Drinking Customs of Old England*, London: Bracken Books.

Harrison, B. 1971, *Drink and The Victorians: the temperance question in England 1815–1872*, London: Faber & Faber Ltd.

Hawkes Smith, W. 1836, *Birmingham and its Vicinity as a Manufacturing and Commercial District*, London: C. Tilt.

Hawkins, R. N. P. 1975, 'Birmingham-made bagatelle tables depicted on checks of public houses', in *Four Studies of British Metallic Tickets and Commercial Checks of the 19th-20th centuries*, British Association of Numismatic Societies, Doris Stockwell Memorial Papers No. 2, London, 35–51.

Hawkins, R. N. P. 1989, *Dictionary of Makers of British Metallic Tickets, checks, medalets, tallies and counters 1788–1910*, London: A. H. Baldwin & Sons Ltd.

Hine, R. 1928, 'Friendly societies and their emblems', *Proceedings of the Dorset Natural History & Antiquarian Society* 49, 114–24.

Hopkins, E. 1998, *The rise of the manufacturing town: Birmingham and the Industrial Revolution*, Stroud: Sutton.

Hudson, K. 1978, *The Bowler Collection*, Bath: Bath Industrial Heritage Museum.

Jones, S. R. H. 1984, 'The country trade and the marketing and distribution of Birmingham hardware, 1750–1810', *Business History* 26:1, 24–42.

Kiddier, W. 1931, *The Old Trade Unions from Unprinted Records of the Brushmakers*, London: Allen & Unwin.

McDonald, M. 1995, *Marketing Plans*, Oxford: Butterworth-Heinemann.

Minnitt, S. C. & Young, D. 1990, *Tickets Checks & Passes from the County of Somerset*, Taunton: Somerset County Council.

Minnitt, S. C., Durnell, J. & Gunstone, A. J. H. 1985, *Somerset Public House Tokens*, Taunton: Somerset County Council.

Monckton Papers, archives of Whitbread & Co., Sheffield, letters written to H. A. Monckton in 1964 about pub tokens in response to a letter in the *Daily Telegraph*.

Neumann, J. 1865, *Beschreibung der Bekanntesten Kupfermunzen* 4, Prague; reprinted 1966, New York: Johnson Reprint Corporation.

Parliamentary Papers 1871 (c.327), XXXVI, Report of the Commissioners appointed to inquire into the Truck System.

Parliamentary Papers 1849 (c.458), XIV, Report of the Select Committee on Friendly Societies.

Parliamentary Papers 1871 (c.452), XXV, Friendly & Benefit Societies: First Report of the Commissioners with Minutes of Evidence.

Poole, R. 1982, *Popular Leisure and the Music Hall in 19th Century Bolton*, Lancaster: Centre for North-West Regional Studies, University of Lancaster.

Rowlands, M. B. 1975, *Masters and Men in the West Midlands Metalware Trades before the Industrial Revolution*, Manchester: Manchester University Press.

Royal Institution of South Wales, 1936–37, Report of the Council.

Sharp, T. 1834, *Catalogue of Provincial Copper Coins, Tokens, Tickets and Medalets in the collection of Sir George Chetwynd*, London: J. B. Nichols & Son.

Smith, R. A. (ed.) 1930, *Catalogue of the Montague Guest Collection of Badges, Tokens, Passes*, London: British Museum.

Spiller, B. 1973, *Victorian Public Houses*, Newton Abbot: David & Charles.

Stanton (Courtney), Y. C. 1983, 'A contemporary tavern token', Seaby *Coin & Medal Bulletin* 782, 252–54.

Stockton, C. 1996, 'Bolton concert hall checks', *Bulletin of the Token Corresponding Society* 5/9, 345–48.

Sydenham, S. 1907, 'Bath pleasure gardens of the 18th century, issuing metal admission tickets', *Proceedings of the Bath Natural History and Antiquarian Field Club* 11:2, 90, 97, 104.

Thompson, R. H. & Wager, A. J. 1982, 'The purpose and use of public house checks', *British Numismatic Journal* 52, 221–23.

Todd, N. B. 1980, *Tavern Tokens in Wales*, Cardiff: National Museum of Wales.

Vaizey, J. 1960, *The Brewing Industry 1886–1951: an economic study*, London: Pitman.

Wager, A. J. 1987, 'Charlotte Charke and the origin of the check system', *Pub Check Study Group Bulletin* 13, 6–8.

Walton, J. K. & Walvin, J. (eds) 1983, *Leisure in Britain 1780–1939*, Manchester: Manchester University Press.

Waters, I. 1976, *Inns and Taverns of Chepstow and the Lower Wye Valley*, Chepstow: Chepstow Society.

Webb, S. & Webb, B. 1920, *The History of Trade Unionism*, London: Longmans, Green.

White, D. P. 1977, 'The Birmingham button industry', *Post-Medieval Archaeology* 11, 67–79.

Wise, M. J. 1959–50, 'Birmingham and its trade relations in the early 18th century', *University of Birmingham Historical Journal* 2, 64–71.

Withers, P. & Withers, B. 1998, *British Copper Tokens 1811–1820*, Llanfyllin, Powys (Wales): Galata.

Wroth, W. 1896, *The London Pleasure Gardens of the Eighteenth Century*, London: Macmillan.

GOODS AND STORES FOR THE WORKERS: THE SHAPING OF MASS RETAILING IN LATE 19TH-CENTURY GHENT

By PETER SCHOLLIERS

INTRODUCTION

Historians and art historians have largely documented the fascination of the elite and the bourgeoisie for material culture.[1] However, most researchers have neglected the viewpoint and the practice of the working classes *vis-à-vis* consumer goods prior to 1914, limiting themselves to mention new forms of retailing (particularly, the consumer co-operative), and focusing on basic needs (*in casu* food and housing). Many historians assume that the European working classes entered the so-called mass consumer society somewhere in the inter-war period, when they started to buy radios, to go to the movies and to enjoy holidays.[2] The timing of 'mass consumer society' has led to debate, in which the question of the 'accession' of the *lower* classes is of course crucial.[3] Only recently have questions started to be asked about working-class interest in consumer goods prior to 1914. For example, the clear-cut 'class identity' of the department store (allegedly, the pinnacle of bourgeois consumption in the second half of the 19th century) has been doubted.[4] I should like to take up this line, arguing that it is urgent to shed light upon the pre-1914 working-class concern with and interpretation of tableware, fashion, furniture, clothing and all sorts of consumer goods. Various types of questions may be asked, that are linked to economic, political, social and cultural issues: did workers give a particular significance to consumer goods, did the buying of certain goods forge a distinct identity, did the non-purchase of reputed fashionable goods cause frustration, was money saved to buy a clock or children's toys, and how much was spent on tableware, clothes, and *things* in general? If such questions cannot be answered, it seems difficult to interpret the history of the labour movement in Europe, the emergence of a 'full' consumer society, the formation of the urban landscape, the nature of the state, the collapse of the Soviet system or, in short, capitalism.

Entering the 'world of goods' of the working classes before 1914 is perhaps more problematic than studying that of the middle and upper classes because of lack of sources (such as testimonies, catalogues, artefacts, etc.). Looking at co-operative stores may be helpful. The range and quality of goods on sale may inform about the workers' viewpoint and practice with regard to consumer goods. This assumes a dialectic, immediate but complex link between supply and demand, that is, a consumption system where each factor (production, design, marketing, distribution, appeal, purchasing power, etc.) influences the other factors.[5] This implies the consideration of the supply of goods by the co-op, the way these were promoted, and the setting where the goods were sold. I propose to do this by using the example of the Ghent Vooruit, one of the big co-operatives on the continent. Earlier I studied the garment store of this co-op, focusing on the work organization, the promotion techniques and the clothing turnover, but hardly looking at the store itself and the goods on sale.[6] Here, I wish to explore the latter aspects, hoping to contribute to questions on the significance of consumer goods for the working classes prior to 1914.

GHENT AND SOCIAL-DEMOCRACY

From the start of mechanized cotton mills in the 1820s, industrial relations in Ghent were tense. Long strikes occurred regularly, and most of the textile barons had a reputation of being hard-liners, while cotton weavers were known for their 'spirit of independence'. It was in this town that the first modern unions (of textile workers) emerged in the late 1850s. Vague social-democratic ideas existed: some unions joined the International Workers Association in the late 1860s, but this had little appeal to the mass of workers. Later, in the 1890s, a strong union movement emerged, that strove for recognition and respectability. Around 1880, a new generation of social democrats had appeared who adhered to the reformist Gotha programme. They aimed at changes in society through solid organizations in order to obtain political power and social legislation. They saw the establishment of a co-operative bakery as an excellent propagandistic and financial tool to support the party and to achieve its aims.

In 1880, Vooruit ('Forward') was set up as a *red* co-operative bakery. It was not the only co-operative that was constituted at that time, but it proved to be the most enduring. In 1881, Vooruit had some 270 members, in 1895 this number reached 5,300, and by 1913 it neared 10,000. Bread was purchased by means of 'bread cards' that were bought in advance. Members (who had to be 'workers', sympathetic to the socialist party, and pay a yearly fee of 0.25 francs) willingly paid a high price for these 'bread cards', but got a discount in proportion to their purchases. This discount was given under the form of more 'bread cards', and thus the discount's advantage was automatically re-invested in the co-op. In the end, the price of Vooruit's bread fell slightly below the city's average bread price, but in the meantime Vooruit supplied itself with an enormous amount of cash. The bread sales skyrocketed thanks to a mix of material and ideological factors: house-to-house delivery, correct weight, discount, advertising, and militant discourse. Because of ultra-modern equipment and good organization, the bakery yielded a net profit of about 30,000 francs a year in the 1890s.[7] This ample sum was used to establish new stores, set up sick and old-age schemes, start a co-operative weaving company and a 'people's bank', finance the party, edit a newspaper, support strikes, and organize balls, a library, gym clubs and concerts. The co-operative formed the financial and ideological core of this *red* network offering members material services, and a sense of self-esteem and of belonging. This did appeal to the workers of Ghent and its surroundings: Vooruit became a genuine force, and it served as a model for other co-operatives in and outside Belgium.

VOORUIT'S GOODS: FORGING A WORKING-CLASS IDENTITY?

Right from the start it was decided to provide co-operators with more than just bread. In 1883, the administrators (among them Edouard Anseele, a masterly organizer and, later, a Member of Parliament and minister) wished to sell groceries, coal, beer, shoes, and medication. However, the first items to be sold next to bread were cotton blankets. This sale started in 1883. It was extremely successful, and it was repeated two or three times a year. In 1885 Vooruit decided that goods would no longer be purchased in a sporadic way, but systematically to have a stock during the whole year. From 1886 onwards the co-operative organized the massive purchase of ready-to-wear clothing thoroughly by sending people to wholesalers and manufacturers in Belgium and aboard. The massive purchases were used in promotion: an advertisement of 1912 read 'Vooruit can supply the most beautiful goods at the lowest price thanks to its huge purchases'.[8] At the end of 1893, the co-op set up a tailors' workshop that manufactured ready-to-wear goods by means of the most modern equipment, trusting to be able to compete with foreign products.

Alongside this supply of cheap goods, however, the co-operative also provided made-to-measure clothing of 'costly cloth'. Not only was made-to-measure manufacturing the traditional way to sell new clothing, but it also met the demand for higher quality. In 1884 Vooruit hired cutters who directed home-working tailors and needlewomen, and this type of work organization developed up to 1914. 'Quality' and 'costly cloth' were asked for in certain periods of the year (from March to May, and in September and October) when seemingly families wished to appear at their best. Often, the Holy Communion and the coming of winter were seen as advantageous periods to sell more luxury clothing. An advertisement of March 1912 in the party newspaper shows the large price gap between plain and costly clothing: a girl's suit cost between 17.75 and 48.75 francs, or almost three times as much.[9]

Next to clothing and cloth, products of a very varied nature were gradually offered by Vooruit. In 1887, an advertisement (one half page, bold printing, various fonts) in the party newspaper indicated the assortment of goods on sale: menswear, women's and children's wear, cloth, shoes, leather goods, overcoats, lingerie, and 'made-to-measure suits within 24 hours'.[10] All items were connected to clothing in one way or another. This did change in the following years, which is shown by the enumeration of all goods on sale in a brochure published on the occasion of the inauguration of the rebuilt store in 1899:

> Large choice of ready-to-wear clothing for children, adolescents, men and women; specialists in wedding suits and dresses. Work outfits in velvet, English leather, linen and cotton; also made to measure, finely finished and delivered in the shortest possible time. Rich choice of cloth for men, women and girls. Plain and fantasy, ecossais, crepon, drap de dames etc etc. Silk, surah, satinette in all colours; ribbons, lace and

braids. Beautiful dresses with or without train. Gold and jewellery. Watches, clocks and alarm clocks, perfume, and various articles of fantasy. Materials for tailors and needlewomen. Large choice of umbrellas for men, women and children very strong and cheap. Wide choice of hats, fine English, German and Italian style. Latest novelties of caps for men and boys at extremely low prices.[11]

This list impressed contemporaries highly. Why did Vooruit so much expand its supply of goods? Right from the start of the garment store, the co-op wished to provide its members with affordable goods of decent quality. The managers cherished this co-operative principle of 'fair trade', and they regularly called upon the members to make comments with regard to quality, price or manufacturing time. Complaints were heard by the board of administrators, and often customers were satisfied.[12] However, Vooruit also wished to make a profit, not — let it be clear — in a capitalistic mode, but to provide capital for the red cause. Buying, and later manufacturing, ready-to-wear clothes on a massive scale was not just seen as an opportunity to offer cheap clothes to the clientele, but also as a means to increase sales and profit. Finally and perhaps crucially, the dress store was also considered as the outstanding way to attract new co-operators and, hence, social-democrat supporters. This latter aim implied a whole programme of diverse techniques to charm as many people as possible. Unlike the bakery, customers of the garment store were not obliged to be a member of Vooruit: as early as 1885 it was decided that non-co-operators would be allowed to purchase at the garment store. Later it was said that 'the lowest possible prices would incite the working class to join us', and that the most commonly demanded goods could be sold with a loss, while profit could be made on other goods.[13] In the same spirit, the managers wished to provide sufficient goods of various style, size and colour in order not to disappoint customers (who then would leave the store to look elsewhere). The huge buildings (see below), the frequent discount sales, the continuous flood of advertising in the party newspaper and through leaflets, the propaganda at meetings, the long opening hours of the store, the discount of two or six per cent, the linking of a pension to a minimum amount of money spent at the co-op and, last but not least, the increasing choice of products all contributed to seduce the people to visit the shop frequently. The only weapon that Vooruit deliberately missed in the modern competitive struggle, was that it did not allow credit, which was central to many dress stores.

These aims and tactics influenced the type of goods on sale at the co-operative. There was both cheap and costly clothing, and luxury goods that may not readily be identified with working-class consumption (jewellery, for example). Also, photographs of the store's interior from around 1900 reveal the rather polished aspect of the co-operative: one photograph, for example, shows the huge, iron stairs on the ground floor in the central hall (Fig. 1).[14] These photographs offer only one, distinct view and are obviously 'artificial', but their overall impression is (deliberately?) much more 'bourgeois' than 'working class'. I put both concepts between quotation marks because I think they have acquired a hazy significance with regard to retailing in Western Europe around 1900. The same would go for the concept of 'fashion'. Up to 1890, advertisements in the party newspaper occasionally mentioned 'fashion', but this was by far secondary to notions as 'cheap', 'good quality', 'nice choice', 'fair

FIGURE 1. Photograph of the interior of Vooruit, Vrijdagmarkt, Ghent. Note the iron pillars, the huge stairs, the display window containing jewellery, and in general the very neat aspect of the store. (E. Sacré, *c.* 1900, AMSAB (Archive and Museum of the Socialist Labour Movement), Ghent, Belgium)

purchase' and the like. After 1900, the publicity contained references to 'splendid colours', 'newest design', 'Winter novelties', 'fashionable' etc. Unlike some other dress stores of the city, Vooruit did not publish drawings of goods on sale prior to 1914. The co-op limited itself to describing its products in very plain words, and it is therefore impossible to look at the style and fashion of clothing sold by Vooruit. Whether these products were indeed of the latest fashion is unimportant; the mere fact that Vooruit hoped to charm the people by referring to 'fashion' is significant.

The cheap goods might have offered a working-class appearance, but it would be hard to characterize the more costly goods as such. It seems to me that Vooruit aimed at a market segment that was large and expanding, but that it also wished to appeal to (lower) middle classes. Vooruit was indeed competing in a new and growing consumer market, where department stores, Christian-democratic co-ops, and traditional sales forms were active and, indeed, aggressive. It is unlikely that products sold by Vooruit differed from those supplied by other retailers, whether cheap or costly goods.

However, it is clear to me that many of Vooruit's customers were well aware of the significance of buying consumer goods at this store. Buying here had a clear social meaning. True, purchasing at Vooruit might have been primarily the result of the consideration of a price-quality balance, but it was undoubtedly linked to ideology, too. The latter was emphasized by numerous observers who (sometimes with envy) noted the very strong dedication of members to their co-operative store. One wrote that Vooruit's success was explained by the appeal of purchasing in an opulent setting, the constant advertising that entailed new longings and, particularly, the sensation of being part of something great.[15] Indeed, since the very start of the garment store in 1884 Vooruit's propaganda stressed this regularly. Vooruit had built a 'palace for the workers', where they could meet in 'their house', and, 'although the co-op is not a communist institution, it is based on the principle of collective property because all members are collectively proprietors of all working tools, buildings and land'.[16] Thus, if the goods sold by Vooruit did not differ from those supplied by other retailers, it seems clear to me that buying at Vooruit had a particular meaning for most buyers, and that this may have forged a separate identity and self-perception.

VOORUIT'S STORES: ICONS OF POLITICS AND COMMERCE

Vooruit's option to diversify and augment the supply of goods, to manufacture clothing, and to buy massively ready-made clothes had consequences for the way the goods were sold. At first, the garment store was set up in a corner of the bakery, which kept the general cost very low. Also, voluntary work was called upon to prolong opening hours of the 'bakery'. Soon, however, this did not suffice. At a board meeting in early 1884, Anseele said that the success of the clothes sales made it necessary to 'buy a separate building' and to 'appoint a general manager for the shop'. Yet the year before, the co-op had moved from a small house (the baking of bread was done in the basement of a café) to an old, transformed factory at the *Garenmarkt* that was soon called 'the temple of all workers'.[17] This large building included the bakery, a spacious café and meeting room, offices, a printing workshop, a library and the dress store. Seemingly, space in this building was too limited for the latter. Regularly, the administrators discussed the possibility of expanding the clothing shop, but no new building was bought.

When Anseele became the general manager of the co-op in 1887, he immediately suggested radical changes. He proposed to 'choose a new direction for the shop [. . .] and to concentrate all selling activities in a central room, so we can vend much more'.[18] Also, he suggested enlarging the range of goods on sale. Later, he wished to expand the shop to the second floor. These changes were radical: they showed the commercial spirit of the administrators who had started truly mass-consumer practices (discount sales, advertising, free entrance). Yet, Anseele and Vooruit had still bigger plans. Sales rose, more employees were enlisted, and more customers visited the store. To diminish the cost, it was decided to start the production of ready-made clothes, which was done by workers at home and, from 1893 on, in a workshop at Vooruit's store. Bringing production together with retailing made the organization of the shop even more complex. Finally, a big step was decided in June 1893, when a building at the *Vrijdagmarkt* was bought to establish the garment store.

Adaptation works to the building lasted for one year. In the meantime the store was re-organized: more people were enlisted (cutters, needlewomen, salespeople and, of significance for Vooruit's view on retailing, a window-dresser), the policy for buying cloth and clothes was fully revised, and modern machinery was installed (e.g. a tool that cut 24 layers of cloth at once). In November 1894 the store was inaugurated with huge celebrations. It had four floors, large display windows, inside and outside electric light, and an elevator. *Red* imagery was affixed to the outside. On a pediment of 16 m² the 'brotherhood of workers' was portrayed, while medallions represented Fourier, Marx, De Paepe and Owen. Finally, the slogan 'Workers of all countries, unite' was written over the total length of the building. Just above the display windows was announced in big characters 'Clothes, cloth, shoes, leather, groceries'. The display windows were filled with tableware and cooking utensils. On the ground floor women's wear was on sale (clothing, underwear, stockings, knitwear and the like), alongside tableware. The first floor was for menswear, but also for the cutters' room, and cabins to change clothes. On the second floor was the workshop for the ready-to-wear clothes and the shoes, while the third floor housed offices and a storeroom. A contemporary observer noted: 'Bref, l'installation du grand bazar moderne'.[19] The store had cost 225,000 francs.

Social democrats presented the opening of the store as a genuine political and commercial success. Particularly, they insisted on the fact that the store belonged to the workers. The monthly review 'Les coopérateurs belges' illustrated this well: 'A wave of electric light submerges the splendid facade of a corner on the Marché du Vendredi. People from the suburbs discuss passionately about the things they see. All this blinking and glancing belongs to them [. . .]. This *petit Louvre de province*, the illuminated facade, the pediment full of symbolic painting, the enormous flag on top and the atmosphere of triumph . . . all this is the result of a generation of patience'.[20] Many more observers wrote in a similar way, expressing their admiration for the modernity of the building, the many innovations with regard to design and commerce, the splendour of it all. Others criticized the new store severely. Christian-democrat, bourgeois and middle-class observers were shocked by the aspect of luxury of the *red* co-operative, while radical socialists condemned the bourgeois style of the store as utterly reformist. The store, its organization and the goods on sale, however, charmed the Ghent workers, judging from the rising sales. Between 1889 and 1894 sales had moved gradually upwards, but in 1895 the growth of sales was sensational with an increase by 60% in one year![21] This was beyond the wildest dreams of Vooruit. In early 1897, the co-op's bi-annual report noted briefly that 'everyone should admit that Vooruit never would have reached such high turnover if it wasn't for the new store on the Vrijdagmarkt'.[22] The declining price of cloth and the gradual rise of purchasing power were other factors that presumably influenced positively the sales of the garment store.

The crucial importance of the type of the store appeared all too obviously in the very same year. A fire destroyed the store completely. Instead of lamenting this misfortune, Vooruit decided to act as soon as possible and to do even better. Yes, the fire was a disaster, but the party newspaper saw this as a way to prove 'the unshakeable trust and extraordinary determination'. Here is how the fire was reported in the bi-annual report of August 1897:

> It took the flames one hour to devour what we so patiently have constructed and what made us proud because of its beauty. However, it will not be a loss to us: our new store shall be even more splendid than the destroyed one. A committee, formed by artist-architects, the manager and a salesgirl, was sent to Paris to visit the department stores Louvre, Bon Marché, Printemps, Pygmalion, Pont Neuf and others, and to see the latest improvements. The committee is now back and indeed very pleased, and it is convinced to present to our members something first-rate.[23]

Insurance covered the rebuilding cost of about 255,000 francs and with additional capital, this allowed the reconstruction without any restriction with regard to the newest sale principles of the Parisian department stores.

In the meantime, the store was re-installed in the old building at the *Garenplaats*. This more modest setting influenced the sales badly, which led the administrators to complaint. In 1898 they stated that the bakery, the selling of coal and medicine, and the various grocery shops did well; however,

> sales in the garment store are declining. Yet, the rich supply of goods hasn't changed, and still some members are not visiting our store because the display windows are gone. That's wrong. A co-operative shouldn't have display windows at all because the members who buy at their own store, should be seduced by absolutely nothing. So, we urge our members to buy at their own store.[24]

Sales dropped by 25% in 1898.

Ferdinand Dierkens was asked to plan the new store. He came up with a design that pleased Vooruit's administrators. Dierkens was known as a conventional architect, working in the eclectic style that was quite popular, but somewhat on the way out by then. The building impressed a lot of people. One contemporary wrote that the store was a 'véritable monument d'architecture originale'.[25] The building was inaugurated in 1899. Three years later a second building was erected next to it, housing the sick fund, the library, various clubs, and many office and meeting rooms. Both the gigantic buildings reshaped the nature of the *Vrijdagmarkt* totally (Fig. 2). The store was characterized by a window in a massive Roman arch (over three floors), while four big Doric columns accentuated the building's height, and a bulging roof with a flat top covered the whole. Art nouveau-like cast-iron supported the huge window. Monuments (representing Labour?), various ornaments, inscriptions ('Vooruit', 'Workers of all countries, unite'), and red flags made clear where the building's roots were. The store had a surface area of 765m.² (45 x 17m.). A huge central hall with inside galleries on three floors, received light through the huge window. Elegant iron pillars supported the galleries and the double iron stairs that had been built in front of the huge window. Goods were displayed on three floors, while offices and storerooms were on the fourth floor; there were two elevators.[26] There was no workshop, and so, all in all, available selling space had expanded *vis-à-vis* the 1894 building.[27]

FIGURE 2. Photograph of the Vooruit buildings, Vrijdagmarkt, Ghent: left, the building (1902) housing the sick fund, the library and offices; right, the store (1899). Postcard, *c.* 1910. (Collection Dexia Bank, Brussels)

Despite the dazzling aspect of the new, gigantic building, the growing range of goods on sale, the constant advertising, and some new selling techniques (such as a two per cent discount for non-members and a eight per cent discount for members), sales stagnated between 1900 and 1906. It was only in 1907 that sales overtook the 1896 turnover. The administrators never commented upon this stagnation. The rise in clothing prices, and stagnating or at least modest real-wage increase of Ghent workers may help explain this weaker growth of sales.[28] Nonetheless, from 1889 to 1913 sales figures at the dress store had risen by 8.5% per year. Compared to the increase of the number of co-operators in the same period (plus 3.8%), this was truly a strong growth. Co-operators may have bought more clothing, or non-members may have purchased more at the store: it seems safe to suggest that probably a mixture of both occurred. Obviously, the Ghent working classes were eager to spend more money on garment goods. The glorious aspect of the buildings did play a role, although the slow growth after the re-opening of the 1899 building would put this into perspective.

CONCLUSIONS: *RED* COMMODIFICATION?

After 1850, the European clothing system changed thoroughly. The changes not only implied production, retailing and cost, but also social meaning, (self-) representation and demand. What this meant for the working classes, may appear through the view of workers who were heard at a session of an investigation board in 1886. For a Ghent linen worker, 'workers are better dressed, at a lower cost, although the quality of cloth has deteriorated', while for a worker from Liège, 'there is a vile rivalry between (women) that spreads a taste for luxury'.[29] After 1850, working-class people wished to dress better (i.e. decent, new, respectable, fashionable, festive, or more varied), and more than before, they were in a position to do so. In other words, the time was there for close and continuous interaction between material culture and social change.[30]

Vooruit reacted promptly to this 'clothing transformation'. After having launched its bakery in 1880, the co-operative opted for the setting up of a dress store in 1883, and by 1894 this store supplied a very wide range of goods (clothing and other) of various quality and price. Both the bakery and the dress store were meant to offer people good quality for a fair price, and to make a profit for the red cause. However, the dress store was also intended to take advantage of people's desire to have better clothes, in order to introduce them into the Ghent social-democratic network (whether this had worked or not, is not at stake here). This orientation to appeal to the broadest possible clientele implied that Vooruit's goods probably did not differ from those sold by other shops that were active in the same market segment. Nonetheless, buying at Vooruit may have had a very distinct significance for a great part of the customers: a conscious act of 'red' consumption which may have provided a feeling of 'us' against 'the others'. The splendid buildings present an adequate summary of the ambiguity of the whole project of Vooruit. The appearance of the store (especially after 1899) was more 'bourgeois' than 'working class', but together it showed obvious socialist images that were familiar to all *Gantois*.

My final conclusion, then, would be that there were many doors to 'enter' the consumer society. Whether Vooruit's customers bought goods as confirmed socialists or not, and whether they gave a particular significance to purchasing goods, in the end they did increase their spending on consumer goods. They were, in a way, properly 'prepared' for the mass consumption of the 20th century. Yet, Vooruit had provided the Ghent workers with affordable clothing sold in splendid buildings, which undoubtedly contributed to the forging of a new self-image of the working classes prior to 1914.

Peter Scholliers, History Department, Vrije Universiteit Brussel, Pleinlaan 2, B-1050 Brussel, Belgium

NOTES

[1] E.g., Brewer & Porter 1993; Schuurman & Spierenburg 1996.

[2] Regarding 'mass consumer society', see Benson 1994, 1–5.

[3] For defining a 'consumer society', see, for example, McCracken 1990, 10–28; Fine & Leopold 1993, 65–70.

[4] Crossick & Jaumain 1999, 27.

[5] For this 'vertical approach' via 'systems', see Fine & Leopold 1993, 4–5.

[6] Scholliers 1999, 71–91.

[7] Up to 1913, one Belgian franc equalled 9 pence.

[8] Vooruit, 1 March 1912, p. 4 ('Vooruit' was the party newspaper from 1884 onwards).

[9] Vooruit, 1 March 1912, p. 4.

[10] Vooruit, 6 October 1887, p. 6.

[11] Vooruit boven al 1899, last page of cover.

[12] Archives and Museum of the Socialist Workers Movement (hereafter AMSAB), Fonds 24, S. M. Vooruit, 14/4, e.g., 29 June 1888: 'Rachel asks whether unsatisfied customers may be reimbursed the next day. Posters will be printed to announce this possibility'.

[13] AMSAB, Fonds 24, S. M. Vooruit, 14/3, 16 October 1885.

[14] These photographs were made by one of the few professional photographers of Ghent, Edmond Sacré (1851–1921), who specialized in winter landscapes, for which he obtained numerous medals.

[15] De Witte 1898, 148.

[16] Volksalmanak voor Noord- en Zuidnederland. Vooruit 1890, 19.

[17] Stallaerts & Schokkaert 1987, 46.

[18] AMSAB, Fonds 24, S. M. Vooruit, 14/3, 4 March 1887.

[19] Duc-Quercy (November) 1895, 4.

[20] Duc-Quercy (June) 1895, 60.

[21] Scholliers 1999, 86.

[22] Verzameling 1920, 176 (February 1897).
[23] Verameling 1920, 187 (August 1897). Unfortunately, the reports of the Board meetings are lacking between 1896 and 1911.
[24] Verzameling 1920, 199 (May 1898).
[25] Charriaut 1910, 294.
[26] Baele & De Herdt 1983; plans of the alteration works of 1956 (kept by the present-day owner of the building, the Socialistische Mutualiteit).
[27] The two buildings still exist today. They were fully renovated in the 1950s; in the 1990s, their façade was altered according to the original plans, but the interior was totally modernized.
[28] There are no estimates by historians of the evolution of clothing prices in this period; contemporaries reported an increase of cloth prices by about 17 per cent between 1902 and 1910 (Avanti 1930, II, 338).
[29] Testimonies before the Commission du travail (set up after the riots of 1886), Commission du Travail 1887, section régionale B, 27; section régionale D, 194.
[30] MacCracken 1990, 27.

BIBLIOGRAPHY

Avanti 1930, *Een terugblik. Bijdrage tot de geschiedenis der Gentsche arbeidersbeweging*, Ghent: Volksdrukkerij.

Baele, J. & De Herdt, R. 1983, *Vrij gedacht in ijzer*, Ghent: Centrum voor Kunst en Cultuur.

Benson, J. 1994, *The Rise of Consumer Society in Britain 1880–1980*, London: Routledge.

Brewer, J. & Porter, R. (eds) 1993, *Consumption and the World of Goods*, London: Routledge.

Charriaut, H. 1910, *La Belgique moderne. Une terre d'expérience*, Paris: Flammarion.

Commission du Travail. Procès-verbaux des séances d'enquête concernant le travail industriel, 1887, Brussels: A. Lesigne.

Crossick G. & Jaumain, S. 1999, 'The world of the department store: distribution, culture and social change', in Crossick, G. & Jaumain, S. (eds), *Cathedrals of Consumption. The European Department Store, 1850–1939*, Aldershot: Ashgate.

De Witte P. 1898, *Histoire du Vooruit*, Brussels: Goemaere.

Duc-Quercy, 1895, *Le Vooruit de Gand, Les coopérateurs belges*, Brussels: Office Coopératif.

Fine, B. & Leopold E. 1993, *The World of Consumption*, London: Routledge.

McCracken, G. 1990, *Culture and Consumption. New Approaches to the Symbolic Character of Consumer Goods and Activities*, Bloomington: Indiana University Press.

Scholliers, P. 1999, 'The social-democratic world of consumption: the path-breaking case of the Ghent cooperative Vooruit prior to 1914', *International Labor and Working-Class History* 55, 71–91.

Schuurman, A. & Spierenburg, P. (eds) 1996, *Private Domain and Public Inquiry. Families and Life-styles in the Netherlands and Europe, 1550 to the Present*, Hilversum: Verloren.

Stallaerts, R. & Schokkaert, L. 1987, *Onder dak. Een eeuw volks- en gildenhuizen*, Gent: Provincie Oost-Vlaanderen.

Verzameling van zesmaandelijksche en jaarlijksche mededeelingen, verslagen, rekeningen, 1920, Ghent: Volksdrukkerij.

Volksalmanak voor Noord- en Zuidnederland, 1890, Ghent: Drukkerij Vooruit.

Vooruit boven al. Beknopte geschiedenis der samenwerking te Gent. Haar verleden, hare bloei, hare toekomst, 1899, Ghent: Samenwerkende drukkerij.

Vooruit. Socialistisch dagblad, 1884– , Ghent: Samenwerkende drukkerij.

RECORDING PEOPLE AND PROCESSES AT LARGE INDUSTRIAL STRUCTURES

By ANNA BADCOCK *and* BRIAN MALAWS

PREFACE

This paper outlines an approach to the recording of large industrial structures and highlights the unique attributes of sites that make up our recent archaeological and industrial heritage. It is an amalgamation of two papers that were given separately at *the Archaeology of Industrialization* conference in Bristol, in October 1999. The themes developed are discussed in relation to two case studies: the RCAHMW recording project at the Cwm Coking Works in South Wales, and the production of a detailed project design for recording at Avenue Coking and Chemical Works in Derbyshire.

INTRODUCTION

The broad-based subject of industrial archaeology includes the studies of architectural, engineering, social, economic, geographic and industrial history and, on the other hand, the archaeological remains. In theory, it draws together many of the present-day specialized aspects of the wide term 'archaeology'. However, in practice, the importance of studying industry through its archaeology has tended to be overshadowed by the architectural and historical aspects of the monuments themselves. This is typified by a common approach to 'preserved' industrial sites where an attractive architectural shell is retained as being of historical significance, whereas the precise nature of the activities carried on within may be poorly understood, recorded or presented. Often, redundant industrial structures are retained only through their re-use for other kinds of development — in our experience those looking for new uses for old industrial sites think largely in terms of 'usable space within an architecturally acceptable envelope'. This undoubtedly has its place alongside preservation of associated machinery in museums, in the continuance of some vestige of the industry's presence. However, the practice of industrial archaeology must be far more than the preservation of interesting facades, or the creation of working museums. It must be more than simply documentary research combined with the study of industrial architecture. Unless we record the processes and human activities that were an integral part of these buildings, we are not practising industrial archaeology at a professional level.

FIGURE 1. Avenue Coking and Chemical Works. (Photo: Stuart Kay)

What makes the two case studies discussed here unusual, in archaeological terms, is the recent nature of the sites. The Cwm Works was still operational when it was recorded by the RCAHMW, and the Avenue Works only fell out of use in 1992. The contribution that oral evidence can make to the study of sites such as these should not be overlooked and indeed should be one of the aspects that makes the study of our more recent past different from the study of earlier periods. This kind of evidence plays a very important role in the understanding of the social relations that were created and reproduced.

The case studies highlight both the importance of understanding the working life of industrial buildings and the constraints (financial, legislative, etc.) that make this ideal hard to achieve. It is hoped that the individuality of each site will show through this text, and demonstrate the need for carefully tailored archaeological approaches that accommodate the kinds of elements particular to such sites.

THE AVENUE COKING AND CHEMICAL WORKS

The Avenue Works is located near Chesterfield in the north Midlands, in the heart of what was once a major coal-producing area. The plant is large, encompassing 188 hectares of land, and comprises a variety of structures, including ovens, reprocessing works, rail sidings, administrative blocks and storage units (Fig. 1). It was built, between 1952 and 1956, to produce smokeless solid fuel (coke) for both the industrial and domestic markets, and its innovative design meant that its own by-products, and some from other plants in the region, could be processed on site. The site layout was planned to accommodate a one hundred percent increase in production, though this expansion never took place, and the plant remained fairly true to its original ground plan. The production of smokeless fuel became an important aspect of the post-nationalization coal industry and the period during which the Avenue Works was built and operated represents the final and most sophisticated form of coke production in the country.[1] Coke production in Britain has declined dramatically in recent years, and almost all remaining plants have been demolished; production at Avenue ceased in 1992 and the works has since been disused.

Building a Design

The Coal Industry as a whole is one of the strategic, national projects that makes up English Heritage's Monuments Protection Programme (MPP). It is hoped that through the study of groups of monuments, in both their immediate environs and their wider landscape context, the most appropriate protection or management strategies can be implemented. It is as a result of this programme that, in 1994, Avenue Works was identified as being of national importance,[2] although a subsequent report rated the national importance of the site as 'moderate/low'.[3] The plant had also been recorded by the Royal Commission on the Historical Monuments of England (RCHME, now part of English Heritage) in 1994. This study comprised photographs of the exterior and interior of the main buildings within the complex, accompanied by a short written description of each building.

In the mid 1990s the plant came under threat from a planning application for proposed opencast coal extraction, and the scheme would have required the complete demolition of the plant. Although the plant is possibly unique, and might, in normal circumstances be afforded protection under Listed Buildings legislation, it is so large that it would be impossible to maintain in its present form; financial constraints and safety considerations alone prevent the site from being preserved in its entirety.

In response to the planning application, preservation by record was deemed the most appropriate course of action, and ARCUS was commissioned to produce a project design for the recording. English Heritage made recommendations to be included within the design. These recommendations were: additional survey of the extant structures to enhance the 1994 RCHME survey; an Industrial Chemist's assessment; the creation of an oral historical record; and an index of the currently dispersed record archive.

So what is it that makes the Avenue Works of national importance? While they may not be particularly distinguished or unusual in themselves, the individual buildings together form a plant that represents technological innovation, and is now a rare example in this country. Like the criteria used for scheduling monuments or assessing the impact of a proposed development, the 'quality' of the plant as a whole can apparently be judged according to the design, function, condition, rarity and group value of its individual buildings. These criteria are important and offer a way to compare sites of a very different nature. However, what these broad terms seem to gloss over, and what we hope this approach develops, is a deeper understanding of the local and personal context of the plant. It is important to see the plant *inhabited* if the record is to have any real meaning. Emphasis should be placed on how the extant building remains were caught up in, and helped to structure, the human experiences of working in a large industrial complex.

It has been argued that industrial archaeologists have been content to analyse the functional aspect of sites and structures, along with their economic and technological context, without consideration of the social or cultural context of production.[4] Archaeologies of inhabitation seem more highly developed for studies of earlier, particularly prehistoric periods, although there are some notable exceptions in more recent industrial archaeological studies.[5] The chance to record a site of this nature comes rarely, and it provides an opportunity to rethink the more traditional approaches, and experiment with different techniques. This is why the creation of an oral historical record is such an important part of the methodology. Ideally, a range of people would contribute to the oral record, bringing together differing viewpoints. Oral evidence not only helps us to understand the physical remains of a site but will give us knowledge of how the plant operated, and the different roles that people played in this operation. In this respect, we are at a great advantage in studying the recent past, particularly when dealing with structures that were in use entirely within living memory.

Mapping Activity

Whilst we were developing ideas about the recording methodology, ARCUS was given a small collection of material which helped to focus these ideas. The material included a selection of works records, original promotional documents and a collection of photographs taken by one of the Works Managers, Mr Stuart Kay, over a period of several years. There were a large numbers of plans, charts and technical drawings which document the original design of the works and some of the changes that were made through time. Schematic diagrams related chemical processes to particular buildings or installations and illustrate how the site functioned as a whole.

The two themes that arose out of the study of this archive material and which help to describe this approach are those of *activity* and *image*. Thomas Markus writes that 'a building's form, function and space each has meanings in the field of social relations, each is capable of signifying who we are, to ourselves in society and in the cosmic scheme of things. And each speaks of both power and bond relations'.[6] A focus on aspects of human activity will draw us away from current methodologies which have a tendency to concentrate on the physical qualities and assigned function of particular structures; this still allows the form and function of a building to be described, as well as the production processes going on within it, but requires that we draw in the human element. If we do not look carefully, the seemingly overt function of particular buildings within the complex may mask the more subtle activities, assumptions and knowledges that were taking place and being formed in these areas. Through a study of activity, we will gain an insight into an understanding of the skill base, which may now be lost, and an idea of what it meant to work there (Fig. 2).

FIGURE 2. Word/deed — layers of work. (Composite picture created by Michael Lane)

In the Royal Commissions, recording at industrial sites has in the past been limited to photographing individual machines and perhaps relating these to a general ground plan; usually little attempt was made to link the components other than through their physical relationship or proximity. Often, a simple industrial installation was separated into component parts, each drawn individually in some detail, but devoid of context. Unfortunately this approach meant that important elements which were not readily measurable or not photogenic might be ignored — such as a piece of baler twine performing a vital function for the control of machinery, or, at the other end of the scale, a mobile crane used to transfer minerals from one part of a process to another. Recording work at Taff Merthyr Colliery in South Wales[7] revealed how different the reality of production was from the idealized process shown on a flow chart (Figs 3 and 4). This experience shows us that changes to original designs of any site would not always have been planned or drafted, especially if they were considered makeshift or temporary. Particularly in terms of minor operations, it is perhaps only through the inclusion of oral evidence that we will know how the 'mapped ideal' was realized on the ground.

While the sequence of production processes would undoubtedly have dictated the plant layout to a large extent, other less obvious factors would also have contributed to the design, particularly on a smaller scale; we must look beyond the 'givens' to find unintended or alternative functions. Not only did Avenue Works consist of a series of functional spaces, it was also a social space, with access governed by a whole series of written and unwritten rules. Perceived and manufactured relations between management, workforce and the public would have been reinforced by the physical space of the buildings and the ways these spaces were dwelt in. Which areas were accessible to whom? How were furnishings and decor used to designate or

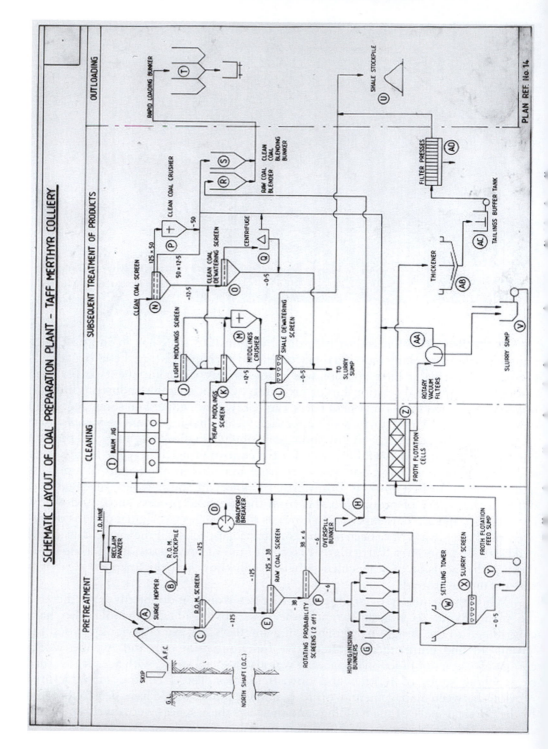

SCHEMATIC LAYOUT OF COAL PREPARATION PLANT – TAFF MERTHYR COLLIERY

PLAN REF. No. 14

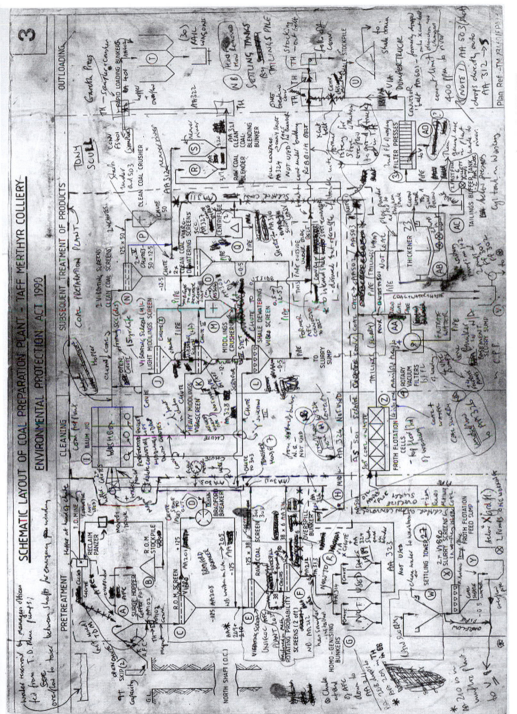

FIGURE 4.   Taff Merthyr Colliery: the process as recorded by RCAHMW. (© Crown Copyright: RCAHMW)

adapt particular spaces? To what extent were surveillance mechanisms (architectural or technological) employed, either for security purposes or personnel management?

The production processes, architecture and workforce relations would have formed routines of activity and movement over a variety of different time scales. Whilst at certain times such activity might be highly structured, at other times it would not be. Access analysis or space syntax[8] gives a method of analysing social relations with reference to the differing penetrability of physical spaces. But this analysis, based upon floor plans and access routes, offers only a partial understanding of the interaction between, people and space. Status, gender, job description and tradition, as a few examples, all govern where and when people move, and it is knowledge of these issues, and the decision to act upon this knowledge, that will enforce or destroy such barriers. This information cannot be gained from building recording alone.

From even a superficial study of Stuart Kay's photographs, it is possible to identify zones of activity and indications of gendered space; out of several hundred images, the only picture of a woman showed an administrative office interior. This is likely to reflect a bias in his photographic record, but it may also hint at the structure of the workforce. While the proportion of men and women that were employed at the plant would need to be investigated, it is likely that their roles were fairly clearly defined in both functional and spatial terms.

Some of the archive files contained figures detailing the output of the plant, efficiency ratings and general running costs. Considered in isolation, these rather dry sets of data are of limited value, but when we tie these figures into our study of activity they help us to focus on the site on different levels. They can pull our view outwards, to build up an idea of the contribution of production at a regional and national scale. We can compare the Avenue Works with other plants, or think about how it related to the different industries that supplied or were supplied by it. Likewise, these data can draw our view inwards to focus on a community level. Wage lists tell us how much was spent on salaries each week, and this gives us an understanding of the financial impact that the closure of the works had on the local economy. These figures are some of the tangible remnants of management and control, and ultimately featured in the decision to close the plant down.

Picturing the Plant

Concentration on *image* enables us to study how the plant was perceived in the past, the role that it played in people's lives and how it could be presented today. The changing image of the plant is another theme that is represented in the archive material. The promotional brochure, which was produced by the National Coal Board in 1956, presented the clean, efficient and technological face of the plant to the public. The NCB was understandably proud of this engineering achievement, saying 'this scientifically planned and integrated smokeless fuel and chemical works is undoubtedly one of the finest in the world . . .'. Along with detailed technical descriptions of coke manufacture and the processing of its chemical by-products, the brochure included photographs of the pristine equipment and new site buildings,

FIGURE 5. Interior view, Avenue Works official brochure. (Courtesy of the NCB)

emphasizing the clean, bright colours of the myriad pipes and towers. We are shown dials, generators and astonishing perspectives. We are given symmetry, standardization, power and control (Fig. 5). The centre pages show a schematic three-dimensional aerial view of the entire works, which isolates the site from its landscape context; there are no hills or houses to be seen, no spoil heaps or smoking chimneys. It is the very model of cleanliness and efficiency.

What are missing from the brochure are the people — out of 71 illustrations, only one contained a person, but we know he did not run the plant by himself. Of course, promotional material has a specific function, and these images were carefully chosen to portray this chosen aspect: technology, efficiency and cleanliness were paramount. It tells us something about the desire of the NCB to inform people, and it almost seems as if they were not promoting so much a product as a technological achievement. The context of post-war Britain is also important here; in a climate of ever-increasing development schemes, ten million pounds for a construction project does not seem a particularly large sum today. But in this case it represents part of the massive investment in the rebuilding of this country's infrastructure. The Avenue

Works was a fine example of a capability to produce large quantities of fuel to power the nation.

Many of these pictures bear strong similarities to drawings and photographs commissioned from American artist Charles Scheeler in the 1920s, to promote the enormous Rouge plant built by Ford, near Detroit. Scheeler's work was commissioned as part of an advertising campaign to promote a new Ford model, although the paintings and photographs he produced were also published as independent artworks. These works served as celebrations of industry, and as commentaries upon a scale of production and physical control over the workforce that had never been seen before. Scheeler also omitted the human subjects from his artworks so as to present the Rouge plant as one 'stupendous, perfectly-functioning, self-operating machine'.[9]

The working reality of Avenue was not, as we know, the clean and colourful ideal promoted in the NCB brochure, and as time went on efficiency decreased, accompanied by an increase in pollution. By the mid 1980s, concern with the public image of the works had grown strong enough to necessitate a 'clean-up campaign'.[10] These concerns were a reflection of a growing awareness of environmental issues, and, perhaps, a direct response to pressures from a Conservative government that was hitting the coal industry hard. A very powerful set of photographs was taken, which, although they are as staged as those seen in the brochure, seem more realistic. They show men at work and the accumulated decades of grime (Fig. 6).

The movement between personal and official archives helps to texture our study. Stuart Kay's photographs give us an image of the plant on an individual level, and give us views that no promotional or official documentation would ever show. They show the plant in various weather and working conditions; some are general overviews, some show particular buildings while others show people at work, or at rest. These photographs are the closest we get to an image of a working plant, improvisation, accidents and all.

Perhaps most poignant are images of the last working day. In September 1992, the last charge of coke was processed. For those watching, this must have been an emotional time (Fig. 7). Avenue Works closed two months afterwards.

An Ongoing Project

As a reflection of recent changes in government attitudes to opencast schemes, the application to develop the Avenue Works site has not been submitted. The proposed archaeological recording work has not yet taken place, and the future of this site is uncertain. At the time of writing, parts of the site have already been demolished for safety reasons, without being recorded. There is every chance that the rest of the buildings will suffer the same fate. However, the ideas worked through during the creation of the project design will not be lost, and should be applied to other industrial sites. Archaeology has an active role to play in the creation of even our most recent histories, and we need more socially informed approaches to our industrial heritage. We need to gain a picture of working sites, that produced smells and sounds which escaped the bounds of the site and, in the case of Avenue Works, required a workforce to be present 24 hours a day. Extant remains may be classified as being of national

FIGURE 6. Working of the oven battery. (Courtesy of the NCB)

FIGURE 7. Workers watching the final charge of coke being processed. (Photo: Stuart Kay)

importance, but placing them in a local context gives them specific meaning. The memories of the people that worked at such places, and even those that grew up around them, are an important part of the fabric of the buildings, and should be allowed to remain so.

CWM COKING WORKS: A CASE STUDY IN PROCESS RECORDING

Current work being carried out by the RCAHMW at Cwm Coking Works in South Wales can be used as a case study to illustrate an approach to industrial process recording and to discuss some methods of presentation. The techniques applied have been developed from pioneer work at Taff Merthyr Colliery[11] and since applied successfully, although not so exhaustively, to various sites including another colliery, an explosives works, a lead re-processing works and a gold mine.

Background

In 1992, faced with the rapid decline of the traditional coal industry, the RCAHMW, with its limited resources, had to make some hard decisions about recording what was arguably the most important industry of South Wales. It was felt that a comprehensive record including details of operation should be made of one colliery to complement the ongoing rapid photographic survey programme which covered several collieries, but not in great detail. From this decision stemmed the far-reaching policy of carrying out process recording to some degree as a normal part of site recording at industrial sites wherever practicable.

In 1997 a decision was made to record Cwm Coking Works, as the last working example of a process used to provide coke for the once extensive iron and steel industry in Wales. The works (Fig. 8) is some 4 km south of Pontypridd in the County of Rhondda Cynon Taff and was opened in 1958, having been designed and built by Simon-Carves Ltd of Stockport for the National Coal Board. Originally, coal was supplied by the adjacent Cwm pit, but this closed in 1986, since when coal has been imported, most recently from the USA and Australia. As a part of the privatization of the British coal industry, the site is currently run by Coal Products Limited and is the sole manufacturer of foundry coke in the UK.

A programme of intensive photography was planned with the dual aims of recording the architectural and engineering features of all site structures and, in conjunction with diagrams and flow charts, illustrating all the stages of coke production in detail. Recording the operation of the works at first hand, rather than putting resources into gathering existing technical records, has so far reinforced the underlying soundness of a policy of recording processes for other industries whilst still operational. When an industry has closed and machinery has been removed or the site cleared, an enormous amount of painstaking archaeological and documentary detective work is required to determine the process; although this can be done successfully,[12] and in many cases there is no alternative, it is much easier and more effective to record at first hand, especially when there are still people on site familiar with and actually operating the processes being studied.

FIGURE 8. Cwm Coking Works: a general view of the site from the north east. Note the truck (centre) preparing to tip into the coal reception hopper. To the left are penned stockpiles each containing coal from different mines (990356/4). (© Crown Copyright: RCAHMW)

On site

All site work was carried out by two Royal Commission staff. Although several large and complex industrial sites have now been recorded in detail, it soon became apparent that operations at the works were much more complicated than originally envisaged. The by-products plant alone is in effect a complete and substantial chemical works; whereas it is relatively straightforward to follow flows of visible materials around a site, liquids and gases in sealed vessels and pipes are a different matter. A site plan was obtained, enabling most ground features to be identified, but unfortunately it did not reflect the essential three-dimensional nature of the buildings and structures. Also there was no process flow-chart to use as a basis for our work, apart from what could be copied from various panels in the site's control centres and a most useful but very technical account of the process as in operation in 1980, compiled by one of the works staff. This latter is being checked against the layout and functions of the installations as they currently operate and adapted and simplified as necessary — it is sometimes easy to forget that we are involved in archaeological

FIGURE 9.   Coal reception area, showing the covered tipping shed for road vehicles and the coal conveyor system supplying bunkers 1–4 (left) (990351/10). (© Crown Copyright: RCAHMW)

research, albeit of a highly technical and specialized subject. Every part of the coke production process, within the site confines, is being followed and recorded: each piece of machinery is being located, photographed as appropriate, its function identified and its role in the context of the whole process noted.

Although only limited areas have been investigated in detail so far, there have been many technical and logistical challenges to face. Professional recording abilities are sometimes tested when trying to inspect, through a haze of coal dust, a noisily vibrating machine, half buried under a heap of spilt coal or coke and operating in a confined area in a very hot and unlit room. Transporting bulky photographic gear along a simple, direct connection on a plan between two machines often reveals in reality that the link represents several changes in floor level and transfer into another building.

The process

It must be made clear that the process described below will, when complete, relate only to that of coke production and associated operations within the area of the works and will do no more than indicate wider aspects of the process such as sourcing of raw materials and onward transport of finished products to customer.

As at all works dealing with continuous flows of materials, the overriding consideration during production is to ensure that one part of the process does not have to stop through delays elsewhere. Normal arrangements allow continuous working by means of overflow and by-pass facilities in the production circuit. It is not practicable to stop the flow should any equipment fail or clogging occur and at Cwm this is overcome in three ways: within the total operation, refining of material necessitates flows to be divided by quality and often a lower standard flow will be fed back to an earlier part of the system for reprocessing; secondly, there are various surge hoppers built into the system which act as buffers against temporary interruptions, the most extreme being the facility to dump overflow material to ground at certain points, notably transfer houses where one conveyor belt tips material onto another, and lastly, those processing machines most likely to cause problems are duplicated so that one can be repaired or unclogged whilst its twin takes the flow of material. The potential bottlenecks are under surveillance by closed-circuit television cameras; the whole system is monitored from various control rooms from where speed and operation of machines and conveyors and also flow diversions can be remotely controlled. Because of the many opportunities to by-pass and recycle material, following the process through from beginning to end is not straightforward.

The basic stages of coke production identified for the purposes of creating an archaeological record of the process are: coal reception; breeze processing; coal and breeze blending and treatment; coking (oven roasting); coke processing; by-products. To date only the coal reception section has been recorded in full; parts of other areas have been investigated and recording commenced.

1: Coal reception, storage and blending

Coal is received by road and distributed to seven storage bunkers or tipped to stockpiles according to grade and origin.

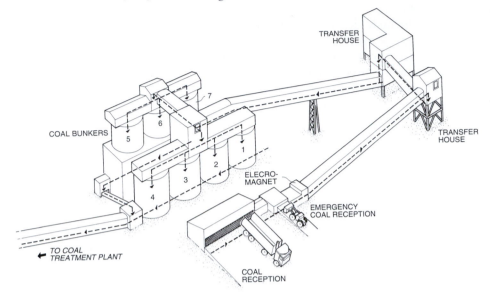

When the coking plant was opened in 1958, coal was supplied from the adjacent Cwm Pit. However, this pit closed in 1986 and since then coal has been brought to the site by road and rail from various sources. Currently, coal is imported from mines in the USA and Australia; the last leg of its journey is by road from Cardiff and Avonmouth docks respectively.

On arrival at the works, each truckload of coal is weighed and the control room is advised as to the origin and amount, both of which are recorded. The destination and available tonnage within the storage system is carefully controlled, as coal from each mine has different properties and needs to be blended to enable a final product to be produced which is most suitable for its intended market. Coal is thus tipped either direct into the conveyor system or to ground storage stockpiles for future use.

Coal is normally tipped through a gridded hopper onto conveyor no. 1, passing under an electromagnet which removes any foreign ferrous objects. Coal retrieved from ground storage enters the system through the emergency reception hopper by dumper truck, similarly passing under the magnet. All coal then passes into a transfer house, where it drops to a short conveyor no. 3, thence to a further transfer house and to conveyor no. 4 which raises the coal to the top of the storage bunkers.

Generally, each bunker holds coal from a particular mine. Information from the prior notification given to the control room as to the origin of each truckload is used to set the distributing conveyors. No. 4A (reversible) runs across between the two rows of bunkers, tipping to conveyor no. 5 which serves bunkers 1–4, or tipping to no. 5A which serves bunkers 5–7. Nos 5 and 5A are reversible and moveable, each complete belt and associated drive being set on a carriage running on rails, to allow access to all the bunkers they serve.

Below each bank of bunkers runs a conveyor, no. 6 underneath 1–4 and no. 6A under 5–7, which collect stored coal via a vibrating weigh feeder set under each bunker, the former delivering directly to conveyor no. 7 and no. 6A via 6B thence to no. 7. Conveyor no. 6 extends back beyond the bunkers to receive crushed coke breeze from two separate storage bunkers (see section 2: Breeze Processing Plant). Conveyor no. 7 takes coal and crushed breeze on to the coal treatment plant (see section 3).

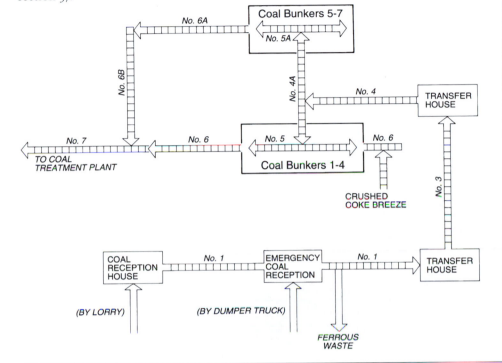

Presentation of results

It is useful to consider the different media that might be employed in the recording and presentation of results, as they too will affect how we think about the site. Information gathered in the field is only of use if it can be interpreted and presented properly — there are many conditions to satisfy that do not apply to a straightforward measured survey, for example. To make available the details of complex industrial processes and activities in a way that is easy to follow on several levels, including technical, graphical and pictorial; is capable of being searched to some degree; contains all relevant aspects to allow further interpretation by others, yet is reasonably concise, requires careful assessment of possible presentation methods before recording work begins.

A conventional written report on specialized and technical processes can make for tortuous reading, although it is relatively easy to produce. Such a report would normally be written at only one level of detail according to the intended audience;

FIGURE 10. Interior of transfer house at the top of conveyor no. 1. Coal is tipped onto conveyor no. 3 (990238/6A). (© Crown Copyright: RCAHMW)

FIGURE 11. A view under the storage bunkers 1–4 showing conveyor no. 6 surmounted by a vibrating weigh feeder which controls the amount of coal released from the bunker (990348/5). (© Crown Copyright: RCAHMW)

even so, a continuous narrative can be difficult to follow and to search for particular areas of interest.

A chart or a series of annotated diagrams is an effective way of depicting process visually but skill and time are needed to produce sufficiently clear drawings and annotations may need to be extensive to explain complex events of low visual content. A single chart has the great advantage of presenting the process in one view, enabling appreciation of the relative importance of the parts and easing the search for particular aspects, but can be visually complicated and even daunting to study.

Photographs are essential for conveying the actual appearance of machinery and are very easy and quick to produce in quantity. Even when recording an operational site, it is doubtful whether photographs alone could convey successfully all aspects of an industrial operation; extensive captioning and explanation would be needed where the nature of the process is not visually apparent.

A website or interactive CD-ROM, which could include text, still and moving images and sound could combine the presentation methods mentioned above. While there are certainly problems with the use of electronic media, there is the potential for creating and presenting a non-linear study. There is no need to conform to traditional reporting or display formats, and a well-designed electronic format which is capable of being studied at several different levels and able to be searched easily will facilitate and encourage individual exploration and enquiry where one person's reading will be different from another's. The possibility for multiple interpretations will therefore flow through the recording *and* the presented results. For Cwm Coking Works, the most practical approach lay in compromise: by careful design, combining the simplicity and economy of paper documents with the interactive principle of electronic media, an illustrated description will be produced capable of being studied at several different levels and able to be searched easily. The example shown above serves to demonstrate the principle: the report headings or illustrations can be searched quickly for a subject or area of interest, which can then be studied at an appropriate level of detail.[13]

CONCLUSION

The survey at Cwm Coking Works is still in progress, and the lessons learned from earlier, similar surveys are proving invaluable. The record being created is both typical and unique, in that coke production is a fairly standard industrial process, yet there is evidence of modification of the standard systems better to fit the local conditions. Due to continuous technical improvements and alterations to working methods, equipment becomes redundant and is often still in place where removal is not urgent. Some parts of the process seemed contorted or unnecessarily complex, until it was realized that a formerly key element had been removed, but the flows of material relating to it had been retained. Two examples will serve to illustrate this at Cwm: because the site was originally supplied from the adjacent colliery, some of the buildings and equipment used also by the coking works have been left behind to fulfil a function only partly related to their original role; also several apparent design oddities, such as the remote position of the coal handling plant, are a legacy from the period when there were extensive railway sidings serving the whole of the site — originally most functions were designed and built to be rail-dependent, but all railway operations ceased some time ago.

The techniques used for this recording exercise are building on those already employed successfully at other sites. As stated earlier, but worth reinforcing, one of the principal aims of future industrial archaeological work at RCAHMW is to ensure that where possible the processes and activities are fully understood and appropriately recorded alongside the architectural and engineering aspects.

ACKNOWLEDGEMENTS

This paper has been produced jointly by Anna Badcock and Brian Malaws. Anna Badcock would like to thank James Symonds for help and advice, Stuart Kay for providing archive material, and John Barrett, Michael Lane and Mel Giles for commenting on versions of the text. Michael Lane produced Figure 2.

The part dealing with Cwm Coking Works has been compiled from current recording work with RCAHMW carried out by Brian Malaws, who would like to thank: Coal Products Ltd and the management of Cwm Coking Works for allowing such free access to the site; staff there who met all requests for information and assistance enthusiastically; colleagues Fleur James who produced superb photographs of often unpromising subjects, and Charles Green for preparing the drawings and flow charts. All illustrations and text relating to Cwm and Taff Merthyr are Crown copyright and are reproduced by permission of the Royal Commission on the Ancient and Historical Monuments of Wales; copies are available through the National Monuments Record of Wales (the Royal Commission's public archive).

Anna Badcock, ARCUS, University of Sheffield, Department of Archaeology, West Court, 2 Mappin Street, Sheffield S1 4DT, UK
Brian Malaws, Royal Commission on the Ancient and Historical Monuments of Wales (RCAHMW), Plas Crug, Aberystwyth, Ceredigion SY23 1NJ, UK

NOTES

[1] Gould 1994.
[2] Ibid.
[3] English Heritage n.d.
[4] Palmer & Neaverson 1998.
[5] E.g. Alfrey & Clark 1993.
[6] Markus 1993, 30.
[7] Malaws 1997.
[8] Markus 1993, citing Hillier & Hanson 1984.
[9] Lucic 1991, 95, citing Stebbins, T. E. Jr & Keyes, N. Jr 1987, *Charles Scheeler: the photographs*, Boston: Museum of Fine Arts.

[10] Kay, pers. comm.
[11] Malaws 1997.
[12] For example, Weddell & Pye 1989.
[13] The Historic American Engineering Record and Historic American Buildings Survey have been successfully recording and illustrating processes in this way for several years; however, there seems little comparable work done in the UK.

BIBLIOGRAPHY

Alfrey, J. & Clark, C. 1993, *The landscape of industry: patterns of change in the Ironbridge Gorge*, London: Routledge.

English Heritage (n.d.), *Coal Industry Step 4 report: Avenue Coking and Chemical Plant*.

Gould, S. 1994, *Coal Industry Step 3 report: Avenue Coking and Chemical Plant*, London: English Heritage.

Hillier, B. & Hanson, J. 1984, *The Social Logic of Space*, Cambridge: Cambridge University Press.

Lucic, K. 1991, *Charles Scheeler and the cult of the machine*, London: Reaktion Books Ltd.

Malaws, B. A. 1997, 'Process Recording at Industrial Sites', *Industrial Archaeology Review* 19, 75–98.

Markus, T. A. 1993, *Buildings and Power*, London and New York: Routledge.

Palmer, M. & Neaverson, P. 1998, *Industrial Archaeology: principles and practice*, London and New York: Routledge.

Weddell, P. J. & Pye, A. R. 1989, *Gawton Mine and Arsenic Works*, Exeter Museums Archaeological Field Unit Reports 98.01 and 89.02.

INDUSTRIAL BUILDINGS AND THEIR EVALUATION

By TAMARA ROGIC

INTRODUCTION

This paper focuses on the evaluation of architectural features of industrial buildings under consideration for protection in England. In the last 20 years, a series of conversions of industrial buildings have been undertaken. These buildings have attracted interest because of the character of their internal space. Industrial buildings have been the object of extensive evaluation under both the Thematic Listing Programme (TLP) and the Monuments Protection Programme (MPP) of English Heritage. It will be argued that through these programmes the character of the internal space of the buildings and sites is not addressed, and that, consequently, these programmes do not inform sufficiently management decisions, particularly regarding the reuse and conversion of the evaluated buildings and sites.

LEGISLATIVE FRAMEWORK FOR CONSERVATION

In England, the ultimate aim of the evaluation process in the conservation field is the statutory protection — that is, scheduling, listing, conservation area designation — of buildings and sites based on the recognition of their national, regional or local significance. During the last 50 years (post World War II) the cultural significance of the evaluated buildings has been established on the basis of historical, social, economic, technological and architectural data collected.[1] Since scheduling is designed primarily for below-ground or ruined archaeological sites (though it is also applied to industrial structures, and occasionally to roofed but non-inhabited buildings), this paper is concerned primarily with listing and the TLP.

The role of the pertinent conservation legislation is to control changes to the protected historic fabrics, resulting from proposed repair works or changes in the original use of a building. In other words, legislation is concerned with the management of protected structures.[2]

Grading, the output of the evaluation process, legally determines management. The approach to the management of Grade I listed buildings is theoretically clear: even with the change of its use, the building should be preserved as found, internally and externally. In other words, the architectural and historic interest of these buildings should stay intact.[3] The scheduling of archaeological sites, in management terms, has the same purpose.[4]

However, most of the protected buildings are Grade II listed. Their lower grade indicates their lesser historical importance in comparison to Grade I buildings. Consequently, Grade II allows for a more ambiguous management approach. In practice, that means that Grade II buildings are more likely to lose their historic character, especially internally, as a result of their change of use, and Grade II listed buildings constitute 94% of the protected building stock in England.[5] Since management depends mainly on the architectural attributes of the building (this will be further argued below), this paper will discuss the extent to which the architectural data collected for the purpose of the evaluation may provide adequate information for future management purposes.

Although management covers a wide range of issues, from a decision on new uses to repair of interior fittings, a decision on a new use may be considered as a starting point for any conversion.[6] All other alterations to the historic fabric will be influenced by this primary decision.[7] In the management guidelines of the legislation, the future life of a building is defined through terms such as 'sympathetic use'[8] or 'sensitive alterations'[9] which would not 'affect the character of the listed building',[10] either external or internal.[11] The proposal for a new use, therefore, is a key issue in the post-evaluation management the process.

Decisions about new uses for abandoned industrial buildings are often taken on the basis of factors such as development schemes, budget, client wishes, and so on, which often do not take account of the architectural potential of a building. In order to preserve or respect 'the character of the listed building', however, a decision on a new use should spring from the building's architectural potential itself, as suggested in PPG 15.[12] One would expect that the data collected during the evaluation process would fulfil the task of revealing the architectural potential of the examined building. However, both the TLP and MPP, the two current evaluation programmes in England, have still not achieved this.

HISTORIC INTEREST OF BUILDINGS

The TLP and MPP[13] originated from the urge to update both the schedule of ancient monuments[14] and the statutory list of historic buildings,[15] by selectively including or excluding evaluated buildings or sites on their lists. In both programmes, building up a 'comprehensive coverage'[16] of a certain examined building type has been recognized as an essential task for the purpose of selecting those buildings and sites which are worth protecting.[17] Developing an understanding of the examined type and, therefore, a research-based evaluation process became a procedure common to both programmes.[18]

The evaluation of industrial buildings and sites, recognized either as a threatened or an under-represented building type on both lists, became one of the first assessment tasks of both the TLP and MPP in the late 1980s: 'Of over 2,400 sites [textile mills] known to have existed, more than half had been demolished by 1992' in Greater Manchester alone.[19] Creating a 'comprehensive coverage' of the examined industrial building type resulted in the growing awareness of the cultural significance of this building type. This change in perception of the cultural significance of industrial buildings is evident through the constant growth of the number of listed and scheduled industrial buildings and sites.[20]

The recognition of the cultural significance and the consequent justification for protection are based on the need to satisfy the selection criteria, such as rarity, historic interest, and so on,[21] of both programmes. A criterion such as 'rarity' is, in fact, related to the age of the building or site.[22] The older the building or site is, the less likely examples are to survive. Pre-19th-century buildings and sites which have survived until today deserve protection according to the criterion 'rarity'. However, when the object of the evaluation is groups of buildings or sites which have survived to our day in the greater numbers, the 'historic interest',[23] rather than the 'architectural interest',[24] becomes the most significant selection criterion.

Industrial buildings and sites present such a group. Historic interest, defined as 'important aspects of the nation's social, cultural or military history; close historical association with nationally important people or events',[25] permits a wide range of justifications for the historic importance of an evaluated industrial building. As a result, the number of listed buildings has rapidly expanded.[26]

The historical significance of anything that belongs to the world around us has become the most important measuring instrument, converting almost unselectively parts of our environment into heritage. It has been suggested that this attitude is more 'backward- than forward-looking'.[27] It may be suggested that it mirrors a more general trend in the world which has been expressed thus: 'Never before have so many been so engaged with so many different pasts spanning the centuries from prehistory to last night.'[28]

A merely historical approach to the evaluation of our environment, like the one described above, would be sufficient if the aim of the evaluation process were statutory protection alone, and the evaluation process were of no consequence for the future life of a protected building or site. Yet, gaining protected status through the evaluation process is considered a starting point for a kind of special care that the protected object deserves through the future management plan. The concern about the extent to which the evaluation process should inform the management plan has not attracted sufficient interest in the conservation field, although the need for this concern has been acknowledged by specialists.[29]

ARCHITECTURAL CHARACTERISTICS OF INDUSTRIAL BUILDINGS

The 'comprehensive coverage' of an industrial building or a site is created in the analysis of historical, archaeological, morphological, architectural, economic, social, and other data.[30] The role of the analysis of the collected data is twofold. On the one hand, the historical and physical context of an industrial building and site is defined, and on the other, the analysis contributes towards justification of the building's place and importance in the pre-defined context.

The data related to the architectural characteristics of a building or site contribute to the establishment of the historical context. However, according to these data a building is categorized on the basis of style and form, rather than analysed in relation to its architectural and spatial potential. Data related to the architectural characteristics of an examined building or site, as collected at the time of evaluation, may be grouped under the following headings:[31]

— spatial organization of individual buildings and sites;
— building materials and construction methods;
— external and internal architectural ornaments.

The most common story line that may be read in order to justify or illustrate the historical architectural importance of a building or site is: in the given area, wrought iron was used *for the first* time as a structural element in this and that mill, allowing the development of the open space floor plan *from that period onwards*; the architectural style/fashion *of the period* or/and the architect is visible in the external and internal decorative features such as wall decorations, staircases fences, and so on, as well as the division and organization of the façade.[32] Although these descriptions refer particularly to the architectural features of a building or site they are always analysed on the historical basis, that is, on the basis of the historical period or the first applications of the technological achievements of a certain period.[33]

It is only through a morphological analysis that the spatial organization of the examined buildings or sites is considered. The internal spaces of the buildings are then described at two levels. Firstly, at the level of describing the plan, for example, 'an open plan space', and secondly, giving the number of storeys, for example, 'four-storey building'.[34] It is always emphasized that the particular spatial organization of the examined industrial building or site is related to the manufacturing process originally housed in the particular building. Occasionally, the spaciousness of a plan is related to the material used for structural elements, that is, steel, wrought iron or concrete columns, beams or slabs, suggesting that the discovery and use of new materials made the particular internal spatial organization possible. Finally, the individual internal features such as staircases, panelling, windows, doors, and so on, and external decorative features are again described and related to the architectural styles of the period in which the building was built and/or to the architectural language of the architect, if known.[35]

It may be suggested that the definition of the character of the examined industrial building is based on the descriptions of the building's external and internal decorative features, and on the analysis of the relation between the manufacturing process and internal spatial configuration. Yet, the spatial configuration — that is, 'open space plan' — is seen only as a result of the need to accommodate a certain manufacturing process and its machinery, rather than being seen as significant in its own right. Accordingly, the internal and external character of the examined building is defined by the building's decorative features only.

The manufacturing process is a generator of the spatial configuration, that is, spatial design, of the examined industrial building. Despite the fact that the manufacturing process has been removed from the building, the quality of the spatial design has not changed. What has changed is the utility of the considered internal space. The spatial configuration, however, remains unaltered. As such, the spatial configuration is an important, if not the most important, element of the character of the pertinent industrial building: 'Internal spaces . . . are part of the special interest of a building and may be its most valuable features.'[36] Yet, the evaluation processes do not take into consideration the possibility that the spatial configuration may contribute to the character and the 'special interest' of the building.

This attitude towards the internal space of industrial architecture mirrors the 'traditional' attitude of industrial archaeology towards industrial buildings. Within this discipline, the building has been considered as a container for machinery, and industrial archaeology deals with 'the machine and the building in which the machine was housed'.[37]

CONCLUSION

Conservation legislation creates a gap between the evaluation process and management. It can be said that one of the reasons is the mere historical justification of the cultural significance of the examined building and site. Even the architectural character of industrial buildings is mainly defined on an historical basis. External and internal architectural features, from the building material and structure to the wall decorations, are evaluated against the main characteristics of the historical period in which the building was built. Interestingly, the internal spatial configuration of industrial buildings is not considered to be an element on which the architectural character of the industrial building depends. Yet, the starting point of a spatial design for a new use, which may be proposed through the management plan, will be the analysis of the spatial configuration of the industrial building.

Further research, currently being undertaken by the author, investigates the contribution of the spatial configuration and design of industrial buildings to their architectural character. Such an approach to the analysis of space in industrial buildings may be seen as a link between the evaluation and management parts of the preservation process. Complementing the historical evaluation of the building, spatial analysis may eventually fulfil two needs: firstly, it may contribute to the investigation of the historical importance of a building, and, secondly, it may inform the design process of conversion.

ACKNOWLEDGEMENTS

I would to express my gratitude to Mr Keith Falconer for his constructive comments on the first draft of this paper, and to Dr Stlyiane Philippou, my supervisor, without whose eagle eye and moral support this paper would never have been finished.

Tamara Rogic, University of Plymouth, School of Architecture, Hoe Centre, Notte Street, Plymouth PL1 2AR, UK

NOTES

[1] See, for example, Robertson *et al.* 1993; see also English Heritage unpublished a, b and c.

[2] DoE/DoNH 1994, 3, Annex C.

[3] Ibid., 3.6.

[4] DoE 1990, Annex 4, vi.

[5] DoE/DoNH 1994, 3.6.

[6] Ibid., 3.9.

[7] Ibid., 3.8–3.15.

[8] Stocker 1995, 109.

[9] DoE 1990, 3.13.

[10] Ibid., 3.2.

[11] Internal and external character of protected building are considered throughout the pertinent legislation (PPG 15).

[12] Ibid.

[13] Both programmes started in the late 1980s.

[14] English Heritage 1996; see also Nieke 1997; Fairclough 1996; Stocker 1995, 105; and Darvill et al. 1987.

[15] Cherry 1997 and 1995, 119; Cherry 1996.

[16] Cherry 1996, 16.

[17] English Heritage 1996; see also Cherry 1996.

[18] Ibid.

[19] English Heritage 1995, 3, see also: Cherry 1997, 12; English Heritage 1996.

[20] Ibid.

[21] DoE/DoNH 1994, 6.10–6.15; DoE 1990, Annex 4, vi.

[22] Ibid.

[23] Ibid.

[24] Ibid.

[25] Ibid.

[26] Saunders 1996, 21, says that the 'total [of listed buildings] had risen from 120,000 by 1969 to 273,000 by the end of 1980. By the end of 1994 the total listings in England were 447,000'. 94% of the total listings are Grade II listed building as it is mentioned earlier in the text.

[27] Lowenthal 1998, 11.

[28] Ibid., 3.

[29] Cherry 1996, 16; private conversation with B. Hoskins and J. Lake, English Heritage Inspectors, London, 23 February 1999.

[30] Cherry 1996.

[31] English Heritage unpublished a.

[32] In the space of this paper, it is not possible to include numerous examples in order to support this and several following statements. Several completed, yet unpublished documents by English Heritage are used as main source of reference: English Heritage unpublished a, b and c.

[33] Ibid.

[34] Ibid.

[35] Ibid.

[36] DoE/DoNH 1994, Annex C.58.

[37] Gould 1995, 52.

BIBLIOGRAPHY

Cherry, M. 1995, 'Protecting Industrial Buildings: the role of Listing', in Palmer & Neaverson (eds), 119–24.

Cherry, M. 1996, 'Listing: Current Developments', Context 51, 16–17.

Cherry, M. 1997, 'Post-war and Thematic Listing: airing the issues', Conservation Bulletin 32, 12–13.

Darvill, T., Saunders, A. & Startin, B. 1987, 'A question of National Importance: Approaches to the Evaluation of Ancient Monuments for the MPP in England', Antiquity 61, 393–408.

DoE (Department of the Environment) 1990, Planning Policy Guidance: Planning and the Historic Environment (PPG 16), London: HMSO.

DoE (Department of the Environment)/DoNH (Department of National Heritage) 1994, Planning Policy Guidance: Planning and the Historic Environment (PPG 15), London: HMSO.

English Heritage 1995, 'Understanding listing: Manchester Mills', London: English Heritage.

English Heritage 1996, The Monuments Protection Programme 1986–96 in Retrospect, London: English Heritage.

English Heritage unpublished a, 'Historic Textile Mills in Greater Manchester, Listing Recommendations'.

English Heritage unpublished b, 'Model Farms'.

English Heritage unpublished c, 'Royal Naval Dockyards'.

Fairclough, G. 1996, 'MPP and Scheduling', Conservation Bulletin 28, 20.

Gould, S. 1995, 'Industrial archaeology and the neglect of humanity', in Palmer & Neaverson (eds), 49–53.

Lowenthal, D. 1998, The Heritage Crusade and the Spoils of History, Cambridge: Cambridge University Press.

Nieke, M. R. 1997, 'Ten Years On — Monuments Protection Programme', Conservation Bulletin 31, 10–12.

Palmer, M. & Neaverson, P. (eds) 1995, *Managing the Industrial Heritage*, Leicester Archaeology Monographs No. 2, Leicester: University of Leicester.

Robertson, M. *et al.* 1993, 'Listed Buildings: the National Resurvey of England', *Transactions AMS* 37, 21–93.

Saunders, M. 1996, 'The Conservation of Buildings in Britain since the Second World War', in Feilden, B. M. & Mark, S. (eds), *Concerning Buildings: Studies in Honour of Sir Bernard Feilden*, Oxford: Butterworth Architecture, 5–33.

Stocker, D. 1995, 'Industrial Archaeology and the Monument Protection Programme', in Palmer & Neaverson (eds), 105–13.

SNAIL AND SNAIL SHELL: INDUSTRIAL HERITAGE AND THE RECONSTRUCTION OF A LOST WORLD

By ERIK NIJHOF

'THE WORLD WE HAVE LOST'

The British social historian Peter Laslett once referred to the agrarian, pre-industrial society, of which he was an outstanding student, as 'the world we have lost'.[1] With the emergence of modern industrial society, not only the traditional way of farming disappeared — the agrarian computerized mass-production is quite a different world — but also the lifestyle and mentality that had remained essentially unchanged for centuries. This change has been so drastic that historians have to make painstaking efforts to record its relics and feelings in combination with the systems of meaning that constitute in their integrity what we now call pre-industrial, agrarian society. Many scientists of varying disciplines are now engaged in this work.

In the last decades we have witnessed a similar process. Many activities, once so characteristic of the triumphant industrial society, like mining, textile manufacturing, steel processing, were ended abruptly, to the bewilderment of the workers involved. The factory buildings with all their belongings have been demolished, often without leaving any traces.

In the remaining industries we see an ongoing process of automation that eliminates the last pockets of manual labour. The continuing spatial separation of industrial and residential functions has banished production to the outskirts of urban conglomerations and to industrial corridors alongside motorways, in pre-fab boxes that bear no resemblance to the former factories. The emergence of the information society creates completely different types of labour with new labour conditions. It will not be long before we will speak about industrial society as 'a world we have lost'. For some trades this is already the situation, other ones are soon to follow. What must we do to in order to be capable of presenting the essential features of industrial society to future generations? What role is to be played by industrial heritage, the material relics and vestiges of this industrial society?

INDUSTRIAL HERITAGE AND ITS INNATE BIAS

Industrial heritage has to do with the representation of the material world of industrial society. The performance of this important mission meets at least two major problems. In view of the alarming speed of disappearance of so many important objects representing essential parts of the industrial past, local and professional groups have been forced to rescue what was possible. The results reflect the necessarily opportunist character of these efforts: more steam engines, always very capable of arousing nostalgic sentiments, than diesel, gas or electric motors; more handicraft tools than heavy machinery; more relics from industries producing goods associated with pleasant living, such as tobacco, chocolate, beer, whiskey, glass and pottery, than dirty industries producing semi-manufactured goods, and heavy or processing industries; more small-scale buildings than huge spatial complexes; more buildings with interesting architectural designs or details than simple and functional ones. There may have been very practical and ponderous arguments for these choices, but the objects that have been preserved do not offer, in their totality, an adequate representation of the material world of industrial society.[2]

A second problem is the actual condition in which all these objects have been preserved. The majority of them have been turned into museums or dwellings, and this transformation was synonymous with restyling their characters into a mixture of respectability and pleasant non-conformity that is particularly attractive to a certain sub-division of the modern 'yuppie' species. Only a minority of these buildings have preserved much of their original character, when used for other productive purposes, or left in a pleasant state of decay.[3]

The combination of both problems has produced a rather distorted image of life in industrial society: it is much too idyllic. When we read contemporaneous testimonies and try to realize what production must have meant for the persons involved, given the imperfect state of the machines and the poor working conditions, we have to correct the picture of the preserved heritage with considerable quantities of dirt, danger, noise and stink. The prevailing atmospheres were either too cold or too hot, too dry or too humid, or simply too poisonous. We have to look for additional knowledge of life in industrial society: the morphology of the few preserved and restyled snail shells will not do. For a deeper understanding of industrial society, we have to turn also to technological and social/economic history, as well as social geography, as will be demonstrated with some aspects of the history of mining in the German Ruhr and in Dutch and Belgian Limburg, two adjacent provinces.

THREE MINING REGIONS

When we travel through these regions with the eye of an historian or geographer, we can observe striking differences. In the Ruhr several mines are still in operation, although mining has long since been ceased to be profitable; this reflects the strong social and political influence of the miners and their organizations in this region. The continued existence of the buildings of mines shut down a decade ago or even longer, however, suggests that there is also some pride in the past, which impression is corroborated by similar projects of industrial rehabilitation. In the vast urban conglomeration we see everywhere distinct neighbourhoods of rustic character: low houses, large gardens, built according to the principles of the 'garden city'. Old photographs reveal the functions of these gardens: the inhabitants grew vegetables

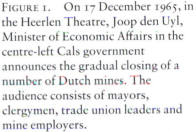

FIGURE 1. On 17 December 1965, in the Heerlen Theatre, Joop den Uyl, Minister of Economic Affairs in the centre-left Cals government announces the gradual closing of a number of Dutch mines. The audience consists of mayors, clergymen, trade union leaders and mine employers.

and potatoes, and they kept pigs and goats that were kept in stables at the end of the yard which are still in use, now for cars.[4] Belgian Limburg shows many similarities, although here all mines have been closed now for several years: many buildings are preserved, the 'terrils' (spoil-heaps) are omnipresent, as are the 'cités' (garden cities). The contrast with Dutch Limburg could not be more striking. With the closing of the mines nearly all material remnants have been demolished. Some last objects are standing lost in the midst of new industrial or urban settlements, one 'terril' is transformed into a slope for artificial skiing.[5] Social and economic history can tell why. While the industrial past is a source of pride and identity in the Ruhr and Belgian Limburg, it is more considered as a transitory stage in Dutch economic development.[6] In Germany and Belgium the closing down of the mines has been an operation that has aroused vehement reactions and required from the politicians a protracted time of tightrope-walking (that in Germany is still going on). In the Netherlands, the closing of the mines was announced by the social-democratic Minister of Economic Affairs Den Uyl in 1965 and realized in the following years; 80 per cent of the redundant miners were declared 'disabled' on a massive scale and received 80 per cent of their wages until their age of retirement or untimely death through anthraco-silicosis from breathing coal-dust.[7] New employment was created in order to restructure the labour market: the DAF motorcar works, the National Statistics Office and the Maastricht State University. Its counterpart was a deliberate policy of cleansing the landscape of the vestiges of its past as a mining region. Even the

FIGURE 2. The Belgian mining companies demonstrated their grip on the daily and spiritual lives of their miners by constructing impressive churches with richly decorated interiors: the churches of Beringen (1940–43) and Eijsden (1935–36) in Belgian Limburg.

FIGURE 3. Central building of the André Dumont Mine at Waterschei, owned by the Société Générale Holding Company.

demolition of all garden cities was considered: renovation was necessary, and why not build new, light and modern houses and do away with the outdated garden city concept? The protestations of the inhabitants, mostly new-comers, because the miners were too old, too sick or too demoralized to protest, prevented this radical policy, together with a growing indignation in public opinion aroused by the blunt treatment of the former miners.[8]

In the Belgian part mining activities have ended too, but much of the 'industrial patrimony' is left. Not all of it will be preserved and the future destiny of several buildings and sites is still uncertain, but at least there is a discussion on the social desirability of preserving parts of the material culture of the mining era. It will be obvious that for the collective memory as a former mining region, it is necessary to have some mining sites, but in Beringen there are also the Casino and the church to remind us of the rich convivial and religious culture of the miners; in addition, the mere fact that both buildings have been constructed by the mining companies as an integral part of the industrial community reminds us of the all pervading patriarchal power system in which the miners had to live. The church has peculiar characteristics. The nave is low and long and has few windows, which deliberately evokes the spatial impression of a mine gallery. A quite inconspicuous small building at the edge of the area tells an interesting story. This is the point where milk was distributed to the miners after their work; although the danger of dust-lungs was officially ignored, it was felt necessary to give the miners a drink to clean their throats and milk was chosen because the white colour contrasted symbolically with the black coal-dust they had been breathing for the hours before. The central building of the Waterschei mining company 'André Dumont' has a rich Art Deco architecture that reminds us of the central positions of the employers as local lords who dominated the city politically as well as culturally.[9] In Germany, some mines are still in operation and some of them have been registered and protected, like Zeche Zollverein XII in Essen, Consolidation in Gelsenkirchen or Zollern II-IV in Dortmund.[10] The Westphalian Museum of Industry has created a network of several restored industrial sites, including Zollern II-IV and two other mines.[11]

GARDEN CITIES

A rich patrimony of garden cities has been preserved everywhere. These show such striking morphological similarities that they must be functional characteristics of the garden cities in the mining regions. Relatively big gardens were indeed intended not only to evoke a non-urban atmosphere to the miners often originating from rural districts, but had also the strict material purpose of enabling the miners to grow vegetables and potatoes and to keep pigs and goats, in order to supplement their poor wages. The houses were not too bad in view of the standards of their respective epochs.[12]

One of the points they had in common was a fairly high number of small rooms: four to six, often one or two in the loft. This was neither an invitation to, nor an anticipation of a more elevated nuptial fertility of miners' families, but a deliberately created opportunity to take boarders: again, this enhanced the miner's income, and it helped to solve the problem of lodging the constant reserve of foreign young, unmarried miners tramping from one mine to another.[13] After 1930, this practice met a growing opposition from the Catholic Church and public opinion concerned with questions of sexual morality. 'Daughters of 14, at best 15 years old are already used by some parents(?) to lure many boarders, for the sake of money', it is reported with indignation,[14] and often the boarders alternated in one bed, according to their successive shifts, if they were not found in the conjugal bed during the miner's shift. Exaggerated or not, the boarding system was prohibited in both provinces of Limburg, but continued to flourish in Germany, albeit under strict rules.[15]

FIGURE 4. House for mining employees in Beringen, built by the architect A. Blomme in Flemish neo-Renaissance style.

FIGURE 5. The 'cité' of Winterslag (B), designed by the famous Brussels architect Adrien Blomme, in the style of the Flemish Renaissance, is considered one of the finest examples of the Belgian garden cities.

The spatial and architectural design of these garden cities can tell us a lot more. They all have a closed character, with their own centre: a church, a square and communal buildings. They all show a distinctive architecture, distinguishing them from the surrounding quarters — if these existed — because often the garden cities were also spatially separated. A gate at the main entrance might accentuate this distinct character. On old pictures the front gardens were uniform, because the mining companies prescribed the design of these gardens, the varieties of plants and controlled their daily maintenance. There were also bigger houses in these cities: these belonged to the overseers and engineers, who also had to live beside the mine and who exerted control on the conduct of the ordinary miners.[16] If we were to fly in a helicopter over all these cities, we would see how many of them there were in Germany, where this type of company town was the normal way for employers to lodge their workers.[17]

FIGURE 6. This aerial view of the 'cité' of Waterschei clearly shows its spatial structure and its spacious design.

MULTI-ETHNIC COEXISTENCE

The living together of miners from so many European regions in rather isolated 'cités' created a laboratory of multi-ethnic relations. Intermarriage and exchange of habits on one hand, and cultural seclusion in ethnic clubs and open rivalries on the other, were the opposing outcomes. But it is interesting to see that nowhere did these tensions evolve into untenable situations of ethnic confrontations of the kind we have become all too familiar with today. Was it because all these groups had some cultural elements in common, despite their differences? It seems so. All of them were Catholic, coming from countries such as Poland, Czechia, Slovakia, Slovenia, Croatia, Hungary, Italy or the Rhineland in Germany. The Catholic church was very active in keeping these young miners in touch with their religion, often sending young priests from their original country on a tour of duty to the cities in Germany, the Netherlands or Belgium, or sending Belgian priests to the countries of the foreign miners, to learn their language.[18] Their common linguistic background is also interesting. Most of the foreign miners who moved to the Ruhr or Limburg in the 1920s and 1930s were able to speak and understand a kind of German. Perhaps they had learned this in Germany, perhaps their provenance from the old Austro-Hungarian Empire acted as a common background, because German was the second language of their parents, that served as a *lingua franca* between the non-Austrian people. Military service in the Austro-Hungarian army may also have played a role. Anyhow, in many cités in Belgian

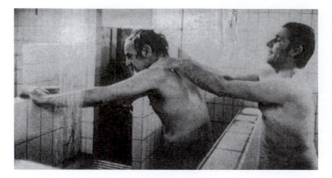

FIGURE 7. Dutch miners washing each other's backs.

Limburg the foreign miners spoke among each other a 'pidgin' that has come to be known as 'cité-German'. Some sources mention also such a common 'pidgin' developing among children, with many French words. After the Linguistic Laws of 1932 these spontaneously created 'pidgins' were on the retreat, as from then on the Dutch language was compulsory in public life and was, therefore, learnt at school by all pupils.[19] In the Netherlands such a 'miners' German' did not develop, mainly because right from the start Dutch was far more prominent as the official language; moreover, the dialect spoken in eastern Dutch Limburg was already very similar to the German language. Besides, many words used underground were purely German.[20]

SOLIDARITY AND PHYSICAL CLOSENESS

One aspect of the miners' culture of mutual co-operation, often neglected in the 'big' histories of miners and their unions, is quite prosaic and indicates that the proverbial solidarity of the miners had also a physical aspect of men working in extreme closeness. When we visit the narrow underground galleries and realize how many workers had to work there, this immediately becomes obvious, but also an inspection of the morphology of the shower facilities can tell us a lot. We see individual cabins, large, undivided bathrooms with showers, and large bathrooms with partitions about 1.5 m high. When the miners had come up after their shift, they wanted to clean themselves, and it was quite natural that they washed the backs of their neighbours. It served as a common ritual of purification, after which the miner could return home and forget about his heavy and dirty job; it aroused much cheerfulness and joking. In the beginning of the 20th century, however, the discourse of public and private morality also reached the mines and the ecclesiastical and civic authorities faced a serious dilemma: it was good that the miners wanted to be clean and were helpful to each other, but they should not see their neighbour's genitals when touching them; hence the erection of the half-high partitions. The design of these bathrooms proves that seeing each other naked when they were drying and dressing was not deemed dangerous. The small private cabins were destined for the overseers and engineers, who apparently were able to wash their own backs.[21] In Germany, there had also been smaller rooms, suitable for several men, but this type was soon condemned as 'Ausbruttstätten der abscheulichsten Unsittlichkeiten'.[22] The morphology of the shower facilities can also be read as the history of the campaign for public and private morality, waged by the authorities of the 20th century.

AFTER WORK

The leisure activities of the miners had quite a particular character. Dennis, Henriques and Slaughter in their study of the Yorkshire miners typified these as 'vigorous and frivolous'. The miners were proud of their physical strength and lived from day to day. This was explained by their precarious perspectives: mine disasters, dismissal, disability and unpredictable wages undermined every inclination to long-term thinking.[23] The miners had their own clubs where they had their pints and discussed their favourite sport, rugby. Women were not allowed, except for dance and music evenings. In other regions the pub was the central meeting place for miners of particular companies: it was here that the first local unions were founded.[24] Interesting was also the phenomenon of the 'Schnappskasinos' in the Ruhr. The new mines being situated in the middle of nowhere, the miners themselves founded co-operative associations that purchased liquors and hired canteen facilities during the changes of the shifts.[25]

To be sure, drinking was an important leisure activity for the miners, especially when unmarried, not only for the alcohol, but also for the sake of conviviality. During the 20th century, stimulated by the mining companies and the church that disliked heavy drinking as leading to bad conduct, and by trade-unions and political parties that wanted to emancipate the miners politically and morally, many cultural associations and sporting clubs were founded. Miners played soccer and rugby, made paintings and staged plays, debated on social questions and performed music. Many of these clubs and associations are still in existence today, although the miners have given way to new members and most of these organizations have changed character dramatically. Nevertheless, it is good to remember how many of these clubs and associations, as well as the many pubs and public buildings, have their roots in the world of mining that now already seems so far away.[26]

ACADEMIC APPROACHES TO MINING

These examples have been selected to show the rich variety of elements constituting the world of mining: memories, habits, experiences and traditions on the one hand, and industrial heritage (buildings and machines), archives, organizations, spatial structures on the other. Accordingly, a great variety of scientific disciplines has studied aspects of the world of the miners:

— social historians have concentrated upon the narratives of social struggles waged by the miners and their unions and have evaluated, from that perspective, the role of the church, political parties, the employers and the authorities;[27]

— historians of technology have outlined the successive technological systems of mining;[28]

— business historians have investigated the economic prospects of mining and the employers' policies;[29]

— geographers have analysed the spatial structures of the mining areas and the problems of the concentration of functions;[30]

— sociologists and anthropologists have studied the social relations and mentalities of miners' communities;[31]

— literature students have analysed the representation of the miner and his world in novels;[32]

— industrial archaeologists have listed the remnants of the mining industry;[33] there have also been efforts to valorize these, as a rule from a technological or from an architectural point of view, but rarely from both together.

As is suggested by this survey, the miners are not a neglected group in the social and historical sciences. On the contrary, the rich variety of studies reflects a deep fascination with these men. This is partly explained by the central role of coal as a source of energy: society was dependent for a long time on these men doing a dirty and heavy job underground. Another feature that attracted attention was the existence of large miners' communities with a distinct proletarian character within a society that grew every decade more orderly and more 'bourgeois'. To many social historians and sociologists, miners are synonymous with a culture of solidarity and common struggle against the mining companies.[34] This attitude is generally ascribed to the necessity of men working underground under difficult circumstances to stick together at any price, and many histories have been told about heroic battles, sometimes assuming mythical proportions, especially from the side of socially engaged scientists, who extolled the inherent revolutionary character of the miner. On the other hand, miners have endured decades of exploitation and coal dust without constant social struggles. This was ascribed by Catholic-inspired authors to the mitigating influence of the church that succeeded in convincing the miners that gradual improvement through harmonious consultation on the basis of social Catholicism and the papal encyclicals offered the best perspectives for the miners' communities. For the Catholic historiography the history of the 20th-century mining communities has proved the success of a deliberate policy of social integration and social control.[35]

SNAIL AND SNAIL SHELL

So each discipline and each approach seems to have its own agenda in studying the miners and their communities; each of them uses its own sources, and an overall picture is lacking. For the practice of academic sciences, this is as normal as it is regrettable, but the actual situation in the mining regions means that this liberal pluralism has become increasingly inadequate. Many mines all over Europe have been closed — or will be in the next few years — and are waiting for a new destiny. When it has to be decided what has to remain and what can be demolished, it becomes imperative to have a method of valorization and a scientific framework to decide upon the image of the world of mining that will be presented to future generations.

Fundamental to any further discussion is the principal statement of the inseparable unity of the material and immaterial elements which constitute the

FIGURE 8. On 23 December 1966, the Belgian government announced the immediate closure of five mines in the Walloon provinces and of the mine of Zwartberg in Limburg. The latter being very modern and certainly not among the loss-making mines, the miners revolted. Heavy fighting resulted in two dead and several wounded. Paratroopers, here against the background of the Zwartberg mine, were called to restore public order.

FIGURE 9. People watching how 'Tall John', the chimney of the Dutch Oranje Nassau Mine No. 1, is pulled down on 21 August 1976. It is not falling in the right direction and will destroy some small buildings.

heritage of the mining epoch. In any representation of the miners' life these elements must complement each other in a balanced and meaningful way. How can one write about the life of a miner and the hardship of his work, if one has never descended in a blinded cage rushing downwards into the depths of the earth and has never felt the dust and heat at 900m. underground? On the other hand, all the material objects are mute and meaningless if one knows nothing about the way they have been used by the miners, as demonstrated before by the example of the shower facilities. So we have to put together an overall picture with pieces coming from the most diverse sources, consisting of fragmented memories and testimonies, houses and industrial areas, machines and tools. We do this as an interdisciplinary project, as historians, anthropologists, industrial heritage experts, technologists, all contributing their own pieces of knowledge and wisdom. But how do all these fragments fit into a general picture? This is not an automatic process; some integrating concepts are needed that might serve as hot-houses for theories and generate new questions for further research.

INTEGRATING THE APPROACHES: 'INDUSTRIAL CULTURE'

In an earlier study, together with Peter Scholliers, the concept of 'industrial culture' was developed, in order to compare and contextualize the Belgian and Dutch industrial heritage. It was defined as '. . . the whole of expressions, material and immaterial, that can be understood as reflections of societal actors on the process of industrialization'.[36] Some basic considerations underlay this definition:

— we look at ideas and habits insofar as they are related to industrial society; in the same way, mere objects do not say anything, however 'industrial' in character: it is the use made of them, and the shaping they have received and the experiences that the people involved have had with them, that constitute their relation to industrial society;

— we see these reflections as an active process by societal actors, involved in the process of industrialization: all these actors, mostly groups and sub-groups, but also some individuals, create their own ideas and habits and have their own specific relationships to the material objects of industrial society;

— we consider all these expressions in their mutual relationships as a dialectical unity, created by industrial society itself, that forced each societal actor to react to the expressions of other actors;

— with the development of industrialization and the mutual influences of the actors the industrial culture itself is constantly changing, just like the perception of it by the actors, the students of industrial culture included.

ORGANIZING THE COLLECTIVE MEMORY

So if we want to preserve the industrial heritage of a certain trade, we must ask, why? And then, how? If we want to do justice to the industrial culture of mining, or any other industry that has been important for the history of industrialization of a country or region, we must try to realize that unity of different sources, of material and immaterial remnants, to provide contextual knowledge. This can be best realized in carefully selected, greater projects, with the industrial heritage as a starting point for creating a centre of study and representation, also as a magnet for tourism and relevant cultural activities. We must be conscious that in creating such a centre, we can never escape the subjectivities and biases of our own era, and as a consequence of what we said about the changing perceptions of an industrial culture, we should not merely try to, but have to be aware of our own biases. If we compare the three mining regions, the Dutch region is the only one to have erased all important vestiges. At the same time, there have been many complaints about the social consequences of the sudden and abrupt disappearance of the mines: many psychological problems, many disabled people who awaited death by silicosis or who felt ostracized by society. Above all, there was much resentment.[37] In my view, this has something to do with the total eclipse of mining from the physical landscape: this indicates that society wants to forget mining, and the miners have interpreted this as a society which wants to forget the miner. It has proved to be very difficult to make the mining era a part of the collective memory of the nation without preserving a good selection of the material remnants of this trade as a starting point for remembering its past. Now we certainly would do things differently, but we cannot undo the demolition of the mining sites. The initiatives around and by the Westphalian Museum of Industry, mentioned above, are very inspiring and encouraging, as are the more small-scale activities in Belgian Limburg. These efforts give the miners their deserved place in our collective memory of the industrial world we have lost.

Erik Nijhof, Instituut voor Geschiedenis, Kromme Nieuwe Gracht 66, NL-3512 HL Utrecht, Netherlands

NOTES

1 Laslett 1971.
2 Nijhof & Scholliers 1996, 48–55.
3 Ibid., 203–10.
4 Steinborn 1991, 21–27; Brüggemeier 1983, 46–52.
5 Cf. Starmans & Daru-Schoemann 1990, 40.
6 Nijhof & Scholliers 1996, 55–60.
7 Paumen 1993, 76–81.
8 Messing 1988, 519–20.
9 Doorslaer 1990; Minten 1992, 126–27, 176–80.
10 Bieker *et al.* 1996.
11 Westfälisches Industiemuseum 1995.
12 *Geschiedenis op zoek* 1991, passim; Minten 1992, 104–10.
13 Also Brüggemeier 1983, 49–52; Zwanniken 1957, 141–42.
14 Dieteren 1959, 74.
15 Brüggemeier 1983, 69–72.
16 Minten 1992, 104–10.
17 Vonde 1989, passim.
18 Bakker 1993, 50–61.
19 Ibid., 98–101; Paumen 1993, 54; Werkgroep 1984, 10–11, 17.

20 Breij 1991, 86–86.
21 Ibid., 122.
22 Brüggemeier 1983, 138–39.
23 Dennis *et al.* 1969, 130–41.
24 Ibid., 141–62.
25 Brüggemeier 1983, 143–47.
26 Minten 1992, passim.
27 For example, Minten 1984, Kreukels 1986, Brüggemeier 1983 and many other books of Beck Verlag on mining history.
28 Cf. the rich bibliography in Minten 1992, 277.
29 Messing 1988.
30 Vonde 1989; Parent and Stackelhaus 1991.
31 Dennis *et al.* 1969.
32 Literair Museum 1982; Kusters and Perry 1999.
33 Starmans and Daru-Schoemann 1990; Doorslaer 1990; Thornes 1994.
34 For example, Kreukels 1986.
35 For example, Dieteren 1954.
36 Nijhof & Scholliers 1996, 18.
37 Messing 1988, 494–516; Paumen 1993, 65–75.

BIBLIOGRAPHY

Bakker, W. 1993, '"Wij zijn allen kompels". Een onderzoek naar de onderlinge verhoudingen tussen verschillende nationaliteiten in de mijncité van Eisden' (unpublished, Utrecht University).

Bieker, J. et al. 1996, Industriedenkmale im Ruhrgebiet, Hamburg: Ellert und Richter.

Breij, B. 1991, De mijnen gingen open, de mijnen gingen dicht, Amsterdam: De Hoeve.

Dieteren, R. OFM 1953, Mens en mijn. Een halve eeuw strijd, groei en bloei van de Nederlandse Katholieke Mijnarbeiders Bond, Heerlen: Winants.

Dennis, N., Henriques, F. & Slaughter, C. 1969, Coal is Our Life. An Analysis of a Yorkshire Mining Community, London: Tavistock.

Dieteren, R. OFM 1954, Grondbeleid en volkshuisvesting in de Mijnstreek, Assen: Van Gorcum.

Dieteren, R. OFM 1959, De migratie in de Mijnstreek 1900–1935, Heerlen: Winants.

Doorslaer, B. van 1990, 'Zwarte monumenten in groen Limburg. Naar een verdiende toekomst voor het mijnpatrimonium', Monumenten en Landschappen 9:4 (juli/augustus 1990).

Geschiedenis op zoek naar waardig vervolg. Studie van de mijnnederzettingen in Waterschei, Winterslag en Eisden 1991, Brussel: Koning Boudewijnstichting.

Jong, H. J. de 1999, De Nederlandse industrie 1913–1965. Een vergelijkende analyse op basis van de productiestatistieken, Amsterdam: NEHA.

Kreukels, L. 1986, Mijnarbeid: strijdbaarheid en volgzaamheid, Assen: Van Gorcum.

Kusters, J. H .W. & Perry, J. F. M. M. 1999, Versteende wouden. Mijnen en mijnwerkers in woord en beeld, Amsterdam: Querido.

Laslett, P. 1971, The World We Have Lost, London: Methuen.

Messing, F. A. M. 1988, Geschiedenis van de mijnsluiting in Limburg. Noodzaak en lotgevallen van een regionale herstructurering, Leiden: Nijhoff.

Minten, L. 1984, 'De stakingen in de Limburgse steenkoolmijnen tijdens het interbellum' (unpublished, Leuven University).

Minten, L. et al. 1992, Een eeuw steenkool in Limburg, Tielt: Lannoo.

Nijhof, E. & Scholliers, P. (eds) 1996, Het tijdperk van de machine. Industriecultuur in België en Nederland, Brussel: VUB Press.

Parent, T. & Stackelhaus, T. 1991, Stadtlandschaft Ruhrrevier, Essen: Klartext.

Paumen, M. 1993, De laatste gang. Het verdwijnen van de Europese mijnwerker, Amsterdam: Veen.

Starmans, J. C. J. M. & Daru-Schoemann, M. M. R. 1990, Industrieel Erfgoed in Limburg. Verslag van een onderzoek naar roerende en onroerende industrieel-archeologische relicten, Leeuwarden/Maastricht: Eisma.

Steinborn, V. 1991, Arbeitergärten im Ruhrgebiet, Dordtmund: Westfälisches Industriemuseum.

Thornes, R. 1994, Images of Industry: Coal, Swindon: Royal Commission on the Historical Monuments of England.

Vonde, D. 1989, Revier der grossen Dörfer. Industrialisierung und Stadtentwickelung im Ruhrgebiet, Essen: Klartext.

Waar de dag nacht is. De steenkolenmijn in de literatuur 1982, Hasselt: Literair Museum.

Westfälische Industriemuseum im Aufbau, Das 1995, Dordtmund: Westfälisches Industriemuseum.

Zwanniken, W. A. C. 1957, Volkshuisvesting en samenleving, Assen: Van Gorcum.

THE ARCHAEOLOGY OF INDUSTRIALIZATION — NEW DIRECTIONS

By DAVID CRANSTONE

The 'Archaeology of Industrialization' conference was a joint venture by the Society for Post-Medieval Archaeology and Association for Industrial Archaeology: two organizations with very different origins and developments, and still, to an extent, different mindsets. For participants at Bristol, this was illustrated by some classic exchanges in discussion; it is a tribute to all my fellow contributors that no such fault-line runs through this volume (though, healthily, several more subtle dialogues do run through many of the papers — some of these are brought out below).

Post-medieval archaeology has developed (as its very name indicates) from within archaeology, and arguably is an important element in the developing maturity of the discipline. Without wishing (or being remotely qualified) to embark on a psychological history of archaeology, it is possible to view the development of the discipline in Britain and northern Europe as that of the relationship of an offspring to the parent discipline of history (similar arguments can be made for the relationship of archaeology to classics in southern Europe, and to anthropology in north America). Until the 1960s, using this analogy, British archaeology acted and thought of itself as an offshoot of history, attempting to use material culture to illustrate and, at best, advance, historically-formulated questions; the underlying mindset is perfectly summed up in the classic description of archaeology as 'the handmaiden to history'.[1] The rise of the 'New Archaeology' in the late 1960s and early 1970s, as well as being an abrupt pendulum-swing from a humanities-based to a science-based view of the discipline, contained a large element of rebellion against the (perceived) repressive parent of history, part of the wider movement of student protest and revolt of its time. This came across clearly (from the author's memory) in the lectures and tutorials of David Clarke; as befits a largely-subconscious process, it is only faintly implicit in his published writings.[2] In this analysis, it is no coincidence that the take-off of archaeology as an intellectual discipline was centred heavily in prehistory; the young adult had to move away from the still-overpowering parent in order to find and develop an independent identity. The development of post-medieval archaeology (which arguably in the 1990s and 2000s has taken over the cutting-edge role within the discipline that prehistory held in the 1970s and 1980s), and of historical archaeology more broadly, is then a sign of real maturity; the younger discipline is now able to re-enter the core territory of the older, as an independent and equal partner.

In its intellectual development, post-medieval archaeology has had particular difficulties in advancing from the empirical stage, due to the sheer bulk of data that exists. The major take-off occurred in the 1990s, very much influenced by American 'historical archaeology',[3] but also centred to an extent round the distinctive voice of Matthew Johnson.[4] To an extent, take-off has seen a leap from data-gathering for its own sake, to a concentration on broad 'big picture' issues (such as capitalism and colonialism) argued by assertion, with only limited and 'top-down' use of archaeological data to illustrate the broader arguments, thereby avoiding the overwhelming nature of the data, but failing to fully integrate 'bottom-up' development and testing of ideas from the data with 'top-down' intellectual concerns, into a genuinely rigorous and analytical discipline.[5] These new approaches have also drawn their inspiration (implicitly and explicitly) from the humanities rather than the sciences; they have also centred on the archaeology of consumption, and have largely failed to engage with production.[6] This mirrors the earlier failure of 'mainstream' archaeology to develop an interest in industrial remains, lagging behind non-academic society in this respect. To return briefly to the psychology of archaeology, I suspect that both failures reflect wider attitudes in middle-class and academic Britain towards industry and manual labour; an attitude all too keen to move rapidly away from the understanding of technology in its own right into the study of more intellectually-respectable social and economic questions (and as so often, the past-present dialectic in post-medieval archaeology rears its head; this attitude uncannily mirrors that of so many industrialist dynasties, moving over two or three generations from entrepreneur via large industrialist to country landowner).

By contrast, industrial archaeology was developed largely by non-academic industrial workers and managers interested in the history of their own industry, with a major input from engineers and an academic linkage with extra-mural departments (to use the contemporary title during the boom years of industrial archaeology), and a great strength in practical conservation (especially of mills and railways).[7] The former link is now being broken, or at least weakened, by the decline of manufacturing industry and the rate of technological change, but the subject retains great strengths in its amateur participation, and especially in the way that this feeds into site preservation. However, its academic side has been slow to develop beyond data-gathering, description, and functionalist analysis of industry and production, and to engage meaningfully with broader social issues in the past, and intellectual currents in the present. It also remains torn between identities as a period or topic discipline,[8] it has yet to develop as a comprehensive period discipline, and remains in many ways a mirror-image of post-medieval archaeology, thus separating production and consumption in the later 2nd millennium into two separate sub-disciplines. To some of its more eminent exponents, at least, the subject enters the 21st century with a real crisis of identity and direction.[9]

Both sub-disciplines have also been constrained, at least in external perception, by their names; 'industrial archaeology' is seen to imply, and even enforce, an emphasis on industry in isolation, whereas 'post-medieval' is seen as implying a focus on the 16th to 17th centuries, and as an inherently negative definition (since it defines the subject by what it is not). The term 'later historical' has therefore been preferred by some recent writers,[10] and 'early modern' is widely used by historians, but both labels, while not negative, are wholly relative, and probably obscure rather than clarify the chronological period involved to those outside the ranks of the specialists who use them. The term 'historical archaeology' has come into occasional use on this side of the Atlantic, reflecting normal North American usage as a synonym for 'post-medieval'; this term, in its period-specific meaning, is surely wholly inappropriate (and indeed inaccurate) in a European context, or indeed in the many other regions of the world where literacy and/or the first appearance of written documentation do not coincide with the period of European expansion from the 15th century onwards. In Britain, 'historical archaeology' can be considered to apply to any period from the later Iron Age onwards, and the term should be kept for that broad division of our subject within which both material evidence and documentary evidence exist, and relate to each other — the matching twin to prehistory.[11] To further complicate the semantic minefield, the recent development of 20th-century archaeology, most notably in military archaeology,[12] has not tended to use any of the above labels, thereby outflanking the whole debate. What is important is that these varied labels, if they persist, aid rather than inhibit debate within a broader study of the archaeology of the later 2nd millennium (the label 'later 2nd-millenium archaeology', though admirably neutral and accurate, lacks all poetry — the present writer prefers to define himself as a post-medieval archaeologist, in the face of strict logic), itself situated within the broader field of historical archaeology.

The archaeology of industrialization, then, has until recently been studied by two rather-separate communities, deriving from different roots and operating in separate sub-disciplines. It is pleasing that this history does not show as a fault-line within the present volume, but rather as one of a series of linked dialogues, both within later 2nd-millennium archaeology and within society more widely: between industrial and post-medieval archaeology; between processual and post-processual theoretical stances; between science-based and humanities-based approaches; between industry and academia; and between archaeology and history. These dialogues, to me, are among the underlying themes of the volume. The last, history and archaeology, is both the most prominent and the least related to the original industrial/post-medieval dichotomy; I will return to it later in this paper. The remainder can all be seen as variations on the theme of 'the two cultures' of the sciences and the arts, though here very much in dialogue rather than in head-to-head opposition. These dialogues and diversities are valuable, so long as there is sufficient common ground for light rather than heat to be shed, and I would suggest that our understanding of industrialization will be deeper if we avoid excessively synthetic and holistic approaches.

Moving on from the history of the subject, and the strands embedded within this volume (though referring back to the latter where appropriate), what future directions can we identify for the archaeology of industrialization?

The first point that should be made, in what is clearly a broadening field, is the continuing importance of understanding the technology in its own right. In order to understand the broader phenomenon of industrialization, we *do* need to research the operation and development of technical processes, in the greatest possible detail and using the range of scientific techniques in conjunction with high-quality archaeological techniques of excavation, building recording, and survey. In this sense, the study of process remains an integral field of our subject, both in its own right and as a basis for understanding the constraints that technology and society imposed on each other, and the processes of innovation and development that lay behind successful industry; Blackburn's analysis of the alternating dominant roles of technological, social, and economic factors, in the lead industry of one Pennine valley, forms an interesting approach to this question (this volume). In this connection, the emphasis on the internal detail of buildings in Badcock and Malaws' and Rogic's papers (this volume) is important; and in standing industrial buildings, it is from internal detail that much of the technology (which in most cases was the *raison d'être* of the building) can be worked out, and much of the dialogue between their users (see below) can be recovered. More generally, we need to beware of the implicit assumption that, since many industrial monuments are so massive in scale, only broad-brush and low level of detail recording are required; as in any archaeology, there is no one-to-one relationship between the physical size and obtrusiveness of the evidence, and its importance (or indeed, the size and obtrusiveness of the original feature that the record represents).[13]

Moving upwards and outwards from the 'internal' study of technology and detail, I would suggest that one of the themes for archaeological study of industrialization should be the processes of experimentation, invention, innovation, and development; it is these, after all, that made the whole 'Industrial Revolution' possible. Here the role of archaeology rather than history remains under-developed; whereas the historical record is dominated by inventions, patents, and the role of the literate industrialist and manager, the archaeological record, particularly when allied with high-quality and problem-orientated archaeological science (notably in examining the process residues that so often form the best surviving evidence for what actually happened on a working industrial, or indeed experimental, site), has the potential to illuminate the unsung contribution of the craftsman or other worker, and the record of the experimentation that so often (deliberately or otherwise) did not find its way into the surviving written record. For example, the forge sector of the iron industry underwent fundamental change in the 18th century, relating to the much better-known development of coke smelting: first the traditional finery process was modified to cope with the different properties and problems of coke pig (a modification that is virtually undocumented historically, and whose significance in the broader development of the iron industry and the Industrial Revolution can therefore only be determined archaeologically); then a series of new processes were developed, with very varying success, to break the log-jams caused by the small-scale, labour-intensive, batch-process nature of the finery process, and its dependence on charcoal fuel, water power, and the craft skill (and therefore industrial strength) of the finer; then the period of diversity and experiment was terminated by the perfecting of the larger-scale, coal-fuelled, and (it was thought by the ironmasters) relatively unskilled puddling process.[14] The role and motivation of the ironmasters in the final development of the puddling process is well documented,[15] but historical documentation of the earlier stages of the sequence is very partial, and probably highly selective; systematic archaeological and archaeo-metallurgical study has the potential not only to elucidate the processes and their technical development, but to balance the historical record of the ironmaster with the material record of the finer, forgeman, and puddler, and to investigate both the practical details and the underlying mindset and psychology of innovation.

A further theme that needs development in the archaeology of industrialization is that of psychology and mindset (developing from the ideas of Uzzell in this volume), though, in the early 21st century, the interaction needs to be as much with cognitive studies and neuroscience as with traditional psychology. This linkage of neuro*science* with the realm of ideas immediately subverts the more extreme (and to this author sterile) versions of the processual/post-processual opposition; the aim is to develop a cognitive archaeology (in the sense advocated by Whitley[16]) of the later 2nd millennium that harnesses scientific approaches (among others) to study the whole range of human activity and imagination, without retreating into the stimulus-response assumptions of the narrower processual approaches. This approach needs to look at the development and expression of human cognition at a much more detailed level than the better-known cognitive archaeology developed for the Lower Palaeolithic by Mithen[17] and others (since it is detailed differences from 'modern' thinking, and between sub-groups and even individuals within our period of study, that we should aim to recover), and a broader definition than that offered by Renfrew's 'cognitive archaeology'.[18] As well as the role of mindset in innovation, and its differences between social, occupational, religious, and ethnic subgroups, it might look at the effects of specific workplace spaces and environments on the behaviour and mental life of their occupants, at how such effects may be socially transmitted between generations and into our own, and more generally at the psychology of past-present interactions within our own archaeology (as touched on above, and by Belford elsewhere in this volume); these last points can be seen as giving analytic rigour to the concept of 'sense of place', currently so widely bandied-about but so rarely defined or used analytically to genuinely advance our understanding either of the past in itself or of its implications in the present.

A further theme, largely off-stage in this volume (though it breaks surface in Gwyn's and Leech's papers), is that of the relationships between industrialization and colonialism and imperialism. At a practical level, overseas trade and colonization, and most specifically the slave trade, offered massive new markets for the products of industrialization, while trading profits (especially from slaves and sugar) provided capital for the massive investments needed to prime the pump of industrialization (a topic covered in detail at the Bristol conference by Mark Horton, whose paper unfortunately could not be included in this volume). The potential role of overseas (and particularly Indian and Chinese) technology and ideas in the 'innovations' of British industrialization also remain understudied; an exception is the probable Indian source for William Champion's 18th-century development of zinc smelting.[19]

But an overriding theme of this volume, as already mentioned, is the relationship between history and archaeology, for a period and topic where both provide evidence of almost overwhelming richness; this appears most explicitly in the papers of Badcock and Malaws, Gwyn, and Nevell and Walker. Approaches to this relationship, in this volume and elsewhere,[20] vary widely. Many can still be characterized as historically led, either intellectually or in the evidence used; conversely, in commercial-sector archaeology the Desk-Based Assessment has developed a genre in which history is used as the handmaiden to archaeology. Others attempt, often very successfully, to integrate both sources into a seamless whole; a synthesis that I now feel can all too often be premature. I would like to propose a third framework; of dialogue between the archaeological and historical evidence, and between the different elements within both, in which no one element is given automatic primacy, and in which discrepancies are seen to be as important and informative as concordances. Relating to this, and developing the concept of 'ownership' of sites used by Nevell and Walker (this volume), I would suggest that we can profitably analyse the archaeological data, at every level from landscape via site to individual excavated feature, artefact assemblage or process residue, in terms of its *authorship*; who produced it, and who controlled its production? Given the richness of the historical data (which itself can be, and sometimes already is, analysed in similar terms), it should often be possible to identify this authorship at least to the level of social/work group (owner, manager, builder, craftsman, worker), and sometimes down to the level of the individual or group of individuals, allowing consideration of occupational, gender, religious, and ethnic factors (an example of the latter might be the structures, features, and artefacts of navvy and construction camps, in relation to the ethnic, gender, and geographic origins of their occupants, and also in relation to the archaeology of nearby settled agricultural and industrial communities). This approach can be used to illuminate many of the themes of industrialization; most notably, to this author, the archaeology of experimentation, innovation, and development,[21] and the archaeology of sub-groups and individuals.[22] The archaeological and historical records can therefore be seen as in complex internal and external dialogue with each other, mirroring (however imperfectly) the dialogues between the groups and individuals who created the record and who formed the past.

These concepts, of dialogue and authorship, may also contribute to one of the major challenges identified earlier: how to move beyond data-gathering on the one hand, and abstract theorizing and the use of cherry-picked field data to illustrate or support 'top-down' theoretical models on the other hand, into a historical archaeology which genuinely and rigorously integrates data and ideas, and uses that combination both to identify what is really different or 'strange' in the past, and to make genuinely original, and even fundamental, contributions from archaeology into the wider intellectual world in which we still find it easier to be borrowers than creators.[23] And, since the material remains of the past are the unique subject-matter of archaeology, and their dialogue with documentary evidence the unique nature of historical archaeology, it is, surely, at least in part 'bottom-up' from the data that those fundamental contributions to the understanding of ourselves and our world will come.

David Cranstone, 267 Kells Lane, Low Fell, Gateshead, Tyne and Wear NE9 5HU, UK

NOTES

[1] Andren 1998, 106 — I have yet to track down the original British source of this much-recycled phase.

[2] Clarke 1973.

[3] To select references from such an extensive literature is invidious, but the papers in Yentsch & Beaudry 1992 and Egan & Michael 1999 form perhaps the best overviews; the former stresses the formative role of James Deetz in American historical archaeology, while the latter looks more closely at transatlantic relations both in the past and within modern archaeology.

[4] Notably Johnson 1993, 1996, and 1999a; Gaimster & Stamper 1997, Egan & Michael 1999, and Tarlow & West 1999 form broader compendia of the developing range of approaches, and Newman *et al.* 2001 is currently the most recent attempt at overall synthesis.

[5] Johnson 1999b, esp. 29–31. I should add (in press) that this paragraph, like the rest of the paper, was written before the publication of Johnson 2002, in which these issues are squarely addressed; the approaches developed in Johnson's study of castles have considerable relevance to industrial sites and the study of industrialization more broadly.

[6] Note the rarity of both science-based and production-centred papers in Gaimster & Stamper 1997, Egan & Michael 1999, Tarlow & West 1999, and Funari *et al.* 1999; but also the attempts to bridge the former gulf by Astill 1998 and Johnson 1998 in the most recent thematic coverage of scientific archaeology (Bayley 1998).

[7] Cossons 2000b, Buchanan 2000; these and other papers in Cossons 2000a form a comprehensive retrospective on the 20th-century development of the subject, while Palmer & Neaverson 1998 forms a current synthesis of its scope and theoretical stance.

[8] See Cranstone 2001, 183–85, for a fuller discussion of industrial archaeology as currently self-defined.

[9] Cossons (2000b, 13) raises the fear that industrial archaeology may be a one-generation subject; the present author's impression from numerous conversations over recent years is that similar fears, if less explicit, are widespread (though by no means universal) within what remains a very distinct industrial archaeology community.

[10] Tarlow & West 1999.

[11] As argued cogently by Funari, Jones & Hall 1999 and Funari 1999 in Funari *et al.* 1999, and forming a main theme of the overall volume.

[12] Brown *et al.* 1995; Cocroft 2000; Saunders 2002.

[13] See for example Cranstone 2001, 184–85.

[14] Cranstone 2001, 195–96, and references cited therein.

[15] Evans 1993.

[16] Whitley 1998a, b; the specific definition of cognitive archaeology is offered in Whitley 1998b, 5–6.

[17] E.g. Mithen 1994/1998.

[18] Renfrew and Zubrow (eds) 1994.

[19] Craddock 1990; Day 1991, 181.

[20] Andren 1998 and Funari *et al.* 1999 illustrate and discuss this range within the broader field of historical archaeology.

[21] An excellent example of a similar approach, using archaeological evidence to challenge contemporary folklore on the self-sufficient mindset of the Ozark farmers, is Stewart-Abernathy 1992.

[22] Matthews 1995.

[23] Again, these words were written before publication of Johnson 2002, which develops, in detail, a different response to a similar identified challenge.

BIBLIOGRAPHY

Andren, A. 1998, *Between Artifacts and Texts: Historical Archaeology in Global Perspective*, New York and London: Plenum Press.

Astill, G. 1998, 'Medieval and later: composing an agenda', in Bayley (ed.) 1998, 169–78.

Bayley, J. (ed.) 1998, *Science in archaeology: an agenda for the future*, London: English Heritage.

Brown, I., Burridge, D., Clarke, D., Guy, J., Hellis, J., Lowry, B., Ruckley, N. & Thomas, R. 1995, *20th Century Defences in Britain: an introductory guide*, York: Council for British Archaeology.

Buchanan, R. A. 2000, 'The origins of industrial archaeology', in Cossons 2000a, 18–38.

Clarke, D. L. 1973, 'Archaeology: the loss of innocence', *Antiquity*, 47, 6–18.

Cocroft, W. D. 2000, *Dangerous Energy: The archaeology of gunpowder and military explosives manufacture*, Swindon: English Heritage.

Cossons, N. (ed.) 2000a, *Perspectives on Industrial Archaeology*, London: Science Museum.

Cossons, N. 2000b, 'Perspective', in Cossons 2000a, 9–17.

Craddock, P. T. (ed.) 1990, 2000 Years of Zinc and Brass, London: British Museum Occasional Paper No. 50.

Cranstone, D. 2001, 'Industrial Archaeology — manufacturing a new society', in Newman et al., 2001, 183–210.

Day, J. 1991, 'Copper, Zinc, and Brass Production', in Day & Tylecote (eds) 1991, 131–99.

Day, J. & Tylecote, R. F. (eds) 1991, The Industrial Revolution in Metals, London: Institute of Metals.

Egan, G. & Michael, R. L. (eds) 1999, Old and New Worlds, Oxford: Oxbow.

Evans, C. 1993, 'The Labyrinth of Flames': Work and social conflict in early industrial Merthyr Tydfil, Cardiff: University of Wales Press.

Funari, P. P. A. 1999, 'Historical Archaeology from a world perspective', in Funari et al. (eds), 37–66.

Funari, P. P. A., Hall, M., & Jones, S. 1999, Historical Archaeology: back from the Edge, London and New York: Routledge.

Funari, P. P. A., Jones, S. & Hall, M. 1999, 'Introduction: archaeology in history', in Funari et al. (eds), 1–20.

Gaimster, D. & Stamper, P. 1997, The Age of Transition: The Archaeology of English Culture 1400–1600, Oxford: Oxbow.

Johnson, M. H. 1993, Housing Culture, London: University College London Press.

Johnson, M. H. 1996, An Archaeology of Capitalism, Oxford: Blackwell.

Johnson, M. H. 1998, 'On science, buildings archaeology, and new agendas', in Bayley (ed.), 211–18.

Johnson, M. H. 1999a, Archaeological theory; an introduction, Oxford: Blackwell.

Johnson, M. H. 1999b, 'Rethinking historical archaeology', in Funari et al. (eds) 1999, 23–36.

Johnson, M. H. 2002, Behind the Castle Gate: from Medieval to Renaissance, London & New York: Routledge.

Matthews, K. J. 1995, 'Archaeological data, sub-cultures, and social dynamics', in Antiquity 69:264, 586–94.

Mithen, S. 1994/1998, 'From domain specific to generalized intelligence: a cognitive interpretation of the Middle/Upper Palaeolithic transition', in Renfrew & Zubrow (eds), 29–39; reprinted in Whitley (ed.) 1998a, 137–56.

Newman, R., Cranstone, D., & Howard-Davis, C. 2001, The Historical Archaeology of Britain, c. 1540–1900, Stroud: Sutton Publishing.

Palmer, M. & Neaverson, P. 1998, Industrial Archaeology: Principles and Practice, London and New York: Routledge.

Renfrew, C. & Zubrow, E. B. W. (eds) 1994, The Ancient Mind: elements of cognitive archaeology, Cambridge: Cambridge University Press.

Saunders, N. J. 2002, 'Excavating memories: archaeology and the Great War, 1914–2001', in Antiquity 76, 101–08.

Stewart-Abernathy, L. C. 1992, 'Industrial Goods in the Service of Tradition: Consumption and Cognition on an Ozark Farmstead before the Great War', in Yentsch & Beaudry (eds), 101–26.

Tarlow, S. & West, S. 1999, The Familiar Past?: archaeologies of later historical Britain, London and New York: Routledge.

Whitley, D. S. (ed.) 1998a, Reader in Archaeological Theory: Post-Processual and Cognitive Approaches, London and New York: Routledge.

Whitley, D. S. 1998b, 'New Approaches to Old Problems: Archaeology in Search of an Ever Elusive Past', in Whitley (ed.) 1998a, 1–28.

Yentsch, A. E. & Beaudry, M. C. (eds) 1992, The Art and Mystery of Historical Archaeology: Essays in Honor of James Deetz, Boca Raton, Ann Arbour, London, and Tokyo: CRC Press.

INDEX

Illustrations are denoted by page numbers in *italics* or by *illus* where figures are scattered throughout the text. The letter n following a page number indicates that the reference will be found in a note.

Abbeydale scythe works (Sheffield) 82, 86, 87
Aberglasney (Carmth.), pottery 193n
Adams, William 211
advertising
    tokens 243–44, 248
    Vooruit 259–61, 262, 265
    see also marketing
agriculture
    improvements in 17
    Moel Tryfan 37, 41–3
    Tameside 66, 68, 72
Ale and Cakes mine (Cornwall) 98, 99–100
Amlwch (Anglesey), Methusalem Jones at 43
Amsterdam (Neth.), pottery 183, 189, 190
Anglesey, copper industry 43, 99, 145
Anseele, Edouard 259, 262
apprenticeships
    cutlery industry 166
    pottery industry 208
archaeological science, application of 15–21; *see also* chemical analysis
architecture *see* industrial buildings
ARCUS 271, 272
arsenic industry 100
Ashton (Tameside)
    Ashton Old Hall 59
    church 67
    location 54
    Lordship of 53, 55, 58, 59–60, 64–66, 72
Ashton family 72
Ashton Carr Wheel (Sheffield) 82
Ashton to Manchester Canal 59, 75
Ashton & Woodhead Railway 75
Association for Industrial Archaeology 1, 137, 313
Atlantic trade
    pottery 189, 204, 211, 212, 214
    slaves 155–62, 317
    sugar 157, 161–62
Austin, John 208
Avenue Coking and Chemical Works (Derbys.), recording project 269, 270, 271
    designing 271–72
    images 276, 277, 278, 279
    mapping 272–76

    ongoing 278–80

Baddeley, John 212
Bagnall, George 208
Barker, John 208
Barnes, Capt. Joseph 161
Barnstaple (Devon), pottery industry 188, 204
Barrett, William 156
Barry, Capt. 160
Bashamere mine (Co. Durham) 131
Bason, Thomas 161
Bath (B. & N.E.S.)
    J. B. Bowler 250–51
    King James's Palace Gardens 243
    pub tokens 247, 250–51
    Spring Gardens 243
Bathurst, Lord 26
Beaminster (Dorset), friendly society 243
Beauchamp family 96
Beauchief Abbey (Sheffield) 80
Beaufort, Duke of 138
Bedford, Duke of 99
Beer Act 247
Beeston (Notts.), pub tokens 250
Bellaers, Tobias 248
Belvoir, Vale of 229
benefit societies 244–45
Beringen (Belgium)
    church 302, 303
    housing 304
Berry Hill (Glos.), settlement 28
Bessemer steel converters 31
Birley Meadows Wheel (Sheffield) 86
Birmingham (W. Mids.)
    Cornish's directory 249
    friendly societies and clubs 245
    Jewellery Quarter 173, 248
    pub concert room 244
    pub tokens
        Commercial Inn 245
        Dial Inn 245
        manufacture and marketing 241, 247–52
Birmingham Copperworks (Swansea) 144, 147
Birmingham Hardware Company 251
Black Country, pub tokens 248

Blackett, William 107, 110
Blaenau Ffestiniog (Gwynedd), quarry 51n
Blaenavon (Blaen.)
    housing 140
    pub tokens 245–46, 252
    see also Nantyglo
Blaenllechau (Rhondda), housing 139
Blaenrhondda (Rhondda), housing 139
blast furnaces
    adoption of 186
    Carnforth 31
    Forest of Dean 27
    residues 18–19
blasting powder, introduction of 109
Blomme, Adrien, buildings by 304
Blour, Bet 208
Bolton (Lancs.), Star Inn and Concert Room 244
Boltsburn mine (Co. Durham) 112, 113
Bon-y-maen (Swansea), housing 144
Booth family 58
Boulton, Matthew 95, 99
Boulton and Watt engines 99
Bourne, John 211
Bowler, J. B. 250–51
Bradfield mill (Sheffield) 79
Bradway mill (Sheffield) 79
Braich quarry (Gwynedd) 43
brass industry 28, 161, 162; see also pub tokens
Brecon (Powys), George Hotel 193n
Brecon Forest (Powys), workers' housing 140
Brickdale, John 160
Bridgnorth (Shrops.)
    clay 208
    port 211
Brightside mill (Sheffield) 79
Bristol
    housing and development 155–62
        Baptist Mills 162
        Broad Plain 158
        Castle Green 158
        Castle Street 158, 161
        Clifton Hill House 155, 162
        Host Street 158
        King Street 157, 158
        Narrow Quay 156, 158
        Old Market 156, 157, 158
        Old Park Hill 160
        Prince Street 155, 158
        Queen Square 155, 158, 159–60, 162
        St Augustine's Back 161, 162
        St James's Barton 158
        St James's Square 158
        St Jude's 161, 162
        St Michael's Hill 158, 160–61

        Trenchard Street 158
        Wade Street 161
        Whitson Court 162
    metal industries 29, 161, 162
    pottery 213, 214
    slave trade 155–62
    sugar industry 157, 161–62
Brittany (France), pottery production 187
Broadbottom (Tameside)
    Broadbottom Hall 59
    Summerbottom 59
Broadhead Wheel (Sheffield) 87
Bryn y Castell (Gwynedd), iron-working 119
Bryncir estate (Gwynedd) 38
Bryngwyn (Gwynedd), railway 45
Bryntirion estate (Gwynedd) 38, 40
Buckton Castle (Tameside) 57
buildings see housing; industrial buildings
Bull, Edward 99
burial societies 244–45
burials, rural 223–24
    graveyards, changes in 232, 233–34, 235, 236,
        237–38
    memorials
        changes in 224, 225–26, 227, 228–29, 238
        consumption of 229–32, 238
Butler, Elizabeth, headstone 226, 227

Cae Ymryson (Gwynedd), enclosure 47
Cae'r Gors (Gwynedd) 45
Caerhays Castle (Cornwall) 145
Caldon Canal Company 213
Camber Castle (E. Sussex), animal bones 17
canals see Ashton to Manchester Canal; Caldon
    Canal Company; Lancaster Canal; Tavistock
    Canal; Trent and Mersey Canal
Canterbury (Kent), pottery production 184
capitalism 56, 66, 181, 182, 190, 204, 207, 210
Carmel (Gwynedd) 38, 47, 48
Carnforth (Lancs.), industrial settlement 29,
    31–2
carriers 189, 211
Castle Neroche (Som.), pottery production 184
Catholicism 305, 308
Cavendish Mill (Tameside) 70
Cefn Eithin farm (Gwynedd) 43
Cefnamwlch estate (Gwynedd) 38, 39
cementation furnaces, steel 19, 173–5
cemeteries, urban 232; see also graveyards
Chacewater (Cornwall), Wheal Busy 98
Champion, William 162, 317
chapels
    Colwyn Bay 150
    Forest of Dean 28

Gwynedd 46, 47–48
Lancashire/Westmorland border 32
Swansea 138, 143, 146, 148, 150–51
Tameside 75
Wrexham 150
charcoal 16, 18, 89, 90, 91, 120, 166
Charlestown (Nevis), excavations 155, 156, 157
Charnwood (Leics.), pottery production 183
Cheetham, George 64
Cheltenham (Glos.), pottery 214
chemical analysis, Rookhope Valley 126, 127
chemical industry see Avenue Coking and Chemical Works; Cwm Coking Works
Chepstow (Mon.), pub tokens 245
Cheshire, pub tokens 248
Chester (Ches.)
    pottery production 184
    river port 211
Chesterfield (Derbys.), pub tokens 250; see also Avenue Coking and Chemical Works
child labour
    copper industry 146–47
    pottery industry 189, 205, 206, 207, 208, 209, 214, 215, 216
    quarrying 51n
Chilvers Coton (Warks.), pottery production 186
churches
    Lancashire/Westmorland border 32
    Moel Tryfan 39
    Ruhr/Limburg, garden cities 302, 304
    Swansea 138, 141, 144, 146, 148, 149, 150, 151
    Tameside 67, 75
    see also chapels
cider making, Forest of Dean 28
Cinderford (Glos.), growth of 29
Clarke, David 313
clay, sources of 204–05, 207–08, 211
clay pipes 156–57, 161, 188
Clifford Amalgamated 95, 98, 100
Cloddfa Cocsith quarry (Gwynedd) 51n
Closure Theory 67, 70–72
clothing production
    Carnforth 31
    Ghent 259–66
    see also hatting industry
co-operative store see Ghent
coal, use of
    glass industry 21
    pottery industry 189, 204
    see also coke; mining
Coal Products Ltd 280
Coalcleugh mine (Co. Durham) 109
cognitive archaeology 317

coke
    coking works see Avenue Coking and Chemical Works; Cwm Coking Works
    use of 18, 19, 316
Collishaw, John, headstone 226, 227
Collishaw, Robert, headstone 226, 227
colonialism 189, 317; see also Atlantic trade
Colwyn Bay (Aberconwy & Colwyn), chapel 150
comb mill 30
Congleton (Ches.), silk mills 70
conservation
    industrial buildings 291–95, 300
    industrial past 300, 310–11
Consolidated Mines 95, 99, 100, 101
Constant, Capt. John 161
consumerism see retailing
Cope, William 208
Copley (Calderdale), planned settlement 25
copper industry
    Bristol/Forest of Dean 29
    Buckinghamshire 145
    Cornwall 95–96, 98–101, 145, 148
    Galloway 120
    North Wales 43, 45, 99, 145
    Swansea 137–52
copperas industry 74
coppicing see woodland, exploitation of
Coppin, W. 245
Corbridge (Northumb.), lead industry 121
Corlett, A. 245
Cosgarne Common (Cornwall)
    clock tower 100, 101
    mining landscape 95, 96–97, 98–101
    Wheal Clifford 95
    Wheal Maid 99
    Wheal Virgin 98, 99
Coster, John 98
cotton industry
    Ghent 258
    Lancashire/Westmorland border 29, 30
    Thameside 55, 59, 62, 64, 65, 70, 71, 74
Court, Wilfrid E. 246
Coventry (W. Mids.), pub tokens 250
Cranstone, David 1
Crawcwellt Common (Gwynedd), iron-working site 119
cremations 231, 237
creolization, theory of 184, 188
Crewe (Ches.), pub tokens 250
Crossley, David, Post-Medieval Archaeology in Britain 1, 56
crucibles 20, 21
Cupboard Hill (Cornwall) 98, 101

currency, pub tokens as 244
Cutlers' Company 79, 166, 169
cutlery industry, Sheffield area
  crofts
    background 166–69
    buildings and spaces 171–75
    as planned landscape 169–70
    protection of 175–77
  historical background 79–82
  water power, use of 79–87
Cwm Coking Works (Rhondda), recording project 269, 270, 280
  background 280
  process 282–85
  results, presentation of 285–88
  site work 281–82, 286
Cwm Dyli (Gwynedd), hydro-plant 43
Cwm Pit (Rhondda) 280, 284
Cwmystwyth (Cerdgn.), mining 119

DAF motorcar works 301
Dafarn Dywyrch (Gwynedd) 45
Daniels, Thomas 99
Darke, N. 246
dating methods 17–18; see also dendrochronology; radiocarbon dating
Davies, David 140
Davis, Joseph, headstone 227, 228
Davis, Sarah, headstone 227, 228
Deetz, James 1, 224
Defoe, Daniel 161
dendrochronology 17, 59, 91
Denton (Tameside)
  Denton Hall 59
  glass furnace 21
  Woolfendens 66
department stores 257, 261, 264; see also Ghent, Vooruit co-operative store
Derby (Derbys.), pottery industry 209
Derbyshire, pub tokens 248
Derwentcote (Co. Durham), slag 19
Detroit (U.S.A.), Rouge plant 278
Devon, pub tokens 241, 248
Devoran Railway 99, 100
Dierkens, Ferdinand 264
Don, river, water power 79, 80, 82, 83, 84, 86, 166
Doncaster, Daniel 172
Donyatt (Som.), pottery industry 204
Dorset, pub tokens 248
Dortmund (Germany), Zollern II–IV 303
Dowlais (Merthyr Tydfil), school 147
Downholme Park (N. Yorks.), coppice 89

dressing floors, Rookhope Valley 109, 110, 112, 113, 121
drover's road, Moel Tryfan 45
Drws y Coed (Gwynedd), industrial settlement 35, 45
Drybrook (Glos.), settlement 28
Dublin (Ireland), pub tokens 245
Dudley (W. Mids.), pub tokens 250
Dukinfield Hall (Tameside), excavations 59
Dulwich Art Gallery (G. London) 145
Dunham Massey (Trafford), lord of 58
Dunraven Colliery (Rhondda) 139
Durham, Bishops of 104, 107, 129
Dutton, Thomas 208
Dwight, John 190

Eastwood House (Tameside) 64
Eccleshall mill (Sheffield) 79
Ecclesiastical Commissioners 111
Edwards, William 38, 47
Eijsden (Belgium), church 302
Ellel (Lancs.), industry 30–31
Ellis, Thomas 162
Engels, Frederich 168
engines/engine houses
  conservation 300
  Cornwall 95–96, 99, 100, 101
  Rookhope Valley 110, 111, 112, 113
  Tameside 59, 60, 74
English, Thomas 248
English Heritage 59, 271, 291
The Enlightenment 69
environmental analysis
  Rookhope Valley 119–33
  use of 16–17
Essen (Germany), Zeche Zollverein XII 303
ethnicity, coal industry 305–06; see also immigration
Evans, John 38
Evans, Llewellyn 156–57
Exeter (Devon)
  pottery 183, 214
  pub tokens 250, 251
    Papermakers Inn 246
    Sawyers Arms 246
    Windmill Inn 245
experimentation, archaeology of 316–17, 318

Factory Act 1833 146
Fairbanks, plans by 83, 84, 85
Fairbottom Bobs (Tameside) 59, 60
farmsteads
  Moel Tryfan 39, 40, 41, 42, 43
  Tameside 59, 61, 62

Featherstone, Elizabeth, headstone 227, 228
Fenton, John 207, 208, 210, 211
Fernhill colliery (Rhondda) 139
Fisher, Paul 155
Flanders, pottery production 187
flint mill 212
fluorspar industry 113, 122
Ford motor corporation 278
Forest Copperworks (Swansea) 139, 144
Forest of Dean (Glos.), industrial settlements 25, 32–33
  industrial hamlets 29
  squatter settlements 26, 27, 28–29
Forge Dam (Sheffield) 83
Foryd (Gwynedd), harbour 35, 43, 45
Francis, Grant 245
Fraser, Joseph and partners 110
Fraser's Grove mine (Co. Durham) 121, 129–30
Fraser's Hush (Co. Durham) 110, 121
Fraser's Quarry (Co. Durham) 121
friendly societies 243, 245
Fron (Gwynedd), industrial settlement 38, 43, 44, 45
fulling mills 29, 79
Furness Railway 30, 31

Galgate (Lancs.), industrial settlement 29, 30, 31, 32
garden cities, Ruhr/Limburg 300–02, 303, 304–05
Garnons estate (Gwynedd) 38
gasworks 32, 74
Gee Cross (Tameside), hatting plank shop 59
Gelsenkirchen (Germany), Consolidation 303
Ghent (Belgium)
  social democracy 258–59
  Vooruit co-operative store 257–60, 261, 262–64, 265, 266
Gill, H. S. 245
Gill family, headstones 229
ginnels, Sheffield 171, 172–73, 174
Glasshouse Green (Glos.), settlement 26, 27
glassmaking
  Forest of Dean 26, 27, 28
  fuel 16
  residues 20–21
  Tameside 59, 66, 74
Gloucester (Glos.), pottery 213, 214
Gloucestershire, pub tokens 241, 248, 250
Glynllifon (Gwynedd) 35, 38, 39, 40
Good Hope Mill (Tameside) 70
Gordano Valley (Som.), peat analysis 120, 131
Gors y Bryniau (Gwynedd), quarry 43, 48
Gorseley Common (Glos.), settlement 28

Gosling, Ralph, map by 166, 168
Gottesdiener, H. 11
graveyards, rural 223–24, 238
  changes to 232, 233–36, 237
  gravestones
    increased consumption 229–32
    production, changes in 224, 225–26, 227, 228–29
  Nonconformist 232, 237
Grayson and Cocker 173
Grenfell family 145, 148, 150
Grenfelltown (Swansea) 146
Griffiths family 39
Grimsby (Lincs.), pub tokens 250
grist mills 29
Groeslon (Gwynedd) 39, 41, 42, 43, 47
Groverake mine (Co. Durham) 109, 112, 113
Guest, W. & H. 173
guilds, potters 187, 191
Gwennap United company 100

haematite mining 31
Hafod Copperworks (Swansea) 140, 142–43, 144, 145, 146, 150
  schools 147, 148
Hamsterley (Co. Durham), Roman settlement 121
Hardy, Thomas, headstone 225
Harkerside (N. Yorks.), hamlet 90
Harlow (Essex), pottery industry 204
Harrison, John (of Sheffield) 172
Harrison, John (of Stoke) 211
Hattersley (Tameside), manor 62
hatting industry 59, 66, 74
Haughton Green glassworks (Tameside) 59, 66
Healaugh (N. Yorks.), manor 90
Hemington (Leics.), pot wain 193n
Henderson, W. O. 151–52
heritage interpretation 10–11
Hickling (Notts.), gravestones 224, 225–26, 227, 228–29
Hiley, Mr 252
Hill, Thomas 207, 210
Hiron, Pope and Cottrill 248
historical archaeology 1, 314, 315
Historical Metallurgy Society 2
Hobley, Revd William 46, 48
Hocking, J. 99
Hodder, Ian 5–6
Hollingworth (Tameside)
  Gunn Inn 65
  weavers' cottages 62, 65
Hollister, Lawrence & Mrs 161
Holme Head Wheel (Sheffield) 86

Holme Mills (Lancs.) 29, 31, 32
Hornblower, J. & J. 99
horse-whims 43, 98, 109
housing
  agricultural
    Moel Tryfan 39, 40, 41, 42, 43
    Tameside 59, 61, 62
  employers/gentry
    Cornwall 145
    Moel Tryfan 39, 40
    Sheffield 172
    Stoke-on-Trent 212, 213
    Swansea 138, 139, 145–46
    Tameside 66
    Taplow 145
  managers
    Bristol 162
    Swansea 138, 139, 145, 146
  merchants, Bristol 155, 156–57, 158–59, 160,
    161, 162
  workers
    Brecon 140
    Bristol 161, 162
    Forest of Dean 29
    Lancashire/Westmorland border 31, 32
    Merthyr area 140
    Moel Tryfan 39, 41, 42
    Rhondda 139–40, 144
    Ruhr/Limburg 300–02, 303, 304–05
    Sheffield, crofts (illus) 165–77
    Sudbrook 139
    Swansea 138–40, 141–43, 144–46
    Tameside 59, 62, 65, 66, 73
  see also slums, perception of
Hull (Kingston upon Hull), pub tokens 246
Hunt, Flower 161
hushes, Rookhope Valley 104–05, 110, 121
Hyde (Tameside)
  Ashton family 72
  Gerrards Wood Mill 59, 70

ice houses 59
immigration 21, 66, 169, 172, 184; see also
  ethnicity
Imperial War Museum 9–10
imperialism 317
industrial archaeology, discipline of 1–2, 314–15
industrial buildings
  change of use 291, 292, 300
  conservation 300
  evaluation 291–95
  recording (illus) 269–88, 316
industrial heritage/culture
  concept of 3, 310

innate bias 299–300
  mining regions as examples 300–10
  preservation 310–11
  reconstructing 299
industrial residues 18, 316
  glass 20–21
  iron 18–19
  lead 19–20
Industrial Revolution
  archaeological study of 55–57, 181–82, 191
  nature of 69–70
industrial settlements, rural
  Forest of Dean 25, 26–29, 32–33
  Lancashire/Westmorland border 25, 29–33
  Moel Tryfan 35, 36, 37–50
  see also housing
industrialization, study of 1–4, 315–18
Inigo Jones slab mill (Gwynedd) 43
institutes 74, 138
Ipswich (Suffolk), pottery production 183–84
iron industry 186, 316–17
  Forest of Dean 27, 29
  fuel 16
  Gwynedd 119
  Lancashire/Westmorland border 29, 31–32
  residues 18–19
  Sheffield 79
  South Wales 140
  Tameside 74
  Weald 120
  Weardale 126, 129, 131–32, 133
  see also steel industry
Ivelet (N. Yorks.), woodland 89, 90, 91

Jackson, Samuel 208
Jamestown (U.S.A.), pottery 218n
Jepson and Co. 173
Johnson, Matthew 56, 314
Jones, John 47–48
Jones, Methusalem 43
Jones, Robert 161

Kay, Stuart 272, 278
Keegan, John 7, 12
Keeling, William 208
Kellington (N. Yorks.), graveyard 232, 233–34,
  235, 236, 237
Kennah, Capt. William and Mrs 160
Kenrick & Sons 249
Killicor Mine (Cornwall) 98
Killifrith (Cornwall), mine 95
kilns
  Barnstaple 188
  Chilvers Coton 186

France 187
Ipswich 183
Midlands 185
Rhineland 188
Staffordshire 189, 191, 205, 207, 208
Kilvey Copperworks (Swansea) 147
Kimmeridge (Dorset), glass furnace 21
Knight, John 157, 161

labour, division of in pottery industry 207, 208, 209, 214–15
Lancashire, pub tokens 241, 248, 250
Lancashire/Westmorland border, industrial settlements 25, 29–32
Lancaster Canal 31, 32
Lancaster–Carlisle Railway 31
Lancaster–Kendal turnpike 29, 31, 32
Landore (Swansea), workers' settlement 150
landscape studies 2
    mining
        Cosgarne Common 95, 96–97, 98–101
        Rookhope Valley 103–16, 119–33
    rural
        Forest of Dean 25, 26, 27, 28–29, 32–33
        Lancashire/Westmorland border 25, 29–33
        Moel Tryfan (illus) 35–50
        Sheffield area 79, 80–81, 82, 83, 84, 85, 86–87
        Swaledale 89, 90, 91, 92
        Tameside (illus) 53–72
    urban (illus)
        Bristol 155–62
        Sheffield 165–77
        Swansea 137–52
lead industry
    Cardiganshire 37
    Galloway 120
    Pennines 120, 131
    residues 19–20
    Sheffield area 80
    Somerset 120, 131
    Swaledale 89, 90, 91, 92
    Weardale/Rookhope Valley 103–16, 120–21, 126, 129–32
Leamington Spa (Warks.), pub tokens 250
leats 16
    Cosgarne Common 97, 98, 100, 101
    Rookhope Valley 110
    Swaledale 89
Leicester (Leics.)
    pottery 184, 189
    pub tokens 250
Leicestershire
    gravestones 224

pottery production 183, 185
pub tokens 248
Leland, John 79
Lemon, William 98, 99
Lescar Wheels (Sheffield) 80
Limbrick Wheel (Sheffield) 83
Limburg (Belgium/Neth.), coal industry 300–01, 302, 303, 304–06, 307–08, 309, 310–11
Lincoln (Lincs.), pottery production 184
linen mills 31
listing 271, 291–92, 293
Liverpool
    clay 208
    pottery 213, 214
    pub tokens 251
Llandaff (Cardiff), Cow & Snuffers 246
Llansamlet (Swansea), collieries 140–44
Lloyd, Squire 38, 47
Llwyn y Gwalch (Gwynedd) 39, 40, 41
Loam, M. 99
Loch Dee (Galloway), sediment analysis 120
Lockwood, Morris & Company 140
London
    Clerkenwell, Mulberry Garden 243
    Craven Head 243
    Finch's Grotto Gardens 243
    Lowe's Grand Hotel 243
    Marylebone Gardens 243
    metalworking 186
    pottery 190, 204, 211, 213, 214
    pub tokens 247, 250, 251
    wet admission tickets 243
    see also Imperial War Museum
London and North Western Railway 30, 31, 32
Longdendale, Lordship of 53, 55, 59–60, 64–66
Louis XV 182
Low Matlock mill (Sheffield) 82, 83, 86, 87
Lowenthal, D. 7–8, 11
Loxley, river, water power 79, 80, 82, 83, 84, 85, 86, 87, 166
Loxley Old Wheel (Sheffield) 82
Ludgvan (Cornwall), Wheal Fortune 98
Lydbrook (Glos.), settlement 29
Lyvedon (Northants.), pottery industry 193n

Maastricht State University (Neth.) 301
Macclesfield (Ches.)
    Childers Inn 245
    silk mills 70
magnetic dating 17
Maiden Way (Northumb.), Roman camp 121
Makin, Thomas 173
Malin Bridge mill (Sheffield) 82, 86–87
Malkin, Jonah 213–14

Manchester
  mills 71, 292
  music saloons 244
  pottery 213
  pub tokens 247, 251
  see also Ashton to Manchester Canal; Oldham;
    Tameside
Manchester to Sheffield Railway 59
Mann, William, headstone 226, 227
Mansel, Bussy 140–44
Mansfield (Notts.), pub tokens 250
marketing
  hardware trade/pub tokens 241, 248–52
  pottery 189, 191, 209–10, 211–14
  see also advertising; price fixing; retailing
Marlow (Bucks.), Grenfell family 145
material culture, interpretation of 5–7
matting production 31
Mayfield mill (Sheffield) 83
Melbourne (Australia), Little Lon 176, 177
Meredith, John 161
Merthyr Tydfil (Merthyr), housing 140; see also
  Taff Merthyr Colliery
Metals Company 98
Metcalf, Ant. 91
Milkwall (Glos.), settlement 28
Miller, W. T. 82
mills, evaluation 292; see also water power
Milnthorpe (Cumbria), settlement 29, 30, 32
mining
  coal
    Derbyshire 270
    Forest of Dean 28, 29
    Ruhr/Limburg 301–03, 304–05, 306–08,
      309, 310–11
    Sheffield 166
    South Wales 37, 139–40, 273, 274–75, 280,
      284
    Staffordshire 212
    Swansea area 138, 139, 140–44, 146, 148
    Tameside 59, 60, 68, 74
    Yorkshire 79, 307
  copper
    Cosgarne Common 95–96, 98–101
    North Wales 43, 45, 99
  haematite, Carnforth 31
  iron, Weardale 129–30
  lead
    Cardiganshire 37
    Derbyshire 120
    Rookhope Valley/Weardale 103–16,
      119–21, 129–33
    Swaledale 89, 90, 91
  silver, Weardale 129

tin, Cosgarne Common 95, 96–101
Moel Tryfan (Gwynedd), landscape study 35,
  36, 37, 49–50
  economy
    agriculture 41–43
    industry 43, 44, 45
    transport 45
  identity
    contestation 47
    craft, skill and technology 48, 49
    facts and fictions 45, 46, 47
    politics 48
    religion 47–48
  landscape
    building typology and spatial distribution
      39, 40, 41, 42
    land-tenure 37–38, 39
    location 37
Monmouth (Mon.), pottery 184
Monuments Protection Programme 271, 291,
  292–93
Morehouse, John and Ann 65
Morfa Copperworks (Swansea) 144–45
Morgan, W. J. 247
Morris family 145–46, 148
  John I 141
Morton, John 189
Moscar Wheel (Sheffield) 79
Mottram (Tameside)
  Black Bull Inn 59
  excavations 59
  industrialization 55
  Old Post Office Farm 59, 61
Mount Gabriel (Ireland), mining 119
Mount Wellington (Cornwall), mining 100
Muker (N. Yorks.), manor 91
Muncaster Head (Cumbria), iron industry 18
museums 10–11
music halls 244, 247

Nantlle (Gwynedd) 35, 45
Nantlle Railway 44, 45, 49
Nantyglo Ironworks (Blaen.) 245–46, 252
National Coal Board 276–77, 278, 280
National Statistics Office (Neth.) 301
Nevern (Pembs.), graveyard 230–32
New Archaeology 313
New Lanark (S. Lan.), housing 151
Newark (Notts.), pub tokens 250, 251
Newcastle upon Tyne, pottery 213
Newcomen, Thomas 99
Newent (Glos.), iron industry 27
Newman, Richard, The Historical Archaeology
  of Britain c. 1540–1900 1

Newnham (Glos.), cider mills 28
Newport (Pembs.), burials 230
Nonconformity
    burial grounds 232, 237
    Forest of Dean 28
    Lancashire/Westmorland border 32
    Moel Tryfan 46, 47–48
    Swansea 138, 148, 150–51
Norden, John 26
Norfolk estate 82
North Wales Narrow Gauge Railway 35, 36
North Wales Power and Traction Company 43
Northampton (Northants.), pottery production 184
Norton mill (Sheffield) 79
Nott, George 244
Nottingham (Notts.), pub tokens 250, 251
Nottinghamshire
    gravestones 224
    pub tokens 248
Nuneaton (Warks.), pub tokens 250; see also Chilvers Coton

Ochr y Cilgwyn (Gwynedd), quarry 38, 43, 44, 45, 49, 51n
Oddfellows 245
Oldham (Old.)
    friendly societies 245
    mills 71
Olive Wheel (Sheffield) 84, 85, 87
Oradour-sur-Glane (France), massacre 9, 10
oral evidence 7, 270, 272, 273
Oranje Nassau mine (Neth.) 309
Orkney, gravestones 230
Owen, Robert 151
Owlerton mill (Sheffield) 79
Oxford (Oxon.), market 185

Padstow (Cornwall), engineering firm 246
Palmer, Marilyn 1
    and Neaverson, Peter, Industrial Archaeology, Principles and Practices 56
paper industry
    Forest of Dean 28, 29
    Lancashire/Westmorland border 29–30
    Sheffield area 85, 87
Paris (France)
    department stores 264
    pottery 188
    tileries 187
partnerships
    pottery industry 204, 207, 208, 210
    slate quarrying 43
peat, analysis of 120

Pen y Groes (Gwynedd), settlement 35
Penrhyn estate 43
philanthropy 144–45, 151–52
Pillowell (Glos.), quarries 26
Pitts, Capt. Francis 161
place-name studies
    Moel Tryfan 37
    Swaledale 91, 92
Plymouth (Devon), pottery 214
Poldice (Cornwall)
    adit 98–99
    mines 95, 98, 99
Poldory mine (Cornwall) 99
politics, Moel Tryfan 48
pollen analysis
    Rookhope Valley 119–23, 124–25, 126–31
    use of 16, 17
pollution
    detection of 120, 130, 131, 132
    Sheffield 172
Poole (Dorset), clay 211
Pope, Thomas 214
population 15
Porter, river, water power 79, 80, 82, 83, 84, 86, 166
ports, river 29, 30, 211
post-medieval archaeology, discipline of 1–2, 15–16, 313–15
Potters Marston (Leics.), pottery production 185
Potterspury (Northants.), pottery industry 189
pottery, dating 17
pottery industry
    Carnforth 31
    Forest of Dean 27
    fuel 16, 189
    long-term change, analysis of 181–91
    Staffordshire potteries, industrialization of 203–18
    Tameside 74
powder houses, Rookhope Valley 110
Price, Thomas 140
price fixing, pottery industry 216–17
Pryce, W. 101
psychological processes 5, 6–7, 11–12, 317
pub tokens 241, 242, 252
    distribution 242, 249
    markets 248–52
    trade context 247–48
    usage before 1830 243
    usage 1830–1920
        documentary evidence 243–46
        oral and anecdotal evidence 246–47
Puiset, Hugh, Bishop of Durham 129

quarrying
  Forest of Dean 26, 28
  Lancashire/Westmorland border 31
  Moel Tryfan 35–43, 44, 45, 46, 47–48, 49, 50
  Weardale 111, 113, 115, 121, 131–32

radiocarbon dating 18, 19, 90, 126–28, 130, 131
Radstock (B. & N.E.S.), pub tokens 251
railways
  Cosgarne Common 99, 100
  Moel Tryfan 39, 43, 44, 45
  slag used in construction of 19
  Weardale/Rookhope Valley 109, 111, 112–13, 115
  workers' housing 32, 140
  see also Ashton & Woodhead Railway; Devoran Railway; Furness Railway; Lancaster–Carlisle Railway; London and North Western Railway; Manchester to Sheffield Railway; Nantlle Railway; North Wales Narrow Gauge Railway
Ravenscroft, George 21
Red Street (Staffs.), glass furnace 21
Redbrook (Glos.), settlement 29
retailing, Ghent 257–66
Rhineland (Germany), pottery industry 187, 188, 189, 191
Rhondda area
  coal industry 139, 144
  pub tokens 251
  see also Cwm Coking Works
Rhos Nennau (Gwynedd), common 38
Rhosgadfan (Gwynedd), settlement 38, 41, 45, 47
Rhostryfan (Gwynedd), settlement 38, 41
Rispey mine (Co. Durham) 11, 111
Rivelin, river, water power 79, 80–81, 82–83, 84–86, 87, 166
Rivelin Bridge Wheel (Sheffield) 86
river courses, changes in 16
  Sheffield area 82–86
  see also leats; ports, river; water power
roads see turnpikes
Roberts, Kate 45–46, 48, 49
Rockley (Yorks.), bloomery site 18, 19
Rookhope Valley
  metal mining and vegetational history 119–21
    interpretation and discussion: chronology of vegetation change 126–28; human disturbance 128–29; metal mining and its impact 129–32
      method 122–23; chemical analysis 126, 127; pollen analysis 123, 124–25, 126; radiocarbon dates 126, 127

site details 121, 122
  summary 132–33
mining landscape, changes in 103, 114–16
  1560s–1680s Moormaster phase 103–07
  1680s–1740s entrepreneurial phase 107–09
  1740s–1810s industrial phase 109–10
  1810s–1930s mechanization phase 110–13
  1930s–2000 destruction phase 113–14
Rookhope Valley Mining Company 112
Roscoe Wheel (Sheffield) 84, 85, 87
Rose Copperworks (Swansea) 144
Ross-on-Wye (Herefs.), King's Head Skittle Club 246
Rouen (France), pottery production 186
Rowleith Wood (N. Yorks.) 89, 91
Royal African Company 159
Royal Commission on the Archaeological and Historical Monuments of Wales 137, 144, 269, 280, 281, 288
Royal Commission on the Historical Monuments of England 59, 271, 273
Rugby (Warks.), pub tokens 250
Ruhr (Germany), coal industry 300–01, 303–04, 305, 306, 307, 311
Rutland, Dukes of 227–29

Sacré, Edmond, photograph by 261, 266n
saggars, use of 188, 189, 205, 207
Saintonge (France), pottery production 185–86
Salt, Titus 151
Saltaire (Bradford), housing 151, 165
Samper, J. 246
Satron (N. Yorks.), woodland 89
Scarborough (N. Yorks.), pottery production 186
scheduling 291, 292, 293
Scheeler, Charles 278
schools
  Moel Tryfan 48
  Swansea 138, 143, 144, 146, 147, 148, 151–52
  Tameside 67, 74
Scriven, S. 216
Seage, Epaphras 245
Seven Sisters (Neath), Seven Sisters Hotel 247
Severn Tunnel 139
Sèvres (France), porcelain production 182
Sharrow Snuff Mill (Sheffield) 82, 86, 87
Shaw, Simeon 207
Sheaf, river, water power 79, 80, 83, 86, 166
Sheffield (Sheff.)
  castle 166
  crofts, perception and protection (illus) 166–77
  Olive Grove Road 174

water power in Sheffield area
 historical background 79, 80–81, 82, 166
 in the landscape 82–84, 85, 86
 water wheels 83, 85, 86–87
 workhouse 169
Sheffield Water Company 82
Shepherd Wheel (Sheffield) 80, 82, 86, 87
Shrewsbury, Earls of 79–80, 82
silk mills 30, 31, 70
silver mining 129
Simon-Carves Ltd 280
Simpson, Elijah 208
Sims, William 99
Skinner, Capt. 160
slag see industrial residues
slate industry see Moel Tryfan
slave trade 155–62, 317
slums, perception of (illus) 165–77
Smith, John, headstone 225
smoke 172
Snake Pass (Derbys.), peat analysis 120
snuff mill 86, 87
social archaeology, Swansea (illus) 137–52
social class, site development influenced by
 62–63, 67–72; see also status
Société Générale Holding Company 302
Society of Journeymen Brush-makers 243
Society for Post-Medieval Archaeology 1, 2, 313
solidarity, miners 306–07, 308
Somerset, pub tokens 241, 248
South Wales, pub tokens 245, 248, 250, 251
Spooner Wheel (Sheffield) 86
squatter settlements
 Forest of Dean 26, 27, 28–29
 pedlars from 189
 Swansea 140
Stafford (Staffs.), pottery production 184
Staffordshire
 pottery industry
  industrialization of (illus) 203–18
  long-term change 183, 184, 189, 191
 pub tokens 241, 250
Staley estate (Tameside) 57, 58, 59
Stalybridge (Tameside)
 Bankwood Mills 64
 Castle Street Mills 64
Stamford (Lincs.), pottery production 184, 186
status, pottery as indicator of 186, 190
steam power
 Cosgarne Common 95–96, 99, 100
 Moel Tryfan 43
 pottery industry 215–16
 Rookhope Valley/Weardale 110, 111, 112
 Sheffield 82, 87

Tameside 70
steel industry
 Carnforth 31
 Derwentcote 19
 fuel 16
 Sheffield 166, 169, 172, 173–75
 see also cutlery industry
Stephen, King 129
Stephens, George 159
Stoke-on-Trent (Staffs.)
 Albion Square 193n
 Burslem 211–12, 213
 Fenton 208
 Ivy House Works 210, 219n
 Old Hall Street 193n
 pottery industry
  industrialization of (illus) 203–18
  long-term change 183, 184, 189, 191
 pub tokens 248
 Shelton 207–08, 211, 212
 Sneyd Green 189
 Spode 219n
 transport 191, 211–12, 213
stone working, gravestones 224, 225–26, 227,
 228–29, 230–32; see also quarrying
Storrs Mill (Sheffield) 82
Stotsfieldburn (Co. Durham), mining 112
Stratford on Avon (Warks.), Mulberry Tree Inn
 246
Styal (Ches.), planned settlement 25
Sudbrook (Mon.), housing 139
sugar industry 43, 157, 161–62
Sunderland (Sund.), pottery 213
Swaledale (N. Yorks.), woodland 89–92
Swansea (Swans.)
 Clasemont 145
 copper industry, social archaeology 137–39,
  151–52
  institutional buildings 146, 147, 148, 149,
   150–51
  workers' housing 139–40, 141–43, 144–45
  workers' housing compared 145–46
 Foxhole, chapel 150
 Haynes Buildings 146
 Maesteg House 145
 Morris Castle 139, 146
 Morriston (Morris Town) 141, 144, 147, 148,
  149–50
 Nott's Garden 244
 Philadelphia chapel 150
 poorhouse 152
 Sketty Park 146
 Trevivian 142–43, 144, 145, 146, 147, 148,
  149, 150

Sydney (Australia), Rocks 176

Taff Merthyr Colliery (Merthyr), recording 273, 274–75, 280
Tal y Sarn (Gwynedd), settlement 35, 48
Tameside, industrialization 53, 54–55
  archaeological database 57, 58, 59, 60–61, 62–63, 64–65
    listed 72–75
  current theory 55–57
  model of 64–66
  theoretical basis
    relationship to other models 67–72
    validity of categorization technique 66–67
Tanner, Robert 243
Taplow (Bucks.), Grenfell family 145
Tarlow, Sarah and West, Susie, The Familiar Past? 56–57
Taunton (Devon), Naval & Military 246
Tavistock Canal 99
Taylor, John 99, 100, 101
textile industries see clothing production; cotton industry; hatting industry; linen mills; matting production; silk mills; woollen cloth industry
Thematic Listing Programme 291, 292–93
thermoluminescent dating 17
Third Coppice Wheel (Sheffield) 86
Ticknall (Derbys.), pottery production 189, 203
tileries
  Paris 187
  Tameside 74
timber, dating 17–18; see also dendrochronology; wood drying kilns; woodland tin industry 19, 95, 96–101, 150
Tingle, Samuel 173
Tirdeunaw Colliery (Swansea) 146
tokens see pub tokens
Townsend, Chauncey 145
toy trade 252
trades unions 48, 258, 307
tramways 75
transport
  Moel Tryfan 45
  pottery industry 186, 189, 191, 193n, 211–13
  see also canals; railways; tramways; turnpikes
Trent and Mersey Canal 212
Trevince (Cornwall)
  mining 96, 98, 99, 100
  Wheal Lovely 98
  Wheal Squire 96, 99
Trevithick, Richard 99
Trevivian see Swansea
Truro (Cornwall), church of St Mary 148, 149
Tryfan Bach (Gwynedd) 38, 47

Tryfan Mawr (Gwynedd) 39
turnpikes 19, 75, 211–12; see also Lancaster–Kendal turnpike
Turton, Thomas 172
Twrog, St 47
Tyddyn Dafydd Du (Gwynedd) 39, 43
Ty'n Llwyn (Gwynedd) 42

United Mines 95, 99, 100, 101
Upper Cliffe Wheel (Sheffield) 82
Upper Forest Coppermills (Swansea) 146
Upper Slack Wheel (Sheffield) 86
Uyl, Joop den 301

Vaynol estate 38
Vivian family 140, 145, 148, 149
  John 99
  John Henry 143

Wade, Nathaniel 161
Wadsley Mill (Sheffield) 79, 86
Wagstaffe family 70
  Nicholas 61
Ward, Mr & Mrs 246
Ware, Isaac 155
Warwick (Warks.), pub tokens 250
water power 16–17
  Cosgarne Common 97–98
  Forest of Dean 29
  Lancashire/Westmorland border 29–31, 32
  Moel Tryfan 43
  Rookhope Valley 110, 113
  Sheffield area
    historical background 79, 80–81, 82
    in the landscape 82–84, 85, 86
    water wheels 83, 85, 86–87
  Tameside 62, 64, 70, 71
water wheels, Sheffield 83, 85, 86–87
Water Works Bill 1831 82
Waters, Ivor 245
Waterschei (Belgium)
  André Dumont mine 302, 303
  city 305
Watt, James 95, 99
Watts, John 173, 175
W. B. Lead Company 107–09, 110, 111, 112
Weald, iron-working 120
Weardale, Moormaster 103–07, 114, 131; see also Rookhope Valley
Weardale Iron Company 111, 115, 132
Weardale Lead Company 112–13
Weardale Minerals Ltd 122
Weber, M. 67

Wedgwood family
    John 210, 212–13
        house of 213
    Josiah
        apprenticeship 208
        Burslem works 191, 219n
        on labour required to fire a kiln 208
        marketing 209
        on number of potteries in north Stafford-
            shire 210
        pottery exported 214
        supports transport improvements 212
        on white salt-glazed stoneware prices 216
    Thomas 210, 211, 212–13
        house of 213
Werneth Low (Tameside) 59
West Bromwich (W. Mids.), Kenrick & Sons 249
Westphalian Museum of Industry (Germany)
    303, 311
wet admission tickets 243, 244, 245, 247, 251
Wharton, Lords 91
Wheal Friendly (Cornwall) 99
Whieldon, Thomas 208, 211
Whirlow Wheel (Sheffield) 87
Whitaside (N. Yorks.), hamlet 90
White Rock Copperworks (Swansea) 146, 151
Wickham, Thomas 157, 158
Wigan Pier Experience (Wigan) 10
Wild, Joseph, headstone 227, 228
Williams, Gilbert 46–47
Williams, Richard Hughes 45
Williams, William 49
Williams family of Cornwall 99, 100
    John 98, 99
    Michael 144–45
    Thomas 99, 145
Willington (Derbys.), port 211, 212
windlasses 98, 103, 105
Winsford (Ches.), port 211, 212

Winterslag (Belgium), garden city 304
Wolfcleugh mine (Co. Durham) 106, 107, 108,
    109
wolfram industry 100
Wolsingham South Moor (Co. Durham), lead
    industry 121, 130
women, role of 49, 189, 276, 307
Wood, Aaron 208
wood drying kilns 89, 91
woodland, exploitation of 16, 119–20
    Forest of Dean 26, 27, 28
    Rookhope Valley 128–29, 130–31, 133
    Sheffield area 79
    Swaledale 89–92
Woolaston Woodside (Glos.), settlement 28
Woolf, Arthur 99
woollen cloth industry
    Forest of Dean 27–28, 29
    Sheffield 79
    Tameside 71
Worcester (Worcs.), pottery industry 209
Worcestershire, pub tokens 241, 248, 249, 250
Worksop (Notts.), pub tokens 250
World Heritage Status 1, 100
Wrenthorpe (Wakefield), pottery production 188
Wrexham (Wrex.), chapel 150
Wynn family, Lords of Newborough 38, 39, 47
    home of 35, 39, 40
    Sir John 38, 39

yards, Sheffield 171–72, 173, 174, 175
Yartleton Woods (Glos.), settlement 26, 27
York, Clifford's Tower 10
Yorkshire, pub tokens 241, 248, 250
Young, Arthur 210

zinc
    detection of 120, 126, 131, 132, 133
    smelting 317
Zwartberg mine (Belgium) 309